REDISCOVERING PAUL

REDISCOVERING PAUL

Philemon and the Sociology
of Paul's Narrative World

NORMAN R. PETERSEN

FORTRESS PRESS   Philadelphia

Biblical quotations are from the Revised Standard Version of the Bible, copyrighted 1946, 1952, © 1971, 1973 by the Division of Christian Education of the National Council of Churches of Christ in the U.S.A., and are used by permission. Where the translation differs, it is the author's.

Library of Congress Cataloging in Publication Data

Petersen, Norman R., 1933–
    Rediscovering Paul.

    Bibliography: p.
    Includes index.
    1. Bible. N.T. Philemon—Criticism, interpretation, etc. 2. Sociology, Biblical. I. Title.
BS2765.2.P47 1985   227'.86067   84–48730
ISBN 0–8006–0741–4

14133I84   Printed in the United States of America   1–741

To the memory of
WILLIAM WREDE
and
RUDOLF BULTMANN

CONTENTS

PREFACE

This book represents an attempt to integrate contemporary literary and sociological capabilities into the traditional philological base of the historical critical method. My purpose therefore presumes that previous literary and sociological applications of the method have been inadequate. In this book, however, my concern is fundamentally constructive. I have tried to show how new literary and sociological approaches can be productive, rather than how the old ones have been deficient. The book is designed to build new bridges, not to burn the old ones behind us.

The twin foci of my literary sociological method, the literary and the sociological, were for many years separate concerns of mine. Just when the two came together for me, I do not now recall; but I do remember some of the principal factors that contributed to their merger. The first was the discovery, at least for me, of the narrative worlds of texts like Mark's Gospel and Luke-Acts. The second was the result of over a decade and a half of teaching texts from the fields of sociology and anthropology, including almost two years in which I served as the acting chairman of the Department of Anthropology at Williams College. This experience led to the recognition that "worlds" are human constructions, whether they are the constructions of societies or of narrators, and that narrative worlds are comprised of the same kinds of social facts—symbolic forms and social arrangements—as so-called real worlds. Thus narrative worlds can be studied like any other world. The third and perhaps the key factor came in connection with classes I have taught on the form of the Pauline letter, where in connection with the events referred to in the letter in Acts 15 and the Letter to Philemon my work on narrative criticism bore surprising fruit—the recognition that letters have stories and that the events of these stories are re-emplotted in the composition of letters, usually with clear rhetorical significance. But the final factor, the final ingredient in the merger of literary and sociological insights, came in the use of some anthropological ideas to make sense of the social problems represented in 1 Corinthians and the Letter to Philemon. This book began as an article on the latter, but when I began to organize the essay it soon became evident that the project involved more than an article and, indeed, more than the Letter to Philemon.

In moving from the article to the book I found that I had to deal in considerable detail with the procedures by which we could transform letters into stories and then relate the two to one another, and this task included a discussion of the sociology of letters, whose rhetorical composition constitutes a form of social relations (chapter 1). But it also became apparent that I had to deal with the sociology of the letter's story, and that this had two aspects, both of which are relevant for letters as letters. One aspect is more narrowly sociological and the other symbolic, or, to use the distinction that is followed throughout the book, one concerns social arrangements, the other symbolic forms. "Social arrangements" have to do with the social structures underlying the social relations comprised of the actions of the actors in Paul's letters and their stories (chapter 2). "Symbolic forms," on the other hand, have to do with the overarching cognitive systems, the systems of knowledge, belief, and value, that define these actors' identities and motivate their actions (chapter 3). In addition to these two sociological aspects, however, it soon became equally clear to me that neither of them could be dealt with without recourse to the other undisputed letters in the Pauline corpus. For most of the symbolic forms and social arrangements represented in the Letter to Philemon are fully comprehensible only in terms of what Paul represents about them in other letters. His Letter to Philemon requires that we understand the sociology of the narrative world represented in all of his letters. Thus, what began as an essay on the Letter to Philemon became a book on the sociology of Paul's narrative world, with the Letter to Philemon becoming a point of departure for an exploration of that world. The final stage of the project is, of course, the one represented in the book's conclusion, where I have tried to show how the sociology of Paul's narrative world can help us to understand more fully Paul's letter to and story about Philemon. Worlds are, after all, places in which people live and act, not mere systems or structures. The exploration of Paul's narrative world is for the purpose of better understanding the actions of the actors who inhabit it.

To acknowledge my indebtedness to those who have contributed to this book is a formidable task partially taken up in the notes appended to each chapter. Let it suffice for me to express here my especial gratitude to my students and colleagues at Williams College for providing me with the opportunity to think new thoughts, to my teachers at Harvard University, Helmut Koester, Arthur

Darby Nock, Krister Stendahl, John Strugnell, and Amos Wilder, for teaching me to respect the thoughts of others and to dare to venture my own, to Robert W. Funk, without whose long-term encouragement and support much of what I have thought would never have come into print, and to Norman Hjelm and John Hollar of Fortress Press, who warmly supplied the print. And last, but not least, I want to express my gratitude to Rosemary Lane, Louise Gilotti, Donna Chenail, and Eileen Sahady, whose caring patience in typing too many corrections of too many pages was above and beyond the call of duty. To my wife Toni and our children, Kristen, Mark, and Joby, apologies rather than gratitude are surely in order. *Mea culpa.*

ABBREVIATIONS

BZNW	Beihefte zur *ZNW*
CBQ	*Catholic Biblical Quarterly*
EKKNT	Evangelisch-katholischer Kommentar zum Neuen Testament
HR	*History of Religions*
HTR	*Harvard Theological Review*
Int.	*Interpretation*
JRH	*Journal of Religious History*
JSOT	*Journal for the Study of the Old Testament*
MTZ	*Münchener theologische Zeitschrift*
NTA	*New Testament Abstracts*
NTAbh	Neutestamentliche Abhandlungen
NTF	Neutestamentliche Forschungen
NTS	*New Testament Studies*
RSR	*Recherches de science religieuse*
SBLDS	SBL Dissertation Series
SBT	Studies in Biblical Theology
SD	Studies and Documents
SNTSMS	Society of New Testament Studies Monograph Series
TF	*Theologische Forschung*
TLZ	*Theologische Literaturzeitung*
ZNW	*Zeitschrift fur die neutestamentliche Wissenschaft*

INTRODUCTION:
NARRATIVE WORLDS,
SYMBOLIC FORMS, AND
SOCIAL ARRANGEMENTS

> Whatever the ultimate sources of the faith of a man or group of men
> may or may not be, it is indisputable that it is sustained in this world
> by symbolic forms and social arrangements.[1]
>
> Clifford Geertz

Today, the map of biblical studies looks different from a map drawn
a decade or so ago. The difference is that today's map has two new
routes on it. Broadly conceived, one route is that of literary criticism and the other that of sociology.[2] My concern in this study is
both to identify an intersection between these two routes and to
explore some of the new territories the intersection opens up to us.
The territories that interest me are what I will call the narrative
world of the Letter to Philemon and the narrative world of Paul. By
using the literary notion of "narrative world," we gain a world to
explore, namely the world referred to in the Letter to Philemon and
the world referred to in the total corpus of Paul's letters.[3] The narrower world of the letter will serve as a case study, a case in point,
but because it occurs within the wider world of Paul we will have to
explore much of that world as well. Just what we will explore in it
will be determined by what in it is relevant to the narrative world of
the letter. The criterion of relevance, however, is as sociological as it
is literary. In terms of the epigram from Clifford Geertz, for instance, we will be examining the symbolic forms and social arrangements by which the faith of Paul and of his communities is sustained in Paul's narrative world. Our considerations will therefore
encompass some fundamental literary, historical, and theological
aspects of Pauline studies, each of which we will look at in a new
light.

The task of this introductory chapter is to prepare for our explorations by making concrete such abstractions as narrative worlds,

1

symbolic forms, and social arrangements. To this end, I want to begin with a story, a story about the Letter to Philemon. This beginning is critical for our entire enterprise because it assumes that in some sense letters "have" stories and because these stories provide us with the narrative worlds we will explore. My assumption that letters have stories will be defended and explained in the course of this chapter and the next one. For the present, therefore, let it suffice to make two observations. First, every commentator on a Pauline letter, whether in a commentary proper, in an introductory handbook, or in an essay, at some point tells a story about the letter, usually under the heading of "the occasion for writing." The events referred to in the letter provide a narrative ("historical") context for understanding the letter. Second, if we as readers were asked to tell someone what the Letter to Philemon is about, we would invariably respond by telling a story. Our story would be based on the same information used by the commentator, and it would be told with the same intent—to explain or interpret the letter. One of my goals is to make us self-conscious about our transformation of letters into stories. Because we do so without realizing it, it is important for us to be aware not only that we do it, but also how we do it. For only when we have become self-conscious about this process will we be able to explore its implications. It is in this light that I tell my story about Paul, Onesimus, and Philemon as a case in point.

THE CASE IN POINT

Once upon a time there was a slave named Onesimus who became a brother to his master and a servant to his father, who was also his brother (as well as a prisoner and ambassador or old man).[4] Onesimus's father, Paul, on the other hand, was both a free man who was nevertheless a slave to a master, Jesus, who had himself been a slave, and a father to and partner with his child Onesimus's master, Philemon, who, like Onesimus, was also Paul's brother. Now one day the father/brother/slave/prisoner/ambassador/partner decided to send Onesimus, his child/brother/servant, back to his master/ brother Philemon, who was, it will be recalled, the father's child/ brother/partner. It seems, however, that the father/brother/slave/ prisoner/ambassador/partner was concerned that the child/ brother/master/partner might not properly welcome the return of his slave/brother, for before becoming Paul's child and his master's brother the slave had run away from the master, and possibly with the family jewels or the like. So it was, then, that the father/brother/ slave/prisoner/ambassador/partner wrote a letter to his child/ brother/partner on behalf of the slave/child/brother/servant in the names of their common master, the slave/son Jesus Christ, and of

2

their common father, God, a slave/brother/son of nobody, appealing to him to receive his slave/brother as he would receive Paul himself, and asking him to prepare a room for him because he would soon be coming to visit.

Now there is, of course, more to the story than this, as any reader of the Letter to Philemon knows. But to deal with any more details at this early point would only complicate matters prematurely. We can leave the complications for consideration later, until we have found some common ground upon which to stand. My purpose in telling the story as I have is simply to highlight what I see as its most distinctive feature, the preponderance in it of social categories which identify the roles, and thereby the actions, of the actors. Again, let it suffice for the moment to say that the social categories are symbolic forms, since they stand for or symbolize social roles, while the roles themselves belong to the realm of social arrangements. Together, the categories and the roles are sociological phenomena, while the actions of the actors have in addition to a literary quality the character of social relations.

This being my purpose, my reason for wanting to highlight these social features is to differentiate my concerns from those of other commentators who also tell the story of Paul, Onesimus, and Philemon, but in a quite different way. In my version of the story the reader is confronted with the problem of trying to figure out both which roles the actors play in relation to one another at any given moment in the story, and what implications their roles have for understanding the meaning of their actions. For example, one wants to know in what capacity Paul sent Onesimus back to Philemon, or perhaps even in what capacities. How do we choose from Paul's roles as father, brother, slave, prisoner, ambassador, and partner? More importantly, how can we tell what Philemon would have chosen from among these roles in his perception of Paul's action and letter? Did Philemon's choice(s) determine the role he found himself playing in response to Paul's actions? Upon hearing Paul's appeal to receive Onesimus as he would receive Paul himself, did Philemon respond as a son to a father, a brother to a brother, a master to a slave, a free man to a prisoner, as a private individual to an ambassador, or as a partner to a partner, or did he respond in terms of more than one of these options? Moreover, did Philemon's choice(s) affect his response by making it an act of obedience, of free compliance, or of disagreement or rejection? From another perspective, we might also ask what it means to be asked rather than commanded to do something by someone who claims the power to command, as Paul does. Or what it means for a master to receive his slave as a brother. Or what it means to be asked to prepare a guest room for a visitor whose actions raised all of these questions in the first place. And last, since in the story Paul has the status of a father and Philemon the status of a master, we need to determine the meaning these roles have for the actors in view of another father in the story, God, and of another master, Jesus Christ, who had also been a slave. Clearly, this story has much to do with the relations between fathers and their children, and between masters and their slaves. Clearly, too, we must understand these symbolic forms (social categories) in order to understand the social arrangements (sociological relations) they represent; and we must understand both of these in order to comprehend the actors' actions, their social relations with one another.

A number of other questions will be raised shortly, but these will suffice to make my point. Through questions like these, readers are caught up in the story, and the world in which we move while captive is that of the story, its narrative world, the world of events and relations to which the story refers. On the other hand, the reader or critic who has finished the story, left its narrative world, and contemplates what happened there, is confronted by problems that are both literary and sociological. Literarily, in order to comprehend the actors' actions we must understand the sociological facts governing their actions, namely, the symbolic forms and social arrangements. The original readers, the church at Philemon's house, probably understood the story as they read the letter or heard it read. But we, coming from other houses, as it were, are confronted with critical problems. We have to reconstruct the symbolic forms and social arrangements of which their world was constructed.[5]

Consider now another version of the story, one which is fairly typical of those that commentators tell about the Letter to Philemon.

> As ordinarily reconstructed, the circumstances were that Philemon's slave, Onesimus, had run away, apparently with stolen money (Philem. 18). He had somehow met St. Paul in prison and had, apparently, been brought by him to accept Christianity, or to return to it after a lapse. Now he is sent back to his master with this letter from the apostle, which was carried, it seems, by Tychicus (Col. 4:7).[6]

The concerns of the teller of this version of the story are clearly as different from mine as are the two versions. His version is immediately followed by a discussion of how and when Onesimus met Paul and was converted, and of when Paul sent him back to Philemon, for the timing of these things bears on Paul's legal responsibilities for

returning a runaway slave. In addition to this legal motive for returning Onesimus, the teller also indicates a moral or religious one
in which Paul acts to repair "the breach between master and slave."
He then concludes this section of his discussion by raising the question of whether Paul expected Philemon to release Onesimus from
slavery. And like some other tellers of the story, this one suspects
that Philemon's Onesimus is identical to a bishop of the same name
mentioned some decades later by Ignatius, an early church leader.
The implication is that Philemon freed *his* Onesimus and that this
former slave subsequently became a bishop. "It is thus possible,
though not demonstrable, that we are given a glimpse of a spectacu-
lar sequel to St. Paul's letter many years later."[7] With this remark
the teller turns to questions of where Paul was imprisoned and of
who the several friends mentioned in the letter were.

It is readily evident from this version of the story and the teller's
discussion of it that his critical concerns are historical and that as a
reader he is caught up in history. Indeed, it is fair to say that for
him, as for most other readers, the story *is* history. It would seem,
therefore, that at the very beginning of our explorations we will
have to decide whether we are going to explore the world of history
or the world of story. The decision is all the more critical because
the customary charge made by historians, both biblical and other, is
that literary criticism and sociology are ahistorical.[8] Literary criticism deals with fictions and sociology with ahistorical patterns,
systems, structures, models, and so on, not with the causal relations
between events in chronological time. Fictions have nothing to do
with history, which is factual, and systems pertain to slices of historical and social time (synchrony) not with temporal sequence (di-
achrony). There is, nevertheless, a certain irony attending all these
criticisms because the recent literary and sociological studies of
biblical texts more often than not claim to be concerned with history, either with the history associated with the writing and/or reading of texts or with the history referred to in them.[9] These concerns
are in fact axiomatic among historians, who have traditionally argued that a text is first and foremost evidence for the time in which
it was written. It is a primary source for that time but only a secondary source for the events referred to in it. In this light, perhaps the
best way to deal with the problematic relationship between story
and history is to consider it from the literary and sociological perspectives I wish to adopt. By proceeding in this way, I will be able to
introduce the issues that are of concern to me, while at the same
time indicating their relevance to historical understanding, and
vice versa.

TEXTS AND CONTEXTS

The distinction between texts and contexts plays a pivotal role in sorting out the problems of relating letters to stories and to history. In literary criticism, the distinction has been at the center of debate for almost a century.[10] At issue in the debate is the question of which should dominate in textual interpretation, the information internal (intrinsic) to the text or contextual information that is external (extrinsic) to the text, like the author's intent, his biography, or the historical and cultural climate of his times. The "New Criticism" first rebelled against contextual interpretation by advocating the "autonomy of the text," and by identifying as contextualist errors an intentional fallacy, which pertains to the overvaluing of the author's textually extrinsic intent in writing, and a genetic fallacy, which overvalues the relevance of historical and social influences (causes) on the author's shaping of a text.[11] For New Critics, the text is a world unto itself, it is autonomous, while the total corpus of literary texts comprises a literary world, the "world" of literature. In response to this radical insistence on separating texts from their contexts in order to concentrate on texts, a mediating position emerged in which texts and contexts are held in some kind of balance, the kind of balance varying from critic to critic and from school to school, but always with an affirmation of the relevance of contexts.[12] Currently, however, the debate among literary critics hinges on the related question of just how determinative even intrinsic textual information is of our understanding and interpretation of texts. One polar position in the debate is that of radical determinacy (e.g., E. D. Hirsch),[13] in which it is believed that valid interpretations can be arrived at; the other polar position is that of radical indeterminacy (e.g., J. Derrida),[14] in which it is believed that we cannot validly interpret a text because texts have many meanings, not merely one right one. Between these positions, there is of course an intermediate one (e.g., W. Iser)[15] which holds that depending on the text sometimes we can validate an interpretation and other times not. The determinists and those inclined in that direction allow, even require, contextual information, as for example from language, cultural conventions, and authorial intent. But the radical indeterminists find that there is no guaranteeing the validity of an interpretation from internal information, and that external, contextual information only further deludes one into thinking one knows what a text is saying. Nevertheless, despite all of these considerable differences of opinion, it remains fair to say that the notions of text and context will continue to remain central to literary critical debate because they refer to the two principal sources of information bearing on the interpretation of texts.[16]

In biblical studies, a corresponding distinction is made in terms of *text* and *history*, as we noted in connection with the twin axioms of historical criticism. Accordingly, when narratives like the Gospels and Acts are the texts in question, their historical context is understood to be that of the time in and for which they were written.[17] This *contextual history* or world, however, is distinguished from the history of events referred to in these texts, such as the events that took place in the time of Jesus and of his followers after his death. Literary and historical critics are therefore in agreement when they associate the notion of context with the time of writing. But what in literary criticism corresponds to the history referred to in our narrative texts? In literary terms, this *referential history*[18] comprises the *narrative world* of the text (or story).[19] The narrative world is that reality which the narrator[20] bestows upon his actors and upon their actions, a reality into which he authoritatively invites his audience, whether he is telling a fairy tale, a spy story, or a great novelistic adventure.

Biblical critics have not yet become accustomed to thinking of the referential worlds of the Gospels and Acts as narrative worlds, but the true critic nevertheless treats them as such by considering them stories that are secondary sources from which history has to be reconstructed. The true critic does not simply assume that the stories of Jesus and his disciples represented in Matthew, Mark, Luke, and John directly represent history as it happened. And the critic does not do so for reasons of both method and evidence. Methodologically these texts are but secondary sources, as we have seen, while evidentially they are not telling the same story even when they seem to be referring to the same events and lives.[21] The history of those events and lives has to be reconstructed from the stories that refer to them.

So unlike the literary critic, the biblical student has to reconstruct from one and the same narrative text both its contextual and its referential history. On the one hand we establish the context of the text from information in it that bears on the time of writing. On the other hand, however, the historian also has to reconstruct a "real world" from the text's narrative or referential world. Later, we will consider some complications that arise when the historian uses information from other texts to assist him in making his reconstructions. For the moment, it remains important to keep to some simple distinctions. Thus, we have seen that the notion of context refers to the time of writing, that narrative worlds are literary constructions represented in stories, and that historical worlds are reconstructions made from the referential, narrative worlds of narrative texts. But what, now, is the relevance for the study of letters of definitions created for narratives? Their relevance is paradoxical because they make it possible both to identify differences between letters and stories and, paradoxically, to do so in such a way as to render the differences superficial. In fact the very evidence for the differences between letters and stories makes it possible to speak of a letter's story. Using the definitions above as a measure, two principal differences, and their superficiality, emerge.

First, it is immediately apparent that in letters there is no distinction between contextual history and referential history corresponding to what we have seen in narrative. The only history *referred to* in a letter is its contextual history, which is the total history envisioned by the writer as relevant for the letter.[22] However, as real as this difference between letter and narrative is, because letters refer to a world they have *referential worlds,* and these are the *narrative worlds,* from which any real-world history must be reconstructed. For example, the events to which Paul refers in his Letter to Philemon have a narrative quality because they comprise a selective sequence of events between which Paul posits certain links.[23] Thus, on this point of difference letters prove to have a narrative aspect in their referential world, while the fact that this world is *also* the letter's contextual world serves only to make the historian's task easier: there is only one world to reconstruct, not two. But having said this, let us also remember that for the historian the narrative world is *a secondary source* for referential history, while the textual evidence for the time of writing, the contextual history, is a primary source for *that* time. What do we do when the narrative world *is* the contextual world? When our historian assumed that the story he reconstructed from the Letter to Philemon was history, he was assuming that the referential, narrative world of the letter was identical with the real, historical, contextual world! For him, the construction of the letter's narrative world was identical with the history he reconstructed.

Clearly, our distinction between contextual and referential worlds, together with our recognition that in letters these worlds are telescoped into one another, poses two problems for a historical approach to Paul's letters. First, the referential-contextual world of the letter has a narrative quality which requires that history must be reconstructed from it. The referential world of the letter is not simply identical with history, any more than it is in narratives. And second, because in letters the contextual and referential worlds are identical, the distinction between primary and secondary sources fails to distinguish between anything.[24] In letters, as well as in nar-

8

ratives, we have to move from the text to its referential, narrative world, and from its narrative world to history.

The second point of difference between letters and stories is the rather obvious one—they look different. Less obvious are the paradoxical implications of why they look different. We can say that on their textual surfaces letters look different from stories because the referential world is formally referred to differently in them. By describing the difference in this way, the key to the paradox is supplied by pointing to an underlying common denominator between letters and stories—a referential world which on the surface of letters and stories is referred to differently. The legitimacy of posing the relationship in this way has already been established when we observed that both letters and stories *have* referential worlds. Since both have them, the problem becomes one of being sure that we understand how letters and stories differ, and with what implications for the study and understanding of letters. Here we can profit from another distinction drawn by literary critics in connection with narrative texts, namely, the distinction between story and discourse.[25] Used of narrative, the distinction refers to the double aspects of narrative in which every story is also a discourse, a message communicated by a narrator to an audience. Discourse refers to the form and content of *telling* someone something; story refers to the narrative form, the *showing*, of something. From a literary perspective, in narrative the form of story dominates the discursive presentation of the message. The narrator speaks, but he speaks in narrative form. Applying this distinction to letters, it becomes immediately apparent that *in letters the form of discourse, of speaking to someone, subordinates the story and its narrative world to the presentation of the message.* Depending on which form and function dominates, referential events are formally distributed throughout a text in different ways. In narratives, the message is in the story. In letters, the story is in the message.

The two principal differences between letters and stories therefore lead to the conclusion that while letters are not narratives they nevertheless refer to narrative worlds. These worlds must be constructed from the events and relations referred to in a letter, and the contextual *history* thus referred to must be *re*constructed from the letter's narrative world. In relation to traditional approaches to the interpretation of Paul's letters, the major conclusion to be drawn is that the narrative world of letters requires attention it has yet to receive, because it has yet to be recognized for what it is. The narrative worlds of letters, like the narrative worlds of narratives, have both literary and sociological dimensions, and it is these with which we are concerned, for the narrative worlds of texts provide their immediate interpretive contexts. But having seen that story is not simply history, let us now take another step on our way by entertaining the provocative opposite of our historian's assumption by considering what it might mean to say that history is story.

HISTORY AS STORY

The idea that history is story is widely held among critics from a number of disciplines, including history, although it is fair to say that it is not a prevailing idea, especially among historians.[26] The idea is important for our purposes for two reasons. On the one hand, it can help us to understand what I have referred to as the narrative quality of a letter's referential world, a world usually construed as corresponding to history as it happened. On the other hand, it can also serve to reinforce the value of our literary concerns by showing that history as it happened is something that can only be grasped by telling stories about it. History in the strict sense is a story about events, not the events themselves, or even a verbal representation of them, since it is impossible to represent the enormous mass of "events" we perceive even in a given day. Because historical stories, like stories in general, are necessarily selective, they construct through story a history that does not exist apart from story. Strictly speaking, therefore, history is always constructed, never re-constructed. So if history is for this reason story, it is all the more important to comprehend a letter's narrative world and its significance for understanding a letter before we jump to conclusions about events as they happened. These events must truly be constructed from such worlds.

Students of narrative are in agreement that narrative or story is probably a universal means of understanding human social actions and relationships in time. While these actions and relationships occur in the real world of everyday experience, our experience of them lacks the narrative form we bestow upon our experience when we think or speak about it. Narrativizing, as some call it, imposes "a certain formal coherence on a virtual chaos of 'events,' which in themselves (or as given to perception) cannot be said to possess any particular form at all, much less the kind that we associate with 'stories.' "[27] The formal coherence achieved by the narrativizing of experience is best represented by what one critic speaks of as the fundamental fictions of narrative—point of view, plot, and closure.[28] "Fiction" in this context merely refers to the construction, the making, of an order which these formal devices make possible. In this sense fictions order facts which themselves lack order, and perhaps even factuality, unless we impute it to them; the facts *may* be factual, but the order *is* fictional because it is an imaginative construction. Even in the natural sciences natural laws have a fictional quality in that they are ordering constructions imputed to facts and factual events. But unlike historians, natural scientists can validate their fictions by experimentally repeating the factual events in order to test the laws they have constructed. Historical events are not experimentally repeatable and therefore the historian's fictions cannot be validated.[29] The natural scientist can demonstrate that her or his fictions represent something "out there," even though he or she has created the fictive "laws." But the historian can only show how such fictions plausibly represent things other people already agree are out there. However, what is out there for the historian are bits and pieces of potential facts and other people's stories of how the facts are related. To this extent historians are in the position of having to adjust their fictions to those of other people. Since historical understanding thus moves from fictions to fiction, we need to see just how constructive of experience the fictions of narrative are.

Point of view refers to the position of a narrator, be it us talking to ourselves or someone talking to others, in relation to the actors whose actions are being described.[30] This position has many aspects, since it can be any or all of a number of things. Temporally, point of view refers to the temporal relationship between the time of the narrator and the time referred to in his story. I can tell a story about today, or yesterday, or about times long past. In all cases, however, the temporal perspective of the narrator is from a retrospective time after the outcome of the events selected for narration. Spatial point of view is more variable, but not unrelated to temporality. While one must be in a different time from the events referred to, one can be in the same place: "It was here that it all happened." But a narrator can also be in a different time and place while telling about events in another time and place. Only one thing is certain. A narrator has to have a time and a place from which to view and describe what has happened. But point of view is perspectival in other ways, too, for point of view also refers to a narrator's principles or values in selecting some events for narration rather than others, in tracing one thematic line through the sequence rather than another, and in drawing one conclusion rather than another about the meaning of the whole sequence. Similarly, the narrator's point of view may reflect her or his ability to tell an audience the feelings, motives, and thoughts of the characters in the story. The narrator may tell an audience such things either directly or allow characters in the story to do so. For all of these reasons point of view may well be the single most important fiction of narrative.[31]

To illustrate the pervasiveness of point of view, imagine, for ex-

11

ample, our experience of events in a single day, and what we do when we respond to the question, "What did you do today?" Our first action is to look back on the day's events from the temporal, spatial, and social perspective in which we are standing when asked the question. We adopt a point of view on events past. Probably simultaneously with this action, we focus on events in which *we* were the principal actors, not others ("What did *you* do?"), and from that moment on we select and arrange for narration those of our actions which from our point of view are significant. In the process, what we deem to be significant takes on a thematic character in the organizing of the selected actions. The theme or themes will provide links of cause and effect or of motivation between the actions we narrate, even though at the time the actions took place those links did not yet exist. They did not exist because we only created them later in response to a question, and as often as not in view of what we think our questioner might consider significant. Chances are that we might even answer with a different story depending on who asked the question: a boss, a traffic policeman, a daughter, a husband or wife, or a fellow jogger or a fellow student.

To illustrate further what is at issue let me use as an example my own still memorable yesterday. Yesterday, I wrote all morning and, uncommonly, well into the afternoon. If asked about my day when I got up from my desk, my answer would have been one thing: perhaps, "a good day's work." But if asked an hour later, after I had discovered downstairs a flood from a broken, iced-up radiator pipe, my answer, and my story, would have been quite different. One difference would have been my interpretation of the significance of having written for a longer time than usual, because, if I had kept to my normal schedule, I could have prevented much of the damage. To take the day a bit further, the pattern of relevance and connections would have changed yet again if the question about my day had been asked after a late evening committee meeting, for the procession of events turned what had started out as a good day into a debacle of sorts. Now the point of this survey is that from the very beginning I have been both highly selective and contrastive. I have not mentioned an enormous number of other things I did, from brushing my teeth to making sure the cat was in before I went to bed. And I started out with something good, saw it turn to bad, and then get worse. I *could* have looked at the rosy side, for example, because there was one.[32] I stopped the flood before any serious damage was caused, and what damage there was was covered by our having "a piece of the rock" (insurance). And the evening meeting was not all that bad. But for whatever reasons, I selected only certain events and cast them in a certain light. The things I have described actually happened, but they were not *all* that happened. They do not tell the whole story, only a story, *a* history, but not history. With the aid of point of view I have told a true fiction, but I have not described history, either of all of the events or of all of the factors which made up my day. Indeed, I could not, and that is why history is story.

The notion of plot has already been alluded to in connection with the selection and arrangement of the events in my "day." But there is more to plot that is useful for understanding why it is a fiction of narrative. Plot refers to the sequence of selected events *as they appear in the story*, regardless of whether or not this sequence corresponds to the sequence in which the events took place, or in which the narrator leads us to believe they took place.[33] A strict chronological sequence would exhaustively follow each and every successive action from the time the alarm goes off in the morning until sleep comes at night. The emplotment of successive actions, however, might begin with the high (or low) point of the day and work around it, or it might begin at the end and treat everything else as a flashback. The point of the variability of emplotment is that it highlights the importance of our being aware *that* a narrator has selected only certain actions for narration because he or she deems *them* relevant. A corollary to this point is a second one, namely that the arrangement of these events is also a matter of choice, which we can sometimes discern when a narrator reports an action *out* of the chronological sequence he or she has led us to imagine. In this connection, Paul's story in the Letter to Philemon is more pertinent than my own, for as we will see Paul was highly selective and equally strategic in his arrangement of references to events in his letter. The notion of plot applies to letters as well as to narratives because letters have referential, narrative worlds that are emplotted in them.

Closure, finally, refers to "the ending that fulfills the story, creates its coherence, and rounds off everything"[34] by satisfying expectations generated in the course of the narration.[35] " . . . [I]t is the postulate of an ending that makes a beginning possible, that makes a meaningful pattern out of the varied items of the story, that fulfills the story."[36] Closure is the relief of a happy ending, the frustration of a last straw, the "now I understand" which comes at the end of an intricate plot, whether we are given its resolution directly by the narrator or led by the narrator to draw an inevitable conclusion for ourselves. In the story behind Paul's Letter to Philemon, for example, we will need to determine its closure by filling the gap left by our ignorance of Philemon's response to the letter. This determination is related to the very last action Paul refers to, the visit he plans to make to Philemon, whom he asks to prepare a room for him. This is the concluding episode in the story, occurring after the arrival of the letter and Onesimus on Philemon's doorstep. But the closure of the total story involves more than just the last few episodes in it. Its closure is also related to the first event in the story, its beginning, as well as to Paul's selection and arrangement of all of the other events in it. The question is, how are these relations established, and what is their significance for understanding the story, even for constructing history from it.[37]

The fictions of narrative show that history is story in a double sense; both in the sense that the historical narrative we construct *from a letter* is a story, and in the sense that the historical narrative we construct *from a letter's story* is also a story, not history in the sense of our historian's judgment that his story about Philemon was history. I have said that historical understanding moves from fictions to fiction. For our purposes, this means that we have to distinguish between Paul's fictions and ours. The story we construct from a letter is Paul's fiction, but the one we construct from that story is ours. But between these two fictions there is yet another one, one that is central to our concerns, namely the fiction of Paul's wider narrative world. This world has further implications for our understanding both of texts and contexts and of story and history.

PAUL'S NARRATIVE WORLD

In discussing texts and contexts, I deferred consideration of some complications that arise when historians use information from other texts to assist them in their historical reconstructions. Now that we have entertained the notion of narrative fictions and their bearing on story and history, we are in a better position to grapple with the complications. For if we understand what it means to say that a letter or a narrative has a narrative world, it is easier to comprehend what it means to say that from the total corpus of Paul's letters[38] we can construct not only the narrative worlds of each of them, but also the narrative world referred to in all of them. *That* is the world I refer to when speaking of Paul's narrative world. With one significant difference, this narrative world is like those historians construct when they attempt to describe the biography of Paul or the history of his mission or, more narrowly, even the nature and development of his thought. The significant difference is, of course, that the character of this world is as much a constructive Pauline fiction as that of the narrative world we construct for any individual letter. It is a referential world from which a historical story must be constructed, but with the help of yet other texts like the Book of Acts,[39] letters and stories by other people, including some stories read by Paul, like those in his Bible, and even evidence of ancient laws and economic and social practice.[40] Strictly speaking, a strict historical criticism should proceed through exactly these stages, moving from the individual worlds of individual texts through the world of an authorially homogeneous corpus of texts, into the broad field of other texts, each of which, and each authorial corpus of which, should be studied in the same way.[41] Our purposes, however, are for methodological reasons more limited than this. Because the first two stages have yet to be explored and because the exploration of them is a sizable task in itself, we will be concerned only with the narrative world of the Letter to Philemon and the narrative world of Paul, as represented in his letters. And for the purposes of our case study, we will be concerned specifically with those aspects of Paul's narrative world that are relevant to the narrative world of his Letter to Philemon. We are concerned with the internal structures and dynamics of Paul's narrative world as it bears on the story of Paul, Philemon, and Onesimus. The results of our exploration of this Pauline world will provide the data upon which our historical constructions would have to be based, or at least in part, the part deriving from Paul's letters.

By isolating the two worlds, the smaller one of the letter and the larger one of its writer, we are affirming for the purpose of our exploration the relevance of the fundamental fictions of narrative for Paul as well as for the individual letters which he wrote. We affirm, for example, that both the story of the Letter to Philemon and the story of Paul are subject in their construction to point of view, plot, and closure. Each story is governed by Paul's point of view, because all we know of each[42] is learned from him, even the points of view of the characters in his stories, who are sometimes allowed by him as narrator to voice their own points of view,[43] but more often have points of view attributed to them by him. Also, Paul is the narrator of both stories in the sense that he alone is the one who has selected and arranged or emplotted all of the events he refers to. Regardless of his historical, contextual reasons for making these selections and arrangements of events, it is Paul who has emplotted them. The discovery, or recovery, of his point of view and plotting, both the devices and the results, is therefore a necessary task for understanding Paul and his letters, but also for constructing history by relating this evidence to that of other, non-Pauline texts. The notion of closure is of no less significance.

The importance of the notion of closure is that at the same time it defines the internal coherence of a story, it sets the story's boundaries by giving it a fictive, that is, constructive, beginning and ending. As we have seen, the open field of events encountered in

15

everyday experience lacks such beginnings and endings. Consider, for example, the creative arbitrariness of identifying the first event in the story of Philemon as Philemon's entering into debt to Paul (Philemon 19), and the last event as a visit by Paul to Philemon (v. 22). We will see in chapter 1 that these two events set the boundaries of Paul's story about Philemon, and that its closure hinges on the significance for Paul, and for Philemon as a character in *Paul's* story, of Paul's anticipated visit. These boundaries clearly differentiate our approach from that of the historian. Not only are we treating Philemon as an actor in Paul's story, rather than as an independent historical agent,[44] but we are also entertaining events for whose historical coming to pass there is no evidence. We do not know from any sources that Onesimus and the letter ever arrived at Philemon's house, how he responded to them, or whether Paul ever made his announced visit. Nevertheless, regardless of our historical ignorance, each of these events is an integral part of Paul's story, because he referred to them, and for this reason they must be understood in terms of their roles in the story. Regardless of "what happened" historically, we cannot understand what Paul says *did* happen prior to the sending of the letter apart from the total framework of the events he envisioned. Paul's motives, strategies, and expectations as an actor in his own story can only be comprehended in terms of the whole story as he envisioned it. Hence the importance both of our constructing that story as carefully as possible, and of our distinguishing between story and history.

The same issues obtain in the wider story of Paul and its narrative world. From the total field of events he might have referred to, he has bounded his personal story, on the one end, with references to events oriented to his call by God to bring the Gospel to the Gentiles (e.g., Gal. 1:13–17), and on the other end, if the letter to Rome is, as many suspect, Paul's last extant letter, with references to a worrisome visit to Jerusalem in which he is going to bring a collection from the Gentiles to Jews. If this action is successful, he plans to visit Rome on his way to Spain, where he will continue his mission (Rom. 15:14–33). Although Paul himself never tells us what happened following his arrival in Jerusalem, *his* story is thematically governed by the relationship between his understanding of his mission and his understanding of the collection.[45] If *we* want to understand *his* story, we have to make sure that we understand *it* before moving on to historical constructions based on information from other texts, like the Acts of the Apostles which tells us *a* story about what happened when Paul arrived in Jerusalem (Acts 21:17–26:32).[46] Likewise, before we can use Acts we also have to understand *Luke's* story, lest we confuse it with Paul's and misinterpret both of them.[47] In order to explore the narrative worlds of the Letter to Philemon, of Paul, or of Luke-Acts, we have to begin with the worlds referred to in the letter, in the Pauline corpus, and in Luke-Acts.

Procedurally, therefore, it is necessary to think of the worlds of the letter and of Paul as concentric, interpenetrating circles, in which the smaller world of the letter is embedded in the larger world of Paul known from all of his letters, and in which this world is embedded in a wider world known from the vast array of other pertinent texts. The historian will deal with all of these, moving back and forth between them in his attempt to construct "history." We, however, will concentrate our explorations in the first two worlds because they are the most clearly related to one another, coming as they do from one and the same person and from a relatively limited period of time, perhaps no more than five years.[48] Were we to introduce other texts, we would be introducing other persons and other worlds, and with them innumerable other problems. In our explorations we will attempt to map the smallest world with care, and with equal care seek to map those portions of the wider world of Paul in which it is embedded.

THE SOCIOLOGY OF NARRATIVE WORLDS

Thus far, our focus has been largely literary. But having gained a more concrete sense of what a narrative world is, we can turn to the symbolic forms and social arrangements that sustain the lives of the actors who inhabit such worlds. Both of these, the forms and the arrangements, are what social scientists call *social facts*,[49] the one because it represents the structures of social relations within a group, the other because it represents the world of meanings maintained by the group. Social life is sustained both by systems of meanings and by systems of social relations, but also by the relations between the two systems. The link between them is linguistic and symbolic because the systems of social relations, like the world in which they occur, are represented in language and symbol, and therefore as "knowledge." Viewing language and symbol as together comprising a symbol system, Clifford Geertz has described symbol systems as models of and for social life and social worlds. They are *models of* such things because they represent both the way social life is in fact lived and the way in which the world is construed within a society. They are *models for* social life and for construing the world in one way rather than another, because they represent for ongoing generations how life is *to be lived* in a society and in a world like the ones represented in the symbol system.[50]

Before illustrating the roles of these social facts in the narrative worlds of Paul and of his Letter to Philemon, we need to locate our concerns with them in relation to the recent sociological study of New Testament writings. Whereas none of the recent literary criticism has attended to Paul's letters,[51] the letters have been the object of considerable sociological study of different kinds.[52]

Our concerns are different from others in two ways. The most significant way is that our focus is on the sociology of narrative worlds rather than of allegedly real or historical worlds, and for all of the reasons given above. None of the sociological studies deals with the narrative qualities of the world Paul or his letters refer to. Many of the conclusions arrived at in these studies are both relevant and valid for us, but because they lack a perception of point of view, plot, and closure, or more narrowly, of Paul's perspective on the world of which he is aware, this perspective, and its sociological implications, remains to be explored.[53]

The second way in which our concerns differ from others is that it is more *social anthropological* than sociological. Apart from the subfield known as the sociology of knowledge,[54] sociology is traditionally devoted to the study of social arrangements, with little emphasis on the symbolic forms or their relationship to the arrangements. It is rather social anthropology which brings together in a single enterprise symbol systems, social systems, and the relations between them.[55] The difference between sociological and social anthropological orientations to social phenomena can be seen by juxtaposing two quotations. The first is from Gerd Theissen, probably the foremost practitioner of sociological methods among New Testament scholars. The second is from T. O. Beidelman, an anthropologist with strong interests in the study of religion. The quote from Theissen contains a definition of what a sociological statement is.

> A sociological statement seeks to describe and explain interpersonal behavior with reference to those characteristics which transcend the personal. First of all, then, a sociological question is less concerned with what is individual than with what is typical, recurrent, general. Second, it is less concerned with the singular conditions of a specific situation than with structural relationships which apply to several situations. Therefore, a sociology of primitive Christianity has the task of describing and analyzing the interpersonal behavior of members of primitive Christian groups.[56]

Now Beidelman:

> A society is a shared way of behavior. We cannot get far in understanding a society before decoding the ways its members communicate their wants and needs to one another, and in order to do that, we must first understand the ways in which these persons see and define themselves and the world in which they live. In this sense, language is

the central and primary problem in social studies, although by language I mean far more than mere grammar, syntax, and vocabulary. What I mean is the sum total of ways in which the members of a society symbolize or categorize their experience so that they may give it order and form and thereby manipulate it and also deal with their fellows who share this experience with them. Language, then, includes not only words but gestures, facial expressions, clothing, and even household furnishings—in short, total symbolic behavior. Those with a common language share common values and perceptions and thus form a moral group, a kind of church.[57]

In Theissen's statement there is nothing that is in principle contrary to what we see in Beidelman's. Both are concerned with what is typical or social in the shaping and expressing of social relations within a society. Yet, from Theissen's statement and from his work in general, it is evident that he is principally concerned with identifying typical patterns of social behavior (i.e., with "social arrangements"), and with the relations between these patterns either over time (i.e., diachronically), as in Christianity's transformation of Hellenistic-Roman culture within the scope of about three centuries,[58] or within a single period of time (i.e., synchronically), as in the conflicts 1 Corinthians identifies in the Corinthian church.[59] Theissen is concerned with the social constants by which one can measure change, conflict, and deviance, all of which are the disciplinary concerns of the field of sociology. His work, moreover, is designed to describe and explain the *historical* sociology of early Christianity, whether it be that of Palestinian Christianity or of Pauline Christianity.[60] Theissen has made major contributions in both areas, and nothing I say is designed to minimize their value. My intent is rather to indicate that *other* sociological contributions can be made by coming at our biblical texts from another angle, one that is both sociological and literary. The quotation from Beidelman suggests how sociological things look from that angle of approach.

Beidelman's sociological interests are evident in his focus on shared ways of understanding and behavior. But his distinctively social anthropological approach is expressed in his perception of the relations between patterns of behavior and patterns of meaning within a closed social situation.[61] Typical of social anthropologists, Beidelman finds it necessary first to "decode" the ways in which a society's members "see and define themselves and the world in which they live." He views these ways as a language "in which the members of a society symbolize or categorize their experience." Such a "language" or system of meanings, such knowledge, enables people to give order and form to their experience and, behaviorally, "thereby manipulate it and also deal with their fellows who share this experience with them." This "language" therefore provides us with a means of comprehending the society's social systems or institutions, the social arrangements pertinent to its social life, such as "the family, kinship systems, political organization, legal procedures, religious cults, and the like."[62] Anthropologists observe directly how these institutions work in the everyday life of a people, and while observing them seek to relate them to one another and to the symbolic forms associated with them. Typically, therefore, the anthropologist moves back and forth between these social facts in order to comprehend the whole that they comprise, and all for the purpose of understanding what it means to be human (*anthropos*) in a world constructed out of these social facts. Which leads us back to narrative worlds. What is the relationship between the worlds explored by anthropologists and the narrative worlds we have been talking about?

The world of a narrative, or of a corpus of authorially related narratives, and the world of a people subject to anthropological scrutiny are first and foremost closed systems.[63] To be sure, neither can be described exhaustively. Each has its grey areas, and each may have predecessors, contemporaries, and successors.[64] But when and as such worlds are experienced, they comprise an internally ordered whole which is the ultimate object of interest, for it is the frame of reference in which the parts make sense. The reader of a narrative is therefore like an anthropologist to the extent that both are participant observers in other worlds.[65] Like the reader of *Anna Karenina* or of a James Bond novel, an Evans-Pritchard among the Nuer, or a Beidelman among the Kaguru, or a Turner among the Ndembu, must suspend both belief and disbelief in these worlds in order to comprehend life as it is lived in them.[66] Both the reader and the anthropologist "learn" these worlds by attending to the things referred to and done in them, to how they are referred to and done, and to why. The anthropologist's informant within a world is even comparable to the narrator of a story, for both tell us about what we see and even show things to us. And finally, as Geertz has argued, the process of anthropological analysis is "like that of the literary critic,"[67] while "anthropological interpretation is constructing a reading of what happens. . . ."[68] Both literary critics and anthropologists are concerned with the meanings of the actors' behavior within the actors' world of meanings. Life in narrative worlds is subject to the same kinds of constraints and motivations as life in "real" worlds.

The relationship between narrative and social worlds can be elaborated further by mapping literary and anthropological concerns on our earlier image of interpenetrating concentric circles. In this way, we can also relate these concerns to those of the historically minded biblical critic or reader.

It will be recalled that the smallest circle was that of the individual letter; for example, the letter to and story about Philemon. This circle is analogous to the single story available from a single anthropological informant, to a single novel, and to the one text the historian has from a certain time and place. The next larger circle was that of the corpus of Paul's letters and the world represented in them. It is analogous to the total repertoire of an informant, like that of the African sage, Ogotemmeli,[69] to the collected works of a novelist, to a corpus of historical texts from a single individual, like the letters of Pliny. In cases where authorial identity is submerged in communal identity, we can extend this circle, to include perhaps the fairy tales of a culture or even Cynic letters and the Dead Sea Scrolls. But this leads us into the largest circle, which in all cases represents the total amount of information available from all "informants" in a closed social and cultural situation. As suggested earlier, each of these circles is a valid object of study independent of the other circles, while ultimately the fullest understanding can only be attained by attending to them all in their interrelatedness. My comparison of anthropology with literary criticism is oriented to all three of the circles, but it focuses on the two smaller circles because they are the ones with which I am presently concerned.

But this view of the anthropologist's work has to be contrasted with another job anthropologists do in their capacity as comparativists, generalists, and theoreticians. Anthropologists study individual societies not only for the sake of describing *them*, but also for the purpose of comparing them with other societies in the hope that comparison will disclose some universal truths about "man."[70] Anthropologists are not concerned only with the culture of the Nuer, the Kaguru, and the Ndembu, but also with what such cultures as these can tell us about human culture as such. Anthropology is traditionally devoted to the study of both the cultures relative to individual societies and cultural universals. It is both relativistic and universalistic.[71] To be sure, many anthropologists view this polarity in terms of doing either one or the other thing, rather than both, but as a discipline anthropology is nevertheless caught up in the activities bounded by these two poles. In my comments thus far, however, I have emphasized the relativistic pole because I am concerned with the narrower worlds of the Letter to Philemon and of Paul. And this, too, differentiates my approach from that of others who in their sociological study have made use of social anthropology. Their tendency has been to apply certain preformed generalizations and theories, universals, to biblical texts and things referred to in them.[72] This practice has its place, and in chapter 2 I will indicate its relevance for us. In general, however, my preference is to employ such universals only where the texts seem to require them. I want to exhaust, as it were, the culture-specific patterns before going beyond them. That is why I have spent so much time trying to make concrete the abstract "universals" represented in the notions of "symbolic forms," "social arrangements," and "narrative world"— to show what kinds of concrete things they refer to. Accordingly, to illustrate further a social anthropological perspective on those social facts of symbolic forms and social arrangements that will concern us, let us consider a few central matters in the strange story with which this chapter began.

In discussing this story earlier, we observed that its most distinctive feature was its marvelous array of social categories. These categories are social facts in the sense that they represent categorizations of social positions acknowledged by Paul, those with him, and by Philemon and the church at his house (Philemon 1–2). Because Paul assumes that the addressees of his letter share these categories with him, we can assume that they represent the ways in which members of one society "see and define themselves in the world in which they live" (Beidelman). The categories thus form a social language, communal knowledge, and Paul's manipulation of them in his letter constitutes a social message encoded in this language. But just what this message is, is problematical because the people (actors) Paul refers to, including himself, occupy several positions simultaneously, in their self-understanding if not also in the process of social life. It appears that Paul's rhetorical manipulation of the categories is designed to secure a certain response from Philemon, but just what this response is, and how he signals his designs to Philemon, is unclear. He wants the master/brother/partner to receive his slave as a brother (vv. 15–17). But what does that mean, and what does it mean coming from Paul, who among other things is known to Philemon as a father/brother/prisoner/ambassador/partner? Does Paul want Philemon to free Onesimus, for whatever purposes,[73] or does he just want Philemon to be lovingly nice to his slave? How can we tell? More importantly, how can Philemon tell? The questions seem simple, but as we proceed with the decoding of Paul's language they become less so, because in the process a vast number of other questions are opened up, questions whose answers reveal much more about the letter and the story than appear on their surfaces.

The problem of decoding is not a linguistic one. With but one exception,[74] the pertinent language is readily translatable; we know enough about fathers, children, brothers, sisters, masters, and slaves to follow what Paul is saying. The problem rather arises when in decoding we attempt to pin down what the words refer to and how the things referred to relate to one another to make transparent both Paul's message and the dynamics of his story. Consider, for example, the strictly sociological, institutional things referred to. The master and slave positions occupied by Philemon and Onesimus clearly belong to a social institution in the story's narrative world. Philemon is literally and institutionally a master over his slave, Onesimus. This is a presupposition of both the letter and the story: Paul intercedes with the master in the slave's behalf because a) the slave has wronged his master, and b) Paul wants the master to treat the slave in a different way from what is presumably socially expected in the domain of master-slave relations. So far, so good. But problems of decoding arise when we see that while Paul is represented as Onesimus's father and Onesimus as his "child," Paul, Onesimus, and Philemon are also "brothers." Sociologically, this is language of kinship and the family. Yet here it is clearly used not literally, like the master-slave language, but symbolically and metaphorically. Paul is *not* Onesimus's father in a literal, that is, biological and legal sense, because he only becomes Onesimus's father (and brother) *after* Onesimus has run away from Philemon. Paul is therefore a metaphorical father, but even as such he is an institutional superior to an institutional inferior, his metaphorical child Onesimus. Let us assume for the moment that this institution is the church and that Paul's fatherhood is a metaphor for a role he plays in it.[75] If so, we now have a superior in one institution (Paul) interceding with a superior in another institution (Philemon) on behalf of a person who is an inferior in both institutions (Onesimus). Now, therefore, we no longer have a merely interpersonal problem, but also and significantly an inter-institutional problem. Paul's role language is used in different ways, that is, literally and metaphorically, to refer to social structural roles in different institutions, those in the world and those in the church. But the problem of decoding the institutional references of his language becomes even more complicated when we observe that Paul, Philemon, and Onesimus are also equals (brothers) within one of the institutions, the church, and that in this institution Philemon is probably also one of Paul's children (cf. Philemon 19b; see further chapter 1, below). Given these roles and relationships, Philemon would be a superior in one system (master), while in another he would be an inferior (child) to his equal (brother), and also an equal (brother) to his inferior (slave) in the first system! Enough said, for now. These examples make it clear that behind Paul's superficially homogeneous language there lies an intricate network of social roles and relationships that spans two different institutional domains. To decode Paul's role language, we need a sociological cipher as well as a dictionary of everyday language.

While enough has been said to indicate the bearing of some strictly sociological issues on the actors' actions, more needs to be said about another aspect of Paul's social categories, an aspect usually spoken of as theological. For whatever reasons we may have individually, I think we would all be inclined to agree that in Paul's story God and Jesus Christ are not actors in quite the same sense that Paul, Philemon, and Onesimus are actors. But regardless of our reasons, if we agree on this point we have another problem. For if God and Christ are not actors in the *same* sense, then in *what* sense are we to comprehend their roles, since the *same categories* used to identify them are used to identify actors like Paul, Philemon, and Onesimus? As in the institutional reference of Paul's language, so also here. There is no lexical distinction between Paul and God as fathers, between Philemon and Christ as masters, and between, for example, Jesus and believers as slaves or as sons. Yet, as in the area of institutional reference, there are clearly significant distinctions to be made between actors like Paul, Philemon, and Onesimus on the one hand, and God and Christ on the other. Since we have agreed on this, we have to take seriously our reasons for doing so. The question is, on what basis are these distinctions to be made? The answer to this question is also fundamental for our entire enterprise.

In examining the institutional reference of Paul's role language we found that he used master-slave terms literally to refer to worldly social institutions and kinship terms metaphorically to refer to churchly institutions. In order to understand the differences between the actors with whom we are now concerned, we must first go beyond the limitations of the institutional example, in which the terms master and slave were used literally, and observe that Paul also uses master-slave terms metaphorically. Christ is the Lord/master of all believers, including Paul, and they are therefore all slaves of Christ.[76] Indeed, in Paul's wider narrative world we find him describing Christ himself as having assumed the form of a slave when he was born in human form, and as having been named Lord of all only after his death in the form of a slave (Phil. 2:5–11). This master-slave language is metaphorical because it is not tied to the worldly social institution of slavery, as the same language is when it is used of Philemon and Onesimus. Jesus is not a master *in* the world and its institutions; he is master *over* all. His being in "the form of a slave" is clearly a metaphor for having the human form of existence, but the idea that there is only one master over all other actors also explodes the literal, worldly understanding in which there are many masters, each with his own slaves. Christ's lordship is therefore neither supported by the social institution in which the idea of master is grounded, nor is his lordship contained within that institution's boundaries. *God* made him master over *all* other actors, be they in heaven, on earth, or under the earth (Phil. 2:9–10). And God, too, is a metaphorical father for the same reasons that Christ is a metaphorical master, for God is not a father either by virtue of or as defined by the kinship institutions of worldly society. Just as Christ's metaphorical lordship renders all believers as his slaves, so also does God's metaphorical fatherhood render all believers as his children, and therefore as brothers and sisters (siblings) of one another.[77] Thus, too, the institutional identity of believers as metaphorical children of God and slaves of Christ is determined by their relationship to God as their father and to Christ as their master. Before we explore this relationship, which proves to be the key to answering the question about the distinction between believers, God, and Christ as actors, we need to update our earlier comments about Paul's literal and metaphorical use of the same terms.

It is now apparent that Paul has borrowed the role names of master, slave, father, child, sons, brothers, and sisters from the kinship and master-slave institutions in the world outside the church. But because he transforms the literal reference of the role names taken from these worldly institutions into a metaphorical reference to roles in the church, we can see that the world and the church are two separate domains within Paul's narrative world. What is more, the relationship between these two domains is one of dependent opposition because one domain, that of the church, has transformed the literal language of the other, the world, into metaphors which represent an opposition between the two domains. The believer's identity as a believer is represented by borrowed language, but the believer is not governed by the institutions from which it was borrowed. The role names are the same in both domains, but in the domain of the world they refer to the literal relationships between actors, namely to many fathers and many masters, each of whom has his own children and his own slaves, all of whom are governed by institutional rules of behavior to be followed by the role players. In contrast, within the domain of the church the same role names are also used to refer to two different sets of actors, one set of which is superior to the other set, but with strikingly different significance. The principal difference is that the actors of one set, God and Christ alone, serve as the father and master of *all* of the actors in the other set. In the domain of the church there is only one father and one master, and all of the other actors are equal to one another as sib-

25

lings and as slaves by virtue of their relationship to the one father and the one master.[78]

Closely related to this point of difference are two others. One is that the father and the master are *not* participants in the concrete social unit comprised of their children and slaves. They are not, that is to say, members of the church as a social institution in the way that worldly fathers and masters are members of the kinship and master-slave institutions. Christ, for example, is not a social presence with his slaves in the same sense that Philemon is a social presence to his slave Onesimus, nor is God present in the social life of his children in the same way that they are present to each other.

The second related point of difference is that in addition to the absence of the father and the master from the social institution of the church there is also an absence in the church of the worldly institutional rules governing the relations between kin and between masters and their slaves. There are, of course, rules governing social relations in the church, but they are not the same rules as those that govern the worldly institutions from which the kinship and master-slave language has been borrowed. The church therefore borrowed considerable language and values from worldly institutions, but it did not borrow or replicate the institutions. Thus, while the church adopted some things from the world's kinship and master-slave systems, it both transformed what it adopted and declined to adopt everything. Kinship and master-slave relations in the domain of the church are therefore *like* the corresponding relations in the domain of the world, but they are so far from being identical as to be opposed. For in the social domain of the church no actors play the superior role of father or master over other actors because all are equals under one father and one master (1 Cor. 8:5–6). Paul's self-proclaimed role as a father of the likes of Onesimus is a sociologically significant exception, but we will find that it is an exception that both proves the rule and opens up the paradox of there being a social hierarchy within the egalitarian community, of the church (see chapter 2, below). Let it again suffice for the present to note that Paul self-consciously minimizes his social superiority as a father by viewing himself as a father who is in enslavement with his children (Phil. 2:22), and indeed as a father who is a slave to his children (1 Cor. 9:19, 3:21–23; 2 Cor. 1:24; 4:5). Paul not only rejects the legitimacy of worldly social distinctions in the institution of the church (cf. Gal. 3:27–28), but he also finds himself terribly uneasy with the distinctiveness of his own social role in that domain.

That all believers are equals as slaves and siblings under the lordship of Christ and the fatherhood of God raises further questions about the relationship between God's fatherhood and Paul's but also between Christ's lordship and Philemon's. These relationships are as relevant to the distinction between believers, God, and Christ as the difference we have just seen between Paul's literal and metaphorical uses of role names, but oddly enough they are relevant because Paul never addresses the questions about them at all. His fatherhood and Philemon's lordship are never spoken of in connection with God's fatherhood and Christ's lordship. Paul's failure to address the questions posed by these at least linguistic relationships is relevant because his failure reflects the qualitative and quantitative differences between his fatherhood and God's and between Philemon's lordship and Christ's. As we have just seen, Paul and Philemon are at best father and master of *some* people while God and Christ are father and master of *all* believers. God and Christ are therefore qualitatively and quantitatively different actors from any others in Paul's stories. To develop this distinction, we have to make yet another.

In addition to the distinction between the different social domains in Paul's narrative world, we also have to distinguish between the different spheres in which the actors act, for these spheres of action entail other differences between believers, God, and Christ. From Paul's wider narrative world known from other letters, we can see that during the time of Paul's stories the sphere in which God and Christ are actors is located in heaven, and the sphere in which both believers and their predecessors and contemporaries are actors is located on earth (cf. Phil. 3:20–21; 1 Thess. 1:9–10; 1 Cor. 15:42–57). Moreover, corresponding to the distinction between these spheres of activity is the distinction between the *form* of the actors who occupy the respective spheres, for God and Christ have an imperishable heavenly form and believers a perishable earthly form (1 Cor. 15:42–57; Phil. 2:5–11; 3:20–21; Rom. 8:12–30; 2 Cor. 4:7—5:10). To be sure, there is, has been, and will be communication between the actors who inhabit the two spheres, but the exceptional character of the communication only underscores the differences between them. Christ's assumption of human form after relinquishing his divine form (Phil. 2:5–11), the gift to believers of God's spirit or his son's (Rom. 8:12–17; Gal. 4:4–7; 1 Cor. 2:12), "revelation" (Gal. 1:15; 2 Cor. 12:1–9), and the return of Christ from heaven in the future (Phil. 3:20–21; 1 Thess. 1:9–10) all represent exceptional transit between the heavenly sphere and the earthly. God and Christ therefore enjoy role names identical to those used in the domains of both the church and the world, but they are actors of a different sort from those who inhabit those two domains of the earthly sphere. Both believers and non-believers inhabit *a social universe* of daily face-to-face encounters with one another, while God and Christ in-

habit *a symbolic universe* in which they do not encounter the inhabitants of the social universe on a daily face-to-face basis. God and
Christ are absent from the social universe but present in the symbolic universe. Indeed, and importantly, they are present in the
social universe only as objects of knowledge, and therefore they are
social facts, not social actors. On the other hand, however, because
God and Christ are known in terms of role names derived from the
earthly social universe, their symbolic universe is also conceived of
by believers in social terms, however metaphorical they may be. For
this reason, if we were to use traditional theological language to
describe these universes we could say that we are interested in both
the theology of Paul's sociology and the sociology of his theology.
But the very fact that our interests *could* be described in this way
raises for us yet another issue, for we are *not* interested in Paul's
theology as such. What concerns us are the two spheres or universes,
the social and the symbolic, and the relations between them in
Paul's stories, and therefore in his narrative world. For the narrative
worlds in which narrative actions take place are comprised of both
social universes and symbolic universes, of both social arrangements and symbolic forms. Our concerns must, therefore, be
sharply distinguished from those of theology.

It is evident from our reflections on the different domains and
spheres in which Paul's actors operate that the relations between
Paul, Philemon, and Onesimus, or between any other set of believers, cannot be fully comprehended by exploring their relations only
in the institutional terms of their social universe. That other sphere
in and from which God and Christ function must also be explored
both in terms of its own internal characteristics and in terms of its
significance in the sphere of the believers' social universe. On the
one hand, this means that we have to modify Geertz's distinction
between symbolic forms and social arrangements by ceasing to
speak of the social categories of everyday life as symbolic, although
they are such in a certain sense, and assign these categories to the
realm of social arrangements. By doing this, we will be able to treat
the symbolic forms in the context of Paul's symbolic universe, in
which God and Christ are the principal actors (see further chapter 3,
below). However, when we speak of God and Christ as actors within
a symbolic universe we also raise the question of the relationship
between this universe and theology, which is the more usual form of
discourse about these actors. In fact, what we are speaking about
in terms of symbolic forms and social arrangements, or of social universes and symbolic universes, can be expressed in
theological terms as the relationship between community theology and community order (Hainz).[79] For this reason, we need to

understand why these theological terms are inadequate for our concerns.

Three points will suffice to explain our avoidance of thinking theologically about Paul's letters and stories. The first two points are related to one another, for (1) Paul not only fails to make a linguistic distinction between the role names given to the different sets of actors in his stories but he also (2) treats God and Christ as *actors* despite their being actors of a different sort from all others. The first point, therefore, is linguistic, and the second is literary. Because the language identifies the roles and relations between a number of characters in Paul's stories, our concern is with the actions of the actors as these are informed both by the emplotment of their actions and by the social roles they play in the stories. Simply, our concern is with *the sociology of narrative actions.* The third point (3) is also a sociological one insofar as we are concerned with *the sociology of the knowledge possessed by the actors* in the social universe of Paul's narrative world.[80] On the one hand, this knowledge pertains to their social arrangements, and, on the other hand, it pertains to their symbolic universe, of which we have glimpsed only a small part in connection with the actors God and Christ. Both kinds of knowledge bear in different ways on the actors' actions, but with respect to the role of theology the knowledge concerning the symbolic universe is critical, for God, Christ, and their actions can be viewed in the terms of either theology or of symbolic universes. What is the difference between these terms?

From the perspective of the sociology of knowledge, theology and symbolic universes are distinguished as representing two different kinds of knowledge.[81] Broadly, a symbolic universe is the "world" *as it is known* and therefore as the knowledge of it shapes one's experience of it, not as something that exists apart from what is known. A symbolic universe is the "world" *as it is viewed,* not as something that exists apart from the way we view it. To be sure, there is something out there outside of us and apart from our knowledge of it, but it is not a "world" apart from what we know about it. In this respect, therefore, "worlds" are like "histories." As we saw in our discussion of history as story, there are events "out there" in the past, but they are not "history" until we compose a story about them. "Histories" are authorial constructions and "worlds" are social constructions. Indeed, "history" is also a part of every symbolic universe, for it also refers to what we know about our total universe. Like knowledge about God and Christ, knowledge about the past is both a social fact and symbolic because it represents realities that are not experienced in everyday life. Theology, on the other hand, is for the sociology of knowledge a kind of knowledge that is the product of systematic reflection upon a symbolic universe, and indeed of reflection that serves to maintain that universe when it is in some kind of jeopardy, as for example from the threats of doubt, of disagreement, or of competing symbolic universes. Theology is, therefore, a kind of knowledge that is produced to defend and maintain the knowledge comprising a symbolic universe, and for this reason we can speak of a symbolic universe as a primary (pre-reflective) form of knowledge and theology as a secondary (reflective) form that is dependent on it. It is in this light, then, that in exploring the symbolic universe of Paul's narrative world we will not be concentrating on his theology but on the universe about which he theologizes. On the one hand, this universe will be seen to have a different *form* from theology, for it has the form of a narrative, or at least of a drama that Paul represents in narrative form—as a story about what God and Christ have done, are doing, and will do in connection with the earthly sphere of the other actors in the story. Paul's theologizing refers to this story and provides argumentative elaborations of it, and for this reason we will often have to work through his theologizing to the symbolic universe it presupposes. On the other hand, his theologizing will concern us more than his theology. It will concern us, however, not in connection with his symbolic universe (chapter 3), but in connection with his social relations (chapter 2). Paradoxically, although theological knowledge is about the knowledge we find in symbolic universes, Paul's theologizing is more important for us than his theology because his theologizing takes place as a form of social relations between himself and other actors in the sphere of their social universe. His theologizing is a means of securing certain kinds of behavior from the other actors by appealing to their shared symbolic universe. Indeed, he seeks to secure certain behavior in order to secure their symbolic universe. Thus, we will consider Paul's theologizing in our exploration of the universe of social relations in his stories, and we will seek to penetrate through his theology in order to explore his symbolic universe.

THE PROJECT

In the following chapters we will explore matters that are traditionally distinguished as literary, historical, and theological. But because we will be bringing new insights to bear on them from the fields of literary criticism, anthropology, and sociology, we will be dealing with these matters in new ways.

Since we have set as our objectives the exploration of Paul's narrative world, our first task will be to transform Paul's Letter to Philemon into a story. Thus, in chapter 1, "From Letter to Story—and Back: Toward a Narratology and Sociology of Letters," we will introduce a method for transforming letters into stories. The method will disclose the actions of the actors in Paul's story about Philemon, thereby making it possible to relate the emplotment of his story to the rhetorical composition of his letter, which will provide us with new insights into both of them. This chapter will also provide us with an opportunity to make some observations about the sociology of the letter as a form of communication between actors in a letter's story, and this will help to prepare the way for chapter 2, "Social Structures and Social Relations in the Story of Philemon." Here we will view the actions of the actors in the story as social relations and seek to determine from these relations the sociological structures underlying them. This will enable us to undertake both a sociology of Paul's story about Philemon and a sociology of his wider narrative world, for in order to understand the story we will have to go beyond its "world" into the "world" of Paul's letters generally. If chapter 2 therefore represents a new approach to matters usually considered in historical terms, chapter 3, "Symbolic Universe and Social Relations in the Story of Philemon," represents a new approach to matters that are usually considered in theological terms. Whereas in chapter 2 we will be interested in the sociological constraints upon the actors' actions, in chapter 3 we will be concerned with cognitive constraints, with the symbolic universe and its systems of meanings which both enable the actors to understand themselves and their world by providing them with *a* world, and motivate their behavior within it. Here, too, we will have to go beyond the letter to and story about Philemon in order to reconstruct the systems of meanings that are alluded to or presupposed in them. Thus, in chapter 1 we will concentrate on the plotted actions of the actors in Paul's letter and story, in chapter 2 on the relationship between these actions, now viewed as social relations, and their underlying sociological structures, and in chapter 3 on the overarching symbolic universe that provides meaning to and motivation for the actors' behavior. In a brief concluding chapter, we will review some of the results of our explorations of Paul's letter and its story.

Finally, it will be apparent in each chapter that the Letter to Philemon serves as a case study for rediscovering Paul through the use of new methods. Exploration of this letter's story and its narrative world leads us into the wider story of Paul and its narrative world because the latter is the most immediate context of the former. To be sure, Paul's wider narrative world has its own context in a yet wider world, but for the methodological reasons given earlier we are limiting our exploration to the world projected by the undisputed letters of Paul. The relationship between this world and its context requires another exploration by explorers who are more suited for it than I am. I will be satisfied if the results of our exploration will assist them as much as I have been assisted by the results of their past journeys. Although I have chosen to follow a different route from theirs, my indebtedness to them is vastly greater than my acknowledgments below can indicate. Our routes are different and our equipment is different, too, but only the results they lead to can tell us how valuable they are. And that judgment, too, must be left for others to make.

NOTES

1. Clifford Geertz, *Islam Observed: Religious Developments in Morocco and Indonesia* (New Haven and London: Yale Univ. Press, 1968), 2.

2. Many forms of literary criticism and sociology are being employed by biblical critics. I know of no survey of current biblical literary criticism, but the range of approaches can be seen in the journal *Semeia*, or in *NTA*, wherever the word "literary" occurs in a title. My own understanding of literary issues may be found in my *Literary Criticism for New Testament Critics* (Philadelphia: Fortress Press, 1978), 9–48; and my "Literary Criticism in Biblical Studies" in *Orientation by Disorientation, Studies in Literary Criticism and Biblical Literary Criticism*, ed. Richard A. Spencer (Pittsburgh: Pickwick Press, 1980), 25–50. Other literary essays are in this volume. For recent surveys of sociological studies and extensive bibliography, see John Schütz's introduction to Gerd Theissen, *The Social Setting of Pauline Christianity: Essays on Corinth*, ed. and trans. John Schütz (Philadelphia: Fortress Press; Edinburgh: T. &. T. Clark, 1982); Robin Scroggs, "The Sociological Interpretation of the New Testament: The Present State of Research," *NTS* 26 (1980): 164–79; and John H. Elliott, *A Home for the Homeless: A Sociological Exegesis of 1 Peter, Its Situations and Strategy* (Philadelphia: Fortress Press; London: SCM Press, 1981), 1–20. For further social anthropological literature on the Bible by both biblical critics and anthropologists, see Gillian Feeley-Harnik, *The Lord's Table* (Philadelphia: Univ. of Pennsylvania Press, 1981), 1–23 (Feeley-Harnik is an anthropologist) and Bruce J. Malina, *The New Testament World: Insights from Cultural Anthropology* (Atlanta: John Knox Press, 1981). As I will indicate below, there are differences between sociological and social anthropological approaches to sociology. *Int.* 37/3 (1982) is devoted to sociology and biblical studies and contains three essays on the New Testament: Bruce Malina, "The Social Sciences and Biblical Interpretation" (229–42); John Gager, "Shall We Marry Our Enemies? Sociology and the New Testament" (256–65); and Wayne Meeks, "The Social Context of Pauline Theology" (266–77). A number of other sociological studies of Paul are cited in chap. 2, below.

3. I exclude from the Pauline corpus the traditionally disputed letters: 2 Thessalonians, Colossians, Ephesians, and the Pastoral epistles, 1 and 2 Timothy and Titus. However, where relevant to the Letter to Philemon, I

will consider certain items in the disputed letters. As for the notion of "narrative world," it is not itself a term usually employed by literary critics, although they do speak of "story world," "worlds of the story," and of the "imaginative world" or "fictional world" of literature. Following Umberto Eco, *The Role of the Reader: Explorations of the Semiotics of Texts* (Bloomington: Indiana Univ. Press, 1979), esp. 200–226, which is on the subject of narrative worlds, I employ the notion to refer to the world as it is represented in narrative texts. In *Literary Criticism for New Testament Critics*, pp. 9–48, I used the notion to represent what Roman Jakobson speaks of as the referential function of messages, and below I will speak of referential worlds and narrative worlds interchangeably. Apart from Eco's very technical work, I know of no literary critical study that focuses specifically on the worlds of narratives, but M. H. Abrams provides some historical background for the idea in a section of *The Mirror and the Lamp* (New York: W. W. Norton & Co., 1958) entitled "The Poem as Heterocosm," 272–85. René Wellek and Austin Warren address the subject in their *Theory of Literature*, 3d, new rev. ed. (New York: Harcourt, Brace & World, 1956), under the heading of "The Nature and Modes of Narrative Fiction," 212–25. Their discussion is strongly influenced by the phenomenological study by Roman Ingarden, *The Literary Work of Art*, trans. George C. Grabowicz (Evanston, Il.: Northwestern Univ. Press, 1973), especially 217–54. Easier to read because less technical is C. S. Lewis, "On Stories," in C. S. Lewis, ed., *Essays Presented to Charles Williams* (Grand Rapids: Wm. B. Eerdmans, 1966), 99–105. See also on the "world" of the fairy tale, Max Lüthi, *Once Upon a Time: On the Nature of Fairy Tales*, trans. Lee Chadeayne and Paul Gottwald (Bloomington and London: Indiana Univ. Press, 1976). The notion of narrative worlds is implicitly dealt with, in connection with what narrators show and tell readers, in Boris Uspensky's *A Poetics of Composition*, trans. Valentina Zavarin and Susan Wittig (Berkeley and Los Angeles: Univ. of California Press, 1973), on which see my " 'Point of View' in Mark's Narrative," *Semeia* 12 (1978): 97–121. Finally, my concern in speaking of narrative worlds is to indicate both that the world of a narrative is a literary construction, and that the events which take place in that world have a narrative quality. This concern will be explained further in the course of this chapter.

4. The alternative readings of "ambassador" and "old man" derive from the ambiguous meaning of the Greek word *presbytēs* in v. 9, which can refer to both "old man" and "ambassador" or "envoy," although another word, *presbeutēs*, more commonly renders the latter. See the commentaries on this verse. My reasons for preferring the meaning "ambassador" are given in chap. 2.

5. Although little critical jargon will appear in this study, its theoretical framework is that of the phenomenological semiotics discussed in my "Literary Criticism in Biblical Studies."

6. C. F. D. Moule, *The Epistles of Paul the Apostle to the Colossians and to Philemon* (Cambridge: Cambridge Univ. Press, 1957), 19.

7. Ibid., 21.

8. Literary historians criticize the text-centered "New Critics" of being

ahistorical because they deny or minimize the relevance of historical contexts for understanding texts. See below on Texts and Contexts. The range of issues involved in the relationship between history and sociology is delineated in: Claude Lévi-Strauss, "History and Anthropology," in C. Lévi-Strauss, *Structural Anthropology*, trans. C. Jacobson and B. G. Schoepf (New York: Basic Books, 1963), 1–27; E. E. Evans-Pritchard, "Anthropology and History," in Evans-Pritchard, *Essays in Social Anthropology* (New York: Free Press, 1963), 46–65; and Robert Bellah, "Durkheim and History," in Robert A. Nisbet, with selected essays, *Emile Durkheim* (Englewood Cliffs, N.J.: Prentice-Hall, 1965).

9. The literature cited in Schütz's introduction to Theissen's *Social Setting* is fully consistent with the historical concerns of the several types of sociological projects programmatically elaborated by Jonathan Z. Smith in "The Social Description of Early Christianity," *RSR* 1/1 (1975): 19–25. See also Robin Scroggs, "The Sociological Interpretation of the New Testament: The Present State of Research." The lack of surveys of biblical literary criticism makes it difficult to document its historical concerns. Suffice it to say that while this criticism is not the traditional historical criticism, it nevertheless respects the historical character of biblical texts. I have tried to relate literary to historical criticism in *Literary Criticism for New Testament Critics*, in which I was asked to deal specifically with this relationship, and in "Literary Criticism in Biblical Studies." For an expression of concern about new critical developments, see Leander E. Keck, on "Will the Historical-Critical Method Survive? Some Observations," in *Orientation by Disorientation*, 115–27.

10. Virtually every book on literary criticism deals with problems of text and context, and Wellek and Warren's classic *Theory of Literature* is structured around the distinction between text (intrinsic criticism) and context (extrinsic criticism); see especially chap. 1, "Literature and Literary Study," and chap. 4, "Literary Theory, Criticism, and History." See also for background to this paragraph René Wellek, "The Term and Concept of Literary Criticism," in his *Concepts of Criticism* (New Haven: Yale Univ. Press, 1963), 21–36.

11. See, e.g., Thomas Daniel Young, ed., *The New Criticism and After* (Charlottesville: Univ. of Virginia Press, 1976); and Robert Detweiler, "After the New Criticism: Contemporary Methods of Literary Interpretation," in *Orientation by Disorientation*, 3–23, which elaborates on the more recent developments referred to below in this paragraph.

12. See Wellek and Warren, *Theory of Literature*, chaps. 1, 4, 7–11, and 19; René Wellek, "The Theory of Literary History," *Travaux du Cercle linguistique de Prague* 4 (1936): 173–91, and the journal, *New Literary History*.

13. I am indebted to Umberto Eco for this sketch of the discussion concerning textual determinacy. He drew it in response to a question of mine during a panel discussion at Vanderbilt University in June, 1981. On E. D. Hirsch, see his *Validity in Interpretation* (New Haven: Yale Univ. Press, 1967) and *The Aims of Interpretation* (Chicago: Univ. of Chicago Press, 1976).

14. On Jacques Derrida, see Jonathan Culler, *On Deconstruction: Theory and Criticism after Structuralism* (Ithaca, N.Y.: Cornell Univ. Press, 1982).

See also Josué V. Harrari, ed., *Textual Strategies: Perspectives in Post-Structuralist Criticism* (Ithaca, N.Y.: Cornell Univ. Press, 1979).

15. Apropos of n. 13, Eco, author of *The Role of the Reader*, locates himself alongside Wolfgang Iser, author of *The Act of Reading: A Theory of Aesthetic Response* (Baltimore: Johns Hopkins Univ. Press, 1978).

16. Psychological interpretation derives other information from theories of mental operations. See, e.g., Shoshana Felman, ed., *Literature and Psychoanalysis: The Question of Reading: Otherwise* (Baltimore: Johns Hopkins Univ. Press, 1982).

17. As noted earlier, commentaries and handbooks always have a section concerned with the occasion for writing.

18. For further discussion of referential history, see my *Literary Criticism for New Testament Critics*, 9–23 and 33–39. An illustration of the problematical relationship between referential history and "actual" history is given on pp. 81–92 of that book. The illustration is relevant for our concerns in the present essay because it provides reason to distrust much of Luke's portrait of Paul's activities.

19. See n. 3, above.

20. For extended discussion of the possible relationships between the authors and narrators of stories, see Wayne Booth, *The Rhetoric of Fiction*, 2d ed. (Chicago: Univ. of Chicago Press, 1983); and Seymour Chatman, *Story and Discourse: Narrative Structure in Fiction and Film* (Ithaca, N.Y.: Cornell Univ. Press, 1978), chaps. 4 and 5.

21. This is readily evident from a comparison of the different representations of the same episodes in Matthew, Mark, and Luke, or of their total picture of Jesus' career, or of any one of the four canonical Gospels with any other of the four.

22. In contrast with letters, there is in narratives no necessary link between the times referred to and the time of writing, although there may be such a link in individual narratives. For example, temporal links are not made in parables like the Sower or the Good Samaritan, whereas a link is relevant, say, in the Gospel of Mark (see my "When Is the End Not the End? Literary Reflections on the Ending of Mark's Narrative," *Int.* 34 [1980]: 151–66). The nature of the continuity each Gospel narrator envisions between the times he refers to and the time of writing differs. But this is a problem for further study. In Paul's letters, however, there is a continuity between the past, present, and future times he refers to. The past and future events referred to contribute to the meaning of the present event of writing. For example, Paul's retrospective autobiographical comments in Galatians 1—2 refer to past events he thinks are pertinent to the occasion for writing that letter. The autobiographical comments respond to a charge made just prior to writing, that he is a man-pleaser, while his references in those comments to his having *dis*pleased certain men, those whom he was apparently charged with pleasing, serve to link his accusers with them. Paul thus uses his autobiographical references to turn his accusers' charges back upon them. Not only did he displease those whom his accusers charged him with pleasing, but the accusers who required the circumcision of Gentile believers were on this point also in agreement with those whom he was

accused of pleasing, since James, Peter, and Barnabas agreed with this requirement. The referential past of Paul's earlier life is thereby linked to the contextual present.

23. See further below on "History as Story," and chap. 1 for a full discussion both of the events referred to in the Letter to Philemon and their narrative quality. Suffice it to say for now that the links are represented in terms of motives, both "because" motives and "in-order-to" motives (on this distinction between kinds of motives see Alfred Schutz, *The Phenomenology of the Social World*, trans. George Walsh and Frederick Lehnert (Evanston, Il.: Northwestern Univ. Press, 1967), 86–96. The event of Paul's writing is (because-) motivated by the past events of Onesimus's running away from Philemon, coming to Paul, and being converted by him, and by the legal obligations Paul has vis-à-vis the returning of a runaway slave. On the other hand, the event of writing is (in-order-to-) motivated by Paul's desire to have Philemon receive the returned Onesimus as a brother, both the return and the reception being future events in the story of Paul, Onesimus, and Philemon.

24. The distinction between primary and secondary sources is best used of original texts and scholarly texts about them, not for making distinctions among original texts, even in narratives, since both contextual and referential history have to be constructed from them.

25. See Chatman, *Story and Discourse*; and for showing and telling, Booth, *The Rhetoric of Fiction*.

26. The literature is considerable. The following are good discussions and surveys containing further bibliographical references: Roy Pascal, "Narrative Fictions and Reality: A Comment on Frank Kermode's *The Sense of an Ending*," in *Novel* 11 (1977): 40–50; Paul Ricoeur, "The Narrative Function," *Semeia* 13/2 (1978): 177–202; Hayden White, "The Narrativization of Real Events," in W. J. T. Mitchell, ed., *On Narrative* (Chicago: Univ. of Chicago Press, 1981), 249–54, and this entire volume, which is comprised of essays that originally appeared in *Critical Inquiry* 7/1 (1980) and 7/4 (1981). See also Hayden White, *Topics of Discourse: Essays in Cultural Criticism* (Baltimore: Johns Hopkins Univ. Press, 1978).

27. Hayden White, "The Narrativization of Real Events," 745.

28. Roy Pascal, "Narrative Fictions and Reality."

29. Hayden White has shown that the appearance of repeatability in "history" is created by imposing on events biographical, evolutionary, or literary models which make the set of events to be explained look like other sets of events we also know or understand in terms of such impositions. See also White's study of nineteenth-century historiography, *Metahistory: The Historical Imagination in Nineteenth-Century Europe* (Baltimore: Johns Hopkins Univ. Press, 1973).

30. The most systematic study of point of view is Boris Uspensky's *Poetics of Composition*. See also Booth, *The Rhetoric of Fiction*; Chatman, *Story and Discourse*; Susan Sniader Lanser, *The Narrative Act: Point of View in Prose Fiction* (Princeton: Princeton Univ. Press, 1981); and for further literature my " 'Point of View' in Mark's Narrative." Pascal speaks more narrowly of the retrospective aspect of point of view.

31. This is certainly the impression one receives from Uspensky's *Poetics of Composition*, but see his comments on pp. 127–29 for other aspects of composition. His notion of the semantic aspect refers to what I am calling the referential aspect, and the syntactic to what I call the poetic. Plot, as I use the term, is both syntactical and poetic, and therefore plot and point of view overlap. Uspensky's pragmatic aspect is related to the notion of closure, since for him pragmatics is concerned "with the relations between the text and the audience" (p. 127). However, semantics, syntactics, and pragmatics, like plot, point of view, and closure, are analytic distinctions, made to isolate different but related aspects of texts. Uspensky's three aspects are also related to Roman Jakobson's communications model discussed in pp. 24–48 of my *Literary Criticism for New Testament Critics*.

32. This option is an example of where psychological criticism may be relevant to compositional analysis. However, psychological interpretation would approach the composition from the contextual perspective of the author/narrator's psychological make-up.

33. On this understanding of plot, see pp. 24–48 of *Literary Criticism for New Testament Critics*. For a recent discussion of problems pertaining to the notion of plot, see Kieran Egan, "What is a Plot?" *New Literary History* 9 (1978): 455–73.

34. Pascal, "Narrative Fictions and Reality," 42.

35. On this addition to Pascal's formulation, see Barbara Herrnstein Smith, *Poetic Closure* (Chicago: Univ. of Chicago Press, 1968). For a study of closure in a biblical text, see my "When Is the End Not the End? Literary Reflection on the Ending of Mark's Narrative."

36. Pascal, "Narrative Fictions and Reality," 42.

37. See further the next section, on "Paul's Narrative World," and chap. 1.

38. On the exclusion of letters of disputed authorship from this corpus, see n. 3 above, and for discussion of individual letters in dispute such introductory handbooks as Werner Kümmel's *Introduction to the New Testament*, rev. ed. and trans. Howard C. Kee (Nashville: Abingdon Press, 1975).

39. For an illustration of this point, see chap. 4, "Narrative World and Real World in Luke-Acts," in my *Literary Criticism for New Testament Critics*.

40. Such information is regularly noted in scholarly commentaries. Probably the best of these on Philemon is by Eduard Lohse, *Colossians and Philemon*, Hermeneia, trans. W. R. Poehlmann and R. J. Karris, and ed. Helmut Koester (Philadelphia: Fortress Press, 1971). For other commentaries, see Lohse's bibliography on pp. 210–14, to which should be added Peter Stuhlmacher, *Der Brief an Philemon*, EKK (Zürich: Benziger Verlag Neukirchener Verlag, 1975). See also his bibliography on pp. 11–16. For a very full description of Paul's social world from a historical rather than literary perspective, see Wayne Meeks, *The First Urban Christians: The Social World of the Apostle Paul* (New Haven: Yale Univ. Press, 1983).

41. Regardless of his conclusions, one of the finest examples of how a historical critic usually works and thinks is Morton Smith's *The Secret*

Gospel (New York: Harper & Row, 1973). For a further illustration see my review of this and a related study by Smith, in *Southern Humanities Review* 8 (1974): 525–31.

42. I am not denying here that we know things about Paul and his "real world" from other sources, like the Book of Acts. The limitation is rather methodological: all we know of the *story* of each letter is learned from the letter.

43. Contrast, for example, the apparent quotations of other points of view in 1 Corinthians with the imputation of other points of view to the addresses in Galatians. See also Romans, where points of view other than Paul's are represented in the form of rhetorical questions. A systematic study of how points of view other than Paul's are represented in his letters would be most useful.

44. Even if we had information about Philemon from other sources than this letter, our method requires us to focus on him as a character in Paul's story. Similarly, we only know Paul himself from what he tells us, or from what we can infer from his role as the narrator of his stories. And here, too, Booth's distinctions between authors and narrators is pertinent (*The Rhetoric of Fiction*).

45. My point here is limited to Paul's personal story. In fact, the total world envisioned by Paul, his symbolic universe, begins temporally with creation and ends with the eschaton; the mission-collection story is meaningful only when it is set in the context of the creation-eschaton story which, as Paul understands it, is God's story. On this, see further the discussion in chap. 3, below. The best study to date of the mission-collection theme in Paul's thought is Dieter Georgi, *Die Geschichte der Kollekte des Paulus für Jerusalem*, TF 38 (Hamburg-Bergstedt: Herbert Reich, Evangelischer Verlag GmbH, 1965). See also Keith F. Nickle, *The Collection: A Study in Paul's Strategy*, SBT 48 (London: SCM Press, 1966).

46. Luke, despite the suggestion that he was present on Paul's arrival (Acts 21:17ff.: "we"), seems to know nothing about the collection. On the other hand, from Luke's description of Paul's arrest upon arrival, it would appear that "historically" Paul's bringing of the collection to Jerusalem resulted in the realization of his worst fears as expressed in Rom. 15:31. On the problems of evaluating Acts 21—26, see, e.g., Ernst Haenchen, *The Acts of the Apostles: A Commentary*, trans. Bernard Noble and Gerald Shinn (Philadelphia: Westminster Press; Oxford: Blackwell, 1971).

47. See the reference cited in n. 39, above.

48. The limitation to five or so years is admittedly extrinsic information, as is that concerning authenticity, although the latter is arrived at by intrinsic analysis. However, the first step of literary criticism in general is to establish the text, its authenticity, and integrity. Cf. Wellek and Warren, *Theory of Literature*, chap. 6. On the various assessments of the dating of Paul's letters, see the useful chart by Joseph A. Fitzmyer in his review article, "Two Views of New Testament Interpretation: Popular and Technical," *Int.* 32 (1978): 309–13. The chart is on p. 310.

49. For a good brief discussion of the notion of social facts, see Jonathan Culler, *Saussure* (Glasgow: Fontana/Collins, 1976), 70–79. Culler shows how

three contemporaries, Freud, Durkheim, and Saussure, independently re-
defined the status of the facts with which their disciplines worked as *social*
facts. Culler concludes: "In short, sociology, linguistics, and psychoanalytic
psychology are possible only when one takes the meanings which are attached to and which differentiate objects and actions in society as a primary reality, as facts to be explained. And since meanings are a social
product explanation must be carried out in social terms. It is as if Saussure,
Freud, and Durkheim had asked, 'what makes individual experience possible? What enables men to operate with meaningful objects and actions?
What enables them to communicate and act meaningfully?' And the answer
they postulated was social institutions which, though formed by human
activities, are the conditions of experience. To understand individual experience one must study the social norms which make it possible" (72). For an
extended essay on social facts that has also influenced me heavily, see Peter
L. Berger and Thomas Luckmann, *The Social Construction of Reality: A
Treatise in the Sociology of Knowledge* (Garden City, N.Y.: Doubleday & Co.,
Anchor Books, 1967).

50. "Religion As a Cultural System," in Clifford Geertz, *The Interpretation of Cultures* (New York: Basic Books, 1973), 87–125. See especially pp.
89–94. On language and symbol, see also Berger and Luckmann, *The Social
Construction of Reality*, 34–41, and 92–104. Wayne Meeks has rightly observed that Geertz's model of/for distinction is a social scientific version of
the theological distinction between the indicative and the imperative. See
Wayne Meeks, "The Image of the Androgyne: Some Uses of a Symbol in
Earliest Christianity," *HR* 13 (1974): 165–208, esp. 182 n. 80, for bibliography on the theological distinction.

51. I exclude here structuralist studies, which are not strictly speaking
literary. Literary criticism is concerned with surface structures and structuralism with deeper logical structures and processes.

52. See the references to surveys of sociological studies in n. 2, above.

53. The one study that comes closest to the project envisioned here is
John Elliott's sociological exegesis of 1 Peter, *A Home for the Homeless*.
However, it too is still oriented to history and lacks the literary dimension I
am concerned with.

54. I am referring here specifically to the landmark treatise by Berger
and Luckmann, *The Social Construction of Reality*, which will be discussed
later in this chapter and in chap. 1 in the section entitled, "On the Sociology of Letters." This book provides a better theoretical basis for the pro-
gram of social anthropology than any anthropological study I know. Clifford Geertz has been influenced by Alfred Schutz, to whom Berger and
Luckmann are indebted. See Geertz, *The Interpretation of Cultures*. On the
scope and history of the sociology of knowledge, see *The Social Construction
of Reality*, 1–18; and Hansfried Kellner, "On the Cognitive Significance of
the System of Language in Communication," in Thomas Luckmann, ed.,
Phenomenology and Sociology (New York: Penguin Books, 1978), 324–42.

55. See, e.g., T. O. Beidelman, "Some Sociological Implications of Culture," in John C. McKinney and Edward A. Tiryakian, *Theoretical Sociology*
(New York: Appleton-Century-Crofts, 1970), 499–527; E. E. Evans-Prit-

chard, *Social Anthropology* (Glencoe, Il.: Free Press, 1952); and Clifford Geertz, "Thick Description: Toward an Interpretive Theory of Culture," in *The Interpretation of Cultures*, 3–30; and Mary Douglas, ed., *Rules and Meanings: The Anthropology of Everyday Knowledge* (New York: Penguin Books, 1973), for an excellent collection of readings. For a theoretical elaboration of the dialectical relationship between symbol systems and social systems, see Berger and Luckmann, *The Social Construction of Reality*, pp. 19–46, "The Foundations of Knowledge in Everyday Life," and pp. 47–128, "Society as Objective Reality."

56. Theissen, *Social Setting*, and Schütz's introduction to this volume.

57. T. O. Beidelman, *The Kaguru: A Matrilineal People of East Africa* (New York: Holt, Rinehart and Winston, 1971), 30.

58. Theissen, *Social Setting*, 176.

59. The essays translated in Theissen's *Social Setting* focus on the Corinthian church.

60. See also Gerd Theissen, *Sociology of Early Palestinian Christianity*, trans. J. Bowden (Philadelphia: Fortress Press, 1978).

61. By a "closed social situation" I mean the array of social facts which are shared within a group, defining it as a group and differentiating it from other groups or from other groups within a more comprehensive group. In this connection, see Alfred Schutz, "On Multiple Realities" and "Symbol, Reality and Society" in Alfred Schutz, *Collected Papers* (The Hague: Martinus Nijhoff, 1973) vol. 1, *The Problem of Social Reality*, ed. Maurice Natanson, 207–59 and 287–356. See also his "Don Quixote and the Problem of Reality," in *Collected Papers* (The Hague: Martinus Nijhoff, 1971), vol. 2, *Studies in Social Theory*, ed. Arvid Brodersen, 135–58. On symbolic universes, see also Berger and Luckmann, *The Social Construction of Reality*, 92–128.

62. E. E. Evans-Pritchard, *Social Anthropology*, 5.

63. On "closed systems," see n. 61. In addition, see Clifford Geertz, "Thick Description: Toward an Interpretive Theory of Culture," and "Religion As a Cultural System," in *The Interpretation of Cultures*.

64. See Geertz, *The Interpretation of Cultures*, 29, on the necessary incompleteness of cultural analysis, which corresponds to the inexhaustibility of texts as objects of literary analysis. Paradoxically, while we can speak of a system, we cannot exhaustively describe or interpret it. From within a system, too, the mode of existence of predecessors, contemporaries, and successors is twofold, on the one hand as present social facts, to the extent that what is known about them belongs to a body of socially shared knowledge, and on the other hand as objects presumably back there, out there, or yet to be. Paul's knowledge of Abraham and his anticipation of Christ's return are cases in point. In chap. 3 we will consider these and other notions as social facts.

65. On participation in narrative worlds, see my "Literary Criticism in Biblical Studies," and Uspensky, *Poetics of Composition*.

66. Social facts are thus like literary facts. Questions of the truth or falsity of claims represented by such facts are irrelevant to the critic, whose concern is with the meaning and significance of the facts for the actors for

INTRODUCTION

whom they are facts. See E. E. Evans-Pritchard, *Theories of Primitive Religion* (Oxford: Clarendon Press, 1965), 17; and Geertz, "Thick Description."
67. Geertz, *The Interpretation of Cultures*, 10. See also Giles Gunn, "The Semiotics of Culture and the Interpretation of Literature: Clifford Geertz and the Moral Imagination," *Studies in the Literary Imagination* 12 (1977): 109–28.
68. Ibid., 18. Cf. W. T. Jones, "World Views: Their Nature and Their Function," *Current Anthropology* 13 (1972): 87. Jones notes that at a conference on world views some anthropologists maintained that "anthropological inquiry was more like a 'sensitive' reading of a novel or a poem" than like inquiry in the natural sciences. Geertz's "Thick Description" is the most self-conscious representation of this position I know of. In "Some Sociological Implications of Culture," Beidelman also frequently cites literary characteristics of certain anthropologists' work.
69. Marcel Griaule, *Conversations with Ogotemmeli* (London: Oxford Univ. Press, 1965).
70. For two views of the comparative methods in anthropology, see Geertz, *Islam Observed*, and Claude Lévi-Strauss, "Comparative Religions of Non Literate Peoples," in Lévi-Strauss, *Structural Anthropology*, trans. Monique Layton (New York: Basic Books, 1976), 2:60–67, and "Social Structure" and "Postscript," in *Structural Anthropology*, 1:269–342. For brief but useful comments on the history of the comparative method in the social sciences, see Robert A. Nisbet, "Development: A Critical Analysis," in McKinney and Tiryakian, *Theoretical Sociology*, 167–204 (189–92, "The Comparative Method"). See further the introduction to chap. 3, below on the comparative method in biblical studies (i.e., in the "history of religions school").
71. In its relativistic aspect anthropology is concerned with cultural "meanings"; in its universalistic aspect it is concerned with the "truths" that find expression in different cultural forms. But these are "truths" about man, not the truths of men, which are usually beyond the pale of anthropological interpretation, except as social facts.
72. Cf. John Gager, *Kingdom and Community: The Social World of Early Christianity* (Englewood Cliffs, N.J.: Prentice-Hall, 1975), and the reviews of this book in *Zygon* 13 (1978): 109–35; and by Cyril S. Rodd, "On Applying a Sociological Theory to Biblical Studies," *JSOT* 19 (1981): 95–106. See also Malina, *The New Testament World*. Social anthropologist Gillian Feeley-Harnik takes a more analytic and historical approach in her book, *The Lord's Table*, and also in her paper "Is Historical Anthropology Possible? The Case of the Runaway Slave [Onesimus]," in *Humanizing America's Iconic Book*, ed. Gene M. Tucker and Douglas A. Knight (Chico, Calif.: Scholars Press, 1982), 95–126.
73. C. F. D. Moule, quoted at the beginning of this chapter, refers to the classic but disputed argument of John Knox, that Paul wanted Philemon to free Onesimus for service in the mission. See John Knox, *Philemon Among the Letters of Paul* (Nashville: Abingdon Press, 1959). For criticism of Knox's argument, see, e.g., Heinrich Greeven, "Prüfung der Thesen, von J. Knox zum Philemonbrief," *TLZ* 79 (1954): cols. 373–78, and E. Lohse, *Colossians*

and Philemon, pp. 186–87 and n. 1 for further bibliography. My own reasons for not being persuaded by Knox's case will be developed in subsequent chapters.

74. For the exception, see n. 4, above.

75. In chap. 2, we will see that this role also has a literal designation, which raises the further question of why so many categories, both literal and metaphorical, are used to identify Paul's position of superiority. The problem is compounded when these categories are related to others that designate his equality and even inferiority.

76. Paul specifically identifies himself as a slave of Christ (Rom. 1:1; Gal. 1:10; Phil. 1:1), and by implication all who call Christ Lord/master are his slaves. Complications arising, e.g., from Rom. 6:22 and 1 Thess. 1:9, where believers are identified as slaves of God, and from 1 Cor. 7:22, where slaves are called freedmen of the Lord, will be dealt with in chap. 3, where the whole range of master-slave terminology will be considered.

77. Ernst Troeltsch, followed by Theissen, speaks of Paul's "patriarchalism." See E. Troeltsch, *The Social Teachings of the Christian Churches*, trans. Olive Wyon (New York: Harper and Brothers, 1960), 1:78 ("Christian patriarchalism"; see further 69–82); and Theissen, *Social Setting*, 37, 107–10, and 139–40. Theissen speaks of Paul's "love patriarchalism." The notion of love will be dealt with in both chaps. 2 and 3, when we consider Paul's kinship language with respect to its institutional referents (chap. 2) and to its symbolic aspect (chap. 3).

78. In chap. 2 the relations between these two domains will be clarified with the aid of Victor Turner's theory that social life is comprised of both social structural and anti-structural relations. Turner's theory will also help to disambiguate the variety of role-names used in the letter to Philemon. See Victor Turner, *The Ritual Process: Structure and Anti-Structure* (Chicago: Aldine Press, 1969), 94–203.

79. See Josef Hainz, *Ekklesia. Strukturen paulinischer Gemeinde-Theologie und Gemeinde-Ordnung*, BU 9 (Regensburg: Verlag Friedrich Pustet, 1972).

80. This third point is important because by orienting ourselves to the knowledge possessed by the actors in the social universe of Paul's narrative world we may seem to be ignoring the knowledge possessed by symbolic actors like God and Christ. We are not ignoring it but rather acknowledging that the entire symbolic universe, including God and Christ, is the content or object of knowledge possessed by the actors in the social universe. Indeed, it *is* their knowledge. While Paul *could* have told his stories in such a way as to represent what the symbolic actors know, he did not. This much is clear, but problems nevertheless arise when we say that Paul's symbolic universe itself has the form of narrative because he represents God and Christ as actors whose actions bear on the actors in the social universe. Because his symbolic universe has these narrative actions we can entertain the sociology of the actions, but because we do not know what the symbolic actors know we cannot explore *their* symbolic universe.

81. On symbolic universes and theology as one means by which they are maintained, see Berger and Luckmann, *The Social Construction of Reality*, 92–128, and both chap. 1, below, on the sociology of letters and the introductory remarks in chap. 3.

1

FROM LETTER TO STORY—
AND BACK:
TOWARD A NARRATOLOGY
AND SOCIOLOGY OF LETTERS

It is usually possible to transform a non-narrative text into a narrative one.[1]

Umberto Eco

Letters have stories, and it is from these stories that we construct the narrative worlds of both the letters and their stories. Our concern in this chapter is to establish methods for moving from letters to their stories, but also for moving back to the letters from the stories, since the whole point of the project is to see what the stories can tell us about the letters. To this end, our focus will be on a narratology of letters, on viewing letters in the light of their narratives. Our concern, however, will also involve a sociology of letters because the writing and receiving of letters are forms of social relations which are dramatized as actions or episodes within a letter's story. Together, our narratological and sociological considerations will lay a groundwork for our later and fuller studies of the social arrangements and symbolic forms governing the narrative world of the Letter to Philemon.

Two letters will serve us as case studies. The first is a very brief Greek papyrus letter, the second the somewhat longer but still quite brief Letter to Philemon. We will work out our methods of operation in connection with the first text, because of both its brevity and its noncontroversial content, and then we will turn to some observations on the sociology of letters. With these discussions behind us, we will have a basis for a fresh look at the Letter to Philemon and its story.

43

A TRIAL RUN

Our first letter is a piece of correspondence on papyrus from a Greek-speaking Egyptian named Mystarion to another man named Stotoetis, who was apparently a priest at an island whose name is missing from the papyrus fragments.[2] According to the close of the letter, which begins with the writer's "farewell," it was written on 12 September 50 C.E., thus making it contemporary with Paul's letters. The letter is of further interest in relation to Paul's Letter to Philemon because both appear to have been dictated by the writer to a scribe and then supplied with a close in the writer's own hand. Mystarion's letter, of which we have the original, is written in two hands, while Paul's letter, of which we only have copies in a single hand, draws to a close with Paul saying, "I, Paul, write this with my own hand, . . ." (v. 19a, and for what *he* wrote in his own hand see vv. 19–25).[3] Mystarion's letter reads as follows:

> To Stotoetis, chief priest,[4] at the island . . .
> Mystarion to his own[5] Stotoetis, many greetings.
> I have sent my Blastus to you to get forked sticks for my olive-gardens. See to it, therefore, that you do not detain him, for you know how I need him every hour.
>
> Farewell
>
> In the year 11 of Tiberius Claudius Caesar Augustus Germanicus Imperator in the month Sebastos 15.

As stories go, the one represented in Mystarion's letter is not likely to win any awards. Yet, the important point is that the letter does represent a story with at least a minimal plot. Since Aristotle's *Poetics*, every notion of story has included the idea of a sequence of actions between which some causal or motivational links establish the story's plot. In narratives these actions are all past or accomplished events because they are narrated from a retrospective point of view. In letters, however, the temporal point of view from which the actions are contemplated[6] is located somewhere in the middle of the sequence of actions. More precisely, the temporal point of view is located at the time of writing, wherever it may occur in the sequence of actions referred to in the letter. In some letters, like Mystarion's, it may come closer to the initial action referred to. In others, like 2 Corinthians 1—7, where Paul refers to a number of events prior to the time of writing,[7] the temporal point of view of the letter writer may come closer to the end of the sequence of events he refers to. But point of view in a letter's *story* is another matter entirely. While it is not identical to the retrospective point of view of a narrator, because all of the actions referred to are not past, the letter's author projects future events which include at least the reception of the letter by the addressee and his response to it. At this point, however, the letter's author becomes the narrator of his story by creating for himself a retrospective point of view like that of a bona fide narrator. He now envisions a story in which his act of writing is but one action whose significance lies in its relations to all of the other actions in the story. Simply, the story explains why he wrote the letter, namely to achieve some purpose in relation to the person(s) to whom the letter is written and sent. This purpose supplies the plot of the story by providing motivational links between the actions. In other words, the expressed *motive(s)* for writing the letter establish a causal relationship between the actions of its story. Consequently, the temporal point of view of the writer of the letter, namely at the time of writing, must be distinguished from the imaginative point of view of the narrator of the letter's story, which is located after the last event referred to in the story. Because of the wishful character of the future events projected by the letter's writer, those events are imagined by the story's narrator as events he desires to become past. For this reason, when we identify the actions referred to in the letter, projected or implied events are as important as accomplished events. All actions referred to are equally actions in the letter's story. These actions and the relations between them must be identified in order to construct that story. Let us consider the actions in Mystarion's story, and their relational emplotment in it:

(1) The first referential action is more a field of actions defining a relationship between Mystarion and Stotoetis that obtained prior to the time of writing. This "action" is referred to at the end of the letter when Mystarion indicates that Stotoetis already knows about Mystarion's need for Blastus. Whatever the relationship between Mystarion and Stotoetis may be, it was established before the time of writing, not by the letter: the correspondents already know each other. Mystarion knows that Stotoetis can supply the forked sticks he needs, thus suggesting that Stotoetis has done so previously, and probably in connection with Blastus, whose importance to Mystarion is also known by Stotoetis. In fact, Mystarion seems to have had a previous experience in which Stotoetis detained Blastus, which is the principal reason for Mystarion writing the letter (see 3, below). By referring to *another story* about a previous mission by Blastus, the first action in Mystarion's story provides a because-motive[8] for writing in addition to the because-motive for sending Blastus, which is provided by Mystarion's need for the forked sticks for his olive gardens. But this need constitutes a second action, one which occurs after Blastus's previous mission.

(2) Mystarion runs out of forked sticks, providing both a second

because-motive and a second theme to the story. The first theme is Mystarion's concern that Stotoetis will detain Blastus again; the second is Mystarion's need for the sticks.

(3) Mystarion writes to Stotoetis telling (commanding[9]) him not to detain Blastus, who is coming to pick up the sticks. Note, now, that *this* is the request stated in the letter, not that Stotoetis give Blastus the sticks. It would appear from the letter that Stotoetis has no choice in the domain of stick-supplying, at least when it is Mystarion who sends someone to get them. This suggests sociologically that while Blastus is an inferior to both of the other principals, each of whom has power over him, Mystarion is Stotoetis's superior in the domain of stick-supplying. More of this later. More pertinent to our present concerns is that the two because-motives *for* writing are transformed *by* writing into in-order-to-motives: Mystarion writes in order to secure the sticks promptly and in order to secure Stotoetis's compliance with his request not to detain Blastus.

(4) Mystarion sends Blastus and the letter to Stotoetis. Blastus's action is also because- and in-order-to-motivated: he acts because he has been told to do so and in order to get the sticks.

(5) Blastus and the letter arrive at Stotoetis's island.

(6) Blastus gets the forked sticks. This precedes (7) because Mystarion's request of Stotoetis is distinguished from Blastus's mission. See further below, on the poetic sequence.

(7) Stotoetis responds to Mystarion's request about not detaining Blastus—because of the request and in order to respond to it.

(8) Blastus returns to Mystarion with the sticks.

(9) Mystarion's olive trees are staked with Blastus's aid or by Blastus himself. Thus both of Mystarion's initial motives for acting have been satisfied and the story arrives at its intended closure.

The implied motivations identified in the story provide links between its several actions and thereby establish its plot, which centers on Stotoetis's potential obstruction of Mystarion's desires. The point of view from which the actions are selected and arranged is Mystarion's, and the only other point of view represented in the story is the one Mystarion imputes to Stotoetis: Stotoetis may look upon Blastus's arrival as an occasion for a chat, or for something else that would detain Blastus from completing his mission promptly. Blastus's point of view is at best implied as a readiness, for whatever reasons,[10] to do as he is told, whether by Mystarion or by Stotoetis. The closure of the story is in the satisfaction of Mystarion's desires that Stotoetis not detain Blastus, and that Blastus return with the sticks so that the olive trees can be propped up.

There remains for us to consider the narrative voice (persona) which tells the story. I have said that the author of the letter becomes the narrator of the story, but in the outline of the story's actions constructed above there is no narrative voice, only a list of actions which can be narrated from the phraseological point of view[11] of more than one narrator. For example, I can tell the story in the third person of an omniscient narrator, or Mystarion can tell it in the first person of a participant narrator. And both of us can tell the story either from a retrospective point of view located after its last action or, consistent with the temporal point of view from which the letter was written, from a temporal location within the sequence of actions. Thus some events would be described as past (actions one through four) and others as intended or expected to come to pass (actions five through nine). But just as the temporal point of view can be located in only one position, so also are there limitations on the number of narrative voices that are possible. Although we can easily conceive of Blastus and Stotoetis telling stories about the same events, because the selection and arrange-ment of actions in our story are determined by Mystarion, Blastus and Stotoetis would necessarily have to be telling *other* stories.[12] Because our outline of actions is derived from Mystarion, there are actually only two possible narrative voices, Mystarion's and ours, and if ours, we would be telling *Mystarion's story*. Thus, the story is in the first instance his and only derivatively ours. It would be an interesting exercise to write both versions, but that would take us beyond our present concerns. Let it suffice, therefore, to remember that we are dealing only with the emplotment of the story's actions, with their closure, and with the temporal and intentional point of view[13] from which they are envisioned. The casting of the story into one or the other narrative voice, and the choice of a temporal loca-tion from which the story is to be told, are variables we need not be concerned with. They do not alter the constancy of plot, closure, and temporal and intentional point of view.

In the process of constructing Mystarion's story we have also seen how the story serves to explain the letter by providing the textual message with a narrative context. Let us call this the text's immedi-ate interpretive context, in order to distinguish it from extratextual "historical" contexts, which in the final analysis must be inferred from the letter's story. Thus, Mystarion's selection, arrangement, and motivation of the actions in his story explain why he wrote his letter and what he expected to achieve by it. Our task now is to develop a method for relating his story to the poetics or composition of his letter. To do this, we have to reflect on and expand the method by which we constructed his story.

Our method for constructing a story out of a letter was simple. We identified the actions referred to or implied in the letter and then represented them in their *chronological* sequence. Technically, this sequence is the *referential sequence* of events represented in the letter.[14] One way of approaching the poetics of a text, be it a narrative or an epistolary text, is to relate the referential sequence of events to the *poetic sequence* of events, by which I mean the sequence of events as they appear in the text. The referential sequence is an abstraction from the text in which events are represented in their logical and chronological order. Poetic order is judged to be poetic or creative by virtue of the ways in which it differs from the referential order.[15] In narratives, it is possible that the two sequences may be identical, that a narrator will describe events in a strictly chronological order. His textual sequence would still be poetic because it is a concrete representation of the abstract referential sequence. But it would not be *very* poetic, in the sense of being very artful. Such, for example, would be the case if we or Mystarion told the story of his letter and followed the chronological sequence discussed above. On the other hand, we or Mystarion might exercise "poetic license" and poetically rearrange the chronological sequence. We could begin the narration not with the chronological first event but, say, with the sending of Blastus (action number four), then refer to Mystarion's having run out of sticks (action number two), and then to his previous experience with Stotoetis (action number one) as the basis for his writing of the letter (action number three). In this way, the referential sequence of actions 1, 2, 3, and 4 would be poetically presented in the sequence 4, 2, 1, and 3. The abstract referential sequence is therefore a constant by which we can measure the poetic variations from it in the text. But what is the purpose of such measurements?

The differences between the poetic and the referential sequence disclose both formal and material peculiarities of the poetic composition. By constructing the referential sequence, we gain a basis for identifying both the actions the writer has selected for his text, and the ways in which he has related them. In this respect, comparison of the two sequences provides us with access to the writer's formal plot devices and the rhetorical strategies they serve. On the other hand, however, comparison of the two sequences also yields material gains. Because the actions enjoy one set of relations to one another in their chronological sequence, the process of rearrangement may represent other than chronological relations between them, and thereby provide further material insights into both the story and the epistolary text. The formal differences therefore lead us to seek their material consequences. To illustrate these points, let us return to Mystarion's letter.

The simplest way of representing the two sequences is to do so in parallel lines, as in the following diagram. In the diagram, those actions that are only implied in the letter are placed in parentheses on the line representing the poetic sequence.[16]

Referential Sequence: 1   2   3 4 5 6   7   8 9

Poetic Sequence: (2) (5) 4 9 3 1 (6) (7) (8)

The most striking thing revealed by a comparison of these two sequences is that out of nine actions in the referential sequence only four have been selected for emplotment in the poetic sequence, in which their order, moreover, is totally different from that of the referential sequence. In order to explore this state of affairs, let us first review the referential sequence, now including the parentheses to acknowledge implied actions, and then turn to a more careful look at the poetic sequence.

Referential Sequence

   1. The prior relationship between Stotoetis and Mystarion.
(2.) Mystarion runs out of sticks
   3. Mystarion writes Stotoetis, telling him not to detain Blastus
   4. Mystarion sends Blastus and the letter
(5.) Blastus and the letter arrive at Stotoetis's island
(6.) Blastus gets the sticks
(7.) Stotoetis responds to the letter
(8.) Blastus returns with the sticks
   9. the olive trees are staked

For the poetic sequence, let us use the wording of the letter for those actions emplotted in it. Also, in order to make clear the poetics of the letter, we can set the emplotted actions off from those that are only implied by indenting the latter.

Poetic Sequence

       (2.) Mystarion runs out of sticks
       (5.) Blastus and the letter arrive
4. "I have sent my Blastus to you
9. to get forked sticks for my olive-gardens.
3. See to it, therefore, that you do not detain him,
1. for you know how I need him every hour."
       (6.) Blastus gets the sticks
       (7.) Stotoetis responds to the letter
       (8.) Blastus returns with the sticks

Before we narrow our focus and concentrate on the emplotted actions in the poetic sequence, a few comments are in order about the relationship between them and the implied actions. It will be recalled that the implied actions are referential actions implied in the letter or logically required by the referential sequence. The outline (above) of the poetic sequence, which includes the implied actions, sheds further light on the method of constructing the letter's story.

Of the five implied actions the most problematical one is number five, the arrival of Blastus and the letter. This action is not implied in the letter, but it is logically required by the referential sequence, for without it actions six through nine could not occur! Because Mystarion envisioned these actions in his story, we have to posit action five in the referential sequence. What is true of the story of this letter, however, is true of all letters: *The event of the arrival of the letter must be posited in the referential sequence of every story constructed from a letter.* For this reason, the arrival of the letter is also the key to the fictional nature of every such story. Regardless of what happened "historically," of whether or not the letter ever arrived at its destination, the arrival of the letter and everything that comes after it in the story is a creative projection by the author.

Less problematical is the location of action five in the poetic sequence, for implied (i.e., unplotted) actions like it and action two occur in their referential order. Action five therefore must follow action two since it, Mystarion's running out of sticks,[17] is the presupposition for the sending of Blastus and the letter, and therefore for their arrival. Similarly, implied actions six, seven, and eight necessarily come after the emplotted actions, since they complete them as closural satisfactions of previously engendered expectations. This is evident from the sequential correspondence between them and the poetic sequence of actions expressed in the letter.

Expectations	*Satisfactions*
4. "I have sent my Blastus to you	
9. to get forked sticks for my olive-gardens.	(6.) Blastus gets the sticks
3. See to it, therefore, that you do not detain him,	(7.) Stotoetis responds to the letter by not detaining Blastus
1. for you know how I need him every hour."	(8.) Blastus returns with the sticks

These observations based on a comparison of the poetic and referential sequences not only illustrate further how stories are constructed from letters, but they also illustrate the way in which the story helps to explain the letter. This becomes evident when we examine the emplotment of actions in the poetic sequence, that is, without regard for the implied actions. What has Mystarion achieved by selecting only four of the nine actions and by arranging them as he has, namely in the sequence: 4/9/3/1? The answer to this question is simple, and perhaps even anticlimactic. For by now it is self-evident that two actions, four and three, are central to the letter, and that the actions which follow them, nine and one, provide the motives for the central actions. Action number nine, "to get forked sticks for my olive-gardens," supplies an in-order-to-motive for sending Blastus (four), while action number one, "for you know how I need him every hour," supplies a because-motive for telling Stotoetis not to detain Blastus (three). Thus each central action is accompanied by a motivation:[18] "I have sent Blastus in order to get the needed sticks. Do not detain him, because you know how much I need him."

From a total field of actions available to him, Mystarion has thus selected those that were directly pertinent to his intent, and he has poetically arranged them in such a way as to make and support his point with unmistakable (and laudable) economy. This letter may not, as Doty says, be "a model of epistolary grace,"[19] but it is both a poetic and a strategic rhetorical composition.

The matter of strategy is both literary and sociological. Literarily, plot, point of view, and closure serve strategic ends in the rhetorical composition of the letter. We have considered these fictions of narrative in connection with the letter's story. Let us see now how they apply to the letter itself. It appears that they are not limited to narratives at all.

One of the most interesting results of our comparison of the poetic and referential sequences is the discovery that events are emplotted not only in narratives but also in letters. Beyond this discovery, however, the poetic emplotment of events in Mystarion's letter discloses other than chronological relations between the emplotted events, namely motivational relations. We have already considered these in discussing the letter's story and again in the discussion of the poetic sequence. Our question now concerns the rhetorical strategies involved in the poetic emplotment of the four referential actions. In this light, it is clear that Mystarion has minimized his need for the sticks, a situation which in fact initiated both the story and the letter. He has omitted reference to *this* need, which is only implied, and simply stated that he has sent Blastus to get more sticks. Mystarion rather focuses on his own expectation that Stotoetis might interfere with his project by detaining Blastus. First, he commands Stotoetis not to detain Blastus, and then he appeals to Stotoetis's knowledge of his need for Blastus's presence. Thus, the chief strategic point of the letter is to address the one thing that might threaten Mystarion's project for his olive gardens—Stotoetis's presumed and probably demonstrated (action number one) readiness to detain Blastus. If Stotoetis complies, Mystarion's need for Blastus will be met, as will his need for the sticks. Importantly, the only reason for Mystarion's selection of action number one for both his story and his letter is its strategic function. In theory, he could have composed both the letter and the story without it. He has selected it because he needed it.

Mystarion's need for this action is reflected both in the point of view governing the letter and in its closure. The governing point of view is Mystarion's, for it is he who has sent Blastus and commands Stotoetis. But Mystarion's command also presumes Stotoetis's point of view about the presence of such people as Blastus. Strategically, Mystarion's command constitutes a showdown between points of view: the command constitutes a rejection of Stotoetis's point of view. The reference to Stotoetis's knowledge of Mystarion's need for Blastus supports this command by indicating that as Mystarion knows of Stotoetis's tendencies, Stotoetis knows of Mystarion's need. Thus a shared experience is referred to. As suggested earlier, the command and the reference to Stotoetis's knowledge imply a previous occasion on which the three men had an experience which Mystarion feared would be repeated. The reference to Stotoetis's knowledge supports the command by reminding Stotoetis that they have all been through this before—so don't do it again.

As for closure, the formal close to the letter is in the farewell that precedes the date of the letter, both of which are written in another hand than the address and the body of the letter.[20] This close is formal both in the sense that it is conventional, like "sincerely yours," and because it contains no personalized embellishments.[21] Even the fact that the formal close is probably written in Mystarion's own hand is a convention of ancient letter writing.[22] Yet, in addition to such a formal close, there is also a material closure to the letter. This is the strategic conclusion to the body of the letter, where Mystarion speaks much more intimately, however threateningly as well, than in the anonymously conventional farewell: "for you know how I need him every hour." This clause provides closure to the body of the letter. We have seen that this intimate comment is also the because-motive for the preceding command, and that it refers as well to Stotoetis's point of view, namely to what he knows about Mystarion. Mystarion assumes for himself the power to command, but in the closure of his letter he acknowledges Stotoetis's freedom to disobey. But here, in the closure, plot, point of view, and closure combine to remind Stotoetis of past events which Mystarion does not want to recur. Thus Mystarion moves from command to appeal, but in such a way that the intimacy of the appeal is governed by the anonymity or distance of the modestly threatening command. At this point, however, we have to shift from literary strategies to sociological issues, for commanding and appealing, with or without threats, and anonymity and intimacy are sociological matters distinctively represented in letters. Mystarion's letter to Stotoetis can serve as a point of reference for some more general observations on the sociology of letters, observations that are necessary at this juncture because we have found that the sending and receiving of letters are not only narrative actions, but also forms of social relations. We have come to a point, therefore, where we can develop further the notions of symbolic forms and social arrangements discussed in the previous chapter.

ON THE SOCIOLOGY OF LETTERS

The starting point for a sociology of letters is the rather obvious fact that letters are surrogates for the personal presence of the addresser with the addressee. In a major historical study of the structure, function, and phraseology of the ancient Greek letter, Heikki Koskenniemi demonstrated that its fundamental structure reflects what happens in the face-to-face meeting of friends: greetings are followed by dialogue, and dialogue by a farewell.[23] From a sociological perspective, and on a more theoretical plane, the letter is therefore an alternative form of social relationship, one which functions to establish or maintain a relationship when the parties to it cannot meet face-to-face. Indeed, some sociologists support Koskenniemi when they see the face-to-face situation as "the prototypical case of social interaction," of which all other cases, like the letter, "are derivatives."[24] However, the derivation of the letter is only the starting point for a sociology of letters.

The letter does not merely represent in writing what might transpire in a personal encounter any more than stories merely represent events. We have already observed the literary roles of the fictions of narrative both in stories and in Mystarion's letter to Stotoetis. Sociological phenomena further intervene between what we see in a text and what we experience in personal encounters, for both the act and the product of letter writing are also governed by social conventions which differentiate the text from the encounter. Koskenniemi, for example, has shown that the phraseological conventions of letter writing in Greco-Roman antiquity lend a tone of impersonality even to those letters which are transmitted between intimately related parties, as in family letters or correspondence between close friends. The conventional language of letters does not, he argues, disclose directly anything distinctively personal about the correspondents.[25] While persons, roles, and relations are represented in letters, they are represented in an anonymously objective form which conceals the very subjectivity which makes them personal in face-to-face encounters. Precisely this point is the one emphasized by sociologist Georg Simmel in one of the few attempts made by sociologists to deal with the letter as a sociological phenomenon.[26] Simmel observes that in the intimate interaction of face-to-face situations, individuals

> give each other more than the mere content of their words. Inasmuch as each of them *sees* the other, is immersed in the unverbalizable sphere of his mood, feels a thousand nuances in the tone and rhythm of his utterances, the logical or intended content of his words gains an enrichment and modification for which the letter offers only very poor analogies. And even these, on the whole, grow only from memories of direct personal contact between the correspondents.[27]

Simmel was concerned with the reduction of the reciprocal subjectivity of the face-to-face encounter to the one-sided objectivity of the letter. The few sociologists who have followed up his concern have been further interested in the letter's reduction of the particular to the typical, and with the relations of the typical to the verbal, namely to language. Following their thinking may seem at times to lead us somewhat off the track of our immediate concern with the sociology of letters, but follow it we must because their thinking is directly relevant to our concern with the world of Paul's letters.

The development beyond Simmel has taken place among those involved in the sociology of knowledge, for which the typical and the verbal play a dominant role in the expressing and shaping of human experience. A key figure in this development is Alfred Schutz, whose comments on letter-writing and memory find their point of departure in the quotation from Simmel. Schutz claims that

> . . . the letter-writer addresses himself to the typification of the addressee as he knew him when they separated, and the addressee reads the letter as written by the person typically the same as the one he left behind. Presupposing such a typicality (and any typicality) means assuming that what has been proved to be typical in the past will have a good chance to be typical in the future, or, in other words, that life will continue to be what it has been so far: the same things will remain relevant, the same degree of intimacy in personal relationships will prevail, etc.[28]

The observations made by Schutz and Simmel are clearly supported by what we have seen in Mystarion's letter to Stotoetis. In it, Mystarion's subjectivity is reduced to verbal objectivity, and he represents Stotoetis not as a flesh and blood interlocutor but as a person remembered as typically behaving in certain ways in certain circumstances. Mystarion addresses not the other person in his subjectivity but a typification of that person based on memory; and the memory itself is a reductive typification abstracted from the totality of the other person's past behavior as encountered by Mystarion. By the same token, the image of Mystarion which is represented in his letter is comprised of a bundle of typifications. He is represented as typically in need both of sticks and of Blastus, and he is perhaps typically one who is forthright rather than meek in expressing his wishes. For these reasons, Mystarion's letter represents a manipulation of typifications that is quite unlike the intimate exchange of a face-to-face encounter such as Simmel described. Yet, Schutz has also shown that even intimate face-to-face encounters are informed by such typifications. Interpersonal relations take place, he argues, in such a way that the relations entail a continual adjustment of the typical we know with the particular that we meet.[29] Knowing is a matter of knowing typifications, but in face-to-face encounters knowledge undergoes adjustments in order to match the "face" presented by the known other. If for Simmel letters reduce the subjectivity of face-to-face encounters to a one-sided objectivity, that of the writer, for Schutz this objectivity consists of typifications that are not subject to adjustment in the process of communication. *Letters traffic completely in typifications because the absence of the writer prevents face-to-face adjustments.* Letters are thus like still-photographs in contrast with cinematic films. But for precisely this reason letters are sociologically interesting. They objectify in language the typifications by which writers and their correspondents live and understand themselves; letters represent linguistically the general social conventions by which individuals sharing that language identify themselves, others, and the relations between them.

Two other sociologists, Peter Berger and Thomas Luckmann, have developed these notions further in connection with a theory of the sociology of knowledge.[30] In agreement with Simmel and Schutz they argue that all forms of social interaction are derivatives of the face-to-face situation.[31] In their theory, social reality is apprehended by the individual in "a continuum of typifications, which are progressively anonymous as they are removed from the 'here and now' of the face-to-face situation."[32] In fact, they claim that "social structure is the sum total of these typifications and of the recurrent patterns of interaction established by means of them."[33] For Berger and Luckmann, signs (language and symbol) objectify the typifications in the form of knowledge. "Participation in the social stock of knowledge thus permits the 'location' of individuals in society and the 'handling' of them in the appropriate manner."[34] Following Schutz, they see much of this kind of knowledge as "recipe knowledge," by which they mean knowledge that provides individuals with the competence to perform routine acts in everyday life.[35] Moreover, because routine acts occur in typical situations, recipe knowledge is divided up into spheres of relevance corresponding to such situations.[36] Communication and interaction, therefore, require not only a common stock of knowledge but also a common understanding of the spheres of relevance in which certain bodies of knowledge are pertinent. Looked at from an analytical angle, the knowledge which is shared in a communication also represents shared spheres of relevance. And in this regard, Mystarion's letter and Paul's Letter to Philemon provide an instructive contrast. The knowledge and spheres of relevance represented in the former are quite simple and limited largely to personal relations between Mystarion and Stotoetis, although some recipe knowledge is presumed both for the care of olive trees and for dealing with the likes of Blastus, who is either a slave or an employee. In Paul's letter, however, the personal relations between the correspondents are deeply embedded in a wider sphere of relevance, that of social relations within the church, which has as its opposite the worldly sphere of relevance associated with master-slave relations. In Mystarion's letter, the social behavior of the actors is governed by a limited sphere of relevance, while in Paul's letter behavior is enmeshed in a collision between two competing spheres of relevance, especially for Philemon and Onesimus, who have a personal identity in both spheres.

Of equal interest on the sociological plane is the profoundly institutional character of the spheres of relevance represented in Paul's letter. The proliferation of role-names (typifications) in the letter represents institutionalized structures of social relations between the actors that are largely lacking in Mystarion's letter. According to Berger and Luckmann, "[i]nstitutionalization occurs whenever there is a reciprocal typification of habitualized actions by types of actors. Put differently, any such typification is an institution."[37] But here we must be careful to distinguish between the typicality of the actors and their actions on the one hand, and the linguistic expressions and representations of them on the other. "Institutionalization" refers to the structured social relations (social arrangements), while the language refers to or represents the institutions. From an analytical angle, we must once again observe that because the structured social relations are objectified in language we, who from our distance have only the language objectified in texts, can only perceive the structures through an analysis of the language. Thus Berger and Luckmann conclude that "[i]f the integration of an institutional order can be understood only in terms of the 'knowledge' that its members have of it, it follows that the analysis of such 'knowledge' will be essential for an analysis of the institutional order in question."[38]

The knowledge we have been speaking of thus far is largely "recipe knowledge, that is, knowledge that supplies the institutionally appropriate rules of conduct"[39] for particular spheres of relevance. We have seen, too, that this knowledge includes the roles or types of actors operative in a given social context. But in addition to the objective, social-structural aspect of roles, there is also a subjective aspect which concerns the individual's self-identification. One knows one's self, or "has" a social identity, one "is" a this or a that, within a differentiated field of roles played in a total society or in a narrower sphere of social relevance. But because in the course of time individuals come to play many roles, one's identity entails more than merely being *a* this or *a* that. Identity consists of a synthesis of roles and of other typifications, like memories of one's past behavior, experience, and relations. To achieve such an identity requires knowledge which goes beyond recipe knowledge, a more comprehensively synthetic body of knowledge whose ultimate form is that of a symbolic universe, a socially constructed world.[40] For Berger and Luckmann, symbolic universes are comprehensive systems of shared knowledge that legitimate the institutions and individual identities whose existence is expressed in and defined by them. "Legitimation not only tells the individual why he *should* perform one action and not another; it also tells him why things *are* what they are. In other words, 'knowledge' precedes 'values' in the legitimation of institutions" and of identities.[41] One *should act* in accordance with what one is in relation to what others are, and what one is and others are is known on the basis of the symbolic universe that legitimates all such social positions. A symbolic universe is therefore a body of traditional knowledge that is known through language and symbol. It is a system of meanings that defines, and thereby creates, a "world," and every "world," both narrative and "real," has such a system. For example, in our introductory chapter we saw an illustration of this function of symbolic universes in the significance of symbolic actors like God and Christ for the definition and legitimation of the roles played by social actors like Paul, Philemon, and Onesimus. The roles, and therefore also the identities, of these social actors as siblings and as slaves are defined by reference to the fatherhood of God and the lordship of Christ. Thus, knowing that one *is* a child of God and a slave of Christ both precedes and determines the behavior of the social actors—as the behavior of a child to a parent or to a sibling and as the behavior of a slave to a master or to a fellow slave.

If recipe knowledge pertains to the realities of everyday life, symbolic knowledge both transcends these realities and encompasses them. But if recipe knowledge can be said to refer to and objectify social arrangements, the question arises as to what is referred to and objectified in symbolic knowledge. As social scientists, Berger and Luckmann are not interested in whether or not what one "knows" about the likes of God and Christ corresponds to some external reality as, for example, "mailman" corresponds to the one who delivers our mail six days a week. For social scientists, it is not what "God" and "Christ" refer to in this way that is interesting, because for them these terms refer to what is known about such actors within a culture's traditional lore. For social scientists, "God" and "Christ" are social facts bound up with other social facts, like what the New Testament or this or that religious community says about them. In this respect, social scientists are like literary critics whose knowledge about a character in a novel is limited to what the novelist allows them to know. Neither "God," nor "Christ," nor Don Quixote is or can be known in the same way as the mailman. But it is precisely this difference between these kinds of knowledge that interests social scientists, especially those concerned with the sociology of knowledge. They want to know how various kinds of knowledge are differentiated and how the different kinds of knowledge affect human experience. Thus Berger and Luckmann distinguish between recipe knowledge and symbolic knowledge, and also, for example, between both of these and mythological and theological knowledge. Let us therefore follow their discussion of these distinctions.

Berger and Luckmann observe that language is capable of transcending the realities of everyday life, that "it can refer to experience pertaining to finite provinces of meaning [or spheres of relevance], and [that] it can span discrete spheres of reality, like those of dreams, fantasy or religious experience. The same language can be used to refer to different 'realities.' "[42] However, a significative theme that spans spheres of reality is "defined as a symbol, and the linguistic mode by which such transcendence is achieved may be called symbolic language. On the level of symbolism, then, linguistic signification attains the maximum detachment from the 'here and now' of everyday life, and language soars into regions that are not only *de facto* but also *a priori* unavailable to everyday experience. . . ."[43] Symbolic language does not refer to the realities of everyday life; it creates them. For "[l]anguage is capable not only of constructing symbols that are highly abstracted from everyday experience, but also of 'bringing back' these symbols and appresenting them as objectively real elements in everyday life."[44] For example, the symbolic language in which God is presented as a "father" and

Christ as a "master" brings back and makes real things not available to everyday experience, namely heavenly "realities," by presenting them in the language of everyday life, namely the language of fathers and their children and of masters and their slaves.[45] And because the symbolic use of this language expresses, defines, and creates the identity of individuals in Paul's communities, namely, as children of God and slaves of Christ, Paul's symbolic language is profoundly sociological in both its structure and its content. In saying this, however, we are confronted once again with the issue of the relationship between "theology" and symbolic knowledge. Although we will deal with this issue fully in chapter 3, it requires some preliminary consideration in the present context.

As we observed in the introductory chapter, from the perspective of the sociology of knowledge it is necessary to distinguish between theology and symbolic universes as two different kinds of knowledge. For the sociology of knowledge, a symbolic universe is the ultimate legitimation of social institutions because it integrates all provinces of meaning and encompasses the social order in a symbolic totality. In it, "*all* the sectors of the institutional order are integrated in an all-embracing frame of reference, which now constitutes a universe in the literal sense of the word, because *all* human experience can now be conceived of as taking place *within* it."[46] This universe is symbolic because the realities of everyday life are comprehended within the framework of *other realities*. Paul's use of the symbols of "father" and "master" to identify God and Christ is a perfect illustration of this because the symbols interpret the reality of everyday life: the believer *is* a son of God and slave of Christ, who are fathers and masters in a different reality from that of the fathers and masters of everyday experience. And it is for this reason that we have to conclude that *this* Pauline language represents a segment of his symbolic universe. What, then, about "theology"?

For the sociology of knowledge, a symbolic universe is the ultimate form by which communal life is rendered valid and real, that is, by which it is legitimated. Technically and strictly speaking, as the *ultimate* form of legitimation it cannot be legitimated by anything else; it can only be *maintained*.[47] In this light, therefore, "theology" is a form of conceptual "machinery" by which a symbolic universe is maintained. Other forms are mythology, philosophy, and science, but each form differs from the symbolic universe because each is a form of systematic reflection upon *it*. The symbolic universe represents reality directly, and people usually take that representation for granted, unreflectively; it is something to be learned and lived "in." In different ways, the several machineries for universe maintenance are at best legitimations "to the second degree"[48] because, as we have seen, they presuppose the universe that is to be maintained. The two forms of universe-maintenance that are of greatest interest to us are the mythological and the theological, and they are of interest because some of Paul's comments make him look more like a mythologist than a theologian. What is the difference between them? For Berger and Luckmann, mythology represents "a conception of reality that posits the ongoing penetration of the world of everyday experience by sacred forces. Such a conception naturally entails a high degree of continuity between social and cosmic order, and between all their respective legitimations; all reality appears as made of one cloth."[49] Theology, on the other hand, is for them characterized by "its greater degree of theoretical systematization" and by a correspondingly greater concern to explain the continuity between the social and cosmic orders. This concern derives, they argue, from the experience in everyday life of a discontinuity between these orders. Like all of the machineries for universe-maintenance, theology responds to the experience of problems in living within the inherited symbolic universe, whether these problems originate in failures of the universe or in competing representations or interpretations of it.[50]

These distinctions between symbolic universes, mythology, and theology require us to remember our earlier decision about how we are to approach Paul's thought. Because symbolic universes are prior to any systematic form of reflection on them, what is said upon such reflection is said about them. Our concern is therefore with Paul's symbolic universe regardless of whether he presents it to others directly in the form of narrative, proclamation or teaching, or more mediately in the form of argumentation based on "mythological" or "theological" reflection. Moreover, in view of our literary concerns we should also recognize that the exploration of Paul's symbolic universe is fundamental for our exploration of his narrative world, for his symbolic universe comprises the "world" in which his narration as well as his thought takes place. Like every other "world" his narrative world has a symbolic universe, one that both bestows meaning on and motivates the social actions of the actors in his story, including his own. It does so by defining and giving meaning to the social arrangements by which they live. Literary criticism must therefore acknowledge the significance of both symbolic forms and social arrangements for understanding the emplotted actions of actors.

Just as symbolic universes are maintained by conceptual, legitimating "machineries" like mythology, theology, philosophy, and science, so also are they maintained in everyday life by actors playing institutional roles in relation to other actors.[51] Here we have to do not only with the objective structures of sociological hierarchy, of superordination and subordination,[52] of superiors, inferiors, and equals, but also with the subjective processes of socialization, of becoming a part of a social unit. Berger and Luckmann identify three kinds of socialization, primary, secondary, and re-socialization, each of which is particularly relevant for the sociology of the letter to and story about Philemon, and, indeed, for the sociology of Paul's narrative world.

In each kind of socialization one learns the symbolic universe of one's society from "significant others" who are in charge of socialization.[53] On the primary level these significant others are parents or their functional equivalents. The child first becomes a member of society in the context of the nuclear family or its equivalent. Here "the individual becomes what he is addressed as by his significant others," and "not only takes on the roles and attitudes of others, but in the process takes on their world."[54] The world into which the child is thus socialized is *the* world. On the other hand, secondary socialization and re-socialization[55] are quite different because they respectively entail entry into sub-worlds or other worlds. Entry into a profession, for example, involves adjustment to a sub-world, that of the profession, while conversion to another religion may involve entry into another world entirely. The problem of secondary socialization is one of relating the world of secondary socialization to the world of primary socialization; the former must be assimilated within the latter. In re-socialization, on the other hand, the world of primary socialization is replaced by or assimilated within the new world. In both cases, however, significant others play a determinative role, although now in a less intimate, more institutionally anonymous way than in primary socialization. But what is of interest to us is the way in which Paul relates his world to the world of primary socialization in which his Gentile constituency lives.

Paul plays the role of a significant other in a process of socialization, namely of converting those who already have a primary socialization, and who, as adults, have also undergone other secondary socializations as well. What is of interest in Paul's behavior as a significant other is that the symbolic universe into which he invites others, and in which he nurtures them, is a universe represented in the language and with the values of the process of primary socialization—the language and the values of fathers and children and of masters and slaves. In Paul's world, individuals were not only born into families and their "worlds," but as often as not into slavery, which for many was as primary a social reality as the family![56] *Paul thus uses the language of primary socialization to represent what is sociologically (i.e., for us) and objectively (i.e., for converts) a process and state of socialization.* By this means, however, Paul's symbolic universe transcends and encompasses both all sub-universes and the symbolic universe of his converts' primary socialization. Conversion is therefore not for him a turning to another world, but a reversion to the only real world. It is a process of re-socialization.

Another sociological vocabulary discloses other aspects of this important *tour de force.* Primary socialization corresponds to what has been called involuntary or existential forms of association, while secondary socialization corresponds to voluntary associations. According to Schutz, in *any* form of association "[t]he system of typifications and relevances shared with other members of the group defines the social roles, positions, and statuses of each. This acceptance of a common system of relevances leads the members of the group to a homogeneous self-typification."[57] What differentiates existential (involuntary) and voluntary associations is

> that in the first case the individual member finds himself within a preconstituted system of typifications, relevances, roles, positions, statuses not of his own making, but handed down to him as a social heritage. In the case of voluntary groups, however, this system is not experienced by the individual member as ready-made; it has to be built up by the members and is therefore always involved in a process of dynamic evolution. Only some of the elements of the situation are common from the outset: the others have to be brought about by a common definition of the reciprocal situation.[58]

Schutz concludes that "it is only with respect to voluntary, and not to existential group membership that the individual is free to determine of which group he wants to be a member, and of which social role he wants to be the incumbent."[59] In this light, we can see that Paul's use of the language and values of primary socialization renders membership in the church in terms of involuntary or existential group membership. For the individual members, however, joining the church *is* a voluntary act, and once in the church they have the problem of adjusting their old identity and world to the new one, much as Schutz describes vis-à-vis membership in voluntary associations. Thus the symbolic universe that Paul describes for members, both before and after their conversion, has the character of a preconstituted system which limits the freedom of the individual to choose his role(s) or to reshape or mold the system.[60] The individual's essential social identity, as a child of God and slave of Christ, is predetermined by Paul and other "significant others." On the other hand, however, because the church is also a voluntary form of association, converts are put in a position in which it is possible for them to think of Paul and the church in terms of secondary socialization rather than of resocialization. Just how Paul handles these matters will be considered in detail in subsequent chapters. For now, it will suffice to conclude that the strategy behind his letters is to reinforce the primary and existential reality of what is for the members of his churches both a new world and a voluntary form of association. For example, in the case of Philemon, the individual who has a foot in two different worlds and an identity in each, Paul's symbolic universe is as much at issue as is Philemon's ultimate identity. And because Paul's universe is threatened by a collision between the two worlds, the church as a whole is threatened. Mystarion only had to worry about his olive trees.

Despite the underwhelming nature of Mystarion's problem, his letter is nonetheless of sociological interest as a case in point. We can use it to illustrate some concluding theses pertaining to the sociology of letters that are also relevant to the sociology of their stories. These theses should be rather self-evident; I state them because they are fundamental.[61]

Thesis 1. Every letter presupposes some form of previous relationship between the addresser and the addressee. Even if there is no prior relationship, a letter initiating a relationship must take the prior non-relationship as its premise. Mystarion's letter is, as we have seen, clearly based on a past and enduring association with Stotoetis. Paul's letter to Rome, on the other hand, is written to a community that he did not found, had not visited, and from which he may not have received personal communications. Thus he introduces himself to the community and thereby establishes a relationship with it (see Rom. 1:1–15; 15:14–33).

Thesis 2. Every letter, once it has been received, constitutes a new moment or event in the relationship between the addresser and the addressee. This is, indeed, the intent as well as the effect of letter writing.[62] The letter becomes a past shared experience to which the correspondents can refer in the same way as they refer to past face-to-face encounters (cf. 1 Thess. with 1 Cor. 5:9–13; 2 Cor. 2:1–4, and 12:14—13:10).

Thesis 3. Every letter implies at least one future stage in the relationship beyond the reception of the letter—the addressee's response. The response may entail an overt action, like doing as requested, or it may simply be a nonactive conclusion drawn in response to a request, like *not* detaining Blastus, or like having a new feeling about or image of the addresser, like knowing that he is alive and well. In the case of the Letter to the Romans, and also of the Letter to Philemon, the response may also include the expectation of meeting (Romans) or of reunion (Philemon).

Thesis 4. Addressers, addressees, and other persons referred to in letters are related to one another within a "system of typifications, relevances, roles, positions, statuses." The possibilities for social relations are limited, although they can become complicated, like in the Letter to Philemon, when the actors occupy multiple roles or positions by virtue of their participation in different spheres of relevance. However, the matrix in which all positions must be located, whether in one sphere of relevance or in several, is quite simple. Actors can be related as:

Addresser		*Addressee*
equal	to	equal
superior	to	inferior
inferior	to	superior

The relations of other actors to the addresser or addressee, or to both, can be mapped upon the same matrix. Thus Blastus relates as an inferior to both the addresser (Mystarion) and the addressee (Stotoetis). The relationship between Mystarion and Stotoetis is more problematical. Mystarion is a superior in the sphere of olive-gardening, and Stotoetis, as a chief priest, enjoys a position of superiority in a sphere of priestly things. Yet it is unclear whether Mystarion writes as an equal, as a superior in one sphere to a superior in another sphere, or as a superior to an inferior in some common sphere. Calling Stotoetis "my own Stotoetis" may represent a family relationship,[63] and Mystarion's commanding Stotoetis not to detain Blastus may represent his superiority over Stotoetis, either within the sphere of the family or by virtue of his having a rank within one sphere that is higher than Stotoetis's rank in his own sphere. The letter does not give us sufficient evidence to decide one way or the other, but it nicely illustrates the kinds of relations that need to be considered.

Thesis 5. The rhetoric, the style, and the tone of a letter correspond to the addresser's perception of his or her status in relation to the addressee. As observed earlier in connection with Koskenniemi's findings, this rhetoric is highly conventional, and therefore the conventions have to be identified. Thus in Mystarion's "my own Stotoetis," "own" may be purely conventional, like "dear" in "Dear John," or "sincerely" in "Sincerely yours." The identification of such conventions in Paul's letters is of critical importance, and the Letter to Philemon offers clues to one such convention. Often in his letters, Paul "appeals to" or "exhorts" (the Greek verb in both cases being *parakalō*)[64] his addressees. In Philemon 8—10, Paul claims to be bold enough in Christ to command Philemon, yet for love's sake he prefers to appeal to him. As we will see, Paul's "appeals" are a convention, also employed by royalty, which replaces a command when used with those who know that he has the power to command.[65] Thus the appeal, which on the face of it would appear to come from an inferior or an equal, has the force of a command because it comes from someone who claims and is recognized to be a superior, that is, who claims or has the power to command. On the other hand, however, the choice of an appeal over a command is also a matter of social style both for the person who makes the choice and for those who receive it. This, too, will call for more comment in the next chapter. For now, let it suffice to conclude our theses by noting that in addition to the complication of relationships resulting from actors playing multiple roles (thesis 4), rhetorical conventions introduce a further complication: they show that different systems of terminology (e.g., commands versus appeals) can represent the same system of roles.

THE LETTER TO PHILEMON:
FROM LETTER TO STORY—AND BACK

To construct the story of Paul's letter to Philemon we can adopt the same procedure followed in our study of Mystarion's letter. A few differences in the presentation will be apparent. Some are made possible by our already having walked through the method step by step; others are prompted by certain peculiarities of Paul's letter, like the smaller number of implied actions (only two) and the greater number of actions in the poetic sequence that appear in their referential order (six). In principle, however, the method is the same. First we will extract the referential actions from the letter and arrange them in their chronological order. Then we will identify the poetic sequence and analyze the relations between the two sequences. As with Mystarion's letter, we will derive the referential actions from the body of the letter (vv. 4–22) and use information from the opening (vv. 1–3) and close (vv. 23–25)[66] only for supplementary purposes. No referential actions are represented in either the opening or the close.

In establishing the referential sequence of actions underlying Paul's Letter to Philemon, the most immediate problem is to determine the very *first action* in this sequence. The task is complicated by apparently multiple story lines, one for each of the actors, and by the question of which line has a chronological beginning that is prior to the others. Because Onesimus's running away from Philemon is often cited as beginning the story, we should observe that Paul's imprisonment may precede it. Paul at least had to be imprisoned before Onesimus could come to him in prison, and from the letter one gets the impression that Paul had been imprisoned before Onesimus ran away. Similarly, Onesimus's story definitely does not figure in the end of the referential sequence, because his return to Philemon is followed by Philemon's response to both Onesimus's appearance and the arrival of Paul's letter, and by Paul's possible visit to Philemon, which is the final action in the referential sequence. For all of these reasons and more, Onesimus's story line is not the one to follow; his story is a story within a story. The question is, whose?

The story, of course, is Paul's, but it is also Paul's story about Philemon and his relationship with Paul. Paul is writing to Philemon,[67] about whom he has heard good reports (vv. 4–7), appealing to him to receive back Onesimus as he would receive Paul (vv. 8–17), offering to pay him Onesimus's debts (vv. 18–19a), expecting some "benefit" from him (vv. 20–21), and telling Philemon to prepare a guest room for him (v. 22). Indeed, Philemon's future relationship with Paul is even made contingent upon his response to Paul's appeal (v. 17). In this light, it is imperative that we recognize a reference to a beginning of this relationship in Paul's reminder to Philemon that he owes Paul his "own self" (v. 19b). That is to say, Paul refers to a moment, an action in the narrative sense, in which Philemon entered into debt to him. This moment is the *first action* in the referential sequence, and it certainly precedes Onesimus's running away and Paul's imprisonment. As most commentators suggest, in a more historical than literary context, Philemon's indebtedness is probably a metaphorical allusion to his having been converted by Paul.[68] This probability is literarily important in a number of ways. On the one hand, it is the second metaphor for conversion found in the letter, the first being Paul's "fathering" of Onesimus while in prison (v. 10).[69] On the other hand, the metaphor is also the second reference to indebtedness, the first being Onesimus's literal debt to Philemon, which *Paul* in effect repays (vv. 18–19a).[70] But of most immediate importance is the fact that no other action prior to Philemon's entry into debt is referred to in Paul's letter.[71] Thus, the story of Onesimus's running away/debt, conversion, return, and of Paul's repayment of the debt occur within the story of *Philemon's* conversion/debt and his projected repayment of his debt in the form of his response to Paul's appeal. The full significance of Paul's selection of Philemon's indebtedness to him as the first referential action in his story will become apparent shortly. Our task now is to determine both the actions that follow it and their referential order.

The *second* and *third referential actions* concern Paul's imprisonment (v. 9; cf. vv. 1, 10, 13, 23) and Onesimus's running away from Philemon, thereby incurring a debt to him (v. 15; cf. vv. 11–13 and 18–19a). As we have seen, it is not clear which of these is second and which third, since Onesimus could have run away before Paul was imprisoned. Nevertheless, it is clear that both must precede the *fourth action*, which concerns Onesimus's conversion by Paul during his imprisonment (v. 10; cf. vv. 11–13), and when we compare the referential and poetic sequences we will find that there is no significance to the relative order of the second and third referential actions.

The *fifth action* appears to be Paul's hearing about Philemon's love and faith (vv. 5–7). The precise source of this information is not given (Onesimus?), but the source is not pertinent to the sequence. It is more important that this fifth action, regardless of the source and regardless of whether the information was received on a single occasion or over a period of time, is located prior to the *sixth* and *seventh actions*, namely Paul's sending Onesimus back to Philemon (v. 12) and his letter appealing to Philemon to receive Onesimus as a brother and offering to repay Onesimus's debt to him (vv. 17–19a; cf. vv. 8–22 for the total message of appeal). Here, too, the relative order of these, the *sixth* and *seventh actions*, is unclear. From one perspective we can see the sending of Onesimus and the sending of the letter as simultaneous acts; from another we can see the decision to return Onesimus as preceding the writing of the letter. What seems to be decisive in determining their referential order is Paul's treatment of them in the poetic sequence. He separates the two actions by interposing an earlier one between them (action three, v. 15) and refers to the returning of Onesimus (v. 12) before making his appeal and offer (vv. 17–19a). Because the relocated action appears to interrupt the referential sequence of the two actions, I consider the returning of Onesimus as the *sixth action* and the sending of the letter as the *seventh*.

The *eighth* and *ninth actions* are the only two apparently implied actions necessary for our referential sequence. We have to envision, as Paul did, both the arrival of Onesimus and the letter at Philemon's house, action eight, and Philemon's response to Paul's letter, action nine. And because Paul in fact refers to Philemon's response in vv. 20–21 it is virtually explicit rather than implied. And last, the *tenth* and terminal referential *action* is Paul's visit to Philemon (v. 22). Whether we prefer to think in historical or in literary terms, Paul's very concrete instructions to Philemon to prepare a room for him are fundamental for understanding Paul's story and the rhetorical effect of his letter on its central character, Philemon. Philemon's response (action nine) to Paul's appeal and to Onesimus's return is set in the context of his expectation of Paul's appearance on the scene (action ten).

Although it may appear that we are putting the horse after the cart, our description of the referential cart can be tested against the poetic horse. That is to say, we can now turn to the poetic sequence of references to referential actions in order to see both what they are and what their poetic order is. By seeing what the actional parts are, it is possible to test our chronological arrangement of them, and by observing their poetic sequence we can obtain a basis for comparing our (or some other) referential arrangement with their poetic order. The list below is provided for the purpose of comparing our referential sequence with the poetic sequence. Since I have indicated my own understanding of the referential order, I will leave the testing of it to those who wish to do so.

Before listing the poetic sequence of actions a few comments are in order. Because Paul's letter emplots more referential actions than Mystarion's did, it would be well to remember that the poetic sequence of actions consists merely of the sequence in which individual actions are referred to in the letter as we read it. For this reason, the poetic sequence will correspond to the sequence of verse numbers in Paul's letter. The correspondence, however, need not be exhaustive; not every verse need be represented because only verses representing referential actions will appear in our list. The problem, therefore, is to identify referential actions, and in particular to distinguish between such actions and those actions that are not referentially significant. Some examples may be of help at this point.

Because actions are linguistically represented principally by verbs, verbs are the most frequent clues to actions. However, not all verbs are referentially significant, or of the same referential value. For example, when Paul says, "*I thank* my God always when *I remember* you in my prayers, because *I hear* of your love and faith . . .*" (vv. 4–5a), we have three verbs which *refer* to actions but only one of them is referentially significant. Paul's thanking God and remembering Philemon do not play a role in the total sequence of actions, whereas his hearing of Philemon's love and faith does. What Paul has heard about Philemon's refreshing the hearts of the saints (v. 7) is the basis of his appeal; he too acts out of the same love demonstrated by Philemon (v. 9), and he wants Philemon's response to his appeal to refresh *his* heart (v. 20b). Thus what Paul has heard is related to other actions in the referential sequence: Paul's appeal to Philemon and Philemon's response. Similarly, in vv. 12–14 there are four verbs referring to actions, but only one of them is referentially significant: "I am sending him back to you" (v. 12).[72] That Paul also wanted to keep Onesimus with him as a servant, and preferred to do nothing without Philemon's consent, is only supplementary to the one referential action which, of course, is a major one in the referential sequence. The following list therefore represents those actions in the poetic sequence that have a referential function. The only (implied) referential action that does not appear in the list is number eight, the arrival of Onesimus and the letter.

The Poetic Sequence		Referential Action
vv. 4–7	I hear of your love and faith	5
v. 9	I am now a prisoner	2
v. 10	I have become Onesimus's father[73]	4
v. 12	I am sending him back to you	6
v. 15	He was parted from you	3
vv. 17–19a	Receive him, charge it to my account, I will repay it	7
v. 19b	You owe me	1
vv. 20–21	Philemon's response	9
v. 22	I hope to visit you	10

Two diagrams will facilitate our comparison of the referential sequence of actions in the story *about* Philemon with the poetic sequence of those actions in the letter *to* Philemon. The simpler diagram is like the one used for Mystarion's letter.

Referential Sequence: 1 2 3 4 5 6 — 7 — (8) (9) 10
Poetic Sequence: <u>5</u> 2 — 4 — 6 <u>3</u> 7 <u>1</u> (8) 9 10

The longer diagram differs from our discussion of Mystarion's letter because Paul's letter emplots more referential actions. The diagram is organized according to the referential sequence and it contains three columns. The column on the left contains a verbal description of each referential action; the center column contains a number describing the action's location in the referential sequence, with verse references added in parentheses; the column on the right represents the referential numbers in their poetic sequence (e.g., the fifth referential action is the first one referred to in the poetic sequence, as in the simpler diagram above). Because several actions in the poetic sequence appear in the same order as in the referential sequence, I have adjusted the horizontal lines to allow this parallelism to be apparent. Dashes therefore appear in each column to indicate where a referential action has been poetically relocated. For example, because action three appears between actions six and

**The Referential and Poetic Sequences of Actions
in the Letter to Philemon**

Referential Sequence		*Poetic Sequence*
Philemon incurs a debt to Paul	1 (v. 19b)	5 (vv. 4–7)
Paul is imprisoned	2 (v. 9; cf. vv. 1, 10, 13, 23)	2 (v. 9)
Onesimus runs away and incurs a debt to Philemon	3 (vv. 15; cf. vv. 11–13 and 18–19a)	———
Onesimus is converted by an imprisoned Paul	4 (v. 10; cf. v. 13)	4 (v. 10)
Paul hears of Philemon's love and faith	5 (vv. 4–7)	———
Paul sends Onesimus back to Philemon	6 (v. 12)	6 (v. 12)
———	—	3 (v. 15)
Paul sends a letter of appeal to Philemon and offers to repay Onesimus's debt	7 (vv. 17–19a)	7 (vv. 17–19a)
———	—	1 (v. 19b)
Onesimus and the letter arrive	8 (implied)	8 (implied)
Philemon responds to Paul's appeal	9 (vv. 20–21)	9 (vv. 20–21)
Paul's anticipated visit to Philemon	10 (v. 22)	10 (v. 22)

seven in the poetic sequence, a dash appears both between actions two and four in the right hand column and between actions six and seven in the other two columns (see also the simpler diagram above).

As we saw in connection with Mystarion's letter, differences between the poetic sequence and the referential sequence are indications of possibly significant features of both the referential story and the poetic letter. A poetically relocated referential action is of potential referential significance because *it* has been selected for relocation, and it is of poetic significance because of its role in the poetic sequence. From our two diagrams it is apparent that the poetic sequence of actions referred to in the Letter to Philemon differs from the referential sequence in only three actions, numbers one, three, and five. Apart from the interruptions caused by the relocation of

70

these three actions, all of the rest of the actions appear in the same order in both sequences. They therefore provide a chronological background for the information distributed throughout the letter. We can begin our study of the differences between the two sequences by looking at the effects of the relocation of the three actions.

First, we should recognize that collectively the relocation of the three actions appears against the background of a story which is represented by the series of actions that the two sequences have in common (i.e., 2 / 4 / 6 / 7 / 8 / 9 / 10). In reading the letter (i.e., the poetic sequence), this background story stands out by virtue of the chronological sequence of its parts. The relocated actions, because they do not chronologically belong where they are, stand in a non-chronological relationship with the actions surrounding them. The reader of the letter is therefore put in the position not of locating them in their proper chronological order, but of relating them to the actions around them. Let us consider first the background actions which have the quality of a story. This story, minus the poetically relocated actions, is striking because of what it does *not* report, as we can see in the following list of the actions the two sequences have in common.

Actions the Two Sequences Have in Common

2 Paul is imprisoned
4 Onesimus is converted by an imprisoned Paul
6 Paul sends Onesimus back to Philemon
7 Paul sends a letter of appeal to Philemon and offers to pay Onesimus's debt to him
(8) Onesimus and the letter arrive
9 Philemon responds to Paul's appeal
10 Paul's visit to Philemon is anticipated

It is immediately apparent that this story is entirely innocent of any complications because it lacks the two actions which would give the story a real plot—Philemon's incurring of a debt to Paul (one) and Onesimus's incurring of a debt to Philemon when he ran away (three). Thus, two of the three relocated actions prove to be focal both to the referential story and to the letter, and each of them is concerned with indebtedness. Indeed, Philemon also proves to be the focal actor because he is both a debtor and a debtee, and the thematic plot of the story concerns debts and their repayment. But what is the precise significance of these two relocated actions, and what is the role of the third, action five, Paul's hearing of Philemon's love and faith? To answer these questions we need to consider each

71

of the poetically relocated actions in terms of their functions in the poetic sequence, that is, in terms of their relations to the actions around them.

The first action in the poetic sequence is the fifth action in the referential sequence. Paul begins his letter by referring to his having heard of Philemon's love and faith among the saints. The significance of this action's appearance in this location derives more from formal and rhetorical considerations than from the poetics of actions. Formally,[74] Paul expresses his thanksgiving for the addressee's love and/or faith at the beginning of at least two other letters, the letter to Rome (1:8; faith) and the first letter to Thessalonica (1:2–3; faith and love). The same expression is found in three other letters whose Pauline authorship is disputed, namely 2 Thessalonians (1:3–4; faith and love), Colossians (1:3–4; faith and love), and 2 Timothy (1:3–5; faith). Actually, for our purposes it is not particularly important at this point whether Paul wrote these three letters or not. If he did, they support the point that such expressions are a matter of form in Paul's letters; if he did not, they are still relevant because it would seem that other writers imitated what they considered to be his epistolary form.[75] It also appears that Paul's *having heard* about his addressee's love and faith is related to his expressions of thanksgiving, because in several letters he introduces in these expressions the source of his knowledge about their faith and love.[76] Rhetorically,[77] on the other hand, Paul's reference to his having heard of Philemon's love and faith functions in terms of the strategy of his discourse, message, or argument. We have already observed that Paul relates what he has heard about Philemon to his own appeal to Philemon, which formally follows his thanksgiving in vv. 8–22. Like Philemon (vv. 4–7), Paul acts out of love by appealing to him rather than commanding him (vv. 8–9), and he wants Philemon to respond by refreshing his, Paul's, heart with an act of faith and love like those that have already refreshed the hearts of the saints (v. 20b; cf. v. 7). Formally, therefore, the letter is structured in terms of the pattern "I have heard/therefore I appeal,"[78] while rhetorically the total discourse is structured in terms of the pattern "you have refreshed the hearts of the saints with your faith and love, now refresh my heart also." There is, however, apparently no significance to the placement of action five in terms of the poetic sequence of actions, since Paul's having heard about Philemon has no direct effect upon action two which follows it, Paul's imprisonment, or upon action four, Onesimus's conversion, which poetically follows action two. Consequently, the poetic location of action five is principally motivated by formal and rhetorical considerations.

The peculiar role of the poetics of actions is better seen in the other two relocated actions. The second action in question, number three, refers to Onesimus's having run away from Philemon, thereby incurring a debt to him (v. 15; cf. vv. 18–19a). Whereas the first poetic action has been brought forward from its later referential position, here we have an early referential action that has been placed later in the poetic sequence, between the sixth and seventh actions (i.e., 6 / 3 / 7). Possibly this comparison reveals more of Paul's rhetorical strategy, since he has relocated into the initial poetic position an action bearing positive information concerning one of the actors, the one to whom he is addressing his appeal, while he relocates in a later position an action bearing negative information about another actor, the one *about* whom he is making the appeal. By locating action three where he has, Paul has deferred negative information about Onesimus until he has presented the positive information that Onesimus has been converted (action four) and then sent back to Philemon (action six). Similarly, he has deferred the "negative" information about Philemon's debt to him, action one, by placing it after action seven and by replacing it in the initial poetic slot with action five, the good news about Philemon, his acts of love and faith among the saints. In both cases, positive information about the actors has been made to precede negative information about them. Therefore, one of the chief effects of the three relocations is to encourage Philemon to act in a certain way, first as a further demonstration of his faith and love (the replacement of action one with action five), and second because his runaway slave is returning as a new man (the deferral of action three). Both relocations supply because-motives for Philemon's response to Paul's appeal.

If placing action three after action six has the effect of diminishing the weight of Onesimus's guilt in Philemon's eyes, the effect of inserting it *before* action seven is virtually to exonerate Onesimus. In action seven Paul asks Philemon to receive Onesimus as he would receive Paul himself, and then Paul commits himself to repaying Onesimus's debt (vv. 17–19a). Onesimus's slate is therefore virtually clean as a result of his conversion, return, and the repayment of his debt to Philemon. And Paul's slate is clean, too, because he has promptly sent the runaway slave back to his master after his conversion.

With action seven Onesimus's story-line comes to an end, but a comparison of the referential and poetic sequences discloses that, depending on one's point of view, there are actually two stories about Onesimus. One story is presumably Philemon's, the other Paul's. Philemon's story is that of the referential sequence, and it hinges on Onesimus's having run away; Philemon presumably sees that event as the beginning of the story, and all subsequent events in relation to it (i.e., 3 / 4 / 5 / 6 / 7). Paul, however, both acknowledges and participates in that story (6 / 7) and rewrites it, for *his* story hinges on Onesimus's conversion, with which he begins his reference to Onesimus in the poetic sequence (4 / 6 / 3 / 7). Philemon's story begins with, and is about, the old man, the useless slave; Paul's story begins with, and is about, the new man, the useful brother (cf. v. 11 and 15–16). For Paul, Onesimus's conversion, which he expresses with a metaphor of childbirth, makes Onesimus a new man by reshaping his story. For Paul, it is not what Onesimus was or did as a slave that is important, but what he is as a brother, both to Paul and to Philemon.

Thus far we have been looking at action seven in terms of Onesimus's story-line and its close in Paul's repayment of the brother's debt. However, at the same time that action seven brings Onesimus's story to a close it also brings Philemon's story-line to a climax. It does so by making Philemon's continued partnership with Paul contingent upon Philemon's response to Paul's appeal: in order to preserve this partnership Philemon must do as Paul says. It is in this context that we come to the third poetically relocated action, for action one, Philemon's incurring of a debt to Paul, follows action seven (v. 19b). The effects of locating this action here are momentous both for Paul's letter and for his story. Besides providing a because-motive for Philemon's response, the juxtaposition of Onesimus's canceled debt to Philemon with Philemon's outstanding debt to Paul is critical because with one stroke it shifts the burden of indebtedness from Onesimus to Philemon, and in the process places three other actions in a new light: Paul's appeal to Philemon, both action seven and the letter as a whole, now becomes Paul's calling in of Philemon's debt; Philemon's response (action nine)[79] is therefore his repayment or default on his debt; and Paul's anticipated visit (action ten) becomes a visit by the debtee to the debtor to see if the debt has been paid. Paul may have lovingly deferred the "negative" information about Philemon until late in the letter, but when he introduced it he did so with devastating effect, using it to transform what looked like one story into another by transforming Philemon the seeming debtee into Philemon the debtor.[80] Further light is shed on this transformation, and therefore on both Paul's letter and story, when we consider when it occurs in the process of the letter's poetic composition.

It is widely recognized that Paul dictated his letter up to v. 19, at which point he took up the "pen" (stylus) himself to write vv. 19–25.[81] This means that in the middle of action seven Paul decided to complete the letter in his own hand. He had brought Onesimus's story to a close when he offered to repay Onesimus's debt in v. 18. But we have also seen that Paul had earlier transformed the story of Onesimus's debt into a story about Onesimus's conversion, and that by using a metaphor of childbirth to describe his conversion Paul located Onesimus's debt in a previous "life" and thereby rendered his conversion the ultimate repayment of his debt. Verse 18 is entirely consistent with Paul's story about Onesimus, even though his initial offer to repay Onesimus's financial debt appears almost as an afterthought appended to his appeal in v. 17: "If he has wronged you in any way, or owes you anything, charge that to my account" (v. 18). Now it is at precisely this point that Paul takes pen in hand and completes action seven in much stronger terms than those of v. 18, "I, Paul, write this with my own hand, I will repay it," and then adds action one: "to say nothing of your owing me even your own self" (v. 19). To this Paul further adds action nine, Philemon's response, and action ten, Paul's anticipated visit: "Yes, brother, I want some benefit from you in the Lord. Refresh my heart in Christ. Confident of your obedience, I write to you, knowing that you will do even more than I say. At the same time, prepare a guest room for me, for I am hoping through your church's prayers to be granted to all of you" (vv. 20–22).[82]

It appears from these additions in Paul's hand that he only came to realize fully his story and its rhetorical possibilities when he finally verbalized his appeal in v. 17. The critical moment came when he casually added to his appeal his willingness to pay Onesimus's debt, for just at that point he took the pen in hand, first to commit himself more strongly to paying the monetary debt and then to identify Philemon as a metaphorical debtor.[83] Paul must have realized at that moment the rhetorical possibilities of the idea of indebtedness—that having canceled Onesimus's literal debt to Philemon, he could now render his appeal to Philemon as a metaphorical calling in of Philemon's "debt" to him. A mere appeal must have seemed too weak, as a command had earlier seemed too strong. A personal debt, however, adds to the appeal for a freely chosen act of goodness (v. 14) a sense of personal obligation that still falls short of the authoritarian command that Paul sought from the beginning to avoid. Be this as it may, to understand the power of the obligation Paul laid on Philemon we have to consider further the metaphor of debt.

The idea of indebtedness in this letter is linked both to the notion of conversion and to the "currency" of repayment. Originally, the idea of indebtedness was associated with Onesimus's monetary, and therefore literal, debt to Philemon. For Paul, Onesimus's conversion was the decisive factor in the repayment of this debt, for it changed his relationship with his master, Philemon. By representing Onesimus's conversion as a metaphorical "birth," Paul achieved two things. First, he located the relationship of indebtedness between the master and slave in the past life of the slave, thereby forcing Philemon to view that relationship as past rather than as current. In addition, by committing himself to repay the monetary debt the relationship of indebtedness was literally terminated. Second, and more importantly, with his "birth" Onesimus entered into a new relationship with Philemon, namely a relationship of brother (cf. vv. 15–16). The current relationship between Onesimus and Philemon is therefore a sibling relationship, which for Paul is nonetheless real for being metaphorical. The problem Paul faced was to get Philemon to acknowledge this relationship by accepting Onesimus as his brother, "both in the flesh and in the Lord" (v. 16). Just what this both/and entails will concern us more fully in subsequent chapters. For now it is only important to see that the mode of Philemon's repayment of his debt to Paul is to receive Onesimus as his brother. We do not yet know how this repayment affects the master-slave relationship between Onesimus and Philemon because Paul never addresses this relationship directly.

The mode of Philemon's repayment of his debt is important because it is linked to the source of his indebtedness to Paul, namely Philemon's own conversion, for which his indebtedness is a metaphor, and by which *he* became a brother to Paul (cf. vv. 7, 20) and to all of the saints regardless of when they were converted. Philemon's obligation, his "debt," is to *be* a brother to the brothers and sisters in the Lord. Upon conversion and entry into the sibling relationship that obtains among the children of God, one becomes a brother or a sister, and behaving as such becomes a responsibility. This sociological understanding underlies the seemingly paradoxical fact that one man's conversion is represented as the source of the repayment of his debt (Onesimus), while another man's conversion is the source of his indebtedness (Philemon). For Onesimus, becoming a brother marks the end of one form of relationship with Philemon. For Philemon, being a brother requires him to acknowledge a new form of relationship with Onesimus, a form that was introduced when Onesimus became a brother.

For Paul, then, the governing relationship among church members is the sibling relationship, the relationship between brothers. He himself relates to those whom he has converted, like Onesimus and Philemon, as a brother (vv. 7, 16, 10), but he also has another role as a "converter," and it is in this capacity that he both sends Onesimus back to Philemon and appeals to Philemon who is, besides being a brother, also Paul's "fellow worker" (v. 1) and "partner" (v. 17).[84] It appears that at the beginning of the dictation of his letter Paul was wrestling with the problem of reconciling his brotherly role as an equal with his other role as a superior, but that when he came to the climax of his appeal in vv. 15–18 he began to see a new way of dealing with his problem in the idea of the brotherhood as a source of obligation (debt) and as a form of payment. This idea gave him further leverage in his appeal by expanding its basis from Philemon's free will and brotherly love (vv. 8–14) to the social reality of the brotherhood.[85] But the expansion also has the effect of returning Paul to his position of authority "in Christ" (v. 8; cf. v. 20), in which he is a "father" as well as a brother. Having backed off from this authority at the beginning of the letter, the idea of Philemon's indebtedness to him for his life in Christ seems to have emboldened him to speak from authority: I want some benefit from you; refresh my heart in Christ; confident of your obedience, I write you, knowing that you will do more than I say (vv. 20–21). The "I" who says these things is the "I" who has the power to command, not the "I" of merely a brother among brothers.

Much of what we have observed about the poetics of actions in Paul's letter also helps us to weigh the actions in his story. If we review the referential sequence in light of our observations thus far, it becomes apparent that the first action in that sequence, Philemon's incurring of a debt to Paul, supplies the suspense which governs the whole story—a debt is incurred, of Philemon's own self. When and how will it be repaid? Because debts have to be paid, the first action introduces the expectation of its closural satisfaction. This expectation is reinforced by actions three and seven, in which *Onesimus's* monetary debt is incurred and then paid by Paul. The poetic relocation of action one then renders action seven the denouement of the story by interpreting Paul's appeal as the calling in of the remaining outstanding debt, namely Philemon's. By the same token, action nine becomes Philemon's repayment of his debt to Paul, but because the story does not tell us how Philemon responded, it comes to a close with a certain ambiguity: Did he repay or did he default on his debt? However, the story does not end with this ambiguity. Rather, it ends with Paul's anticipated visit which provides us with two possible endings to the story, one for each of Philemon's alternatives. If Philemon pays his debt, Paul will come as a brother and as a partner. If he does not, Paul will come to collect his debt personally. Action ten is therefore both a carrot and a stick.

In terms of the sociology of both the story and the letter, the ending in action ten suggests the conclusion that both Philemon and other readers should draw. Viewed in the context of the whole story, the ending requires an action by Philemon that will either preserve his equality with Paul as a brother and as a partner, or render him an inferior as a debtor to Paul—and to the brotherhood. One of the consequences of Paul's new insights at the moment he took the pen in hand was that there was more than Philemon's partnership with Paul at stake in Philemon's response to Paul's appeal. Partnership with Paul only involves Philemon's relationship with Paul. But if Philemon refuses to accept a brother as a brother, then Philemon's status in the brotherhood is at stake, for *he* has not shown himself to be a brother. This, I believe, is the underlying issue in Paul's letter as it stands. Paul's visit to Philemon involves not only Philemon's decision to be or not to be a brother, but also Paul's response—to say, "You are a brother." Or, "You are not a brother." Clearly, Paul wants Philemon and other readers to conclude that only one response is reasonable for Philemon—to be, and to remain, a brother by being a brother to Onesimus.

Nevertheless, because Paul has not openly addressed the master-slave relationship between Philemon and Onesimus, we cannot from our literary considerations yet see what other reasoning is involved for Philemon. It remains for us to determine from further sociological considerations both what Philemon's problem actually was and the constraints influencing both his decision and the story's outcome. We have seen that Paul's story about Philemon is constructed around the themes of indebtedness and repayment as these occur within the brotherhood of Christ, and that these themes, however literal or metaphorical, raise the fundamental issue of the economy, the integrity, of the brotherhood. Further consideration of the full range of social arrangements and symbolic forms governing the story's narrative world should help us to get a clearer picture of the social economy of the brotherhood. Perhaps from this picture we will be able to determine whether Philemon's problem is to figure out how he can be *both* a master *and* a brother to Onesimus, or whether it is to decide *between* being a master and a brother—and a partner.[86]

NOTES

1. Eco, *The Role of the Reader*, 13, cf. 29–31.
2. The letter is P. BGU 37. The translation is my own, based on the text and accompanying photograph printed in Adolf Deissmann, *Light From the Ancient East*, trans. Lionel R. M. Strachan (New York: Doran Press, 1927), 170–72. A different translation based on an uncorrected transcription of the original text is given by William G. Doty, *Letters in Primitive Christianity*

(Philadelphia: Fortress Press, 1973), 4. For the correction, see Deissmann, p. 171, n. 2. The chief difference is in the verb used to describe what Mystarion wants Stotoetis to do. Doty has Mystarion telling Stotoetis to see to it that Blastus does not *loiter*, but the correct verb, as is clear in the photograph of the letter, has Mystarion telling Stotoetis not *to detain* Blastus. Depending on the verb, we therefore have not only two different messages but also two different stories.

    3. Deissmann, *Light From the Ancient East*, 172, drew this connection between Mystarion's letter and Paul's. For discussion and further literature on dictation and additions in the author's own hand, see Doty, *Letters in Primitive Christianity*, 40–41. On the Letter to Philemon, see Lohse, *Colossians and Philemon*, 204–5; and Stuhlmacher, *Der Brief an Philemon*, 50. Commentators differ in their views on just how much Paul added in his own hand, e.g. v. 19a, v. 19, or vv. 19–25. The significance of Paul's taking up the pen where he did is discussed in the last section of this chapter.

    4. The Greek word translated "chief priest" (*lesōnis*) is itself a translation of an Egyptian word used to refer to the chief administrator of an Egyptian temple (cf. Deissman, *Light From the Ancient East*, p. 171, n. 1).

    5. Deissmann saw no relevance of the expression "my own" (*idios*) for the relationship between Mystarion and Stotoetis (*Light From the Ancient East*, p. 171, n. 3). More recently, Heikki Koskenniemi, *Studien zur Idee und Phraseologie des griechischen Briefes bis 400 n. Chr.* (Helsinki: Suomalaien Tiedeakatemie, 1956), 104, arrived at a more ambiguous conclusion from his study of Greek papyrus letters. On the one hand, he cites our letter as illustrating a usage which designates a close connection between a sender and a receiver when it appears with the receiver's name in the opening or address of the letter (from the first-century c.e. and after). The word is used both of familial relatives and of slaves. On the other hand, however, in letters having to do with economic relations, as ours seems to do, Koskenniemi sees no evidence that the word implies a close relationship between the correspondents. Consequently, because the word "my own" may represent no more than a convention of letter writing we cannot use it as a source of sociological information bearing on our story.

    6. This actual temporal point of view is not to be confused with the phraseological temporality of the so-called epistolary aorist, on which see n. 72, below.

    7. Because 2 Cor. 2:14—7:4 interrupts the continuity of 1:3—2:14 with 7:5–16, it is probably an insertion into that continuous text. But whether or not it is an insertion, Paul's temporal point of view is in the time after Titus has returned to him with news of Corinth (7:6ff.). All other events referred to took place prior to this.

    8. On because-motives and in-order-to-motives, see n. 23 of the introductory chapter.

    9. The verb *hora* is an imperative.

    10. Whether Blastus is a slave or free(d)man employee is not clear, either from "my Blastus" or from anything else in the letter. It is clear, however, that he is in a position of social inferiority to both Mystarion and Stotoetis, who have the power to manipulate him for their own ends.

11. On the relationship between point of view and narrative voice, see Chatman, *Story and Discourse*, 151–58; and Uspensky, *Poetics of Composition*, 17–56.

12. For example, while Mystarion sees the encounter between Blastus and Stotoetis in terms of whether or not Stotoetis will detain Blastus and delay the work in the olive gardens, the other two principals could view the encounter in totally different terms. The problem here is not one of historical ignorance on our part, i.e., of exactly what was *really* going on; rather, it is a problem of remembering that we are in the first instance dealing with Mystarion's story, not with Blastus's story or Stotoetis's story, and not with history. The story we construct from a letter is the writer's story, and he is like the first person (involved) narrator of stories generally. Unlike third person narrators, who independently of the actors tell us about each of them, even represent their individual points of view, the first person narrator is an actor in his own story and everything he tells us is told from his perspective. This conclusion may weaken the historical significance of letters, but it does so rightly. The stories we construct from letters are stories of how the writer/narrator views things, and of how he wants things to turn out. We need other letters or other stories from other points of view in order to be able to begin to plot history, as, for example, in the correspondence between Pliny and Sabinianus, whose freedman had fled to Pliny (see the texts in Lohse, *Colossians and Philemon*, 196–97).

13. What I have called intentional point of view is termed ideological point of view by Uspensky, *Poetics of Composition*, 8–16.

14. The distinction between referential and poetic sequences is derived both from Roman Jakobson's referential and poetic functions and from the Russian Formalist distinction between story (*fabula*) and plot (*sujet*), on which see my *Literary Criticism for New Testament Critics*, 33–48. The distinctions correspond respectively to what I called story time and plotted time in chap. 3 of that book.

15. In addition to the reference in the preceding note, see Linda R. Waugh, "The Poetic Function in the Theory of Roman Jakobson," *Poetics Today* 2 (1980): 57–82; and Wellek and Warren, *Theory of Literature*, 20–28. For critical discussion see also Barbara Herrnstein Smith, "Narrative Versions, Narrative Theories," and the responses by Nelson Goodman and Seymour Chatman in *On Narrative*, 209–32 and 255–65. In my own use of the distinction between referential and poetic sequences, the differences serve as a heuristic device, not as a measure of the quality of artfulness.

16. A slightly more complicated diagram, which will be employed in our discussion of Paul's story about Philemon, represents the degree to which the two sequences follow the same order. This agreement is important in some letters, like the Letter to Philemon, but not in all, as in Mystarion's letter.

Referential Sequence: 1 2 3 — 4 5 — — — 6 7 8 9
Poetic Sequence: — (2) — (5) 4 — 9 3 1 (6) (7) (8) —

17. Simply, "to get forked sticks" implies that the need for them has arisen.

18. Like the possible significance of agreements in the order of the referential and poetic sequences, the significance of the juxtaposition of actions and of motivating actions is something disclosed by the differences between the two sequences; it is not required by the differences as such. Methodologically, one has to determine in every letter whether or not agreements or disagreements between the sequences signify anything at all. We should also note at this juncture that our study of the poetics of actions does not explain the difference and relationship between the two sets of actions and motivations (i.e., between 4/9 and 3/1). Although we can see that the body of the letter is divided into two parts, the poetics of actions moves us to another level of analysis, one which is formal and rhetorical, or both (on which see nn. 74 and 77, below). Linguistically, the conjunction "therefore" (*oun*) in "See to it, therefore," indicates a transition between the two sets of actions. In terms of the form and rhetoric of the total message, this transitional word renders the first set of actions (4/9) the because-motive for the second set (3/1). Thus the first set becomes the premise (because I have done X) and the second the consequence (I want you to do Y). The difference between the poetics of actions and such formal and/or rhetorical functions will concern us more fully in the Letter to Philemon. In the present context it is only important for us to realize that more than the poetics of actions is involved in the composition of a letter. That is, of course, to be expected, since we are dealing with texts that are *not* narratives.

19. Doty, *Letters in Primitive Christianity*, 4.

20. See n. 3.

21. Cf. Koskenniemi, *Studien zur Idee and Phraseologie des griechischen Briefes*, 151–54, 168–69; and Doty, *Letters in Primitive Christianity*, 39–41.

22. Ibid.

23. Koskenniemi, ibid., 155–205, summarized by Doty, ibid, 11–16.

24. Berger and Luckmann, *The Social Construction of Reality*, 28; cf., 28–34 and 154.

25. Koskenniemi, *Studien zur Idee und Phraseologie des griechischen Briefes*, 202.

26. Georg Simmel, *The Sociology of Georg Simmel*, trans. and ed. Kurt H. Wolff (New York: Free Press, 1950), 352–55, "Written Communication." Koskenniemi does not cite Simmel in his bibliography, nor does he deal directly with sociological issues. Nevertheless, Koskenniemi provides a wealth of material for sociological reflections on the letter. For a more general hermeneutical discussion of the relationship between face-to-face speaking and writing, see Paul Ricoeur, *Interpretation Theory: Discourse and the Surplus of Meaning* (Fort Worth: Texas Christian Univ. Press, 1976).

27. Simmel, *The Sociology of Georg Simmel*, 353. On the differences between epistolary and personal presence, see 2 Cor. 10:8–11.

28. Schutz, *Collected Papers*, 2:112, from the essay "The Homecomer," which deals with presence and absence (106–19).

29. The most convenient source of Schutz's comments on typification

may be found in the volume edited by Helmut Wagner, *Alfred Schutz On Phenomenology and Social Relations: Selected Writings* (Chicago: Univ. of Chicago Press, 1970), 111–22. See also pp. 200–235 for selections dealing with interpersonal communication and indirect social relationships. For a brief description of the dialectics of the typical and the particular in interpersonal relation, see Berger and Luckmann, *The Social Construction of Reality*, 30–33.

30. Berger and Luckmann, *The Social Construction of Reality*.

31. Ibid., 28.

32. Ibid., 33.

33. Ibid.

34. Ibid., 42.

35. Ibid.

36. Ibid., 45. Cf. Wagner, ed., *Alfred Schutz On Phenomenology and Social Relations*, 111–22. For a more extended discussion, see Alfred Schutz, *Reflections on the Problem of Relevance*, ed. Richard M. Zaner (New Haven: Yale Univ. Press, 1970); and Ronald C. Cox, "Schutz's Theory of Relevance: A Phenomenological Critique," *Phaenomenologica* 77 (The Hague: Martinus Nijhoff, 1978).

37. Berger and Luckmann, *The Social Construction of Reality*, 54.

38. Ibid., 65. Cf. Clifford Geertz: "The anthropological study of religion is therefore a two-stage operation: first, an analysis of the system of meanings embodied in the symbols which make up the religion proper, and, second, the relating of these systems to social-structural and psychological processes" (*The Interpretation of Cultures*, 125). See also the discussion of the sociology of narrative worlds in the introductory chapter, above, especially in connection with T. O. Beidelman.

39. Berger and Luckmann, *The Social Construction of Reality*, 65.

40. Ibid., 95–96, (cf. p. 40 and n. 69), and more broadly, 92–128. In n. 69 the authors note the proximity of their notion of symbolic universe to Durkheim's notion of religion, i.e., as a collective representation of collective "sentiments."

41. Ibid., 93–94. This distinction between knowledge and values is closely related to the notions of model of/model for and of indicative and imperative referred to in n. 50 of the introductory chapter, above.

42. Berger and Luckmann, *The Social Construction of Reality*, 40.

43. Ibid.

44. Ibid. See also Schutz, "Symbol, Reality and Society," in *Collected Papers*, 1:287–356; and more briefly, *Alfred Schutz on Phenomenology and Social Relations*, 245–52; and Geertz, *The Interpretation of Cultures*, 89–94.

45. How this symbolic use of everyday language is related to everyday life will be discussed in chap. 3, below.

46. Berger and Luckmann, *The Social Construction of Reality*, 76 (cf. 75–76).

47. Ibid., 104–16.

48. Ibid., 105.

49. Ibid., 110.

50. Ibid., 110–12. See further, Peter Berger, *The Sacred Canopy* (Garden

City, N.Y.: Doubleday & Co., Anchor Books, 1969), and especially the appendix on "Sociological and Theological Perspectives," 179–85; and on symbol systems and symbolic universes, Clifford Geertz, "Religion as a Cultural System," in his *The Interpretation of Cultures*, 87–125.

51. For extended discussion, see Berger and Luckmann, *The Social Construction of Reality*, 116–28 and 129–47.

52. See Simmel, *The Sociology of Georg Simmel*, Part Three, "Superordination and Subordination," 181–303.

53. Berger and Luckmann, *The Social Construction of Reality*, 131.

54. Ibid., 132; on primary socialization, see further pp. 129–37.

55. Ibid., 138–57, on secondary socialization, and 157–63, on re-socialization.

56. On the institution of slavery in first-century Greece, see, e.g., S. Scott Bartchy, *Mallōn Chrēsai: First-Century Slavery and the Interpretation of 1 Corinthians 7:21*, SBLDS 11 (Missoula, Mont.: Scholars Press, 1973), 37–125.

57. Schütz, *Collected Papers*, 2:252 (cf. 251–54).

58. Ibid.

59. Ibid., 254.

60. It is essential not to confuse what Paul says the church and life in it is, which derives from his symbolic universe, and the sociological reality of the church and life in it. Paul describes life in the church in the language of involuntary associations, but the people in the church as often as not act as though it were a voluntary association. Perhaps the best example of this distinction is 1 Corinthians, where members of the community are building up among themselves a "system of typifications, relevances, roles, positions, and statuses," to which Paul responds by telling them how things really *are* and therefore *should be.*

61. Most of the theses are sociological elaborations of points made by Koskenniemi and elaborated by Doty and others.

62. This is one of Koskenniemi's central observations. See *Studien zur Idee und Phraseologie des griechischen Briefes*, 88–95.

63. See n. 5, above, and thesis 5, which concerns the language and rhetoric representing social relations. Koskenniemi's studies are invaluable aids to seeing actual relations behind the conventional language of ancient Greek letters.

64. Whereas Koskenniemi covered a wide range of epistolary language, Carl J. Bjerkelund concentrated on just this one term, *parakalō*, in his *Parakalō: Form, Funktion und Sinn der parakalō-Saetze in den paulinischen Briefen*, Bibliotheca Theologica Norvegica 1 (Oslo: Universitetsforlaget, 1967). For a brief description in English of Bjerkelund's findings, see Hendrikus Boers, "The Form Critical Study of Paul's Letters: I Thessalonians as a Case Study," *NTS* 22 (1976): 140–58, especially 154–56.

65. See Boers, ibid., 155.

66. I include in my understanding of the body of the Pauline letter the initial thanksgiving (*eucharistō*) section, which I also see as extending right up to the transition to the appeal or exhortation (*parakalō*). Thus I view the body of the Pauline letter as consisting of two main parts, which are lin-

guistically introduced by thanksgiving and appeal formulas. I believe that
Bjerkelund, *Parakalō*, was the first to sense this structure, although he did
not rigorously follow it up. Doty, *Letters in Primitive Christianity*, adequately represents alternative views, which are oriented to the formulaic
character of several parts of the Pauline letter. I prefer Bjerkelund's more
organic approach to the atomizing approach, and would rather consider
the smaller parts within the framework of the whole. It is fair to say that at
least among American critics there is a clear tendency towards a more
organic, holistic perception of the Pauline letter. This is evident, for example, from a comparison of Robert Funk's survey of scholarship prior to 1969
("The Letter: Form and Style," in his *Language, Hermeneutic & Word of God*
[New York: Harper & Row, 1969], 205–74); Doty's *Letters in Primitive Christianity* from 1973; and Boers's essay, "The Form Critical Study of Paul's
Letters," from 1976. See also John L. White, "The Structural Analysis of
Philemon: A Point of Departure in the Formal Analysis of the Pauline Let-
ter," in *The Society of Biblical Literature, 1971 Seminar Papers—28–31*
(SBL, 1971), 1:1–47. Holism also characterizes another approach which is
oriented to the extrinsic rhetorical models of Greco-Roman antiquity: F. F.
Church, "Rhetorical Structure and Design in Paul's Letter to Philemon,"
HTR 71 (1978): 17–31; Hans Dieter Betz, *Galatians* (Philadelphia: Fortress
Press, 1979); idem, "The Literary Composition and Function of Paul's Let-
ter to the Galatians," *NTS* 21 (1975): 353–79. Wilhelm Wuellner, "Paul's
Rhetoric of Argumentation in Romans," *CBQ* 38 (1976): 330–51; idem,
"Greek Rhetoric and Pauline Argumentation," in *Early Christian Literature
and the Classical Intellectual Tradition: Inhonorem Robert M. Grant*, ed. William Schoedel and Robert L. Wilken, Theologie historique 53 (Paris: Beau-
chesne, 1979), 177–88; idem, "Paul as Pastor: The Function of Rhetorical
Questions in 1 Corinthians," in *Colloquium Biblicum* (Louvain, August
1984, to be published). Despite this tendency, however, Bjerkelund's contribution remains to be fully appreciated, let alone developed, and there is no
consensus on how to relate insights derived from the formulaic character of
Paul's letters, from the relationship between these formulas and those of
other contemporary letters, from the composition of Paul's letters, both
individually and collectively, and from generic conventions influencing the
composition of several different types (genres) of letters known from antiquity. That is to say, the study of Paul's letters suffers from the same problems as the study of biblical narrative—an inability yet to perceive the
literary whole and its parts as functions of the whole. Our identification of
intrinsic rhetorical features can serve as a basis for further comparative
study. See also, George A. Kennedy, *New Testament Interpretation through
Rhetorical Criticism* (Chapel Hill: University of North Carolina Press, 1984),
unavailable prior to the completion of my manuscript.

67. Despite the naming of Paul and Timothy as addressers and of Philemon, Apphia, Archippus, and the church in Philemon's house as addressees,
Paul speaks in the first person singular to Philemon alone. See further
below on the possible significance of the collective identifications.

68. There seems to be no alternative to this interpretation of Philemon's
debt to Paul. Stuhlmacher, *Der Brief an Philemon*, 50–51, notes an impor-

tant parallel to Philemon's indebtedness in Rom. 15:26–27, where the sharing/partnership of the Gentiles in the spiritual blessings of the poor among the saints in Jerusalem places the Gentiles in debt to them. Perhaps more significant is the implied debt to the spirit by which the believer becomes a son of God; see Rom. 8:12 in the context of 8:2–25. This amazingly rich passage will be considered further in chap. 3.

69. In v. 10 Paul uses the verb for giving birth (*gennaō*), thereby implying his fatherhood, which in fact he claims in 1 Cor. 4:14–15. From the context of 1 Cor. 1:10—4:21, it is apparent that "fatherhood" is a metaphor describing one who brings an individual into the church, whether through preaching or through baptizing, or through both. The metaphor, however, is far from strictly Christian, being widely used in antiquity. See Pedro Gutierrez, *La Paternité Spirituelle selon Saint Paul* (Paris: Gabalda, 1968); and Bengt Holmberg, *Paul and Power: The Structure of Authority in the Primitive Church as Reflected in the Pauline Epistles* (Philadelphia: Fortress Press, 1978), 77–79; and chap. 2, below, on "Father and Debtee."

70. See, e.g., Lohse, *Colossians and Philemon*, 204–5, who describes v. 19a as "a promissory note."

71. Neither are any implied actions required by the referential sequence, which makes Paul's letter and story quite different from Mystarion's.

72. Linguistically, the verb translated "I am sending back" is in Greek in the aorist tense (*anepempsa*), i.e. "I sent back." Commentators and grammarians call this an "epistolary aorist." Literally, it is related to what we earlier spoke of as phraseological point of view. In the epistolary aorist, the temporal point of view is from the time when the letter was read by or to the addressee(s); thus the prior time of the sending of Onesimus (and Blastus!) is referred to in the past or aorist tense. See F. Blass, A. Debrunner, and R. W. Funk, *A Greek Grammar of the New Testament and Other Early Christian Literature* (Chicago: Univ. of Chicago Press, 1961), no. 334, p. 172. On the meaning of *anepempsa*, see Lohse, *Colossians and Philemon*, p. 201, n. 39.

73. See n. 69 above.

74. By form I mean the conventional organization of the letter into its main parts (see n. 65, above). The parts, however, are here understood as mandated by convention, not by the structure of the writer's message or argument, which is a matter of rhetoric. Formal and rhetorical structure intersect in any given letter, but they are nevertheless distinct aspects of its composition. On the form of the Pauline letter, see n. 66, above, and for discussion of the thanksgiving section and related literature, see, e.g., Doty, *Letters in Primitive Christianity*, 31–36 (on the thanksgiving and the body); and Boers, "The Form Critical Study of Paul's Letters," 141–53. As indicated in n. 66, I agree with Boers in seeing the thanksgiving as a part of the body, indeed as comprising the first section in it, the second being the appeal or exhortation section. Doty, *Letters in Primitive Christianity*, 27, outlines the usual division of the letter into its formal parts. The classic study of the more narrowly conceived thanksgiving section, which is analogous to Bjerkelund's study of the appeal section, is Paul Schubert's *Form*

and Function of the Pauline Thanksgiving, BZNW 20 (Berlin: Töpelmann, 1939). Subsequent literature is referred to by Doty and Boers.

75. The absence in other letters of faith and/or love as that for which Paul is thankful is related to the particular issues with which those letters are concerned. First Cor. 1:4–9 deals with the spiritual gifts that were becoming a problem in Corinth; 2 Cor. 1:3–7 refers to suffering, affliction, and comfort in relation both to Paul's experience and Corinth's, as described in 1:8—2:13 and 7:5–16; Gal. 1:6–9 is an anti-thanksgiving, because the Galatians have turned to another gospel (cf. 1:10—4:31/5:1a); and Phil. 1:3–11, while shaped in relation to 1:12—2:29 (cf. 2:35–36 and 4:10–20), does eventually offer a prayer for the Philippians' love (1:9), and Paul's thanksgiving for their "partnership in the gospel" is probably a variant of thanks for the addressee's faith.

76. Cf. Rom. 1:8, Rome's faith is proclaimed in all the world; Col. 1:4, "We have heard"; 1 Thess. 1:8, "Your faith in God has gone forth everywhere"; 2 Tim. 1:4–5, "Paul" remembers Timothy's faith. In other letters, Paul's source of information derives from some person who has just come from the church in question.

77. See n. 74 on the general distinction between form and rhetoric. If Church, Betz, and Wuellner (see n. 66) are correct in seeing Paul as following rhetorical conventions, as well as the formal conventions of letter writing, the structure of the message or argument is doubly determined. Penetrating Paul's rhetoric is not merely a matter of following the logic of his argument, but also of decoding the argument on the basis of the rhetorical code book that he followed. And when stylistic codes are also taken into consideration, e.g. chiasm, interpretation becomes even more complex (on stylistic studies, see, e.g., Funk, *Language, Hermeneutic & Word of God,* 258–63). Be this as it may, when I speak of rhetoric I am referring to the verbal flow of Paul's message, regardless of whether or not the flow is governed by conventional models. Since especially Church and Betz do not agree on which rhetorical models Paul followed (Church, "Rhetorical Structure and Design in Paul's Letter to Philemon," p. 19, n. 11), our description of the flow of the message itself will have to suffice. Stylistic observations, on the other hand, are a more accessible aspect of Paul's rhetoric.

78. This is the *eucharistō-parakalō* structure referred to in n. 66.

79. Action 8, the arrival of Onesimus and the letter, is not poetically emplotted and is therefore omitted.

80. The relationship between Paul's use of the metaphor of indebtedness and the rhetoric of his appealing rather than commanding will be considered in chap. 2.

81. See n. 3 above. "I write" is also an epistolary aorist (*egrapsa*); cf. n. 72. Critics are divided in opinion as to just how much of the letter was written in Paul's own hand. Because we do not have the original letter, we will probably never know for sure what he actually wrote. However, most critics agree that he at least wrote v. 19a, and probably v. 19b as well. I see no reason why he could not have completed the letter, once he began to write. But my argument is not dependent on whether he wrote all of vv. 19–25 or only some of it. The point is that when he completed v. 18 he "saw"

something and took pen in hand to verbalize it. Even if he continued dictating after v. 19a, vv. 19b–22 reflect a change of direction, if not of mind, in the rhetorical strategy of the letter. The possibility of a second change of hands is far less important.

82. On the formal ending of the body of the letter in v. 22, see White, "The Structural Analysis of Philemon," 32–33 and 38–47. Endings at v. 20 (e.g. Lohse, Stuhlmacher) are based on content, i.e., the end of Paul's appeal, not on form. White's notion of the body's ending with a formal reference to Paul's visit (Funk: "apostolic parousia") is less convincing than his formal arguments for the close, which is comprised of greetings and a benediction. On the nature of references to Paul's future visits, see Terence Y. Mullins, "Visit Talk in New Testament Letters," *CBQ* 35 (1973): 350–58.

83. The idea that Paul saw new possibilities for his argument while offering to pay Onesimus's debt is, I believe, a new one. However, it is not inconsistent with observations others have made about changes that occur in vv. 19ff. Indeed, it provides an explanation for those changes. For further discussion of the change of direction taken in v. 19, see below, chap. 2, 106–109, 131–151, and the conclusion, 289–296.

84. See chap. 2 on the sociological structures underlying all of these role-names.

85. In view of the argument that Paul arrived at new insights while dictating his letter, we should note that the communal dimension was in mind from the very beginning. Although his thanksgiving and appeal are related solely to Philemon, Paul addresses the letter not merely to him but also to Apphia, Archippus, and the entire church that meets at Philemon's house (vv. 1b-2). By making the letter public knowledge among the brothers and sisters who congregate at Philemon's house, Paul exerts public pressure on Philemon to do his bidding. Similarly, the scope of this knowledgeable public is expanded in the opening and the close of the letter when Paul lists Timothy as a co-addresser (v. 1a) and sends Philemon greetings from Epaphras, Mark, Aristarchus, Demas, and Luke (vv. 23–24). Paul's appeal is therefore not a private matter, nor the letter a private or personal letter. See Ulrich Wickert, "Der Philemonbrief—Privatbrief oder apostolisches Schreiben?" *ZNW* 52 (1961): 230–38. On love as an obligatory debt between the brothers, see Rom. 13:8–10; the intent and result of love is the upbuilding or edification of the other (Rom. 15:1–6, and for a specific application of the law of edifying love, 1 Corinthians 12—14).

86. The rule attributed to Paul in Col. 4:1 is not applied by Paul in our letter, nor does it seem relevant to the dynamics of Paul's story: "Masters, treat your slaves justly and fairly, knowing that you also have a master in heaven." Neither does Col. 3:22–24 seem to fit the role of Onesimus in Paul's story: "Slaves obey in everything those who are your earthly masters, not with eyeservice, as men pleasers, but in singleness of heart, fearing the Lord ("master," in 4:1 is the same Greek word as "Lord," *kyrios*). Whatever your task, work heartily, as serving the Lord and not men, knowing that from the Lord you will receive the inheritance as your reward; you are serving the Lord Christ." On these rules, see Lohse, *Colossians and Philemon,* 154–63. Although I agree with Lohse in denying Paul's authorship of

Colossians, it is only fair to note that its rules for masters and slaves may not envision the problem we see in Philemon, where a master and his slave are members of the same church or are both believers, regardless of their church. The rules in Colossians may be for masters and slaves whose slaves and masters may not be believers. However, since Col. 4:9 mentions an Onesimus as a faithful brother, Paul, if he wrote Colossians, does not seem to have envisioned the problem of the Letter to Philemon when he wrote Colossians. Be this as it may, the letter to Philemon does not represent the rule for masters and slaves found in Colossians.

2

SOCIAL STRUCTURES AND
SOCIAL RELATIONS
IN THE STORY
OF PHILEMON

> The object of social structural studies is to understand social relations
> with the aid of models.[1]
>
> Claude Lévi-Strauss

Now that we have constructed a narrative from Paul's Letter to
Philemon, we are in a position to explore the sociology of the narrative's world. Our task is both to map out the structures of its social
arrangements and to show how the structures inform the actions
(social relations) of the actors in the story. The structures are represented in the roles and relations referred to in the story, both by the
names given to individual roles and by other language indicating
the nature of the relationships between the roles. This language of
roles and relations comprises the actors' knowledge of their social
world,[2] and from their knowledge we can determine how their social life is arranged, the options they envision for themselves as
social actors, and the significance of the options they choose to act
upon. The last of these will prove to be of particular importance for
understanding Paul's social style. We will begin, therefore, with a
survey of the knowledge shared by the actors, and from it identify
the structures of social arrangements underlying their actions. After
surveying the individual features of this social terrain, we will bring
them together by producing some maps of the whole and by plotting
the actors' actions on them.

As we approach our survey of social arrangements it should be
remembered that we are reserving for discussion in the next chapter
the roles of God and of Jesus Christ. In the introductory chapter, we
saw that they are actors of a different sort from people like Paul,
Philemon, and Onesimus. And in chapter 1 we saw that symbolic
language like the fatherhood of God and the lordship of Christ spans

different spheres of reality by using the language of everyday experience to represent in it realities that are not part of everyday experience. Thus God, who in the story is not experienced in the same way as another person, is nevertheless represented as a person of a certain sort, a father, namely of *all* people who acknowledge him as father and thereby become children of God and brothers and sisters of one another. Similarly Christ, who since his death is physically absent from the everyday experience of the actors, is represented as presently being the heavenly master of all who acknowledge him as such and thereby become his slaves. The fatherhood of God and the lordship of Christ are therefore symbols that shape Paul's symbolic universe, but God and Christ are not social actors subject to the social arrangements of everyday life. For this reason we will not give much attention to them in this chapter.

SOCIAL POSITIONS AND THEIR RELATIONS:
A PRELIMINARY SURVEY

Because of the complexity of the social roles[3] and relations in our story, it is necessary for us to know what they are before we can map them and interpret our actors' actions in relation to them. It will be recalled from our previous considerations that the decoding of the language of roles is complicated by several factors. The actors play multiple roles, apparently simultaneously. These roles belong to at least two different social domains, those of the church and of the world outside the church. And the language used to describe roles in the church is largely the metaphorically transformed literal language of worldly roles. But whether in the church or in the world, the roles are hierarchically and therefore structurally related to one another in terms of superior, equal, and inferior. Due to all of these factors, it is not always clear as to the capacity in which a given actor is acting at any given point in the story. And Paul's rhetoric only complicates matters further when, for example, he asserts his authority to command yet prefers to appeal, or when he refers to his child as his brother or tells Philemon that his slave is his brother "both in the flesh and in the Lord." So in order to perceive the structures underlying the social arrangements affecting our actors' actions we need to identify the roles they play, the hierarchical status[4] of the respective roles, and the domains in which they function. To this end, a number of lists will help us to sort out just who is who in relation to whom.

The first list is an inventory of all of the roles attributed to the characters in our story. With three exceptions, the list represents each role in the order in which it is referred to in Paul's letter. (1)

Because Jesus Christ the master/Lord is referred to nine times, eight of the references to his role are cited in parentheses after the first reference to it. (2) Because Paul does not in our story explicitly refer to believers as the children of God or slaves of Christ, these implied roles are added to the references to God as father and Christ as master. And (3) because the relationship of indebtedness is not stated in the form of nouns, they are added where the relationship is indicated.

List 1: *An Inventory of Roles*

Verse

1	Paul, a prisoner (*desmios*)
	Timothy, brother (*adelphos*)
	Philemon, our[5] fellow worker (*synergos*)
2	Apphia, sister (*adelphē*)
	Archippus, our fellow soldier (*systratiōtēs*)
3	God, our father (*patēr*); those included in the "our" are his children
	Jesus Christ, the lord/master (*kyrios*; cf. vv. 5, 6, 8, 9, 20, 23, 25), in relation to whom all are slaves
7	Philemon, brother (*adelphos*)
9	Paul, an ambassador/old man (*presbytēs*)
	Paul, a prisoner of Christ Jesus (*desmios Christou Iēsou*;[6] cf. v. 13, for the gospel, *tou euangeliou*)
10	Onesimus, Paul's child (*teknon*; cf. v. 12, my very heart, *ta ema splangchna*)
	By implication, Paul is Onesimus's father (cf. *tou emou teknou hon egennēsa*)
16	Onesimus, Philemon's slave (*doulos*)
	By implication, Philemon is Onesimus's master
	Onesimus, brother (*adelphos*) to both Paul and Philemon
17	Philemon, Paul's partner (*koinōnos*)
18–19a	Onesimus, a debtor to Philemon, his debtee
19b	Philemon, a debtor to Paul (*opheilō*), his debtee
20	Philemon, brother (*adelphos*)
23	Epaphras, fellow prisoner (*synaichmalōtos*)
24	Mark, Aristarchus, Demas, Luke, Paul's fellow workers (*synergoi*)

In addition, we should note one collective name, "the saints," (*hoi hagioi*, vv. 5, 7), and one implied role, namely Philemon's role as head of the house in which the church meets. We can ignore the former because it defines the quality of living, that is, as holy, rather than a role,[7] but we will consider the latter when we deepen our survey of the roles in subsequent sections of this chapter.

The second list identifies the roles played by each of the principal actors, Paul, Philemon, and Onesimus, in relation to other actors.

List 2: *Roles Played by the Principal Actors*

Paul's roles:
> prisoner of Christ
> brother to Timothy, Apphia, Philemon, Onesimus
> fellow worker of Philemon, Mark, Aristarchus, Demas, Luke
> fellow soldier of Archippus
> son/child of God as father
> slave of Jesus Christ as Lord
> ambassador/old man (of Christ?)
> partner with Philemon
> father of Onesimus
> debtee of Philemon
> fellow prisoner of Epaphras

Philemon's roles:
> fellow worker of Paul
> brother of Paul and of Onesimus
> master/lord of Onesimus
> child of God
> slave of Christ
> partner with Paul
> debtee of Onesimus
> debtor to Paul

Onesimus's roles:
> child of Paul and of God
> slave of Philemon and of Christ
> brother of Paul and of Philemon
> debtor to Philemon

The next list classifies the fourteen roles of the first list in terms of their hierarchical structural positions as superior, equal, or inferior.[8]

List 3: *The Hierarchical Status of the Positions*

Superior:
> Father, master/lord, ambassador,[9] debtee

Equal:
> brother/sister, fellow worker, fellow soldier, fellow
> prisoner, partner, saint

Inferior:
> prisoner, child, slave, debtor

The fourth and last list represents the roles and the principal actors who play them according to both the social domains in which they function and the literal or metaphorical mode of reference of the role names. It should be noted that literal reference occurs only in the domain of the world and metaphorical reference only in the domain of the church.

List 4: *The Domains and Modes of Reference of the Role Names*

World (literal reference)	*Church* (metaphorical reference)
	father: God, Paul
	children: all in the church, Onesimus
	brother: Paul, Philemon, Onesimus
master/lord: Philemon	master/lord: Jesus
slave: Onesimus	slave: all in the church
debtee: Philemon	debtee: Paul
debtor: Onesimus	debtor: Philemon
prisoner, fellow prisoner: Paul	prisoner of Christ: Paul
	ambassador: Paul
	fellow worker: Paul, Philemon (cf. v. 24)
	fellow soldier: Paul
	partner: Paul and Philemon

DEEPENING THE SURVEY

Our preliminary survey enables us to take a further step in our exploration. By examining now the actions of the principal actors in light of the structural roles they play in relation to the other role-players, we can deepen our understanding of both the structures of social arrangements operative in our story and the sociological issues that inform its plotted actions. In this deeper survey we will deal separately with each role or set of related roles, and after we have surveyed them we will map their relationships to one another. Because the roles belonging to the domain of the world are both few and literally represented, we begin with them.

The Worldly Roles: Master, Slave, Debtee, Debtor, Prisoner

It is clear from our last list that only two of the principals, Philemon and Onesimus, relate to one another in terms of their worldly roles. Because they are structurally related as master and slave and as debtee and debtor, Philemon is doubly superior to a doubly inferior Onesimus. However, as a result of Onesimus's having run away and incurring a debt to Philemon, each form of their relationship is characterized by an incompleteness that requires closure; each form entails certain expectations that must be satisfied. On the one hand, because the master-slave relationship has been broken off by Onesimus's running away, the expectation is that it will be restored. From a sociological perspective, Onesimus's flight is a relational breach that must be repaired because his action is not in conformity either with the sociological structure or with the social system (institution) that defines the ways in which slaves are to relate to masters. Simply, Onesimus's social relations are not in conformity with the sociological structure of his institutional relationship with Philemon. Here it is important to distinguish between this *sociological* perspective and the more concrete institutional perspective[10] from which Onesimus's action is seen as a breaking of the law. While he has surely broken the law, we should remember that the *social system* of institutionalized laws, punishments, and officials functions to preserve the *sociological structures* underlying desirable *social relations*.[11] Onesimus's action, therefore, poses a threat both to the institutionalized social system and to the sociological structures it serves, and it is in this light that we can best appreciate the state of tension that surrounds the relationship between Onesimus and Philemon and encompasses people like Paul who have gotten involved with the guilty party. The tension persists until the relationship between the slave and his master is brought back into conformity with its structural ground by bringing the slave's behavior into conformity with the pertinent laws. Onesimus must return to his master as a slave and endure whatever punishments the social system prescribes.

The relationship of indebtedness, on the other hand, also exists within a system of laws, punishments, and officials, but it does not involve a structural or legal violation unless the debtor defaults on his debt.[12] Whereas the master-slave relationship is by definition a closed one except when violated, the relationship of indebtedness is by definition an open one until it is closed by repayment within a prescribed period of time. A structural and legal violation occurs only when the temporal limitation is exceeded and the debt is not paid. The underlying structure of the relationship therefore specifies a temporally limited openness, and when the relationship is closed by repayment of the debt this form of relationship ceases to exist and the structure is no longer relevant to the actors. Consequently, the tension of expectation derived from an unfulfilled obligation, which is abnormal in the master-slave relationship, is normal in the relationship of indebtedness.

Now in our story both forms of relationship are initially encountered while they are in a state of suspenseful openness which moves toward closure. When Paul in effect pays Onesimus's debt, the relationship of indebtedness between Onesimus and Philemon is both closed and terminated.[13] Similarly, when Paul sends Onesimus back to Philemon it appears that the master-slave relationship is about to be closed by being brought back into conformity with its structural ground. Precisely at this point, however, the narrator frustrates our expectations by failing to satisfy them. Instead of bringing the master-slave relationship to its expected closure, he makes its closure ambiguous by introducing another form of relationship and another sociological structure from another domain, the role of brothers in the domain of the church: "Perhaps this is why he was parted from you for a while, that you might have him back forever, *no longer as a slave but more than a slave, a beloved brother, especially to me but how much more to you, both in the flesh and in the Lord*" (vv. 15–16). The very next sentence complicates matters yet further by introducing relations between *Paul* and Philemon: "So if you consider me a partner (*koinōnos*), receive him as you would receive me" (v. 17). Without anticipating too much our later discussion of structural roles in the domain of the church, let us see if the distinction between sociological structures, social systems, and social relations can help us to figure out just what Paul expects of Philemon, the master, brother, and partner.

The first observation to be made is that "both in the flesh and in the Lord" refers to two social domains, that of the world ("in the flesh") and that of the church ("in the Lord").[14] The second is that vv. 15–17 refer to both social structural positions and social relations. The role-names "slave," "brother," and "partner" refer to structural positions, the first in the domain of the world and the second and third in the domain of the church. Social relations between the role-players are indicated by the verbs "parted" (*echōristhē*)[15] and "have back" (*apechēs*) in v. 15, and by the verbs "consider" (*echeis;* literally, "have" or "hold") and "receive" (*proslabou*) in v. 17. In addition, in v. 16 we find that Philemon is to have Onesimus back no longer "as" (*hōs*) a slave but (by implication, "as") a brother, and in v. 17 that Philemon is to receive Onesimus "as" he would receive Paul.[16] The word "as" is important because commentators usually see its presence in v. 16 as meaning "act as though Onesimus were a brother," but without regard for what he *is* as a slave. As in 1 Cor. 7:21–24, so the argument goes, Paul is concerned with what one is in the church, not with what one also is in the world. In other words, Paul is not out to change the worldly social positions of believers, nor does he think believers should worry about them.[17] Because this interpretation depends on a text (1 Cor. 7:21–24) which does not address the problem posed by the relationships between Philemon and Onesimus,[18] we can best approach the question of Paul's expectations of Philemon by starting with the problematical "as."

The usual interpretation of vv. 15–16 rightly points both to Paul's primary orientation to brotherly relations and to the fact that Philemon and Onesimus are also related as master and slave. However, its concentration on "as a brother" fails to do justice to "no longer as a slave." The interpretation properly emphasizes Paul's expectations about Philemon's new *relations* with his slave, but it too hastily dismisses the idea that these relations entail a *structural* change in their relationship as master and slave. A sociological interpretation follows a different line of argumentation and arrives at a different conclusion.

Sociologically, we begin with the fact that Onesimus now plays two social structural roles in relation to Philemon—as his slave in the world and as his brother in the church. Second, when Paul tells Philemon that he will have Onesimus back as a brother, and that he is to receive Onesimus as he would receive his partner Paul, the message is in both cases, "relate to him as an equal,"[19] not "as though he were an equal." On the one hand, this message means that by relating to Onesimus as his equal Philemon will bring their *relations* in the church into conformity with their *structural* ground. When a brother relates to a brother as a brother, structural equals relate as equals. On the other hand, however, this message and meaning also define the remaining problem in new terms: how does the conformity of relations with structures in one domain affect the problem of relations and structure not only within the other domain but also between the two domains? Simply, can Philemon relate to his slave as a brother and still remain his structural master? Theoretically, the answer is probably yes,[20] but theory must be measured against what Paul says. What he says in his appeal to Philemon focuses on Philemon's new structural relationship with Onesimus resulting from the latter's conversion, and Paul never explictly refers to Philemon's role as a master. We can see in the following diagram that what Paul says, and what he does not say, undercuts the structural ground of the master-slave relationship. In this diagram role-names represent the structural ground and directional arrows indicate the relations derived from the role on which Paul focuses.

Philemon: brother   master

Onesimus: brother   slave

Paul's expectations of Philemon can also be approached from another perspective, one from which the social relations verbalized in vv. 15–16 are mapped onto their underlying social structure.

	World	*Church*
social relations		Philemon will have Onesimus back forever
social structure	no longer as a slave but more than a slave,	a beloved brother both
	in the flesh and	in the Lord.

In this diagram it is apparent that the conformity between social relations and social structure in the church is complemented by: a) the lack of reference to social relations in the world, b) a denial of Onesimus's social structural status as a slave (i.e., "no longer as a slave"), and c) a displacement of the role of slave "in the flesh" by the role of brother, "both in the flesh and in the Lord." Thus, in the first diagram we see the social structural ground of the master-slave relationship undercut by the elimination of the role of master, and in the second diagram we find the structural relationship between master and slave further undercut by the elimination of the role of slave.

Viewed in this light, it appears that Onesimus's new social structural role as Philemon's brother has three related consequences: (1) Philemon must relate to Onesimus as a brother both in the church and in the world; (2) he must, therefore, *not* relate to him as a master in the world; and (3) this puts in question the social structural ground of the master-slave relationship between the new brothers. Why? Because by relating to one another as the equals they now are, they cease to *be*, that is, structurally, superior and inferior, except only in the residual legal sense of having the identities of master and slave in the world. And once we see that the structural ground of their worldly relationship is already at issue in Paul's appeal, we can also better understand the troublesome v. 21. There, Paul expresses his confidence in Philemon's obedience to his appeal, but also in Philemon's doing *even more than Paul says*. If Philemon's obedience responds to both the relational and the structural aspects of Paul's appeal, the "even more" that Paul refers to in v. 21 in all probability concerns the legal vestiges of the old relationship between the master and his slave. The "even more" would therefore refer to Philemon's bringing the legal aspect of his worldly relationship with Onesimus into conformity with the social structural ground of their new churchly relationship, presumably by legally freeing Onesimus.[21] This means, of course, that the sociology of our story radically differs not only from 1 Cor. 7:21–24, which we will discuss in greater detail later, but also from three other letters attributed to Paul—Colossians, Ephesians, and 1 Timothy. In contrast with the Letter to Philemon, each of these three letters *affirms* the social structural ground of the master-slave relationship and addresses rather the quality of Christian behavior appropriate to masters and their slaves. In our story Paul does not tell Philemon to treat his slave Onesimus justly because he, too, has a master in heaven (Col. 4:1; Eph. 6:9). And neither does Paul indicate that Onesimus has been instructed to obey his master Philemon as though he were serving the Lord (Col. 3:22–24; Eph. 6:5–8) or fellow believers (1 Tim. 6:1). Indeed, precisely because Paul says none of these things to Philemon, nor what he says in 1 Cor. 7:21–24, we must conclude that he is doing something quite different in his appeal to Philemon. Lacking confirming evidence, we cannot prove our sociological interpretation, but it makes more sense of our story than interpretations based on other letters. But whether our conclusion is right or wrong, it is based on sociological matters that have to be attended to in any interpretation.

Although Paul's introduction of the relationship between brothers in vv. 15–16 creates some ambiguity about the closure of the master-slave relationship, it also unambiguously transforms the social problem of our story. Initially, Onesimus was focal because he illegally broke off his relationship with Philemon and entered into debt to him. The responsibility for closing both forms of relationship fell upon Onesimus, and with Paul's help he did his duty by having his debt paid and by returning to Philemon. Thus, with Onesimus's responsibilities fulfilled, with his return as a brother, and with the arrival of Paul's appeal on his behalf, the spotlight now shifts to Philemon. Two forms of relationship still remain open, that of master and slave and now also that of brothers, but the responsibility for closing them falls upon Philemon. It is now his responsibility to act in such a way as to bring *his* social relations with Onesimus into conformity with both their structural ground and the social systems that function to preserve the structures. In order to appreciate Philemon's new position in the story, we have to consider the social contexts that inform his situation.

In principle, Philemon can satisfy the requirements of the worldly social system and its structure in a number of ways. He can remain Onesimus's master and exact whatever penalties the system prescribes. He can lend his slave to someone else like Paul, which may be implied in vv. 13–14.[22] And he can free Onesimus. In the world, therefore, Philemon has a number of options and he is relatively free from social pressure from that quarter as long as he takes up one of the options. Not so within the system of the brotherhood.

In the brotherhood, Philemon really has only one option, to receive his brother as his brother, and social pressure is on him to do so from the moment Onesimus and Paul's letter arrive at his doorstep. This option is both structurally and socially required of him by virtue of his own position in the church as a brother. What is "required," "right," or "fitting" (*to anēkon*, v. 8)[23] in this instance is that Philemon receive Onesimus as his brother, and Paul claims the authority to command Philemon's obedience in this matter (vv. 8 and 21, *tē hypakoē sou*), even though he prefers for love's sake to appeal for Philemon's free act of goodness (v. 14, *to agathon sou*). Sociologically, therefore, an objective structural and social deficiency (*to anēkon*) exists in the community until Philemon acts to correct it, either out of obedience or out of goodness.[24] And it is precisely the *communal* nature of the deficiency that is the source of local pressure on Philemon to do what is required, because the community needs to have *its* problem resolved. If Philemon does not act as he should, the ball will then be in the court of the community to correct the deficiency. The logic of its decision-making process is painfully simple. If Onesimus is a brother and Philemon refuses to acknowledge him as such, Philemon will be the one who is not acting like a brother. Thus the community, if it is to be consistent with its social structure and its social system, will have no choice but to expel Philemon in order to preserve the brotherhood. We can safely assume that this message was understood by all concerned, certainly after the reception of Paul's letter, which identifies the social situation and both explicitly and implicitly cultivates social pressure in support of his appeal.

Social pressure on Philemon is secured most conspicuously by Paul's addressing his letter not only to Philemon but also to Apphia, Archippus, and the entire church that meets in Philemon's house. Although Paul speaks almost uniformly to Philemon,[25] the letter's collective address makes it a *public* letter, and we must therefore assume public knowledge of its content.[26] From Onesimus's presence the community knows of his return as a brother, and from Paul's letter it learns that this fact must be translated into action, if not by Philemon, by them. And because Paul's visit will be to them as well as to Philemon (see the plural "you" in v. 22b), they are as accountable to what is required as Philemon is. They, too, are illuminated by the spotlight focusing on Philemon.

The communal context of our story's social problem is further characterized by other local and even translocal factors. On the local level, we have to consider the significance of the community's meeting as a house church. From what is known of house construction at the time, the size of the group that could meet in a house numbered between only ten and thirty individuals,[27] thus creating a relatively intimate atmosphere in which social tensions could be even more personally experienced than they might be in a larger group. In addition to this factor, however, we also have to reckon with the fact that as the master of the house in which the community meets, Philemon plays (*de facto* if not *de jure*) a role that differentiates him from other members, if only as their host.[28] As master of the house and as the church's host, some degree of deference is due him, and practically speaking there is no little awkwardness involved in the possible expulsion from the church of the man in whose house the church meets! To expel Philemon from the church its members would have to leave *his* house and, not incidentally, find another one. Consequently, in the purely practical terms of social relations, the return of the house-master's slave as a born-again brother requires that the rest of the community renegotiate its relations with *each* of them. Household tensions must be somewhat acute in such circumstances, and they must contribute to the social pressure to resolve the problem. Paul's letter, I suspect, is written in full cognizance of this situation and also of the temptation of the community to act in worldly terms by taking Philemon's side. His letter serves, among other things, to remind *them* of the terms of *their* communal existence and its responsibilities.

In addition to the local pressure on Philemon, we also have to observe that Paul explicitly puts him in a conspicuous position in relation to others than the members of his own church. As in 2 Corinthians 8, where Paul tells the Corinthians that others know what he is asking of them and that the eyes of others in the extended church are upon them, so also in his Letter to Philemon. Paul first identifies his fellow worker Timothy as the co-writer of the letter (v. 1a), and then sends Philemon, whom he addresses as their[29] fellow worker, the greetings of five other fellow workers: Epaphras, Mark, Aristarchus, Demas, and Luke (vv. 23–24).[30] Thus, in the opening and the close of the letter, Paul places the local issues in the church at Philemon's house in a social context that is translocal or, as we might say, international. With this wider public cognizant of the local problem, the pressure on both Philemon and his church is magnified. The problem is not his or theirs alone. Others know about it and await its resolution. Therefore, if the other members of Philemon's church have any inclination to defer to Philemon because he is Paul's fellow worker and master of the house in which they meet, the wider public named in the letter, in addition to Paul's own intervention, should tilt the balance of their thinking in favor of Paul's appeal. Minimally, they have to decide what to do by balancing the position of one of Paul's fellow workers, Philemon, against the position of Paul and a half-dozen of his other fellow workers. And just as Philemon's status in his own church hinges on *his* decision, so does the status of his church in the extended brotherhood hinge on its decision concerning whom to support.

A more implicit aspect of the total social context also contributes to the social climate of our story. Beyond the problem of social relations that arises upon the arrival of Onesimus and Paul's letter, there is also a problem pertaining to the church's symbolic universe. This problem concerns the *idea* of equality,[31] which is important because it is a fundamental feature of the symbolic universe Paul shares with his people. It is fundamental because it is grounded in the ideas of the fatherhood of God and of Christ as the heavenly master of all who believe.[32] For this reason, Philemon's refusal to accept Onesimus as his brother would not only disrupt the social fabric of the community, but it would also threaten the whole rationale, the "reality," of the international brotherhood.[33] Philemon's options and actions are therefore significant because of what they mean as well as for their more immediate effects on social relations in his church. It is, I think, only in this light that we can fully appreciate the apparent paradox that in defense of the structures and relationships of equality in the church Paul acts from his position of structural superiority in the church—tactfully, to be sure, but nevertheless clearly and forcefully. That he acts from this position is already evident in the last of the worldly roles on our list, Paul's role as a prisoner.

In Philemon 9 Paul refers to himself as "an ambassador/old man and now also a prisoner of Christ Jesus (cf. v. 1, and v. 13, "for the gospel"). Later, we will consider this statement in its entirety. For now, it is important to recognize that although Paul relates to Onesimus and Philemon *during* his imprisonment, he does not relate to them in his social structural role *as* a prisoner, as he does, for example, to Epaphras, his "fellow prisoner" (v. 23).[34] At the most, Paul's literal powerlessness as a prisoner renders him an inferior in the world, and as such he is both an equal to Onesimus the slave and an inferior in the same world in which Philemon the master is a superior. This is surely relevant for the interpretation of Paul's rhetoric and strategy in his letter,[35] but it is, nevertheless, precisely Paul's rhetoric which indicates that he views his present inferior status in the world from the perspective of his superior status in the church. That his imprisonment is for him a form of churchly service is indicated by his description of it as being "a prisoner of Christ" and "for the gospel."[36] As in Phil. 1:12–14, this refers not to the charge for which he was arrested or convicted, but to the charge for which he was called—to proclaim Christ among the Gentiles as an apostle of Christ (cf. Gal. 1:15–16 and Rom. 1:1–6). It is in this structural role that while in prison Paul "fathered" Onesimus through the gospel (Philemon 10; cf. 1 Cor. 4:14–15) and writes to Philemon, claiming in effect that even as a prisoner he retains his authority *in Christ* to command Philemon to do what is required of him, his choice of appealing to him notwithstanding.[37] Therefore, Paul, a prisoner in the world, does not relate to Onesimus and Philemon *as* a prisoner, but as a "father" and as one who has the power to command in churchly matters even those who like Philemon are superiors in the domain of the world, as long as they are also members of the church.

The Churchly Roles

Because our narrator, Paul, views the world from within the church, we have had to entertain in a preliminary way certain churchly roles in discussing the worldly roles in his story. Therefore, little more needs to be said about the role of brothers, which we have seen to be the primary social category in the church's social arrangements. Every member is a brother or sister to every other member, and despite the metaphorical reference of this kinship language it renders members as equals. However, in addition to this fundamental axis of equality we have noted the apparent sociological paradox of Paul's structurally hierarchical role of apostle, in which capacity he functions as a "father," not as a brother, and with the authority to command, even though he chooses to appeal. As we turn now to the churchly roles in our story, two issues will therefore inform our concern with them. One has to do with the relationship between the axes of equality and hierarchy (stratification) in the churches' social organization, the other with the metaphorical use of language to describe the roles belonging to each axis. These two issues are inextricably related because metaphor is a rhetorical trope, an element of speaking style, and because the speech with which we are concerned is that of Paul, the hierarchical apostle who is our narrator and letter writer. For these reasons, our sociological exploration of Paul's rhetoric will tell us as much about the style with which he played his apostolic role as about the social arrangements of the church. His rhetoric is a form of his social relations, and we must determine from it the sociological structures underlying his relations with others. Their roles, when not explicitly identified by him, can frequently be seen as implied by his own roles.[38]

Finally, in view of the long-standing discussion of the degree to which churchly roles are institutionalized in Paul's time,[39] the distinction we have made between sociological structures, social systems (i.e., of institutions), and social relations proves to be most useful. Thus, while institutionalization into "official" roles belongs to the category of social systems, our focus is rather on the sociological structures underlying the social relations of the actors in Paul's story, including the relations represented in Paul's rhetoric. Our interpretation of these social relations is therefore based on the relationship between social relations and their structural ground, not on hypotheses about institutionalized roles. On the other hand, the results of our exploration will provide evidence for a hypothesis about the state of institutionalization in Paul's narrative world, although providing such a hypothesis is not a major issue for us, not least of all because it would match those of others who find little evidence for institutionalization in Paul's letters.[40] Indeed, his letters are sociologically interesting because in them we see social groups whose social systems are only beginning to take shape. On the one hand, this is interesting because the letters show how behavior is motivated and controlled in the absence of official authority acknowledged by all. On the other hand, this is interesting because the letters show how official authority emerges by securing the assent of all to the leadership of some.[41] We have had a glimpse of both of these phenomena in the preceding section. In the remainder of this chapter they will be fully before us.

Fellow Worker and Partner

Paul explicitly identifies Philemon by only three role-names—brother, fellow worker, and partner. The initial identification comes in the letter's address to "Philemon the beloved, our (i.e., Paul's and Timothy's) fellow worker" (v. 1b). This is followed by references to him as "brother" (*adelphē*, in the vocative, vv. 7 and 20; cf. v. 16)[42] and as "a partner" (v. 17). Before we explore the sociological significance of these role names in other letters, let us consider the significance of their social structural reference for the social relations between Paul and Philemon that are represented in Paul's letter and story. This will provide some direction for our investigation of his use of these role names elsewhere.

Thus far we have concentrated on the closure of relationships of equality in Paul's story. The relationships of brothers and partners require closure by a brotherly act on Philemon's part (vv. 15–17),

103

and Philemon's status as a fellow worker among Paul's other fellow workers (cf. vv. 1 and 24) appears to be equally contingent upon his performing this same act of goodness (v. 14) and obedience (v. 21), which is also represented both as Philemon's payment of his debt to Paul and as a benefit Paul desires from him (vv. 19–20). However, we have also begun to see that despite his egalitarian rhetoric Paul relates to both Onesimus and Philemon as a structurally hierarchical superior, namely as a father (v. 10) and as one who has the authority in Christ to command Philemon to do what is required (vv. 8–10; 21). Later we will attend to the sociological implications of Paul's commanding and appealing. Now we need to see that the rhetoric of his letter discloses a hierarchical structural relationship behind the notions of partner and fellow worker, and that this relationship affects the social meaning of the other egalitarian notion of brother. By exposing this relationship and its effects, we will gain access both to some of the structures of social relations in Pauline churches and to Paul's administrative style. What we can learn from the letter to and story about Philemon can then be supplemented by information from other letters.

In v. 17 Paul says to Philemon, "So if you consider me a partner, receive him (Onesimus) as you would receive me" (*Ei oun me echeis koinōnon, proslabou auton hōs eme*). The translation of *koinōnon* by "partner" represents a sociologically significant interpretation of this somewhat ambiguous Greek word. Semantically, while it denotes a relationship of sharing between two or more persons, it can also connote a relationship of companionship, even friendship, as well as of partnership.[43] That the latter connotation is the one represented in v. 17 is suggested by the fact that there is no indication in the letter that Paul and Philemon are "companions" in the literal sense of "fellow travelers." Rather, they are "associates" or "colleagues," namely, "partners" in a common enterprise. This is suggested already in the initial identification of Philemon as a "fellow worker" (*synergos*) in v. 1, and it is supported by the only other instance of *koinōnos* in Paul's letters in 2 Cor. 8:23, where Titus is also identified by Paul as his "partner and fellow worker" (*koinōnos emos kai eis hymas synergos*).[44] Here "partner" and "fellow worker" are virtually synonymous, as are "fellow worker and fellow soldier" in Phil. 2:22[45] and "servants of Christ and stewards of the mysteries of God" in 1 Cor. 4:1.[46] Paul and Philemon are therefore fellow workers and partners in a common enterprise, and it is the common enterprise that defines the nature of their work and of that in which they participate as partners. The enterprise appears to be represented in the thanksgiving section of Paul's letter (vv. 4–7) both as the sharing (*koinōnia*) of faith in the Lord Jesus and as acts of love commensurate with that faith. More of the enterprise later. The point is that by designating a relationship of partnership between himself and Philemon, Paul implies a social structural relationship of equality which is also expressed in the designation of Philemon as a fellow worker. "Fellow worker" and "partner" therefore represent synonymous relationships of equality. So much is semantically connoted by the two designations.

However, once we have seen this we also have to observe a number of sociologically interesting things about these relationships that are reflected both in the rhetoric of Paul's statement in v. 17 and in its rhetorical context in the letter. First, the statement itself. Two points are focal. (1) Paul makes the continuation of the relationship of partners contingent upon Philemon's receiving of Onesimus as he, Paul, requests.[47] (2) The orientation of the statement is to what Philemon construes as and values about his relationship with Paul. Of these two points, the first is the critical one because it is Paul, not Philemon, who sets the conditions for an action by Philemon that will properly express the relationship of a partner, just as it is Paul who, by this statement, renders the relationship contingent upon Philemon's response to him. The first point, therefore, reveals the actual social dynamics underlying this verbal transaction and discloses the second point, the orientation to Philemon's view of things, as a rhetorical tactic. Strategically, Paul sets his conditions for continuing the relationship of partners between himself and Philemon. Tactically, however, Paul's rhetoric shifts the focus from himself onto what *Philemon* considers and values. Notwithstanding the rhetorical play, it is quite clear that if Philemon does not do what *Paul* says, it is not only Philemon who will break the relationship of partners, but also Paul. In effect, Paul is saying, "If you do not receive Onesimus as you would receive me, you will prove to me that you are neither my partner nor a brother."[48] Nor, since "fellow worker" and "partner" are synonymous, will Philemon prove to be a "fellow worker." In communicating this message to Philemon, Paul reveals that despite the connotations of equality in the notion of partner, he is the *senior partner* in the relationship,[49] and that as such he is Philemon's social structural superior.

The rhetorical context of the statement in v. 17 confirms this conclusion and provides further insights into the relationship between Paul's view of his social structural position and the style of his social relations. The statement not only occurs within the hortatory or, following Bjerkelund, the *parakalō* section of Paul's letter, but it also constitutes the subject of Paul's appeal or exhortation. In

105

v. 10, he announces that he is appealing to Philemon concerning[50] Onesimus, but it is not until v. 17 that he tells Philemon what it is that he wants him to do, namely, to receive Onesimus as he, Philemon, would receive Paul. Although in its present form the appeal extends from v. 8 through v. 22, the appeal proper can be reduced to something like the following: "I appeal to you, brother, concerning my child, Onesimus (v. 10) that you receive him as you would receive me" (v. 17b).[51] In this light, it is apparent that Paul has rhetorically developed his appeal in three areas: he prefaces the beginning of the appeal with vv. 8–9, interrupts what he has begun with the material in vv. 11–17a, and supplements the completion of the appeal with vv. 18–22. In each of these areas, we—and Philemon—can witness Paul's adjustments of his rhetoric to his social structural position, on the one hand, and to his motives, on the other. The most obvious and critical example of this, for both the original readers and ourselves, is in vv. 8–10. There Paul claims the authority[52] in Christ[53] to command Philemon to do what is required, but then says that, motivated by love,[54] he prefers to appeal to him.[55] In these two verbal moves, Paul strategically shifts from a position of authority to a tactical posture of love in order to secure another loving act from Philemon (cf. vv. 4–7), who himself is in a position of authority in the domain of the world over the slave on whose behalf Paul speaks. In these moves Paul mediates the conflict between his authority in the church and Philemon's authority in the world by appealing to the nonauthoritarian value of love which they share.[56] Nevertheless, Paul's expression of his authority to command Philemon is from the very beginning of his exhortation a fact of the social interaction represented by the letter and in Paul's story. Indeed, it is also a fact of their past relationship as well, for despite Paul's address to Philemon as his fellow worker, this fellow, Philemon, is subordinate to Paul because Paul has, and has had, the authority to command him. Thus, in this social transaction between them Paul does not allow Philemon to forget the structure of their relationship, nor does Paul permit Philemon to miss his preference to treat Philemon as an equal. Behind rhetoric that is openly grounded in a posture of love stands the authority of Paul which is equally openly grounded in his social structural position.

It is on the background of vv. 8–10 that we must read Paul's other elaborations of his appeal, for they set the tone of the others. Thus, in vv. 12–14 we find Paul saying that he has not kept Onesimus with him as he wished, but that he has sent Onesimus back to Philemon because he preferred that Philemon do his good deed freely rather than by compulsion. Here Paul replicates what he has done in

vv. 8–10. He has refrained from exercising his authority to compel Philemon to do as he wished, and he has also refrained from doing what he himself really wanted to do with Onesimus. He has not done either what he wanted to do or could have done, and now it is Philemon's turn to reciprocate. Similarly, in vv. 15–17, the motifs of love, brotherhood, and equality are reiterated, climaxing in v. 17. However, v. 17 renders the state of equality between Paul and Philemon contingent upon Philemon's acknowledgment of the state of equality between himself and Onesimus. What is objectively required (v. 8), Philemon's act of goodness (v. 14), is now expressly demanded by Paul in order for Philemon to preserve his social status as a fellow worker, brother, and partner. And last, in his supplements to the climax of his appeal (vv. 18–22) Paul reverts to the description of things from his own superordinate perspective, which was only rhetorically abandoned in vv. 8–10 and 12–17. The overt reversion begins in v. 18 when he offers to pay Philemon whatever Onesimus owes him. But it is fully present in vv. 19–22 when he reminds Philemon of his debt to him (v. 19b), demands some "benefit" from Philemon in the Lord, summons him to refresh *his* heart (v. 20; cf. v. 7), and expresses his confidence in Philemon's *obedience* to him, even to the point of doing more than Paul has "requested" (v. 21). Paul's own perspective continues to govern the remainder of the letter as he tells Philemon to prepare a room for him, indicates his expectation of prayers for him, sends greetings from *his* fellow prisoner and *his* fellow workers, and pronounces a concluding benediction upon Philemon and the church in his house (vv. 22–25). And this benediction, of course, is reminiscent of Paul's expression of *his* approval of Philemon's demonstrations of his faith and love in the thanksgiving that opens the body of the letter. Paul, therefore, conceals his sense of his role only rarely, and then not very subtly; more often than not he asserts it, either directly or indirectly. Throughout, he presents himself as a social structural superior, and if Philemon and the church in his house acknowledge his self-representation, he will be a social structural superior not only in his own mind, but he will also be such institutionally. In such transactions as those represented by the Letter to Philemon, we can see how institutional authority and even "official" positions emerge, both for Paul and for Philemon. For if Philemon accedes to Paul's "appeal," his position will be strengthened in the community as much as Paul's. Perhaps this is why, from a sociological perspective, Paul went to such pains in the composition of his Letter to Philemon. Paul needs his fellow workers and partners in order to further their common work.

Our analysis of v. 17 and its context in Paul's letter indicates that despite the egalitarian implications of the notions of brother, fellow worker, and partner, Paul also claims a position of hierarchical superiority both over brothers and sisters and over his own fellow workers and partners. But the Letter to Philemon also seems to suggest that while all members of the church are brothers and sisters, those brothers and sisters who are fellow workers and partners also have a position of hierarchical superiority over those who are not.[57] The first indication of this in our letter is that fellow workers are such by virtue of their participation in *Paul's* work, and therefore to some extent in his authority. Philemon is the fellow worker of Paul and Timothy, who in Rom. 16:21 is described as *Paul's* fellow worker (*synergos mou*), and in Philemon 24 four other people are identified as *his* fellow workers (*synergoi mou*). At least from Paul's point of view, fellow workers are not simply a class of equals among whom he is but one, like a brother among brothers. Fellow workers are equals in the sense that they do the same "work," but sociologically they are *Paul's* fellow workers, not God's.[58]

In what, then, does Philemon's work consist? We have seen that in Paul's thanksgiving section he applauds Philemon's love and faith, in which his sharing of his faith promotes among others the knowledge of all the good that accrues from being in Christ, and in which his love has refreshed the hearts of the saints.[59] Because Paul addresses this thanksgiving to Philemon as "brother" (v. 7), we might be inclined to see his work as that of a brother. To do this, however, would be to miss two important points, for Philemon's actions are those of a brother who is also Paul's fellow worker and partner (vv. 1 and 17), and his actions are those of one who is the host[60] of the church that meets in his house (v. 2; cf. v. 22). Paul, therefore, writes his letter both to a fellow worker and to the church of which that fellow worker is host. From this it appears that the place where Philemon performs the work which he shares with Paul is his own home. Clearly, as the church's host Philemon plays a role in it that is not played by any other of its members, not even by Archippus, Paul's "fellow soldier" (v. 2) and a member of that church. Philemon would, therefore, seem to have a *special* responsibility both for promoting the knowledge of all the good that is to be found in Christ and for refreshing the hearts of the saints. Indeed, he is doubly superordinate insofar as he is both Paul's fellow worker (and partner) and the host of a church, and both roles may well derive from his having been converted by Paul (v. 19b). Such, at least, is the case with Stephanas of Corinth, whose household, baptized by Paul, was the first to be converted in Achaia. They dedicated themselves to the service of the saints, which includes the refreshing of spirits, and

Paul urged the community to subordinate itself to such fellow workers and laborers as these (1 Cor. 1:16; 16:15–18).

The example of the household of Stephanas makes it apparent that the further we explore the letter to and story about Philemon the more necessary it is to move further into Paul's wider narrative world for a fuller picture of the things we see in the letter.[61] By the same token, however, what we have seen provides us with directions for what to look for in that world. In particular, our exploration of the role of fellow workers and partners in the letter has made it evident that the notion of work is central, for it is a primary metaphor in Paul's representation of both his activities and those of his associates. Therefore, as we turn to other Pauline letters, our focus can be on the sociological implications of the metaphor of work.[62]

Some Sociological Implications of Paul's "Work" Metaphors

Consideration of the Letter to Philemon suggests several areas where additional information would be useful. Although the following areas cannot always be kept separate, it is important to keep them in mind as we move into Paul's wider narrative world: the nature of the "work"—what is it, who assigns it, who performs it, and to what end? Who is superordinate and who is subordinate to whom? What is the relationship between the translocal superordinacy of Paul and his traveling associates and the local superordinacy of people like Philemon and Stephanas?

Although Paul is fully aware of the literal sense of "work" (*ergon, kopos*; cf. 1 Thess. 4:10–12),[63] even that "those who proclaim the gospel should get their living from the gospel" (1 Cor. 9:14),[64] he distinguishes between it and metaphorical work, even by emphasizing that he "works" at preaching the gospel without literal pay (1 Cor. 9:18; 2 Cor. 11:7–11; 12:13). "Work" is for him primarily a metaphor for the noneconomic productivity of believers among believers (cf. 1 Cor. 15:58; 1 Thess. 1:3) and particularly for the productivity of those believers like himself who have a special role to play in relation to the gospel. The richest text bearing on this is 1 Cor. 3:5–17.[65]

The initial problem dealt with by Paul in 1 Corinthians is bound up with the divisive allegiances some Corinthians have to people like himself and Apollos (1 Cor. 1:10—4:21). In 1 Cor. 3:5–17 he employs a number of metaphors associated with work in order to lay out his view of the roles of Apollos and himself in relation to God,[66] on the one hand, and to the Corinthian community, on the other. The metaphors comprise an economic system involving a boss who employs workers to tend his field and build his building, and who will determine his workers' wages according to their labor and the quality of the work they accomplish. Let us examine this system and the way in which Paul applies it to the situation in Corinth.

Decoded, the system described above represents God as the boss, Apollos and Paul as his hired workers, the Corinthian community as the product of their labor, and the day of (eschatological) judgment as payday. Within this system, Paul makes a number of distinctions, the most important of which sociologically are related to the equality of and differences between the principal workers.

As God's employees, his workers are equal to one another (*diakonoi*, v. 5; *hen eisin*, v. 8; *theou . . . synergoi*, v. 9;[67] cf. 4:1), and in light of the total economic project in which they participate they are subordinate in significance both to the owner-boss and to the product of their labor (3:21–23). Their value and their wages hinge on the match between their products and the jobs assigned them, but this value is viewed from two perspectives, God's and the community's. God will judge the worker by his product, the community, and the community should judge the worker by the way he fulfills his job, keeping in mind the job he has been given, and by whom, and not viewing the worker independently of his economic role (cf. 2 Cor. 4:5)—as they had in identifying themselves as belonging to Apollos or to Paul, which Paul also implies is a false wage. The community is *God's* field and building, not Apollos's or Paul's. Therefore, the community's allegiance to Apollos or Paul is a false wage; God alone is their paymaster.

If people like Apollos and Paul are thus equals as fellow employees hired by God (i.e., as fellow workers), they are also clearly differentiated sociologically by the jobs they have been given. In both agricultural and building construction metaphors, Paul depicts his job as temporally prior to and as of more fundamental significance than Apollos's. While both of them are servants through whom the Corinthians "believed" (v. 5), it is Paul who "planted" and Apollos who "watered." On one level, that of jobs that have to be done, both workers are equally subordinate to God who employed them and provided the growth. Yet, on another level, the implied seeds cannot be watered and cannot properly grow unless they have first been planted properly. That Paul views his job as the "planter" as one of higher value than Apollos's is only implied in this agricultural metaphor, but his view is made explicit when he shifts to the construction metaphor in vv. 9ff. There the community is described as God's "building" (*oikodomē*),[68] and it is Paul who has been given the job

110

(*charis*)[69] of laying a foundation like "a skilled master builder" (*sophos architektōn*), while another, presumably Apollos, is building upon it (v. 11). To be sure, on the level of jobs to be done there is in principle no difference between the value of a foundation and the value of what is built upon it. Both are integral parts of the building, and Paul is aware of it. But here, as in 2 Cor. 10:13–18 and Rom. 15:17–21, Paul represents himself as a planter and as a foundation layer, not as a waterer or as one who builds on another's foundation. In his view, the foundation that *he* lays is the only one that can be laid, Jesus Christ, and therefore anything that is built upon it must fit it. Indeed, each of his letters can be read as an attempt to build upon his own foundation or to restructure what others have built upon it. Here in 1 Corinthians, he is doing both. No sooner does he describe his job and refer to the one who came on the job after him than he warns every man to take care how he builds upon the foundation which has been laid (v. 11 end). He asserts that no other foundation *can* be laid than the one that has been laid, namely by himself, and that what is built upon it will have to pass God's judgment, as will the builder before he gets paid. Paul is confident about how well he has done his job, but he is clearly less confident about what Apollos has done, and equally so about what yet other members of the Corinthian community are doing to God's building, God's temple. By thinking too highly of themselves and what they believe they have gained from people like Apollos, they are destroying God's temple, for which God will destroy them (vv. 16–21a). The whole letter attempts to lead the community back to the foundation laid by Paul in order to rebuild what has been constructed upon it in his absence. Whatever Apollos did in Corinth, Paul considers that community *his* work (*ergon*) in the Lord (9:1).[70]

Paul speaks of the community as his work in the Lord, as a monument to his labors which also publicly validates his understanding of his job (1 Cor. 9:1–2). The community is evidence of his apostolic role; it would not be there if he had not preached, and they accepted Christ. In this sense, Paul's "work" in the Lord is the *product* of his labor. Viewed as *project*, however, his work, as the job assigned to him, is God's work.[71] And from this perspective, too, the product of Paul's labor is also the building, the *oikodomē*, of God, who commissioned the project. The community, therefore, is Paul's work, but not his work! In this seeming contradiction, theology—a symbolic structure—is closely integrated with sociology, but the two must be carefully distinguished. The theology refers to the frame of reference, the field of knowledge, within which Paul understands and undertakes his social actions, but because it is the sociology of his

111

actions that presently concerns us, we must not be distracted from it by the symbolic and theological language through which Paul rationalizes sociological matters. Sociologically, the community *is* his work in the Lord. It is also true, however, that his work is neither complete nor even his alone.

It is evident from our discussion of 1 Cor. 3:5–17 that the community (*oikodomē*) founded by Paul is a dynamic rather than static social structure, one that is, until God's judgment which Paul envisions as imminent, in the process of construction and conservation. Throughout this process, from the very laying of the foundation, the ongoing building activity requires sociologically both superordinate and subordinate actions[72] by the total labor force, including both local residents and translocal figures like Paul and his emissaries. The work of constructing and maintaining the communal edifice is, sociologically speaking, both horizontal and vertical. Horizontally, it is the responsibility of each member to build up and integrate into the community "building" every other member by acts of love.[73] The general rule is perhaps best stated in 1 Cor. 10:24: "Let no one seek his own good, but the good of his neighbor."[74] Vertically, on the other hand, Paul gives greater emphasis to the constructively "edifying" roles of superordination and subordination, and it is this dimension of his rhetoric that is of greatest concern to us. Both dimensions entail the ethics of social responsibility in the churches, but the vertical dimension also entails the social structure of life in the churches.

As the foundation layer Paul has the ultimate superordinate authority. There is no indication in his letters that he believes there is any social authority higher than his own in the churches founded by him.[75] While he acknowledges that there are many apostles who preach the gospel (e.g., 1 Cor. 15:3–11), he not only thinks that he has worked harder than any of them, but he also views his mission to the Gentiles as the distinctive feature of *his* apostolic job (see Rom. 1:1–6, 11–15; 15:15–24; Gal. 1:15–17; 2:1–10; contrast 2 Cor. 10:7—11:29).[76] His authority in the Gentile churches founded by him is directly exercised when he founds the churches or later visits them, but also indirectly when he contributes to the edifice built upon his foundation through his letters and through the efforts of his fellow workers, some of whom are itinerants like himself (e.g., Timothy and Titus) and others of whom are local residents, like Philemon and Stephanas.[77] The Corinthian correspondence is throughout evidence for the full range of ways in which Paul exerts his authority and also of the process by which it is established.

Second Corinthians 10—13 is particularly interesting because in it Paul addresses a direct challenge to his job and therefore to his authority.[78] Some in Corinth have apparently been persuaded by other apostles that Paul's exercise of his authority in Corinth is overbearing and not matched by his personal qualifications. Some say "His letters are weighty and strong, but his bodily presence is weak, and his speech of no account" (2 Cor. 10:9; cf. 10:1; 1:24). The other apostles not only claim to be less oppressive and stronger in body and speech but also to have jobs equal to Paul's (11:12). His response is extensive, weighty, and strong, but the sociologically critical points are his denial of their equality—they are "false apostles, deceitful workmen, disguising themselves as apostles of Christ" (11:13–14)—and his claim that authority (*exousia*) has been given him by the Lord for the purpose of building the community up (*oikodomeō*), not for tearing it down (10:8; 13:10). Each of these points deserves attention.

First, Paul repudiates the other apostles' claims to have the same job he has by challenging their understanding (10:12). What they lack is an appreciation of his own understanding of *his* job, which is to lay, as he has, the gospel of Christ as a foundation for the community (cf. 10:5–7, 13–18; 11:1–2). By contrasting the form of Paul's presence with their own and by preaching another gospel than his (11:4), they doubly convict themselves in Paul's eyes. *His* knowledge of the gospel (11:6) and his confirming experiences of it (12:1–10) subordinate the forms of personal appearance to the gospel of Christ as Paul knows it (10:18). Moreover, the "truth of Christ" that he knows is not that of the Christ proclaimed by the others (11:10). On the basis of *his* knowledge and of *his* experience, he claims that Christ is speaking in him (12:19; 13:3), not in them. It is not the publicly verifiable accuracy of the gospel that either Paul or his opponents preach which is the ultimate criterion upon which his judgment is based but his personal certainty of the rightness of *his* understanding, which is in turn based on his own experience (Gal. 1:15–16; 1 Cor. 15:3–11;[79] cf. 2 Cor. 12:1–10).[80] In his view, because he has preached Christ to the Corinthians, Christ is also in them; therefore they should also know what he knows (cf. 1 Cor. 9:1–2). If they do not recognize the truth of Christ that is in himself and in them, he is prepared to deal with them in terms of sheer authority and power (13:1–10). What forms that may take he does not indicate, although from 1 Corinthians we know that he claimed the authority to expel people from the church, and that claim becomes social power if he succeeds in exercising it (cf. 1 Cor. 5:3–5; 16:22; Gal. 1:8; Rom. 9:3).[81]

The second point is that previous demonstrations of Paul's authority and power (cf. 1 Corinthians *passim*, the prior events referred to in 1 Corinthians 10—13, 2 Cor. 2:14—7:4, and 2 Cor. 1:23—2:11) have been construed by some Corinthians as destructive of what *they* have built up. Paul insists to the contrary that his authority has been given him for purposes of building up, not for tearing down (10:8; 13:10). From what we have seen, it appears that from Paul's perspective the tearing down of an edifice that does not match its foundation is, like demolition prior to rebuilding, a constructive act (see also 1 Cor. 3:3–5), an act of love (2 Cor. 2:4–11).

The two points raised by 2 Corinthians 10—13 tell us much about how Paul viewed and expressed his authority, but without 2 Cor. 1:3—2:13 and its continuation in 7:5–16 we could not know whether this authority has any social reality beyond his claims, whether this authority translates into power. Because this section of 2 Corinthians was written after 2 Corinthians 10—13, it shows that what Paul sought to achieve in it succeeded.[82] It shows that the Corinthians accepted his efforts and thereby confirmed the authority he claimed and established his power among them. Thus, through his personal presence, his letters, and his emissaries, Paul succeeded in his job and in the process established the very authority and power that had been challenged. The Corinthians' assent to Paul's claims socially validates them, and their response to Paul achieves what Philemon's response to Paul can also achieve. But in both cases it is also evident that in his transactions with his communities Paul's authority is in as much of a process of taking social shape as are the social structures of the communities themselves. Indeed, despite Paul's rhetoric about having laid a foundation through the preaching of the gospel, the Corinthian correspondence shows that both the symbolic (e.g., the gospel) and the sociological foundations of the community are shaky (contrast 1 Thessalonians). The foundations are, in this correspondence, undergoing repair at the same time that the social edifice is being constructed upon it.[83] For this reason, Paul's actions cannot be understood properly apart from the process of social formation in which they occur.

The same is true, of course, for the actions of Paul's fellow workers, whose authority is derived from his own and whose very designation as fellow workers derives from *his* role as the foundation layer. With them, however, we have to reckon with two roles, namely as subordinates to Paul and as superordinates in the communities by virtue of their association with him.

The subordinacy of the fellow workers to Paul is principally reflected in the fact that Paul usually initiates their actions. This is not entirely clear in all references to fellow workers, since some are only

114

referred to as such or are merely mentioned as having worked with him.[84] Nevertheless, in all other cases Paul's role as the initiator of action is evident, even in the interesting case of Apollos, who may well be the exception which illustrates the rule. For despite Paul's questioning of this fellow worker's work in 1 Corinthians 1—4, Apollos apparently enjoyed a sufficient independence from Paul to decline his appeal (*parakalō*) that he visit Corinth (1 Cor. 16:12).[85] If so, Paul's authority may not have been acknowledged by Apollos, and Paul's identification of him as a fellow worker in 3:5–23 may reflect Paul's attempt to get the Corinthians to view Apollos as *his* subordinate. Certainly, the other two fellow workers mentioned in 1 Corinthians are represented as Paul's subordinates.[86] But that Apollos declined Paul's appeal is also related to a question some critics have raised about the sociological difference between appealing to someone to take a trip and sending him on one.[87] Titus, Paul's partner and fellow worker (2 Cor. 8:23), is a better example of this problem than Apollos because of his closer association with Paul, especially during the period encompassed by 2 Corinthians (see also Gal. 2:1, 3).[88]

According to 2 Corinthians 8, Paul appealed (*parakalō*) to Titus to undertake a mission to Corinth concerning the collection (v. 6), and Titus graciously accepted (vv. 16–17). Just how much authority is behind Paul's appeals is a matter we will go into more fully later when we consider the rhetoric of his commanding and appealing. The point of note here is that after referring to his appeal to Titus, Paul says that he is *sending* along with (*synpempō*) Titus two "brothers" whom other churches have appointed to travel with Paul and participate in his work (*charis*) on the collection for Jerusalem (8:18–23). Similarly, in 2 Corinthians 9 Paul says that he is sending brothers (v. 3), but then he confuses the apparent distinction between sending and appealing by saying that he had also appealed (*parakalō*) to those whom he sent to go on ahead of him (v. 5)! That this distinction is more rhetorical than sociological is suggested by 2 Cor. 12:17–18. There Paul refers to *those* whom he sent to Corinth (v. 17) and then he more specifically says that he had appealed (*parakalō*) to Titus and sent the brother with him (*synpempō*) in v. 18. Thus, he may have "appealed" to Titus (v. 18), but it also appears that he "sent" him (v. 17). In fact, in all three cases (2 Corinthians 8, 9, and 12) Paul uses the verb "appeal" when he describes to others what he said to the agents but "send" when he tells others who initiated the agent's trip. He tells others that he sent Timothy (1 Cor. 4:17; cf. 16:10–11; 1 Thess. 3:2; Phil. 2:19–23) and Epaphroditus (Phil. 2:25–30), but he never reports what he said to *them*. The

115

fact is that Paul sends all of his emissaries because they are *his* emissaries. They go from him, work for him where they are sent, and return to him (cf. 1 Cor. 16:10–11; 2 Cor. 2:12–13 and 7:5–16; 1 Thess. 3:1–8). The case of Epaphroditus is only a variant on this since he had been sent by the Philippians to Paul, and Paul sent him back to them after he had served him for a time (Phil. 3:25–30; 4:14–20). And as for Paul's reports of his appeals to his fellow workers, the Letter to Philemon represents an extended appeal in direct speech. But this letter is also decisive with regard to the alleged sociological difference between sending and appealing, because in it Paul tells Philemon that he has the authority in Christ to command him to do what is required but prefers for love's sake to appeal to him. The distinction between appealing to and sending his fellow workers is therefore rhetorical rather than sociological. It reflects Paul's rhetorical style, not different roles and relations. As Paul's emissaries or representatives, the fellow workers are like his letters (cf. 2 Cor. 10:8–11; 13:10; 1 Cor. 5:3–5); they are a form of *his* apostolic presence because they participate both in the same work and in his authority as the one who sent them.[89] And all of this suggests that because Apollos did not accede to Paul's "strong appeal" (*polla parekalesa*, 1 Cor. 16:12), Paul *could* not send him to Corinth. Whereas other fellow workers acknowledged their subordination to Paul, Apollos apparently *did not*, which again brings into question Paul's intent in telling the Corinthians that Apollos and he were fellow workers.

Sociologically, the superordinacy of Paul's bona fide fellow workers in the local churches also derives from their being his emissaries or his representatives, a form of *his* presence in the communities. In sending Titus to the Corinthians in connection with the collection, Titus is described to them as "*my* partner and fellow worker among you," whereas the brothers he has sent are "apostles of the churches" (2 Cor. 8:23). Similarly, in sending Timothy[90] to Corinth, Timothy is described to them as "*my* beloved and faithful child in the Lord," who will remind you of "*my* ways in Christ, as *I* teach them everywhere in the church" (1 Cor. 4:17). And later in the same letter: "When Timothy comes, see that you put him at ease among you, for he is doing the work of the Lord, as I am. So let no one despise him. Speed him on his way in peace, that he may return to me; for I am expecting him with the brethren" (16:10–11). It was Timothy, too, whom Paul sent to Thessalonica to establish that community in its faith, to exhort them not to be moved by afflictions, and to report back to Paul on the state of their faith (1 Thess. 3:1–6). And again it is Timothy who is to be sent to Philippi to find out how that church is faring. In a sociologically insightful description of Timothy to the Philippians, Paul says: "I have no one like him, who will be genuinely anxious for your welfare. They all look after their own interests, not those of Jesus Christ. But Timothy's worth you know, how as a son with a father he has served with me in the gospel" (Phil. 2:20–22). What is interesting about this statement is that despite its coming from a difficult period in Paul's career, when he is imprisoned and with some question about his fate (Phil. 1:12–25), his singling out of Timothy corresponds to the contrast between Paul's many references to him and the vastly fewer references to other fellow workers. Of all those whom he identifies as such, only Titus seems to have stayed with him for any nearly comparable period of time. Euodia, Syntyche, and Clement apparently worked with him for a short time (Phil. 4:2–3), as did those named in Romans 16 and Philemon 24; Silvanus may have served longer (2 Cor. 1:19; 1 Thess. 1:1).[91] It appears that most of Paul's fellow workers must have been more loosely associated with him, perhaps either as residential rather than as itinerant workers, or as having settled down in local communities. Whatever the case may be, it is clear that few of Paul's fellow workers were continuous associates throughout the missions through Asia, Macedonia, and Achaia. Indeed, none of them appears to have been present for each of these phases.[92] One can rightly wonder, therefore, how many of Paul's fellow workers shared his sense of *his* mission, even, perhaps, submitted for long to his superordinate self-image. Paul's apparently unidirectional personality, and the evident passion that accompanied it, may have affected the response of his fellow workers to him, as it did a community like Corinth, where Timothy and Titus may also have done more to effect reconciliation and acquiescence than Paul's letters suggest. Without Timothy and Titus, we would have to assume that the Corinthians responded directly to the rationality of Paul's arguments, or to his threats. Yet Timothy and Titus are the ones who mediated Paul's presence, his arguments, and his threats to that community, and in that capacity they played a superordinate role in the community.

Paul's admonitions to the churches concerning resident fellow workers must be viewed in light of the picture we have sketched of their itinerant brothers, for even fewer residents are mentioned than itinerants. In fact, apart from Philemon the only residential fellow worker we hear much about is Stephanas of Corinth.[93] He and his household were the first converts (*aparchē*) in Achaia, they were baptized by Paul (1 Cor. 1:16), and they put themselves in the service of the saints (*eis diakonian tois hagiois etaxan heautous*, 16:15).[94] Like Philemon, the three Corinthians, Stephanas, Fortunatus, and Achaicus, had refreshed the spirits of their community

(16:18a), and now they have refreshed Paul's spirit by visiting him, probably even reporting to him.[95] But what is most striking in view of the divisions of the community into (at least) Paul's people and Apollos's people is that Paul appeals (*parakalō*) to the Corinthians to subordinate (*hypotassō*) themselves to such men "and to every fellow worker and laborer" (*kai panti tō synergounti kai kopiōnti*, 16:16), and to give recognition (*epiginōskō*) to them (16:18b). Here Paul unequivocally urges subordination to such people because of the jobs they are doing, but it is curious that in urging such subordination he does not say as he did earlier, that they were converted by him (cf. 1:16; Fortunatus and Achaicus may have been members of Stephanas's household, which is referred to in 1:16 and 16:15). Indeed, the two references to the household of Stephanas are significant for understanding social problems in Corinth, because given the divisions in the community that were addressed in 1 Corinthians 1—4, *Stephanas and his household,* together with Chloe's people (1:11) and Crispus and Gaius (1:14), *are prime candidates for membership among those "belonging to Paul."* It is not clear as to which of the groups originated the "I belong to" slogan, but Stephanas is publicly identified with Paul, not with Apollos. Consequently, for those who see themselves as belonging to Apollos, the superordinacy of *Paul's* converts must have contributed strongly to the divisions in the community. For example, Apollos's people would have been all the more resentful if the "service for the saints" (*diakonia tois hagiois*) to which Stephanas and his household set themselves concerned the "collection for the saints" (*logeia eis tous hagious,* 16:1) initiated by Paul. Although critics are not inclined to make this connection, two factors support it. First, in 2 Cor. 8:4 and 9:1 (cf. 9:12, 13) the collection is described in the same terms as Stephanas's "service" (*diakonia eis tous hagious*), and second, the topical formula introducing 1 Cor. 16:1 (*peri . . . tēs*) suggests that the collection was one of the subjects about which the Corinthians had written Paul (cf. 7:1, 25; 8:1; 12:1; 16:1, 12).[96] Therefore, if Stephanas exercised a superordinate position in the community by virtue of his having been baptized by Paul as the first convert in Achaia, and if he participated in taking a collection from Corinth and for Jerusalem as directed by Paul (16:1-4), Stephanas looms as a pivotal figure, however innocent, in the community's divisions. And in this light 1 Corinthians must be seen as indicating the potential for conflict in the local communities that results from the dependence of some of their residential members on the translocal authority of Paul. The Letter to Philemon, on the other hand, reveals another side of the same problem, since there Paul makes the con-

118

tinuation of a resident's local authority dependent upon his reaffirmation of his relationship with Paul. In both cases, the tenuous state of the emergent structures of authority, both local and translocal, is clearly evident.

In 1 Cor. 16:15–18 Paul does not specifically identify Stephanas as a fellow worker, but he implies as much by including him among those who work and labor within the community. Subordination to such individuals is reiterated in 1 Thess. 5:12–13 without mention of particular individuals by name. There Paul exhorts (*erōtaō*)[97] the Thessalonians: "respect those who labor among you and are over you in the Lord and admonish you, and . . . esteem them very highly in love because of their work. Be at peace among yourselves" (*eidenai tous kopiōntas en hymin kai proïstamenous hymōn en kyriō kai nouthetountas hymas kai hēgeisthai autous hyperekperissou en agapē dia to ergon autōn. eirēneuete en heautois*).[98] Similarly, Paul tells the Philippians to "honor such men" (*tous toioutous entimous echete*, 2:29) as Epaphroditus, one of their own people whom they had sent to Paul for the work of Christ, and whom Paul is returning to them (2:25–30). However, beyond these references we see little of Paul's attempts to secure the positions of others, although his recommendations that the churches receive certain people because of their work with him may have that effect (cf. Rom. 16:1–2; Phil. 4:3), as may his greetings in Romans 16 and 1 Cor. 16:19 (cf. Philemon 2). But what is of most interest in texts like 1 Cor. 16:16; 1 Thess. 5:12–13; and Phil. 2:29 is that Paul urges subordination to those who perform certain jobs in the local churches. It is one thing to say "be subordinate to Stephanas," another to say "be subordinate to those who labor among you, are over you in the Lord and admonish you." The former has an ad hoc character related to an individual person, the latter an incipiently institutional character because different persons can perform such jobs. Because the jobs have a social structural position of superiority independent of the persons who perform them, the fate of the building project depends on certain work being performed, regardless of by whom. But this aspect of the social structure of the church in Paul's narrative world requires us to consider two other texts in which Paul speaks about the kinds of work performed in the churches, Rom. 12:3–8 and 1 Corinthians 12—14. Despite some significant differences between these two texts, they share more similarities between them than either does with the texts considered thus far. Both employ as an image for the community the metaphor of the body (*sōma*) as a unity of different members (*melē*), each with its own function (*praxis*, cf. Rom. 12:4–5; 1 Cor. 12:12–31),[99] and both speak of these functions as "gifts" (*charismata*, Rom. 12:6, 1 Cor. 12:4–11, 31).

In Rom. 12:3–9, Paul says that the gifts (*charismata*) differ according to the grace (*charis*) given to each member (12:6). He himself speaks by the grace given to him (12:3), and this is the same "grace" by which he laid the foundation of Jesus Christ, namely his call to be an apostle of Christ Jesus (1 Cor. 3:10–11; cf. 1 Cor. 15:9–10 and Rom. 15:15–21). "Grace" (*charis*), therefore, once again connotes the *job* God has assigned, while "gift" (*charisma*) connotes the individual's ability to perform the assigned task or play the assigned role. A "gift" is the functional or operational manifestation (i.e., in *praxis*) of one's job, as distinct from the "job description" (*charis*).[100] The gifts envisioned in Rom. 12:6–8 are as follows: prophecy, service (*diakonia*), teaching (*didaskalia*), exhortation (*paraklēsis*), giving (*metadidōmi*), supervision (*proïstēmi*), and consolation (*eleeō*).[101] Of these, we have already seen "service," "exhortation," and "supervision." New are "prophecy," "teaching," "giving," and "consolation." Unlike the role of apostle, which is not mentioned in this list, all are functions performed by members of the local churches, and Paul apparently does not attempt to rank them according to their socially hierarchical value. His point is simply to urge, in performance of the job given to him to be an apostle of Christ,[102] that church members perform their own functions well and without overestimating their own importance. The ranking of functions is but one of several differences between 1 Corinthians 12—14 and Rom. 12:3–8.

In 1 Cor. 1:4 and 7 Paul also sees gifts (*charismata*) as the manifestation of the grace (*charis*) of God given to individuals in the church. However, in 1 Corinthians 12—14 we find a change in his description of the origin of the gifts, and this change apparently reflects a distinctively Corinthian view of its own social differentiation. For them, the gifts directly result from the reception of the spirit at baptism (cf. 12:4–13; 14:12).[103] In 1 Corinthians 1—4 Paul dealt with social divisions in the community that are related to the members' allegiances to their baptizers. Here he deals with other divisions related to the spirit they received at baptism, a spirit probably construed by some as having been given or mediated to them by their baptizer. Be this as it may, in 1 Corinthians 12—14 Paul seeks to restructure an emergent social hierarchy that he finds detrimental to the construction of God's building. His focus is on what transpires in communal worship (see also 11:17–34),[104] but in the process of trying to introduce an acceptable order into the Corinthians' worship (14:26–36, 39–40), he undertakes a much more comprehensive restructuring of their sociological orientation (1 Corinthians 12).

As Paul sees it, the root problem is the Corinthians' enthusiasm for manifestations of the spirit (*charismata*) they had received at baptism (cf. 14:12; 12:13; 1:12—3:4).[105] The two manifestations he focuses on in 1 Corinthians 13—14 are prophecy and speaking in tongues (*glossalalia*). Apparently speakers in tongues have disruptively dominated worship services, and possibly there are women among them.[106] To correct this situation in communal worship, Paul commands that speakers in tongues should seek to become interpreters of tongues (14:13), and in any event to defer to prophets, for prophecy is a higher gift than speaking in tongues (14:1–5, 26–33a, 37–40; cf. 12:27–31). Each member should be governed by what "edifies" (*oikodomeō*) the whole community, not by what edifies him or herself as an individual (cf. Rom. 12:3). Love, according to Paul, is that quality of edifying, upbuilding behavior which each person should exhibit and also seek in others. And because love is concerned with the building up of the community, it should lead one to defer to those with higher gifts (*ta charismata ta meizona*, 12:31) than one's own (12:31—14:1, 5). Because prophecy is a higher gift than speaking in tongues, speakers in tongues should defer to prophets when the prophets have something to say. But why is prophecy a higher gift than speaking in tongues? One answer given by Paul is communicability. Prophecy is superior because it enables edifying communication between members of the group. Whereas the speaker in tongues addresses God in speech that is unintelligible except to God and to some interpreters, the prophet "speaks to men for their upbuilding and encouragement and consolation" (*oikodomēn kai paraklēsin kai paramythian*, 14:3; cf. 14:1–25). In addition to communicability, however, Paul offers a second answer to the question of why one gift is superior to others, and this answer locates the two focal gifts within a more comprehensive hierarchy of gifts and jobs.

Lest there be any question about which gifts of the spirit are higher or lower than others, Paul provides a hierarchical ranking of them which he attributes to God: " . . . God has appointed in the church first apostles, second prophets, third teachers, then workers of miracles, then gifts of healing, helpers, administrators, speakers in various kinds of tongues" (12:28; cf. 12:30, which adds after speakers in tongues, "interpreters of tongues"; see also 12:10). This list differs not only from that in Rom. 12:3–8,[107] but also and more importantly from another list that appears just before it in 1 Cor. 12:8–10. The differences between these two lists suggest that the first list represents functions operative in the Corinthian community and the second Paul's revision of it. The first list is, like that of Rom. 12:3–8, according to gifts (*charismata*), now understood as "spiritual gifts" (cf. *pneumatika*, 1 Cor. 14:1), and they are not expressly hierarchical in the order of their appearance. Their order is: the utterance of wisdom (*logos sophias*), the utterance of knowledge (*logos gnōseōs*), faith, gifts of healing, the ability to perform miracles, prophecy, the ability to distinguish between spirits, speaking in tongues, and the interpretation of tongues. The second list, however, is not of *charismata* but of *jobs*, and it has a hierarchical order: first, second, third, then, then. This list adds four jobs to those implied in the first one (apostles, teachers, helpers, administrators) and deletes four (the utterance of wisdom, the utterance of knowledge, faith, and the ability to distinguish between spirits). Moreover, in a repetition of this list in vv. 29–30 Paul omits from his own list in v. 28 helpers and administrators, and he adds "interpreters" at the end, which is also the last of the gifts listed in v. 10. The differences between v. 28 and vv. 29–30 are probably not significant, and certainly not as significant as those between the lists of gifts and of jobs.

Although the list in 12:8–10 is not systematically organized according to an existing hierarchy of gifts, it is likely that the first two or three gifts, those concerning the utterance of wisdom and knowledge and faith, are high on the list of those people involved in the divisions within the community referred to in 1 Corinthians 1—4, for these gifts are there expressly associated with the divisions (cf. 1:4–7, 17—3:4, 18–23; 4:6–13). Paul challenges them in chaps. 1—4 and he omits them in his own list in 12:28 (and vv. 29–30). As in chaps. 1—4, wisdom, knowledge, and faith seem to be the functions of apostles, who replace them in Paul's list of jobs in 12:28 and 29. On the other hand, the location of speakers in tongues at the bottom of both lists in 1 Corinthians 12, and after prophecy and prophets, may reflect Paul's own ordering of the list of functions in 12:8–10, since 1 Corinthians 14 suggests that some Corinthians had a higher regard for speakers in tongues than Paul, who subordinates them to prophets both in chap. 14 and in his list in 12:28 (and vv. 29–30). But the most important difference between the two lists in 1 Corinthians 12 is Paul's assertion that in the church God has appointed in the highest position apostles—first, apostles (12:28).

The role of apostles as Paul represents them entails a radically different sociological orientation from that of the Corinthians because it is based on God's grace (*charis*) not on God's gifts (*charismata*). Regardless of how the Corinthians ranked apostles (cf. 1

Corinthians 1—4), Paul *had* to omit apostles from the list of gifts in 12:8–10 because for him apostleship is not a function of the spirit received at baptism (*charisma*), but a product of God's decision (*charis*) that a certain function be performed by certain individuals, especially by Paul (1 Cor. 1:1, 17; 3:5–10; 4:15; 9:1; 15:9–20; cf. Rom. 15:15–21). This, I think, is true of all of the jobs Paul lists in 1 Cor. 12:28 and Rom. 12:3–8. They are not, as some Corinthians think, the products simply of the baptismal spirit, although the spirit is the source of the power for performing most if not all of the jobs God or Christ assigns. Ultimately, because all of the jobs are assigned by God, Paul has to distinguish between grace (*charis*) and gift (*charisma*) and subordinate the latter to the former. At least in terms of the differentiation of roles in the church, baptism is simply not as central for Paul as it is for the Corinthians (or for Luke!), as Paul indicates in 1 Cor. 1:14–17 and 4:15. Yes, the spirit comes to all only at baptism, and it is the same spirit that is operative, in different ways, in each person, but the Lord is over all forms of service and God is behind everyone's actions (12:4–6). The baptismal spirit is for Paul the source of social equality among the brethren, while God is the source of social differences among them. Baptism is indeed fundamental, but as a baptism into what God has done in Christ (Rom. 6:3–11; cf. chapter 3, below). This seems to have eluded the problem-people among the Corinthians.

Apostleship is therefore not a product of the baptismal spirit, but neither is it a local function like the other positions represented in the lists found in 1 Corinthians 12 and Romans 12. The apostle and his traveling fellow workers operate within communities, but as itinerants rather than as residents, and their authority derives from outside of the communities in which they serve, namely from those who commission and send them (cf. the "apostles" of the churches in 2 Cor. 8:19, 23, and Phil. 2:25). Paul is commissioned and sent by God, and his fellow workers are commissioned and sent by him. But because God has also commissioned the jobs performed by the residents of local communities, he is the ultimate source of authority behind every job. For this reason, what Paul says of worldly authorities in Rom. 13:1–7 also applies to all of the jobs in the differentiation of labor within the church.[108] Every person, Paul says, must be subordinate (*hypotassō*) to the governing authorities (*exousiai*) because there is no authority except from God, and those that exist have been instituted (*tassō*) by him. Consequently, those who resist such authorities resist what God has ordained and will incur God's judgment for it. Authorities are God's servants (*diakonoi*) for the communities' good (Rom. 3:1–4; cf. 1 Thess. 5:12–13). In this light, the jobs we have been considering are to be seen as divine authorizations to perform certain functions, and as such they render the persons who perform them as authorities to whom other individuals must necessarily subject themselves. This is what Paul is asserting in 1 Corinthians 12—14, and also in all of the other texts dealing with the subordination of some church members to others. His hierarchical list of authorities in 12:28 specifies what is evident in the whole letter, and indeed in all of his letters: since all are to defer to those with higher "gifts," gifts grounded in *God's* differentiation of social functions, the Corinthians must defer to Paul's exhortations because his apostolic commission is higher than any they possess. First Corinthians, like the Letter to Philemon, therefore represents the imposition of translocal authority upon the local forms of social differentiation and the behavior that follows from them. First Corinthians shows, too, just how resistant a local church can be to other than indigenous authority, and also how susceptible a local church can be to other influences than Paul's upon its social life. The Pauline churches, including the one at Philemon's house, are very much in the process of construction, even of remodeling during the construction process.

Paul's Roles

Our investigation of the roles of fellow workers and partners, and of the metaphor of work, has shown that the structure of relations represented in the two egalitarian role names is in fact hierarchical. Moreover, the investigation very quickly led us to Paul's superordinate apostolic role by virtue of which some brothers become his metaphorical fellow workers and partners. These names, therefore, rhetorically mask a relationship other than the one they imply. They imply a relationship of equality between persons who are in fact related hierarchically. Fellow workers and partners are sociologically inferior to Paul, whose use of these egalitarian metaphors is a matter of his administrative style, a style both motivated and legitimated by his symbolic universe. The most immediately pertinent segments of this universe are the metaphorical systems oriented to work and to the human body, but principally to work.

The role-names "ambassador," "prisoner of Christ Jesus," "father," and by implication "debtee," are also metaphors that rhetorically mask Paul's apostolic role, and for the same motives that inform his work metaphors. Paul uses the name "apostle" literally, as we can see, for example, in the lists of role-names in 1 Cor. 12:28–30 (cf. 1 Cor. 15:3–9), where "apostle" is as literal in its reference as "prophet" and "teacher." But because Paul uses the noun "apostle" as though his readers understood what it meant, critics have largely concentrated on exploring the meaning of that word outside of Paul's letters, especially to see if it refers to an *institutional* role or office.[109] However, that it does not have such an institutional reference *for Paul* is clearly evident from Gal. 1:1 (cf. 1:11—2:21), where he claims that *his* apostleship is not derived from human institutions but from Jesus Christ and God.[110] As we can see from his references to other apostles or messengers of individual churches (2 Cor. 8:23; Phil. 2:25; cf. 4:18), he uses the word to refer to a role, namely of one who is sent by someone to someone else for some purpose. But his role does not necessarily connote an institutional "office," and he in any event denies that his role has any institutional origin at all. What is significant for him about *his* apostleship is that he has been called and sent by God to preach Christ among the Gentiles (Gal. 1:15–16; Rom. 1:1–6; 15:15–21; 1 Cor. 1:1; 2 Cor. 1:1). For Paul, to be an apostle is to be called (commissioned) and sent to do a job, and that is apparently the knowledge he presupposes among his audiences, together with the knowledge that in the church many are sent (cf. 1 Cor. 15:3–11), although not all who are sent have exactly the same job. Peculiar to *his* job, as we have seen, is its origination with God and its destination to non-Jews. And as we have also seen, the authority entailed in his job derives from his "employer." Overlapping these work metaphors, however, are other metaphors that help us to see yet more about Paul's literal role in the church and the style with which he plays it. Because the metaphors of "ambassador" and "prisoner of Christ" are closest to his literal role, we will begin with them and then attend to those of "father" and "debtee," both of which refer to a more particular aspect of the literal role.

Ambassador and Prisoner of Christ Jesus

We take up once again the notion of prisoner because of its qualification, "of Christ Jesus" (Philemon 1 and 9; cf. v. 13, "for the gospel"),[111] but also because of its conjunction in v. 9 with *presbytēs*, which can be translated as either "ambassador" or "old man."[112] As noted previously, commentators are divided over the proper translation of this ambiguous Greek word. Those preferring "old man" do so because it is the more common meaning of *presbutēs*, which differs by only a single letter from *presbeutēs*, the word for "ambassador," and because they do not read the letter to Philemon as a product of Paul's apostolic authority.[113] On the other hand, those who prefer the translation "ambassador" do so because they see the Greek word as an allusion to Paul's apostleship, which in 2 Cor. 5:20 he describes as "working as an ambassador for Christ" (*hyper Chris-*

125

tou oun presbeuomen), here using the verb *presbeuō*, which is also
employed in the Deutero-Pauline Letter to the Ephesians to describe
Paul as an ambassador in chains (*presbeuo en halysei*, Eph. 6:20).[114]
Since these three passages are the only places where the noun or the
verb occur in the Pauline corpus, evidence from Paul's usage is
minimal. But if it is minimal for the notion of "ambassador," it is
also nonexistent for the notion of "old man," for Paul never refers
elsewhere to his age. To see Philemon 9 as a reference to old age has
only lexical support from outside of Paul's letters, but not from
either lexical or conceptual evidence within them. To see Philemon
9 as a reference to his ambassadorship, on the other hand, has only
the lexical and conceptual support of 2 Cor. 5:20 and Eph. 6:20. In
the final analysis, therefore, it is the context that we introduce as the
basis for our interpretation which is critical.

Two contexts strongly support the translation of *presbytēs* as ambassador. One is the rhetorical context of the Letter to Philemon, the
other is the context of Paul's self-identifications in other letters.
Both cases make "ambassador" a more sensible translation than
"old man" because Paul relates to others as an ambassador of
Christ, not as an old man, let alone as "an old man of Christ." Each
case offers further insights into Paul and his administrative and
rhetorical style.

One of the distinctive features of the rhetorical context of the
reference to Paul as a *presbytēs* is that it contains a series of semantic
contrasts between two terms, the second of which is contrasted with
the first. "*Presbytēs* and prisoner of Christ Jesus" forms the second
set of contrasted terms in a series that begins in v. 8 and ends in
v. 16. The series therefore begins at the beginning of Paul's appeal
and ends just before its climax in v. 17, which is itself a bipartite
conditional sentence.[115] The series of contrasts is as follows:

vv. 8–9a	bold enough to command	I prefer for love's sake to appeal
v. 9b	*presbytēs*	a prisoner of Christ Jesus
v. 10	my son	whom I fathered
v. 11	formerly useless	now useful
vv. 12–13	whom I sent to you	whom I wanted to keep with me
v. 14	not by necessity	by free will
v. 15	he was parted from you for a while	that you might have him forever
v. 16a	not as a slave	as a beloved brother
v. 16b	especially to me	so much more to you
v. 16c	in the flesh	in the Lord

In this series it is of further interest to note that the two contrastive sets in vv. 14 and 16a are grammatically marked by a negative plus "as" (*mē hōs; ouketi hōs*) preceding the first term and the strong adversative "but" (*alla*) preceding the second term. But Paul also repeats other constructions, such as the three *hina* (in order to) clauses in vv. 13, 14, and 15, and the parallel relative (*hon*) clauses in vv. 12 and 13, which comprise one of our contrastive sets. In view of these grammatical repetitions, it is especially interesting to see that the construction of the set with which we are concerned, "*presbytēs* but now also (*nyni de kai*) a prisoner of Christ Jesus," (v. 9b) is repeated in v. 11: "who was formerly useless to you, but now also (*nyni de kai*) is useful to you and to me."[116] If there was any doubt about there being a contrast between the terms in v. 9b, this parallelism should end it. The question that remains, however, concerns a translation of *presbytēs* that is a credible contrast to "prisoner of Christ Jesus." The status reversal suggested by the contrast between ambassador and prisoner is much more obviously consistent with the list of contrasts in which it appears than is the relationship between "old man" and "prisoner," which is not a contrast at all. Indeed, because the contrast may also be governed by *both* terms being qualified by "of Christ Jesus,"[117] it would not make much if any sense to speak of being "an old man of Christ."

The rhetorical context offers us yet further assistance. In the first three sets of contrasts Paul is represented (1) as one who has the authority in Christ to command, yet prefers to appeal (*parakalō*), (2) as *presbytēs*, and (3) as a "father." The first of these is a direct expression of Paul's apostolic role, the last is clearly a rhetorical mask for it. What, then, about *presbytēs*? We know from 2 Cor. 5:20 that it is as an "ambassador" for Christ that God makes his appeal (*parakalō*) through Paul (cf. 6:1), and from 1 Cor. 4:15–16 that Paul also appeals (*parakalō*) to the Corinthians as their "father" in Christ Jesus. So also in 1 Thess. 2:11 (cf. 2:1–12), where Paul reminds the Thessalonians that "like a father with his children" he exhorted (*parakalō*), encouraged (*paramytheomai*), and charged (*martyromai*) them to lead a life worthy of God. These texts therefore combine with the content of Philemon 8–10 to support the translation of *presbytēs* as ambassador because Paul's appeal derives from the apostolic masks of "ambassador" and "father," not from his being an old man.

When we turn to Paul's self-identification in other letters we find more support for this translation. First, in speaking of his imprisonment for Christ in his letter to Philippi, Paul describes his imprisonment as being a form of his apostolic activity, that is, his preaching of the gospel (Phil. 1:12–18). The apostle is now also a prisoner, but nonetheless an apostle. But in this letter Paul also employs another mask, another metaphor of inferiority, namely that of slave (*doulos*, 1:1; cf. 2:22, *douleuō*),[118] which introduces a second form of self-identification bearing on our problem. In Rom. 1:1 and Gal. 1:1, 10 he describes himself as both an apostle and "a slave" (*doulos*) of Christ Jesus." Thus, for Paul "slave" and "prisoner of Christ" are functional equivalents, as are "apostle" and "ambassador," and therefore "ambassador and prisoner of Christ" is also the functional equivalent of "apostle and slave of Christ." The contrast between the terms in the latter set synonymously corresponds to the contrast between those in the former set.

In light of all of this evidence "old man" is simply not a viable translation of *presbytēs*. In representing himself as an ambassador, but now also a humbled and obedient prisoner of Christ Jesus, Paul is fully consistent with the strategy we have already observed. Until v. 19b he consistently enacts in his rhetoric the very humility and obedience (cf. Phil. 2:1–13) he expects from Philemon. Thereby, Paul sets himself as a model for Philemon to imitate, probably even to the point of suggesting that by renouncing his worldly authority over Onesimus he will, like Paul, retain his superordinate authority in the church—as Paul's fellow worker and partner, and as host to the church that meets in his house.

Father and Debtee

Earlier, we saw that in the Letter to Philemon "father" and "debtee" are synonymous metaphors representing Paul's superordinate role in relation to those whom he converts. Because the metaphor of debt is peculiar to this letter and has already been discussed, we can concentrate on Paul's metaphorical paternity and the corresponding designation of church members as his children.[119] These metaphors occur elsewhere in his letters, and because they entail more than the relationship of converter to convertee they refer to more than the relationship of indebtedness.

In Philemon 10 Paul refers to Onesimus as his "child" (*teknon*, cf. v. 12, "my very heart," *ta ema splangchna*), whom he has "fathered" (*gennaō*) while in prison. In other letters, Paul similarly refers to church members, indeed, to whole churches, as his children (1 Cor. 4:14, 17; 2 Cor. 6:13; 12:14–15; Gal. 4:19, with Paul as mother; 1 Thess. 2:7, with Paul as nurse; 2:11), but the most illuminating references occur in 1 Cor. 4:14–21. Here Paul represents himself as father both to the Corinthians and to Timothy, both of whom are also explicitly identified as his children. This passage offers almost as rich an insight into the kinship metaphor of apostolic paternity as 1 Cor. 3:5–17 did into the work metaphor.

Paul begins this section of his exhortation concerning the divisions in Corinth by shifting from a depiction of himself and Apollos as servants of God laboring among the Corinthians to a representation of *himself* as their father.[120] Thus the superordinate position we found to be latent in 1 Cor. 3:5–17 now becomes fully manifest. Paul claims that he is not writing to shame (*entrepō*) the Corinthians, as he later does (6:5; 15:34),[121] but to admonish (*noutheteō*) them as beloved children (*tekna*, 4:14). For while they have countless guides (*paidagōgous*) in Christ, they do not have many fathers (*pateras*), and it is he who fathered (*gennaō*) them "in Christ Jesus through the gospel" (v. 15; cf. Philemon 10). On this basis (*oun*), Paul appeals (*parakalō*) to them to become imitators of him (*mimētai mou*, v. 16), and to this end (*dia touto*) he announces that he has sent to them Timothy, his beloved and faithful child in the Lord (*mou teknon agapēton kai piston en kyriō*, v. 17; cf. Phil. 2:22, "how as a son with a father he has served [*douleuō*] with me in the gospel," and 1 Thess. 3:2). Timothy is to remind them of Paul's ways (*hodous*) in Christ, as he teaches (*didaskō*) them everywhere in every church (v. 17). Paul then refers to the arrogant among the Corinthians, accuses them of acting as though he were not coming again to Corinth, announces that he will come and that when he does he will measure their talk against their power, for the kingdom of God consists not in talk but in power (vv. 18–20). He concludes by asking, "What do you wish? Shall I come to you with a rod (*en rhabdō*) or with love in a spirit of forbearance (*praütētos*)?" (v. 21). The alternative of his opening words, shame or admonition, is echoed in his closing words, with a rod or with love.

To these comments we can add information from other letters. In addition to the paternal admonishing and appealing in 1 Corinthians, we find Paul reminding the Thessalonians about how, like a father with his children (*hōs patēr tekna heautou*),[122] he and his companions appealed (*parakalō*) to each one of them and encouraged (*paramytheomai*) them and implored (*martyromai*) them to lead a life worthy of God, who has called them into his own kingdom and glory (1 Thess. 2:11–12). In the context of this statement we also see Paul addressing the fact that he did not make financial demands upon the Thessalonians (2:1–9;[123] cf. 1 Cor. 9; 2 Cor. 11:7–11; 12:13). In 2 Cor. 12:14 this issue is represented in kinship terms when Paul says that he does not want to be a burden (*katanarkaō*) because he seeks not what belongs to the Corinthians, but the Corinthians themselves, "For children (*tekna*) ought not to lay up for their parents, but parents for their children." Because of his own paternal love, he is willing to spend himself on the Corinthians (12:15), which sounds very much like 1 Thess. 2:8, "So, being affectionately desirous (*homeiromai*) of you, we were ready to share with you not only the gospel of God but also our own selves, because you had become very dear to us." This, however, follows another metaphor, one in which Paul claims that he had been gentle among them, "like a nurse taking care of her children" (2:7). Paul was therefore not limited to paternal metaphors of affection and care; elsewhere he even compares himself to a woman in labor with his churchly offspring (Gal. 4:19).

From these texts it is evident not only that the notion of "father" metaphorically describes Paul's apostolic role (1 Cor. 4:15; cf. 1 Thess. 2:4), and that the generation of his metaphorical children is through the "seed" of the gospel he preached, but it is also evident that the parent-child metaphoric complex expresses a hierarchical social structural relationship. Indeed, it is a form of Paul's social relations that explicitly expresses his social structural relationship with the churches. This superiority is most clearly represented in the power of the "rod" he holds over the Corinthians (1 Cor. 4:21), but it is also represented in his appeal to them to imitate[124] *him* (4:16), in connection with which he sent Timothy to remind them of *his ways* in Christ, *as he teaches them* to all (4:17). Paul's superordinate position is further demonstrated both in his ability to shame (*entrepō*) his children (4:14; cf. 6:5 and 15:34; 2 Cor. 6:11–13; 10:6; 13:2–10; Gal. 4:19–20) and in his preference rather to appeal, admonish, cajole, and so forth (cf. 1 Cor. 4:14, 16; 1 Thess. 2:11–12). Although the metaphor of "father" is one of ambiguous superiority, Paul expressly prefers to admonish rather than to shame, to be gentle rather than firm, to give of himself rather than take from his children. On the other hand, however, although Paul is ready to spare the rod, he is not prepared to spoil the child. Throughout, love is the familial or kinship quality that expressly motivates his behavior, but for Paul, love can also be expressed in shaming, just as edification can be expressed in tearing down. And Paul can use the rod and even receive from his children (cf. Phil. 4:14–19). He makes full use of the ambiguity of the metaphorical paternal role.

Paul's paternal affection is to be reciprocated by his children.[125] Whereas he affectionately admonishes them, they should affectionately comply with his admonitions (cf. 2 Cor. 6:11–13; 7:5–16; 12:15). However, Paul says surprisingly little about this reciprocity. More often than not, the behavior of his children has to be inferred from his appeals. Thus, in the texts we have looked at, his children are to imitate their father, follow his ways and teachings, heed his appeals, and lead a worthy life. Compliance with his appeals, if not obedience to the father, is the proper response of the child to the father.[126] That the behavior of both the parent and the children is governed by love and affection only softens their hierarchical relationship. It does not replace it.

Paul's relations with Philemon are all the more interesting in view of the father-child metaphors. They are interesting not least of all because Paul neither identifies himself nor relates to Philemon as *his* father, even though the metaphor of Philemon's indebtedness to Paul suggests that he is Philemon's father in the same sense that he is Onesimus's father—and Timothy's, and the Corinthians', and the Thessalonians', and so on. Similarly, he does not employ the metaphor of slavery to represent himself, Philemon, or even Onesimus, although they are all metaphorical slaves of the master Jesus Christ. Why Paul does not use either of these metaphorical systems can perhaps best be understood by contrasting them with the metaphors that he does use. The most conspicuous of these are, of course, those designating relations of equality: brother, fellow worker, partner. To be sure, the last two of these have proved to mask a hierarchical relationship explicitly expressed in Paul's claim to have the authority to command Philemon's obedience. Nevertheless, the rhetorical tone of his letter (up to v. 19) is clearly one which backs off from his superordinacy and stresses equality. It is, I believe, precisely this flexibility of movement which accounts for Paul's *not* using father-child or master-slave language with respect to Philemon, for those systems are inherently hierarchical in their implications. They do not allow for the change of positions that Paul represents for himself and Onesimus and that he desires for Philemon. But if this is the correct interpretation of Paul's rhetorical strategy, it also suggests that when he does use the father-child metaphors he does so in the exercise of his loving yet superordinate position. And indeed this appears to be the case in all of the texts we have looked at. Paul's authority is at issue in each and every case. His fatherhood is therefore a rather transparent mask for his apostolic role, much more so than the metaphor of ambassador, which locates his authority not in himself or in his job, but in the one whose ambassador he is.

Commanding and Appealing, Rhetoric and Reality[127]

Whatever language of appeal Paul employs, his appeals are rhetorical acts that proceed from the ambassadorial and paternal masks of his apostolic authority. His appeals are forms of his social presence and therefore exhibitions of his social style. To be sure, individuals within the churches appeal to and exhort one another (cf. 1 Thess. 4:18; 5:11, 14), and Paul's fellow workers exhort the congregations as he does and with his backing (cf. 1 Thess. 3:2). But when *Paul* appeals, he does so as an expression of his apostolic role, and because his appeals proceed from the masks of this role the appeals equally mask it. The Letter to Philemon is the most concrete example of Paul's style to be found in his letters, for there he says outright that he, who has the authority in Christ to command Philemon, prefers for love's sake to appeal to him (vv. 8–9).[128] As an expressed substitute for commanding, the appeal only very thinly masks a command, for behind the formal appeal is the stated authority to command. But what is true of vv. 8–9 is also true of the entire appeal which extends from v. 8 through v. 22. The sociological reality includes the rhetorical character of Paul's mask because it is disclosed to Philemon as such. This reality can be represented in two ways.

One way represents the chiastic rhetorical sequence in which Paul performs his appealing action.

A	B	B[1]	A[1]
command /	appeal /	consent /	obey
v.8	vv.9–10	v.14	v.21

More fully described, Paul begins his extended "appeal" by informing Philemon of his authority in Christ to command (*epitassō*) him and then indicates his preference to appeal (*parakalō*) to him for love's sake. Love therefore determines the form of Paul's rhetorical action. This form is continued when he speaks further about Philemon's response in terms of consent (*gnōmē*) based not on necessity (*kata anankēn*), which resonates with the possibility of commanding, but on Philemon's free will (*kata hekousion*), which resonates with the preference to appeal. Nevertheless, Paul's "appeal" comes to a conclusion with a reference to Philemon's response being an expected act of obedience (*hypakoē*), that is, as to a command that Paul could have made but did not. Or did he? As the object of Paul's action, Philemon is cast as receiving initially its severity (command) and then its affectionate substitute (appeal) when Paul, as it were, steps down from the position of commanding to the position of appealing. Yet the steps remain and even in the course of the appeal

Philemon is reminded of the necessity of his responding affirmatively to Paul's "request." And at the end, Philemon knows that the severity of Paul's intent remains. The last word is obedience.

A second way of representing the social reality underlying Paul's action separates the actional masks from their sociological ground. Here we can assign the actional language to Paul's apostolic role on the one hand, and to his ambassadorial and paternal masks on the other, and for each of these we can represent Philemon's actions and motives as projected by Paul.

	apostle	*ambassador/father*
Paul's action	v. 8 command	
		vv. 9–10 appeal
Philemon's action		v. 14 consent
	v. 14 by compulsion	out of free will
	v. 21 obedience	

Taken together, the two representations of the sociology of Paul's rhetoric show that rhetoric and reality are not two distinct things but only one. The rhetoric is a part of the sociological reality because Paul employs it in his social relations, and because it is an element of *his* social relations it is not independent of his actual social role. His rhetoric is the form through which he exercises his role, and Philemon, like ourselves, apprehends the role through the form in which it is expressed. He can be no less aware of the total reality than we are.

Because the rhetoric of Paul's appeal to Philemon so beautifully illustrates the social reality of Paul's actions, we can use the insights it opens up to help us understand his social style in other cases. These other cases will in turn supplement what we have seen in the Letter to Philemon. Since we have already explored some of the key examples of Paul's appeals and admonitions, we can concentrate on cases in which he employs his authority to command. These confirm what is already evident in the Letter to Philemon, namely that *Paul's rhetorical style serves to mediate the paradox that the egalitarian social structure of Paul's churches is complemented by a hierarchical axis.* This axis is not merely a matter of Paul's pretensions, for in acquiescing to his appeals the Corinthians affirmed its social reality, first in the reports from Chloe's people and by Stephanas in 1 Corinthians and then in the Corinthians' response to Titus's embassy described in 2 Corinthians (2 Cor. 7:5–16). So also in Timothy's report to Paul concerning the Thessalonians (1 Thess. 3:6–10) and in Epaphroditus's mission to Paul on behalf of the Philippians (Phil. 4:14–19; cf. 1:3—2:30). And Romans 16, whether originally addressed to Rome or to Ephesus,[129] implies further acceptance of Paul's role by members of one of those communities. The several communities may have been divided in their estimate of Paul at one time or another, but the evidence suggests that his self-proclaimed superordinacy over them was affectionately acknowledged by many.

Outside of the Letter to Philemon Paul nowhere else so explicitly links his own authority to command to the obedience of those whom he commands. Although obedience is probably implied when he issues commands, it is usually referred to in connection with a whole community's obedience to the faith (Rom. 1:5), to the Lord Christ (Rom. 16:18–19; 2 Cor. 10:5), to the gospel (Rom. 10:16; cf. 2 Cor. 9:13), or to the standard of teaching (*typon didachēs*) to which a church has committed itself (Rom. 6:17; cf. 16:17). Nevertheless, Paul also considers that this obedience has been achieved through him. Just as God appeals (*parakalō*) to the brethren through Paul and his fellow workers (2 Cor. 5:20), so also is it by virtue of his job, the grace and apostleship given him through Christ, that *he* brings about obedience to the faith among all the Gentiles (Rom. 1:5; 15:18–19). This he does by word and by deed, by the power of signs and wonders, by the power of the Holy Spirit (Rom. 15:18–19; cf. 2 Cor. 10:5–6; 12:12). Our concern is with his words.

In addition to his appeals, Paul's words consist of literal commands as well as of preaching.[130] While his mission is to preach Christ, he also says that Christ speaks through him in the form of commands (2 Cor. 13:3–4 and 12:19 in the context of chaps. 10—13). First Thessalonians offers a good introduction to Paul's speech and its relationship to Christ's speaking in or through him. In the thanksgiving (*eucharistō*) section of this letter (1:2—3:13), he reminds the Thessalonians both of his earlier preaching to them and of his fatherly exhortations (*paraklēsis*, 2:3; *parakalō*, 2:11) that they lead a life worthy of God. He also says that after he had left them his concern for them led him to send Timothy back to Thessalonica to firm up (*sterizō*) their faith and exhort (*parakalō*) them not to be moved by afflictions. The content of both the gospel and their faith is probably represented in that for which Paul commends the Thessalonians in 1:9b–10, where he says that they responded to his preaching by turning "to God from idols, to serve a living and true God, and to wait for his son from heaven, whom he raised from the dead, Jesus who delivers us from the wrath to come." The content of his exhortation, on the other hand, is referred to in the hortatory (*parakalō*) section of the letter (4:1—5:22).[131] Paul begins his exhortation by appealing to the Thessalonians to continue doing the things they had learned from him concerning how to live and how to please God. Importantly, these things are described as "instructions" (*parangelia*) that he had given them "through the Lord Jesus" (4:1–2). One of these instructions, concerning love, is referred to in 4:9–12, where Paul exhorts (*parakalō*) the Thessalonians to continue doing as he had "charged" or "instructed" (*parangelō*) them on this subject. For our purposes, the content of his instructions is less important than the way he refers to them, and already a number of interesting observations arise from these brief references in 1 Thessalonians 4.

First, during the time of his founding of the church in Thessalonica Paul and his fellow workers "charged" (*parangelō*) the Thessalonians with "instructions" (*parangelia*) about how to live (*peripateō*) and to please God. The seriousness of these instructions is indicated both positively, as pleasing God, and negatively. For example, on the matter of immorality Paul says that "the Lord is an avenger in all these things, as we solemnly forewarned you. For God has not called us for uncleanness, but in holiness. Therefore, whoever disregards this [instruction], disregards not man [Paul] but God, who gives his Holy Spirit to you" (4:6–8). Thus, one who is called into God's kingdom and glory must lead a life worthy of God, or confront the Lord as an avenger in the wrath to come upon his return. But by supplying his instructions with such a conceptual context, Paul integrates his social instructions within a *symbolic* universe rather than a social one, for the consequences of compliance or noncompliance are not determined socially, that is, by social actors, but eschatologically by the Lord. In this respect, therefore, the force of Paul's instructions is derived from a symbolic universe which makes them nonnegotiable and gives them the status of commands.

Second, in social terms it is nevertheless Paul and his fellow workers who bring these instructions to the Thessalonians. They claim to have issued instructions "through the Lord Jesus" (4:2), which seems to be only a variant of their speaking "in the Lord Jesus" (4:1).[132] Both expressions refer to their being apostles (2:6), that is, to their having been "approved by God to be entrusted with the gospel" (2:4; cf. 2:2), and it is from this "trust" that their "appeal" (*paraklēsis*) also derives (2:3–4). However, by grounding *his* position in relation to the Thessalonians within the same symbolic universe as his instructions, Paul's position assumes an authority

135

which matches the force that universe lent to his instructions. His status is as nonnegotiable as his instructions, and it is the status of one who commands. Paul is the social presence of a transcendent, symbolic authority; he is its ambassador. When he confronts an audience he presents himself, his preaching, and his instructions in the framework of the symbolic universe that legitimates[133] both himself and his words.

Third, once Paul has delivered his instructions they assume a virtually legal objectivity because they become social facts, something that is communally known and can be referred to as authoritative. Thus, in 1 Thess. 4:1–2 he refers to instructions he had given to the Thessalonians, and in 4:9–12 he appeals to them to continue doing as he had instructed. We know that most of the topics of Paul's appeals in 1 Thess. 4:1—5:22 have become social facts because Paul refers to the Thessalonians' knowledge of them: the instructions concerning immorality and holiness (4:2–8), love of the brethren (4:9–12), times and seasons (5:1–10), and probably the miscellaneous collection of topics in 5:12–22. Only the problem of brethren dying before the return of Christ (4:13–17) may not be a topic previously addressed, since Paul does not, as in the other topics, indicate his approval of what the Thessalonians already know and are doing. Indeed, he specifically says that on this subject he does not want them to be uninformed (4:13). On the other hand, however, once Paul delivers "a word of the Lord" (*logos kyriou*, 4:15) on this matter, that "word" becomes a social fact. And in this light, it is of further interest to note that in his Letter to Philemon, Paul addresses another topic which had yet to become the subject of instruction. In this case, however, the topic is a subject of appeal, and Paul's words do not have the forms of instruction. Paul's appeal to Philemon to receive his brother as a brother is not expressed in terms of an instruction applicable to a whole community (cf. Phil. 4:23). In contrast with Col. 3:22—4:1 and Eph. 6:5–9, Paul does not generalize about master-slave relations. He has no "instruction" to give Philemon on this matter, only an ad hoc appeal/command, which is legitimated by his authority in the Lord.

Paul speaks "in the Lord," but in 1 Thess. 4:9 he also refers to the Thessalonians' having been "taught by God" (*theodidaktoi*),[134] and in 4:15 to his speaking "a word of the Lord" (*logos kyriou*). These expressions introduce another aspect of Paul's speech because speaking "a word of the Lord" is at least rhetorically different from being "taught by God." The latter is bound up with the more general notions that Christ is speaking in Paul (2 Cor. 12:3) and that God is making his appeal through him (5:20).[135] The former suggests more specifically that while all of Paul's instructions are "in the Lord," some of his instructions come from the Lord and some from himself. This is most clearly expressed in 1 Cor. 7:10 and 12. In 7:10, Paul responds to a question about divorce by saying, "To the married I give charge (*parangelō*), not I but the Lord . . .," and then he continues in 7:12, "To the rest I say, not the Lord. . . ." What is of interest sociologically is that Paul's own instructions, which he distinguishes from the Lord's, are apparently no less binding on the communities than the words of the Lord which he reiterates. But while this should not surprise us in view of Paul's role as the ambassadorial presence of the Lord, it does call for further examination because Paul seems to have had exceedingly few "words of the Lord."

Because Paul distinguishes between his words and the Lord's, it is striking that 1 Thess. 4:15 is the only place where he uses the expression, "a word of the Lord" (*logos kyriou*), and there it is accompanied both by a quotation of something the Lord *said* (4:15) and by Paul's description of a sequence of events that will commence when the Lord descends from heaven to begin the last days (4:16–17). In 4:15 the Lord is therefore both the object of the words Paul quotes and their subject.[136] However, this word by the Lord is in any event a "word about the Lord," and while that is quite different from what we might have expected from 1 Cor. 7:10 and 12 it is very much like the words of the Lord quoted by Paul in 1 Cor. 11:23–25. The entire section, 1 Cor. 11:17–34,[137] is not only in Paul's words but it is also governed by the fact that it contains *Paul's* instructions. He introduces his comments on the celebration of the Lord's supper as his instructions (*parangelō*, 11:17), and he concludes by saying that he will direct (*diatassō*, 11:34) the Corinthians on other and presumably related matters when he comes to Corinth. Between these two boundary markers, Paul first describes and chastises the Corinthians' practices (11:17–22) and then says that on this subject he had delivered (*paradidōmi*) to them what he had also received from the Lord (*parelabon apo tou kyriou*, 11:23a). What he received and passed on is quoted in 11:23b–25,[138] following which he concludes (*hōste*, 11:27) with his own judgments and instructions about the celebration of the Lord's supper (11:27–34). What Paul quotes as having been received from the Lord is like the "word of the Lord" quoted in 1 Thessalonians 4. However, while he describes what Jesus did and said on the night of his betrayal, *Jesus'* words now form only a part of Paul's quotation (vv. 24b and 25b), not the whole. What Jesus *did* is described as coming from the Lord, but only what Jesus *said* is in Jesus' words. First Corinthians 11 therefore joins

137

with 1 Thessalonians 4 to raise the question of exactly what Paul means when he says that he is speaking a "word of the Lord" or repeating something he had "received from the Lord."

At least the social aspect of the answer to this question comes from the language of receiving and delivering employed by Paul in the introductions to his quotation in 1 Cor. 11:23ff. and also later in 15:1ff. This language is focal because in 11:2 he uses it in a more general context to refer to the "traditions" (*paradoseis*) that he had delivered (*paradidōmi*) to the Corinthians. Here we find that what Paul himself received "from the Lord" and then delivered to others were *traditions*, things passed on within the church and therefore "in the Lord" in the social connotation of this expression,[139] such things as the words about the Lord's supper in 11:23–25, about the gospel Paul preached in 15:3–7, and about the resurrection of the dead upon the Lord's return in 1 Thess. 4:13–17. The authority of such traditions is clearly derived from their anchorage in the symbolic universe where they are associated with "the Lord" in the symbolic connotation of this expression,[140] either (or both) as coming from the past time of Jesus or from the present of his heavenly lordship. Conversely, there is no evidence in Paul's letters to suggest that the traditions derive their authority from institutional transmission, and therefore from the human "authorities" who transmit them.[141] Paul does not say who delivered the traditions to him but suggests that they are a part of the churches' sacred lore, and as such they are "from the Lord."[142] The traditions are therefore equally authoritative no matter who delivers them, as Paul implies in his letter to Rome, a community that did not receive them from him. In Rom. 6:17 he gives thanks that the Romans[143] have become obedient to the standard of teaching (*typon didachēs*) that had been delivered (*paradidōmi*) to them. For our purposes, however, it is equally important to reiterate that Paul envisions no practical difference between the communities' obligations to heed what comes "from the Lord" and to heed what comes from him. His comments to the Philippians in 4:9 are to the point: "What you have learned and received (*paralambanō*) and heard and seen in me, do." And corresponding to this lack of difference is the ability of Paul to add his own words to the Lord's or to the traditions, as in 1 Thess. 4:13–17; 1 Cor 11:23b–29, and 15:3b–8. All words spoken in the Lord are equally authoritative.

While it is striking that Paul only once refers specifically to an instruction as "a word of the Lord," it is equally surprising that it is only in 1 Corinthians that he elsewhere attributes "words" to the Lord, and then only a very few of them compared with the many "words" of his own. His instructions in this letter open up yet further insights into his language, into his social style, and into the sociology of the churches. Let us therefore return to 1 Corinthians 7, where Paul begins his responses to questions raised in a letter from Corinth (7:1a).

The first topic dealt with in 1 Corinthians 7 concerns sexual behavior (7:1–7). We do not learn just what the Corinthians asked Paul, but his response to one question in their letter describes what is "good" (*kalos*, 7:1b, "a man should not touch a woman"; 7:6a, 32–35b),[144] what is bad (7:2a, immorality; cf. 7:5), and what is proper since people lack self-control (7:2b–5, marriage). He concludes by expressing the wish that all could be celibate as he is, but acknowledges that God has not given everyone the same gifts (*charismata*, 7:7). However, before expressing his wish he describes his words as a concession (*syngnōmē*), not as a command (*epitagē*, 7:6). He is not commanding marriage but permitting it as a concession to those who lack self-control. Similarly, he is not commanding sexual abstention. Nevertheless, it is apparent that his *authorization* of sexual relations between those who are married implies a command: no sex outside of marriage.

Paul's reference to a "command" (*epitagē*) requires us to recall two other texts. The first is 1 Thess. 4:1–8, in which Paul refers to his words on immorality and marriage as "instructions" (*parangelia*). Because the content of these words conveys the same rules as his implied command in 1 Cor. 7:1–7, "commanding" (1 Corinthians 7) and "instructing" (1 Thessalonians 4) are functionally synonymous words. The second text is 1 Cor. 11:17–34. It will be recalled that Paul describes the whole section as "instruction" (*parangelo*, 11:17), using the verbal form of the noun for instruction employed in 1 Thessalonians 4, and that he ends the section by speaking about "giving directions" (*diatassō*) on other matters when he comes to Corinth. From this it appears that "giving directions" is also functionally synonymous with "commanding" and "instructing." Therefore, despite their lexical differences these terms are, like Paul's language for appealing, virtually synonymous. The words that both he and "the Lord" pronounce are equally binding regardless of whether they are called "commands," "instructions," or "directions."[145] This is evident in the rest of the texts to be considered.

Following his comments on immorality and marriage in 1 Cor. 7:1–7, Paul addresses widows and those who are unmarried, communicating the same message as in the preceding verses but without any explicit language of commanding, although his opening words, "I say," lend the authority of a command to what he says

(7:8–9).[146] This authority is indicated in the next section, 7:10–16, which Paul begins by saying, "To the married I give charge (*parangelō*)," but then reverses himself and says, "not I but the Lord" (7:10). There follows a command about divorce, including a parenthetical addition by Paul (7:10b–11). In 7:12, however, Paul resumes his own speech by saying, "To the rest I say (*legō egō*), not the Lord," following which he gives his instructions.[147] Thus, not only do we find both Paul (cf. 1 Thess. 4:2, 11) and the Lord giving "charge" or issuing instructions (*parangelia*), but we also see that when Paul "says" something imperatival it is an "instruction," "command," and "direction." And again, what Paul says is as binding on the community as what the Lord says. This is evident in 7:17–24, which he introduces by referring to the directions he gives (*diatassō*) to all of the churches (7:17b), and in 7:25–40, where he says that although he has no "command of the Lord" (*epitagē kyriou*), he gives his "opinion" (*gnōmē*) "as one who by the Lord's mercy is trustworthy" (7:25) and as one who thinks that he has "the spirit of God" (7:40). What Paul says about his opinions concerning marriage in 7:35 pretty well covers everything he says in his commanding speech: "I say this for your own benefit (*symphoron*), not to lay any restraint (*brochos*) upon you, but to promote good order (*euschēmon*) and your undivided devotion to the Lord" (cf. 2 Cor. 1:24). This is, of course, yet another instance of Paul's paternal attitude and rhetorical style, for he softens the restraints he has in fact placed upon the Corinthians by setting them in the context of the communal good that they serve. While he exercises his authority for the purpose of building up (*oikodomeō*) the community, not for tearing it down (2 Cor. 10:8; 13:10), he does in fact exercise it.

Another area of Paul's commanding speech concerns not moral problems but the collection of money from the Gentiles for the saints in Jerusalem. In 1 Cor. 16:1–4 he tells the Corinthians that he had "directed" (*diatassō*) the churches in Galatia to take a weekly collection, and that they are to do the same (*houtōs kai hymeis poiēsate*, 16:1). Here there is no equivocation like that in the rhetoric of 1 Corinthians 7, and Paul's role in the collection is unequivocally central. In addition to his "directions," he says that when he comes to Corinth, *he* will send the gift to Jerusalem with the church's emissaries, and that if it seems advisable (to whom?) he will go with them. From 2 Corinthians 8, however, and apparently after a visit by Paul (2 Cor. 1:1–3, 13:2),[148] we learn that a year has gone by since 1 Corinthians (2 Cor. 8:10) and the collection has yet to be completed. Titus is, therefore, being sent to complete the job (8:6), and Paul is writing to tell the Corinthians about it. Just how he tells

140

them is not without interest for understanding his style. He begins by telling them how the impoverished Macedonians gave beyond their means, giving even themselves to the Lord and to Paul and his fellow workers (8:1–5). Then, after referring to Titus, he tells the Corinthians to see to it that they excel (*hina perisseuēte*) in this matter as in others of which they are proud—their faith, speech, knowledge, zeal, and love (8:7). The imperative command is obvious, so much so that Paul immediately says, "I say this not as a command (*kat' epitagē*), but to prove by the zeal of others that your love is also genuine" (8:8). The Macedonians proved their love by giving generously; the Corinthians can prove their love by doing the same (cf. 8:24). By their giving, they will offer proof to other churches whose representatives will accompany Titus (8:16–23). But their giving will prove more than their love. It will, Paul says, prove to Titus and to the representatives of the churches that he was right to boast about the Corinthians' love (8:24). The Corinthians' gift will therefore be "honorable not only in the Lord's sight but also in the sight of men" (8:21).

Paul's strategy in 2 Corinthians 8 is almost a carbon copy of his strategy in his Letter to Philemon. A command is indicated, then rhetorically retracted and replaced by a public test in which the social status of those tested hinges on their behavioral reaffirmation of the churches' symbolic universe (cf. 2 Cor. 2:9 and 13:5–10). Indeed, obedience to Paul's command constitutes proof of their acceptance of this universe and validates their social position within it. Regardless of whether 2 Corinthians 9 is also to Corinth or to other churches in Achaia (9:1),[149] Paul reiterates this point when he says that passing the test of the collection will document obedience (*hypotagē*) to the gospel of Christ like a confession of faith (9:13). The saints who receive the gift will acknowledge this confession with thanksgiving to God (9:11–14) and, no less importantly, other churches will acknowledge that God's grace is in the givers as well as in themselves. The latter is implied in a significant example of Paul's rhetorical tactics in 9:3–5.

> I am sending the brethren so that our boasting about you may not prove vain in this case, so that you may be ready, as I said you would be; lest if some Macedonians come with me and find that you are not ready, we be humiliated—to say nothing of you—for being so confident. So I thought it necessary to urge the brethren to go on to you before me and arrange in advance for this gift you have promised, so that it may be ready not as an exaction (*pleonexia*) but as a willing gift.

Clearly, the brethren and the Macedonians will judge the Achaians' status in Christ by their response to Paul's test. On the other hand, however, more is at stake than the Achaians' status, for it is also clear from these comments that *Paul's* status with both the Achaians and the Macedonians is equally at issue in the Achaians' response! That Paul's suggestion that the collection could be construed as an "exaction" indicates his awareness of some resistance to giving *him* money for Jerusalem, and although his sending of others to collect the gift takes some of the onus off himself, an onus remains insofar as he also fears personal humiliation if Achaia does not produce a gift. Sociologically, this humiliation entails more than his merely seeming to have been boasting vainly about Achaia, for if the Achaians refuse to produce a gift they will also be rejecting Paul's "direction" (1 Cor. 16:1) and "command" (2 Cor. 8:7–8). For this reason, behind all of the rhetoric of 2 Corinthians 8 and 9 there lies the possible rejection of Paul's authority to command, an issue which is equally present in Paul's Letter to Philemon. Earlier we considered the effects of Philemon's failure to comply with Paul's "appeal" and concentrated on its consequences for Philemon's status in the church. And we also saw that the public nature of the letter put the church on the spot, too, for Paul's testing of Philemon was also a testing of the church that meets in his house. But 2 Corinthians 8 and 9 now show that when Paul puts others to a test, *his* authority is being tested to the same degree that the obedience of the others is being tested. If they obey, his authority is confirmed; if they do not obey, his authority is challenged if not terminated among the disobedient, and it is potentially weakened among the witnesses Paul has summoned from other churches. If those tested do not pass, *Paul* stands to lose not only a brother like Philemon or a church like the one in Philemon's house or in Corinth, but he also stands to lose his own power to win the obedience of others. His rhetoric in the Letter to Philemon and in 2 Corinthians 8 and 9 suggests that he was not unaware of what was at stake in those communications.

The letter to Rome contains not only the last of Paul's words about the collection for Jerusalem, but also the principal testimony to his readiness to risk all for the symbolic universe in which both his mission and the collection are grounded. Indeed, in Romans his symbolic universe is in the foreground and his role in the background. Paul is not seeking to secure a contribution from Rome but reflecting on the significance of his mission on the eve of his departure for Jerusalem with the collection from Macedonia and Achaia (15:25–27). Following his delivery of the collection, he plans to go on to Spain by way of Rome, which is apparently the immediate reason for writing this letter (1:8–15; 15:14–33). But on the eve of his departure Paul discloses information that is important for understanding the contribution this letter makes to our picture of Paul's position in his social world. The information that he has received funds from Achaia, which includes Corinth within its boundaries, indicates that his efforts in 2 Corinthians 8 and 9 were successful, and that both the Achaians' love and Paul's authority among them were confirmed. However, when at the end of Romans 15 Paul expresses anxiety about his reception by both the nonbelieving Jews of Judea and the saints of Jerusalem (15:30–33), we learn that his trip to Jerusalem entails yet another confrontation in which his own role will once more be in jeopardy. We do not know whether he personally delivered the earlier collection from Galatia (cf. 1 Cor. 16:1), but we do know that when he wrote 1 Corinthians he had not yet decided whether or not he would go to Jerusalem with the collection from Macedonia and Achaia (1 Cor. 16:3–8). Romans therefore informs us that Paul made a decision to go to Jerusalem despite the possibility of his being rejected by both nonbelievers and believers, and this possibility of a two-fold rejection presents us with two new aspects of his social world. We have observed his actions among the Gentiles; now we have to attend to his relations with both nonbelieving and believing Jews. His decision raises for us the question of what this social risk meant to him, and what made the risk worthwhile. And to answer the question we have to deal both with Paul's world of meanings, that is, his symbolic universe, and with certain aspects of his personal story (biography) that are pertinent to his trip to Jerusalem. Romans is central to our concerns, but portions of the letter to Galatia are also relevant. We begin with Rom. 15:14–33 and the relationship between Paul's mission and the collection.

In Rom. 15:16 Paul says that the job (*charis*) God gave him (15:15b) was "to be a minister (*leitourgos*) of Christ Jesus to the Gentiles in the priestly service (*hierourgounta*) of the gospel of God, so that (*hina*) the offering (*prosphora*) of the Gentiles may be acceptable (*euprosdektos*), sanctified by the Holy Spirit." In 15:17–24 he describes the completion of one stage of this service to the Gentiles, saying that Christ has wrought through him obedience (*hypakoē*) from the Gentiles, from Jerusalem to Illyricum, leaving him free to move on to new territories (15:18–24). He says, however, that before moving on he is going to take the collection to Jerusalem (15:25–29). Rhetorically, therefore, 15:17–24 expands on his description of his ministry in 15:16a, and 15:25–29 expands on his reference to the Gentiles' "offering" in 15:16b. And conceptually, the reciprocal nature of the relationship between the mission and the collection already suggested in 15:16 is confirmed in 15:27, when Paul says that "if the Gentiles have come to share in their [the Jerusalem saints'] spiritual blessings, they ought also to be of service (*leitourgeō;* cf. 2 Cor. 9:12, *leitourgia*) to them in material blessings" (cf. 2 Cor. 8:14; 9:11–14). Paul's "service" (*leitourgia,* 15:16) is therefore to bring the gospel to the Gentiles, and the Gentiles' "service" (*leitourgia*) is to give material gifts to Jerusalem.[150] In addition, because it is the purpose of his mission to enable the Gentiles to make an acceptable offering (15:16), his presentation of it in the form of the collection will publicly represent the success of his mission. This is confirmed in 15:30–33 when Paul concludes by requesting the Romans to pray with him that he may be delivered from the nonbelievers in Judea, and that his service (*diakonia,* 15:31) may be acceptable (*euprosdektos,* 15:31b; cf. v. 16b) to the saints in Jerusalem. Because the acceptable offering of the Gentiles in 15:16 here becomes the acceptable service of Paul, we can see yet again (cf. v. 16) that Paul's job includes both the mission and the collection. At least in Romans the two are inseparable.

Rom. 15:14–33 clearly shows that Paul fears his "service" may *not* be accepted by the saints in Jerusalem, which means that their rejection of his service would be a rejection of his understanding of the job God gave to him. But these verses do not indicate either why the saints might reject Paul's service or why he fears the nonbelieving Jews. Romans 9—11 helps to solve the latter problem but offers little assistance toward our solving of the former one.

Chapters 9—11 of Romans disclose a portion of Paul's symbolic universe that indirectly explains the relationship between Paul's mission, the collection, and his possible rejection by the nonbelieving Jews. Here Paul says that God has sent to the Gentiles the message of salvation that was formerly the property of the Jews (among whom are the saints in Jerusalem), and that God did so for the purpose of making the Jews angry and jealous at seeing the Gentiles enjoy their religious heritage and inheritance (see especially 10:17–19; 11:11–15).[151] According to Paul, this jealousy should lead some nonbelieving Jews to acknowledge what God has done in Christ and thereby be saved from God's impending judgmental wrath upon the world (cf. 11:11–36). This perhaps strange idea is undergirded by a temporal scheme that is fundamental for our understanding of Paul's mission as well as of his anxieties on the eve of his trip to Jerusalem. The scheme is partially represented in Romans by the expression "to the Jew first, and also the Greek" (1:16; cf. 2:10), in which "the Greek" represents the Gentiles.[152] This sequence is implicitly expanded in Romans 9—11 by two further stages, then the Jew and then the end (cf. 11:11–36). Together, these four stages constitute a temporal periodization that in Romans governs Paul's understanding of key moments which begin with Christ's death and resurrection and end with his return (see 1 Cor. 15:3–24 for another periodization). "To the Jew first" refers to the opportunity the Jews had to acknowledge the redemption God offered to them in Christ's death and resurrection (cf. Rom. 3:21–26; 5:1–11; 15:8–9; etc.), a redemption to be completed when Christ returns, which marks "the end" (cf. 8:18–23; 11:15). According to Paul, because many Jews declined this opportunity God determined to give them one more chance by provoking them into an acceptance of his actions in Christ.[153] "Also the Greek" refers to the message of salvation coming to the Gentiles as the means of provoking the Jews into a jealousy that would lead some of them to obedience (cf. 1:16; 11:11), and in Romans Paul represents himself as the agent principally responsible for bringing the message to the Gentiles. He is the one who is apostle to the Gentiles par excellence, even though he did not found the church in Rome. Yet, neither Paul's role nor the moment referred to by "also the Greek" is exhausted by his bringing the message of salvation to the Gentiles. As we have seen in Rom. 15:14–33, his mission's ultimate goal is to produce from the Gentiles an acceptable offering (15:16), one that will publicly testify to their glorification of God for his mercy to them (15:9; cf. 2 Cor. 9:12–13). "Also the Greek" therefore refers to the combined activities of Paul's mission to the Gentiles and the collection from them for Jerusalem. "Also the Greek" is the provocative moment which at its climax will produce anger and jealousy among the Jews, and Paul's decision to go to Jerusalem with the collection from the Gentiles of Macedonia and Achaia is made with the understanding that doing so will provoke this anger and jealousy among the Jews, and perhaps faith among some of them. His delivery of the collection will, therefore, inaugurate the third stage of his temporal scheme, "and then the Jews." Little wonder, then, that Paul is anxious about his reception by the Jews in Judea. Their rejection of his service will constitute a rejection of what he understands God to be doing through him in the mission and the collection. Their rejection of him will be a rejection of his symbolic universe as well as of his role in it.[154]

The relationships between Romans 9—11 and 15:14–33 explain why Paul fears the nonbelieving Jews of Judea, but it does not explain his concerns about the believing Jews, the saints of Jerusalem. The relationships show that the collection for the saints is a sign of the Gentiles' glorification of the God of both believing and nonbelieving Jews. From this, it is easy to see why the nonbelievers might reject the sign, but it is still difficult to see why the saints might reject it. To solve this problem, we have to step back from the texts for a moment before turning to another one, the letter to Galatia.

The basis of the temporal scheme seen in Romans is the worldly social distinction between Jews and Gentiles. The distinction is fundamental for Paul because for the Jews to become jealous of the Gentiles, the Gentiles cannot become Jews.[155] If they did, they could not become a provocation to the Jews and there would be no reason for the Jews to become angry or jealous. Because Paul sees the Gentiles as agents of provocation, he insists that the Gentiles not become Jews, as we can see in Galatians 3—6 and Philippians 3. All of this is rather self-evident, but it raises some important problems for us not least of all because Paul also insists that *in the church there is no distinction between Jew and Gentile* (cf. Romans, *passim;* 1 Cor. 7:18–19; 12:13; Gal. 3:28). How, for example, can he insist on the distinction in one situation and deny it in another? The answer to this is that for Paul the church is an extension of the people of God in which God has both added Gentiles and created new ground rules for their admission to this social body. "Israel" is no longer comprised of born Jews and Gentile converts to Judaism, and participation in this Israel no longer requires circumcision and adherence to the laws of Moses as the price of admission, only faith in what God has done in connection with Christ (e.g., Rom. 3:9—8:39; 9—11; Galatians 2—6; Philippians 3). Paul can therefore insist that in joining the church a Gentile cannot become a Jew in the old way, and in this sense one remains in worldly terms a Gentile. By the same token, however, the Gentile who joins the church without becoming a Jew in the old way acknowledges his obedience to the same God worshiped by nonbelieving Jews, and in so doing he is in a position to provoke nonbelieving Jews to anger and jealousy. This understanding of the relationship between Jews, Gentiles, and the church is basic to Paul but also a problem for others, both Jew and Gentile, and even for Jewish believers like the saints at Jerusalem.

In considering Romans 9—11 we saw why Jews might reject Paul's understanding of things (see also 1 Cor. 1:22–24), and from Galatians and Philippians 3 we can see that some *Gentile* believers did reject it, either knowingly or ignorantly, and sought to become Jews by being circumcised and following the Law of Moses. Why some Gentile believers did this is not explained by Paul, but the reason is clear upon a little reflection. Simply, because Paul represented the church as an extension of the Jewish religion (Israel), not as a different religion ("Christianity"), Gentiles must have assumed that they were becoming Jews of some sort. After all, in Paul himself they were confronted with a Jew who preached about a Jewish king, explained this king's death, resurrection, and return in terms of a Jewish symbolic universe[156] and Jewish scriptures, proclaimed that Gentile believers were sons of Abraham, and initiated a collection from them for residents of Jerusalem. In this light, the response of some Galatians, and perhaps Philippians, to Jewish preachers is not surprising, for they were only completing the process of becoming Jews that they had begun when they joined the church. But it is in this same light that we can also see why some of the saints in Jerusalem, who were largely if not solely Jewish believers, might have rejected Paul's appearance with the collection for Jerusalem and all that it signified, for some of them also drew the same conclusion as some of the Gentiles about the social reality in which they were participating. For some of them, being a believer in Jesus means being a Jew, and therefore they concluded that it was necessary for Gentile converts to become Jews by being circumcised according to the Law of Moses. In Galatians 1—2 Paul tells us about these people and in the process reveals the reason for his anxiety about his reception by the saints at Jerusalem.

In Galatians 1—2 Paul provides autobiographical information concerning his relations with the leaders of the saints at Jerusalem, James, Cephas (Peter), and John. His principal point in his narration is to establish his independence from the Jerusalem leadership, and to this end he recounts the origins of his mission in a revelatory call and cites two widely spaced visits to Jerusalem in which he received the approval of the leadership. Not himself a Jerusalemite, he first visited the leaders three years after his call to preach Christ to the Gentiles, and then he went again some eleven or fourteen years later.[157] On this second visit, he says that he told the leaders about the gospel he was preaching to the Gentiles and even brought with him Titus, an uncircumcised Gentile believer whom we have encountered as Paul's fellow worker and partner. Despite the presence in Jerusalem of some pro-circumcision believers, Titus was not required to be circumcised, and the Jerusalem leadership acknowledged Paul's mission to the Gentiles. The only qualification they placed upon Paul was that he "remember the poor," which is apparently a reference to what Paul later speaks of as the collection "for the poor among the saints at Jerusalem" (Rom. 15:26; cf. Gal. 2:10). Paul warmly accepted the qualification. Thus the link between the collection and the mission dates to this meeting in Jerusalem, and Paul's missions to Asia, Macedonia, and Achaia, during which he gathered the collection, all commenced after this meeting. However, apparently before he began this series of missions another critical event took place.

Immediately after describing his second visit to Jerusalem, Paul recounts an episode that took place in Antioch, his "home base" and a community comprised of both Jewish and uncircumcised Gentile believers (Gal. 2:11–21). Cephas is present on a visit, and the community is partaking of meals that are in contradiction of the Jewish law that circumcised Jews cannot eat with those who are uncircumcised. This practice lasted until "certain men came from James," following which Cephas and the rest of the Jews, except for Paul, ceased eating with the uncircumcised Gentiles, "fearing the circumcision party" (2:11–12). Paul responded to Cephas by accusing him of behavior that was hypocritical in view of the gospel that he and James had acknowledged back in Jerusalem, a gospel which holds that there is no distinction between Jew and Gentile in the church, and that Gentile believers do not have to become circumcised. Paul does not describe the outcome of this confrontation, and that fact is critical for our understanding of the anxiety he expresses about his reception by the saints at Jerusalem in Rom. 15:31. For if Cephas and James had responded favorably to his protest he would have had nothing to fear from the saints at Jerusalem. On the other hand, however, if they did not respond favorably Paul, on the eve of his departure for Jerusalem with the collection, was facing not only a hostile leadership that either represented or feared the circumcision party, but he also faced a showdown with the leadership that would conclude one way or another the earlier confrontation in Antioch. What is more, although this new confrontation will be over the same principles as at Antioch, the issues are magnified beyond what they were then because Paul has spent about a half-dozen years on a mission that had been affirmed at the second meeting in Jerusalem, and he is now coming to Jerusalem with the very collection its leaders had requested at that meeting. Consequently, because he has spent over half a decade doing what God had called him to do and what the Jerusalem leaders had earlier expected of him, his presentation of the collection in Jerusalem will be as much of a provocation of its leaders as of the Jews. In his magnification of his service (*diakonia*) to the Gentiles as a means of provoking his fellow Jews to jealousy (Rom. 11:13–14), he has also magnified the provocation that will be created by his delivery of the collection from the uncircumcised Gentiles to the saints at Jerusalem, whose reception of his service (*diakonia*) is of concern to him on the eve of his departure (15:31).

Delivering the collection from Macedonia and Achaia to Jerusalem is thus the ultimate example of the provocative dimension of Paul's social style, a dimension also evident, as we have seen, in the Letter to Philemon and in 2 Corinthians 8 and 9. In all of these cases he intentionally creates a situation in which others have to act in ways that can result in Paul losing as much as he can gain. The collection is the ultimate example because of the magnitude of what he could lose, and in this regard the loss resulting from a rejection by the nonbelieving Jews of Judea pales in comparison with the loss resulting from a rejection by the saints at Jerusalem. A rejection by the nonbelieving Jews would signify their rejection of his symbolic universe, but that would only mean that the time was not yet at hand for the Jews to move from jealousy to obedient faith, and Paul could then go on to Spain as he planned. A rejection by the saints, on the other hand, would also signify their rejection of Paul's symbolic universe, but *that* would mean vastly more to Paul. A rejection by the nonbelieving Jews can be understood *within* the scope of his symbolic universe, but a rejection of it by the saints cannot. Indeed, a rejection by them would split and therefore destroy his "world" because it would deny both the message and the function of his mission as he explains them in the letter to Rome. His entire vision of the relationship between Jews and Gentiles would be undercut by the withdrawal of the believing Jews from the vision. Consequently, Paul's anxieties as he prepares to go to Jerusalem with the collection are those of a man on the brink—on the brink of seeing his "world" confirmed or split, and therefore destroyed. In every sense, therefore, Paul faces the possibility of his world coming to an end in Jerusalem.[158]

Now, in reviewing Paul's role in connection with the collection we began with his activities among the Gentiles and ended with his relationship to the saints in Jerusalem. As we bring to a close our consideration of Paul's commanding speech and his apostolic style, we have to return briefly to his relations with the Gentiles of Corinth and Galatia.

In 1 Corinthians 9 Paul addresses the topic of the material support the churches owe not to Jerusalem but to those who proclaim the gospel.[159] Two issues are central, the first being that some Corinthians resent the fact that Paul does not work for a living (9:1–7), the second, that he does not seek the material support due him (9:12b, 15–18; see also 2 Cor. 11:7–16; 12:14–18). In response, he argues that apostles have the authority (*exousia*) to claim food and drink from the churches. This authority does not originate in him or in some human institution (9:8a), but in both the Law of Moses (9:8b–10, 13) and in the "direction" (*diatassō*) by the Lord "that those who proclaim the gospel should get their living by the gospel" (9:14). However, having established this apostolic authority, which is his by virtue of his apostolic vision of Jesus the Lord (9:1–2), he claims that he has *not* exercised it because he does not want to put any "obstacle in the way of the gospel of Christ" (9:12b). In his preaching he makes the gospel free of charge and does not exercise his "authority in the gospel" (*tē exousia mou en tō euangeliō*, 9:18).

Paul's argument is interesting because he claims authority from the Lord to command support but does not use it. What is of interest is not merely that his behavior in this matter is analogous to his appealing instead of commanding, but that at least with regard to himself he disagrees with "the Lord." Whereas "the Lord" directed that apostles be supported, Paul sees such support as a reward for work originating in himself and finds this to be a contradiction of his own sense that *his* work originates elsewhere than in himself (9:17). His reward in making the gospel free of charge (9:18) is in his sharing in the blessings of the gospel, the saving of others (9:23). His strategy here is therefore comparable to his disengaging of himself from the collection for Jerusalem by involving others in it (1 Cor. 16:1–4; 2 Cor. 8:9), so that people will not think he is seeking monetary gain for himself (2 Cor. 12:14–18; cf. 4:5). This strategy is doubly motivated because in addition to his constructivist self-understanding derived from his symbolic universe (e.g., 2 Cor. 10:8; 13:10) he is also concerned to avoid criticism of being self-seeking. The latter, however, is also comprehended within his symbolic universe because Paul does not wish to deflect the attention of others from the gospel onto himself. That would prove to be an obstacle in the way of the gospel (9:12b) which would hinder the carrying out of his task. Paul is therefore free to ignore an authority given to him by the Lord, because by publicly denying it he can better do the Lord's work, and this is the principle that links 1 Corinthians 9 to Paul's preference for appealing rather than for commanding. His style is not merely to do one thing rather than another, but to let his audience know that while he has the authority to do the other, he prefers not to. This style is designed to secure goals rather than power, and Paul's only interest in power is for the purpose of securing his goals, which are selflessly benign when viewed in the context of his symbolic universe. He only runs into problems when his actions are viewed apart from that context.[160]

Viewing Paul's actions apart from that context is an issue in the last of the texts to be considered, his Letter to the Galatians, where criticism of Paul is linked to another symbolic universe, another gospel (cf. Gal. 1:6–10 and *passim*). Our interest in this letter, however, is not focused on either the criticism or the other gospel but on Paul's unmasking of his authority in dealing with these matters. The letter shows that despite the fact that Paul's imperative commands are almost always softened by being prefaced with the masking language of appeal, when the occasion demands he can drop the mask and openly command his people. Such is the case in Gal. 5:1—6:10. Corresponding to the absence in this letter of a thanksgiving (*eucharistō*) section, which is explained by his having nothing to be thankful for in the Galatians' behavior (1:6–9), is the related absence of the usual "therefore I appeal to you, brethren . . ." at the beginning of its hortatory (*parakalō*) section in 5:1—6:10.[161] Lacking this, the entire tone of the section is transformed. In place of the formula that usually marks the transition from the first part to the second part of the body of his letters, Paul employs but redistributes all of the features of the formula except the verb for appealing (*parakalō*). Thus, in the ending of his non-thanksgiving section he refers to the Galatians as "brethren" (4:31)[162] and then, after a bridging clause in 5:1a (cf. "freedom" in 4:31 and 5:1a), he employs the transitional "therefore" (*oun*) to introduce the now unqualified imperatives, "stand fast" and "do not again submit to a yoke of slavery" (5:1b). And last, the grammatical first person which normally appears in the verb of appeal now appears in 5:2 in the form of an authoritative personal judgment: "Behold! I, Paul,[163] say to you that if you receive circumcision, Christ will be of no avail to you."[164] This is followed by a legal-sounding oath, "I testify (*martyromai*) again to every man who receives circumcision that he is bound to keep the whole law," and by a further judgment, "You are severed from Christ, you who would be justified by the law; you have fallen away from grace" (5:3–4). We need not go further. In most of the remainder of his "hortatory" comments to the Galatians Paul lays down the "law of Christ" (6:2). It is sufficient to note as a conclusion to this section of our exploration that in the Letter to the Galatians Paul's paternal mask is off and the apostle speaks. This is clear even at the one point when he slips back into kinship language, 4:19–20: "My little children, with whom I am again in travail until Christ be formed in you! I could wish to be present with you now and to change my tone, for I am perplexed about you." He was not present with them and he did not change his tone.

STRUCTURE, ANTI-STRUCTURE, AND PAUL'S SOCIAL STYLE

Our deep survey of social positions and relations has exposed the individual features of the social terrain of Paul's narrative world.

Our task now is to produce some maps that will represent the relationships between all of these features. But before we can produce such maps, we have to organize our material in such a way as to account for two sets of relations, one between the church and the world, and the other within the church. And we have to do this for two reasons. The first is that Paul uses metaphorical language that has a literal reference in the world (e.g., kinship, master-slave, and work language); the second is that his metaphorical language implies an egalitarianism that masks hierarchical structures. To assist us in rendering a sociological account both for the two sets of relations and for these two peculiarities of Paul's language, we can take advantage of some very relevant ideas suggested by an anthropologist, Victor Turner.[165] Rather than review Turner's whole theory, I will concentrate on those aspects of it that are directly relevant to our concerns, and I will illustrate their relevance from Paul's letters rather than from Turner's African field work and historical research.

The key terms in Turner's contribution to a theory of society are "structure" and "anti-structure." They refer to two different modes of social relations that are not only found, he says, in every society, but are also necessary for the continuing existence of any society. The structural mode of relating is governed by the system of hierarchically and segmentarily differentiated roles that can be played by a society's members. As Simmel argued, no society can function without some form of superordination and its corresponding subordination in the distribution of labor and of responsibility.[166] Turner, however, goes beyond this truism on the basis of his study of ritual practice. His observation of the ritual suspension, even inversion of hierarchical roles, led him to the conclusion that a society's members also frequently relate to one another not merely in a *non*-hierarchical fashion, but in an *anti*-hierarchical, *anti-structural* fashion. For Turner, anti-structural relations serve to humanize social relations and social existence by providing a communal intimacy, which he calls *communitas*, as an antidote to the often dehumanizing anonymity of structured relations. The force of the prefix "anti-" in this anti-structure is critical because it signifies that the forms of anti-structural behavior and the contents of anti-structural language and symbols are the opposite or the inverse of structured behavior and of the language and symbols associated with it. Turner further argues that the opposition between these forms consists of a dialectical relationship between them because each, as it were, constitutes the other. Anti-structure is dependent for its terms on the terms of social structure, and over time the social structure responds to its anti-structural opposite. Indeed, the dialectical relationship can be seen both in individual moments in a society's history and in its ongoing history. It is evident in individual moments like rituals of status elevation or status reversal, but it is also evident in the emergence and ongoing social history of a group like early Christianity, or like the Franciscan monastic movement studied by Turner.[167]

In order to show the relevance for our enterprise of the dialectically related notions of structure and anti-structure, we can divide our considerations into two parts. The first concerns the structures of the world and the anti-structures of the church; the second concerns structure and anti-structure within the Pauline churches. The first part will address Turner's theory that when new social groups emerge, they often do so in the form of anti-structural responses to the social structural world around them.[168] The second part will address the notion that once anti-structural groups emerge, it is necessary for them to develop their own internal structures in order to enable the groups to survive over time. Thus anti-structure has two faces, one directed outside the group, the other inward.

The Structures of the World and the Anti-Structures of the Church

In order to appreciate the anti-structural relationship between the church and the world it is first necessary to recognize that in Paul's symbolic universe the two are *conceived* as being spatially distinct from one another. In recognizing this, it is equally important to distinguish between conceptual and physical "space," because the churches' physical boundaries are different from their conceptual boundaries. While the physical boundaries of the house church are obviously rigid for architectural reasons, members physically move in and out of such churches more readily than they move in and out of their conceptions of themselves as church members. On the other hand, however, their physical movement back and forth between the church and the world appears to have produced problems of both a conceptual and a behavioral ("physical") nature. A classic illustration of this is represented in 1 Cor. 5:9—6:6,[169] which both establishes the conceptual distinction between the church and the world and lays the groundwork for identifying the anti-structural character of the church's relationship to the world.

In 1 Cor. 5:9–13 Paul addresses one question, in 6:1–6 another, but the two are related by the topic of judgment and by his anti-structural response to the second question. The first question concerns the Corinthians' misunderstanding about earlier instructions that they should not associate with immoral men or with the greedy, robbers, and idolaters. Some Corinthians understood this to mean the immoral, and so forth, of the world, but Paul was referring to "brothers" who are guilty of these vices. He argues that in order to disassociate oneself from the immoral of the world, one would have to leave the world (*ek tou kosmou exelthein*, 5:10)! The "world" is therefore something that is defined by these vices (cf. 1 Thess. 4:1–8; 1:9–10; 2:10–12), which Paul also refers to elsewhere when contrasting "walking according to the flesh" with "walking according to the spirit" (cf. Gal. 5:16–26). Here, however, Paul contrasts the "space" of the church with the "space" of the world outside it. He and other church members have the responsibility for judging those "inside" (*esō*) the brotherhood; God is the judge of those "outside" (*exō*) of it (5:12–13a). Paul concludes by citing from Deuteronomy the injunction to drive out the wicked from among them (5:13b). Spatially, therefore, the church exists within the "world" and it has boundaries that can be crossed both physically and conceptually by becoming a member or by being expelled by the membership. The "world," on the other hand, is here depicted as having *no* external boundaries, and for this reason one cannot leave it by going outside of it. If one is in the world, one can only move within it—into the church. But one's place in the church is also personally precarious because it is contingent upon one's behavior. One can be thrown back into the world where, from Paul's perspective, one no longer can have either hope or choice. Thus, the spatial distinction between the church and the world in Paul's symbolic universe reinforces the process of resocialization. But so, too, do his anti-structural statements, as we can see in the further development of his argument.

The distinction between the church and the world is the presupposition of Paul's next comments in 6:1–6, which are on the matter of brothers taking disputes between them to worldly courts. One part of his argument is that disputes between brothers should be decided by brothers and not by nonbelievers. But another part is more interesting because it posits an anti-structural relationship between the church and the world. Whereas from the worldly perspective its courts judge matters in the world, in which the church exists, Paul anti-structurally inverts the responsibility for judgment by arguing that *the saints*, among whom are the Corinthian believers, *will judge the world* (6:2). To be sure, this judgment is eschatologically future, but it is nonetheless an expression of an anti-structural conception and sentiment. So also is Paul's view of marriage in 1 Corinthians 7.

For social anthropologists, marriage is not only a major form of social institutionalization, but it also represents a fundamental sociological structure of relationships between the males and females of human societies.[170] Shortly we will see that Paul anti-structurally denies the validity of the distinction between males and females in the church. Now we need to see that his prohibition of sexual relations outside of marriage joins with his own commitment to remain unmarried (cf. 7:1–9) in rendering his affirmation of celibacy as another expression of an anti-structural conception and sentiment. In social structural terms, celibacy is an anti-structural opposite of marriage.[171] For Paul, marriage is a part of the "scheme" (*schema*) of the world (7:31), and married men and women are anxious about the worldly concern for pleasing one another. Believers, however, should rather be anxious about pleasing the Lord, and they cannot be this if their concerns are divided. Because this world is passing away, the Lord should take priority over the world, and this means that the sexual relations which are legitimated by the institution of marriage should be suspended as much as possible. Those who have wives should live as though they had none (7:29; cf. 7:25–35). Paul's instructions on marriage in 1 Corinthians 7 are, therefore, predicated on the opposition between a worldly social structure and a churchly anti-structure. His concessions and refinements of the opposition both deviate from it by allowing marriage and revert back to it for the definition of a "better" marital relationship: "he who marries his betrothed does well; and he who refrains from marriage will do better" (7:38).

In the midst of his instructions on marriage and sexuality Paul introduces two other instances of his anti-structural conceptuality (7:17–24).[172] In 7:17 he cites a principle that he employs in instructing (*diatassomai*) all the churches: "let every one lead the life which the Lord has assigned to him, and in which God has called him" (cf. 7:20, 26). This principle is then illustrated by two examples. The first concerns circumcision and uncircumcision, which for Jews like Paul differentiate Jews, who are circumcised according to the Law of Moses, from Gentiles, who are not usually circumcised (7:18–19). The issue, therefore, has to do with a social distinction in the world outside of the church. Paul's principle of not changing the marks of this distinction is not in itself anti-structural, but its basis is, for he argues that in the church "neither circumcision counts for anything nor uncircumcision, but keeping the commandments of God" (7:19). Thus the church's practice is anti-structurally opposed to a social structural distinction obtaining outside of the church. Again, we will see another example of this in a moment.

The second illustration of Paul's principle concerns slaves and freemen, which are terms representing yet another social structural distinction in the world (7:21–23).[173] In treating this distinction Paul is quintessentially anti-structural because each of these terms is literally inverted: he who was called in the Lord as a *slave/* is a *freedman* of the Lord; he who was *free* when called/ is a *slave* of Christ (7:22). A slave in the world is a freedman of the Lord, and a freedman in the world is a slave of Christ, like Paul who though "free from all men" has made himself "a slave to all" (9:1, 19).

Male and female, Jew and Gentile, slave and free comprise three sets of fundamental social structural distinctions that Paul sees in the world and that he also sees as anti-structurally opposed in the church. With one very interesting exception, the three sets come together in two different places in Paul's letters, 1 Cor. 12:12–13 and Gal. 3:28,[174] and in both places in connection with baptism which is the rite of initiation into the social body of the church, a rite that for Paul marks one's passage from the world into the church and ultimately into the kingdom of God. Since we have been considering Paul's comments to the Corinthians, let us look first at 1 Cor. 12:12–13. In 12:12 Paul describes the church, "Christ," as one body with many members, and then in 12:13 he says: "For in one spirit we were all baptized into one body—Jews or Greeks, slaves or free—and all were made to drink of one spirit." The second place the sets come together is in Gal. 3:26–28, which may be quoted in full because in it all three sets are cited: "in Christ Jesus you are all sons of God, through faith. For as many of you as were baptized into Christ have put on Christ. "There is neither Jew nor Greek, there is neither slave nor free, there is no male and female; for you are all one in Christ Jesus." A few verses later, Paul also speaks about the believers having received the spirit, as in 1 Corinthians 12, only here the spirit serves as the experiential confirmation that each believer is a son of God. The spirit is the source of the apparently ritual cry of believers at baptism, "Abba! Father!" (4:6; cf. Rom 8:14–17).[175] Thus, in both 1 Cor. 12:13 and Gal. 3:27–28 the spirit is the source of a unity among believers that is anti-structurally opposed to the worldly social-structural distinctions between Jew and Greek, slave and free, male and female.

That Paul does not address the worldly distinction between male and female in 1 Cor. 12:13 is interesting for two reasons. One is that his denial of the validity of this distinction for church members in 1 Corinthians 7 is consistent with Gal. 3:27–28, and therefore it would seem to deserve mention in 1 Cor. 12:13. Paul's failure to mention it there could be related to problems posed by women speaking too much in church, to which Paul responds in 1 Cor. 14:33b–36 by subordinating them to men. However, 14:33b–36 may well be a later interpolation, and thus not from Paul.[176] But while this possibility leaves us without a clear explanation of 1 Cor. 12:13, it does lead to a second reason for our interest in 12:13, and now also in Gal. 3:27–28. For if 1 Cor. 14:33b–36 were original to Paul, it would set up a hierarchical, social structural relationship between males and females in the church. What is of interest in this possibility is that for Paul the worldly distinctions between Jew and Greek, slave and freeman, and male and female are segmentary[177] rather than hierarchical distinctions. They belong to the horizontal rather than the vertical axis of social differentiation. Consequently, Paul does not address such hierarchical relations as those between masters and slaves (cf. 1 Cor. 7:22 and Philemon in contrast with Col 3:18—4:1 and Eph. 6:1–9). This peculiarity is probably to be explained by Rom. 13:1–7, where all hierarchical positions are represented as "authorities" (*exousiai*), which are in turn all instituted by God, even in the world outside the church (13:6–7). For this reason, Paul insists that believers subordinate themselves to such authorities (13:1, 5). Paul's anti-structural conceptions and sentiments therefore do not extend into the field of worldly hierarchical structures, and this fact explains much about why Paul did not say to Philemon that worldly masters are in the church slaves of the Lord!

There are other instances of Paul's anti-structural proclivities, as we can see, for example, in his opposition of foolishness to wisdom (e.g., 1 Cor. 1:17—3:4; 4:10a) and of weakness to strength (e.g., 1 Cor. 4:10b; 2 Cor. 11:20–30; 12:9). But a more all-pervading anti-structural opposition in his thought is the one expressed in Gal. 3:26—4:7, in which the unity of believers in Christ is represented by the sociological metaphor, "sons of God." This metaphor is the basis for Paul's more widely used sibling terms of "brother," "sister," and collectively, "brothers" or "brethren."[178] Such language is anti-structural because it renders all believers as siblings to one another in opposition to the diverse social structural roles they play in the many family units that are a fundamental part of the social structure of every social "world." In the church there is but one family, and all members are brothers or sisters, not fathers or mothers, sons or daughters, grandparents, in-laws, uncles or aunts, nephews or nieces—or cousins, that favorite of social anthropologists.

Having begun with the spatial distinction between the world and the church, and having explored a number of examples of Paul's anti-structural conceptuality and sentiments, we can now draw a few conclusions. First, baptism is the initiatory rite of passage between the two social spaces of the world and of the church.[179] Second, Paul envisions the road between these spaces largely as a one way street leading from the world into the church, but he also insists that for the wrongdoer in the church the traffic can become two way; the ultimate penalty prescribed by his discipline is to "drive out the wicked person from among you" (1 Cor. 5:13b; cf. 5:3–5).[180] And third, Paul's vision of social relations in the church is heavily influenced by anti-structural concepts and sentiments. Because he links these to baptism, they are a feature of his post- if not pre-baptismal teaching, and in this teaching, whether in person or by letter, the concepts function as symbolic forms by which he seeks to shape the social arrangements of the churches. The primary anti-structural symbol, which will concern us more fully in the next chapter, is that of sibling relations. It establishes an egalitarian social structural axis upon which individuals are differentiated as brothers and sisters but without any hierarchical axis based on age, sex, or generation. The social relations corresponding to this structure are sibling oriented, and they are symbolized by the notion of non-erotic love. Finally, we have also observed two other features of Paul's anti-structural conceptuality, his acceptance of the world's hierarchical structures as valid for church members in their "dealings with the world" (1 Cor. 7:3), and his introduction of hierarchical structures within the anti-structural church (1 Cor. 11:2–12; 12—14). The latter brings us back to the churchly social structures we have been examining throughout most of this chapter, but it also enables us to go forward by reexamining those structures in light of the anti-structural character of the church. The notion of anti-structure will prove to be of yet further assistance in our attempt to understand Paul's social style.

Structure and Anti-Structure in the Anti-Structural Church

Since we have already spent considerable time exploring social structures in the church, we can now presuppose both *that* they exist and *what* they are. This will free us to inquire more narrowly into the ways in which the anti-structural aspect of the church affects its own internal social structural aspect, which is but another way of describing the problem earlier posed in terms of the paradox of hierarchy in an egalitarian society.

The first and most important observation to be made is that anti-structure assumes different forms depending on whether it faces outward upon the social structural world or inward upon the social structural church. Facing outward, because it is opposed to certain worldly social structures, it denies their validity within the church. Facing inward, however, because it affirms the validity of the church's social structure it cannot and does not oppose them in the same way. Facing outward, anti-structure has an ideological purity deriving from a simple inversion of worldly distinctions, and its power derives from this radical contrast between opposites. But facing inward, anti-structure loses this ideological simplicity and must therefore find its power elsewhere than in the mere polarization of opposites. It is, on the one hand, confronted with structures than it does not reject, and it is, on the other hand, confronted with concrete issues that defy simplistic antithetical solutions. Paul's compromise over marriage in 1 Corinthians 7 and his Letter to Philemon are good examples of his ability to back off from outward facing anti-structural oppositions when dealing with problems internal to the church: he permits marriage despite its bases in worldly distinctions between male and female, which he ideologically rejects, and he declines addressing Philemon the master as a slave of Christ. But if anti-structure is not antithetically oppositional when facing inward upon the church, what *is* it and from what sources does it derive its power? Indeed, can we really speak of anti-structures to the church's own social structures?

To answer these questions we can refer first to two of Paul's devices for dealing with problems raised by structural stratification within the church, his metaphors of work and of the body (cf. 1 Corinthians 12; Rom. 12:3–8).[181] These are "symbolic forms" that affirm structural hierarchy yet serve to establish a quality of social relations that is based on a mutuality of affection and responsibility rather than on the power of superordinates over subordinates. In the metaphors of work, for example, focus on the superordinacy of individuals performing certain structural jobs is redirected, on the one hand, to God as the employer and project director, and on the other hand, to the community as the product and beneficiary of the laborers' work. In this way, the superordinate individual is construed as one part of a whole that includes those who are subordinate to him or her and in which *he* or *she* is also a subordinate. The priority of the whole over the parts is reinforced behaviorally by the responsibility of each part, both superordinate and subordinate, to act in such a way as to edify, build up (*oikodomeō*), or construct the whole, the communal edifice (*oikodomē*). Mutual and communal edification is for Paul a symbolic value that motivates the social relations of each structural member. The same conceptions and sentiments are represented in another form in the metaphor of the body. In describing the church as a human body, Paul again affirms social structural differences within the church and again renders them as parts, namely as members of a whole body which is of greater value than any of its individual members, each of which must perform its own functions and respect the functions of other members in order to make the whole functional—as a whole. Each part both suffers and enjoys the fate of the whole, and because even the least function is indispensable to the whole, it is as valuable as the highest function. The motto of the Three Musketeers is appropriate: all for one, and one for all.

Now we can ask if these two metaphorical systems are anti-structural, and if so, in what ways. Clearly, both systems affirm the differences between superordinate and subordinate parts, while also subordinating the different parts to the unity of the whole. In their affirmation of differences, they are social structural because a social structure is by definition a system of differences between parts. But in their subordination of the different parts to the whole the metaphorical systems are anti-structural because *the unity of the whole is the anti-structural opposite of difference.* The two systems are fundamentally anti-structural, moreover, because the social differences that are affirmed are viewed from the perspective of their anti-structural unity. Therefore, the first conclusion to be drawn is that antithetical opposition is also present in the inward facing direction of the church's anti-structures, and these also derive their power from the opposition between two terms, here the parts as opposed to the whole. The second conclusion to be drawn is that the dialectical relationship between the church's structures and anti-structures obtains within a single social unit, the church, and not between two discrete social units, the church and the world. Paradoxically, while Paul does not anti-structurally oppose the hierarchical structures of the world, he does so oppose the hierarchical structure of the church in which, in his mind, he plays a superior superordinate role. We will return to this paradox in a moment. A third and final conclusion to be drawn concerns Turner's view of the roles of structure and anti-structure in the history of a social group, for the two faces of the church's anti-structures represent the social history of Paul's churches. The outward facing anti-structures represent the emergence of the churches as a new social unit that is opposed to certain worldly social structures, and the inward facing anti-structures represent the churches' formation of their own social identity. The combination of structure and anti-structure within a single group is for Turner normative for any group that would maintain itself over time. But in this regard we must not overlook the fact that Paul's letters show the churches' social identity to be only in the process of formation, not yet an accomplished fact. Each letter reveals one form or another of competition with or resistance to the social identity Paul is seeking to create. Turner's categories are therefore eminently useful both for identifying stages in the process of the churches' early social history and for locating the positions of Paul and his churches in this process.[182]

A final question before us concerns the paradox that Paul, who believes that every hierarchical authority is instituted by God (Rom. 13:1–7; cf. 1 Corinthians 12), anti-structurally opposes the very hierarchical system in which he himself plays a superordinate role. The question here is not about the paradox, because we have seen that Paul never denies his social structural role but rather, for love's sake, chooses to act in a less severe way than his role allows. The question rather concerns the anti-structural character of Paul's choice and of the actions that follow from it. Are they anti-structural, and if so in what ways? The answers to these questions are the keys to Paul's social style and the basis for the maps we will draw of the social positions and social relations found in his narrative world. The metaphors of work and of the body represent anti-structural features of his thought, but also of his social style because he employs them in relating to others. However, these metaphorical systems do not exhaust the anti-structural features either of his thought or of his style. In the next chapter we will attend further to the relationship beween his thought, his symbolic universe, and the actions of the actors in his narrative world. Now we have to consider other anti-structural aspects of his style of social relations.

In our attempts to relate social structures to social relations and vice versa, we have seen that Paul's style consists of forms of social relations that are grounded in his social structural role as apostle to the Gentiles. We have also seen that such forms of self-representation as "ambassador," "father," "brother," and "foundation layer" and as one who "appeals" rather than commands, serve as masks of his social structural role. Our task now is to see that *Paul's masks are anti-structural forms of social relations*. To achieve this goal, we have to be careful to keep track of what is opposed to what in the several forms of Paul's anti-structural representations. In dealing with his outward facing anti-structures, we found that certain worldly structures are antithetically opposed within the church, which is socially and conceptually separated from the world. In his inward facing anti-structures, on the other hand, the church's social structural parts were found to be opposed to the social whole to which all of the parts were subordinated. When we turn to Paul's masks, however, what we find in opposition are different sets of structural relations. For example, relations between the apostle and the Gentiles are opposed by relations between a father and his children, and the latter is opposed by relations between brothers. While these sets of relations are clearly opposed or contrasted in Paul's letters, they are not as self-evidently anti-structural as the other forms we have examined. Perhaps Turner can help us to see that Paul's masks are also anti-structural.

From Turner we learned that anti-structural conceptions and relations resolve or mediate social structural differences by mitigating the harshness of living in a system of anonymous, bureaucratic, social structural differences. These differences are anonymous because they are structured roles, objective slots in a social matrix, that can be played or filled by different *persons*. Anti-structural relations are such because in one form or another they emphasize that all role-players are persons and that they must ideally relate to one another as such. This is what Turner means when he says that anti-structural relations humanize social structural relations. In principle, people are to relate to one another as people and not solely in terms of their structural roles, and forms of intimacy are therefore opposed to forms of anonymity. In this light, one person relating to another as a metaphorical father to a metaphorical child, or as a metaphorical brother to a metaphorical brother, is relating more intimately than he would if he related to the other as a literal apostle to a literal Gentile. For this reason, Paul's paternal and sibling masks are anti-structurally opposed to his structural role as apostle to the Gentiles, which he confirms when he says that he chooses to use these masks for love's sake, a value more intimate than any known to humankind. Paul, therefore, anti-structurally substitutes more intimate forms of social relations for a more anonymous one and, indeed, he does so progressively. For while the father-child relationship retains a connotation of social structural superiority, the sibling relationship does not, at least as Paul views it. The kinship relationship between brothers and sisters not only represents the egalitarian axis of the church's social structure, but it also represents the ultimate form of anti-structural relations in the repertoire of Paul's social style. Love is, at least ideally, first and most purely developed in the family. Among siblings, and between parent and child *agapē*-love is, Freud notwithstanding, unencumbered by *erōs*, erotic love.

These conclusions about the anti-structural character of Paul's social masks can best be sharpened and developed by mapping the several systems of relations we have been exploring.

MAPPING THE SOCIAL TERRAIN OF
PAUL'S NARRATIVE WORLD

In order to draw maps we have to think visually as well as conceptually. Turner has helped us with the conceptual organization of our data, but for visual aid we have to turn to another anthropologist, Claude Lévi-Strauss. While Turner often refers to Lévi-Strauss, he does not do so at a point that is critical for us, namely, at the point of relating his notion of anti-structure to his French colleague's notion of the mediation of oppositions.[183] The reason for Turner's omission is probably due to his concentration on social structures, whereas Lévi-Strauss developed his notion of mediation largely in connection with cognitive mythological structures. But because social structures are structured through knowledge and its linguistic vehicles, the gap between the two anthropologists on this matter need not exist. Turner argues that anti-structure humanizes social structural oppositions, and Lévi-Strauss argues that although people have to live in social and symbolic worlds that are constructed out of oppositions between differences, life can only be made tolerable by *mediating* radical oppositions. Turner and Lévi-Strauss are therefore clearly arguing similar points. But my concern is not to make them come to terms with one another. It is rather to show that Lévi-Strauss's method for dealing with the mediation of oppositions is directly relevant for our mapping of the social structures and anti-structures of Paul's narrative world, and especially of the relations between Paul's social structural role and his anti-structural masks. The maps illustrate certain sets of roles played both by Paul as an *agent* of resocialization and by Gentile believers who are the *patients* of resocialization.

What I have metaphorically called sociological "maps" are more properly identified by Lévi-Strauss as models, namely, of the social structures that underlie and are implied by social relations. To repeat the epigram at the beginning of this chapter: "The object of social structural studies is to understand social relations with the aid of models." Our "maps" will therefore represent the social structures underlying the social relations, the narrative actions, of the characters in the story of Philemon, and not a little of other actors in Paul's narrative world. We can begin with a simple map in order to introduce both the form of Lévi-Strauss's model of mediations and a selection of key mediations in the domain of the church. The several positions on the map are represented by role names beneath which are some of the verbs designating the kinds of behavior (relations) associated with them. Each vertical column represents the social structural opposition between roles. Visually, in the column on the left the opposed terms represent the most radical form of opposition and are therefore farthest apart. In the center column, however, because the opposition is less radical the terms are less far apart. The relationship between the terms of this column thus serves to mediate, that is, to reduce, the opposition between the terms in the column on the left. And last, the column on the right represents the final mediation of the oppositions in the first two columns because it posits no hierarchical opposition between terms at all. In order to see the similarities and differences between Lévi-Strauss and Turner, we should also note the different oppositions each refers to. For Lévi-Strauss, the oppositions are in this case between the *terms* of a relationship, but for Turner the oppositions are between the *sets* of relationships. Thus, for Turner the central column is anti-structurally opposed to the column on the left, and the column on the right is anti-structurally opposed to the center column.

Map 1

Structure		*Anti-Structure*
apostle (command)		
	father (appeal; love)	
		brother/sister; saint (appeal; love)
	children (comply; love)	
Gentiles (obey)		

From this simple map of social positions and their relations we can plot Paul's rhetorical movements back and forth between his three principal roles as apostle, father, and brother. Moreover, because his rhetorical movements can be translated into narrative actions, we can observe the changes in character that he makes at any given moment. But equally important is the effect of his adopted identity at any given moment upon those with whom he is relating, for every time *he* assumes a given role the other actors are also forced to assume a corresponding role in relation to him. Their identities therefore depend on the identity that he assumes, or at least that is the way that Paul would have it. For example, if he speaks as an apostle, the other person is to assume the role of "Gentile"; if he speaks as a father, the other person is to assume the role of his child; and if he speaks as a brother, the other person is to assume the role of a brother or a sister. As Berger and Luckmann put it, one becomes what one is addressed as. Therefore, by following Paul's rhetorical and narrative moves on a map like this one, we can better appreciate the relationships between his strategies and tactics and their intended effects. And in this regard, perhaps the most surprising and interesting result of using such a map in this way is not its disclosure of Paul's versatility of movement, but of the effects on the implied reader. Contrast, for example, the relative stability of the implied reader's position in any of Paul's other letters with the ever-changing position of Philemon, an implied reader of Paul's letter to him. Philemon begins as Paul's beloved fellow worker (v. 1), shifts to being a brother (v. 7), then a "Gentile" (v. 8), then the recipient of the message of an ambassador who is also a prisoner (v. 9), then a junior partner (v. 17), a debtor to Paul (v. 19), a brother (v. 20), and a "Gentile" (v. 21). If the effect of these constantly changing roles is to make Philemon wonder who he is, then perhaps Paul made his point, for as we have seen, it is Philemon's social identity that is at issue in Paul's letter to him.

Let us now make our first addition to our simple, base map. The positions and relations in question are those of debtee and debtor, which our narrative analysis in chapter 1 showed to be critical for Paul's story. The two roles are, moreover, peculiar to the Letter to Philemon. The question is, where do these roles belong on our map? Are they synonymous either with apostle and Gentile or with father and child, as suggested earlier, or are they totally independent of these and, if so, how are they related to these? Because Paul does not use the terms "debtee" and "debtor" but only implies them by employing the verb "to owe," we can focus on the verb as the designation of the debtor's side of the relationship of indebtedness. The other side, the debtee's, is implied by Paul's calling in of Philemon's debt (v. 19). Thus we can now ask, are *these* terms synonymous with either commanding/obeying or appealing/complying, or are they independent of these and, if so, how are they related to these two sets of terms? First, it is evident that calling in/owing a debt is not synonymous with either set. Calling in/owing a debt is here metaphorical, not literal like commanding/obeying, and the former is also a relationship of more limited duration than the latter. More importantly, calling in/owing a debt is more personally intimate and less anonymous than commanding/obeying. And even though both connote a relationship of power between a superior and an inferior, calling in a debt is semantically less comprehensive than having the more general power to command. On the other hand, in terms of anonymity and intimacy calling in/owing a debt is more anonymous and less intimate than appealing/complying. For these reasons, the relationship between debtee and debtor in Paul's story is a form of mediation that is intermediate between the first two columns in Map 1. And Paul, in using the metaphor of debt in v. 19, can be seen to have moved rhetorically from an intimate position of near equality as a "partner" (v. 17) to a more anonymous position that is but one step away from his social structural role as apostle.

Map 2

Structure			*Anti-Structure*
apostle			
	debtee		
		father	
			brother
		child	
	debtor		
Gentile			

The next positions to be added to our map largely supplement the positions already on it. They are of two kinds, one representing Paul's colleagues, his "fellow workers" and "partners,"[184] and the other his own role as an "ambassador" and "prisoner of Christ." The key to the location of Paul's colleagues on the map is their subordinate relationship to yet another of Paul's roles that must be added, that of "foundation layer," which is synonymous with his role as "father," since both are metaphorical masks for Paul's comprehensive role as apostle. Therefore "foundation layer" must appear in the same position as "father," and "fellow workers" and "partners" must appear beneath them in order to indicate their subordination to Paul. Also, to complete the positions deriving from Paul's metaphor of work, we may add to the position of "child" the communal metaphor of "building." And as for Paul's roles as "ambassador" and "prisoner of Christ," they are also synonymous with "father." Finally, the several positions literally identified in 1 Corinthians 12 (cf. Rom. 12:3–8) should follow the descending order given there: first apostles, second prophets, third teachers, and so forth.

In *Map 3* the roles of debtee and debtor have been omitted because they are not typical roles in Paul's narrative world.

Map 3

Structure	*Anti-Structure*	
apostle		
prophet	father; ambassador; prisoner of Christ,	
teacher	foundation-layer	
etc.	fellow workers; partners	
		brothers;
		saints
	child; building	
Gentiles		

In connection with *Map 1* I referred to the movements of actors from role to role in the Letter to Philemon. *Map 4* now plots the several roles played by Paul, Philemon, and Onesimus. In order to avoid cluttering up this map, only the names of the actors appear, but in order also to avoid getting lost we should remember that the *first* column represents the apostle/Gentile relationship, the *second* the relationships of indebtedness, here including Onesimus's indebtedness to Philemon along with Philemon's indebtedness to Paul. The *third* column represents the relationships of both father/child and of foundation layer, fellow worker and partner, and the *fourth* the relationship of brothers.

Map 4

Structure		*Anti-Structure*	
(1)	(2)	(3)	(4)
Paul			
	(Philemon) Paul		
		Paul	
		Philemon	
			Paul, Philemon, Onesimus
		Onesimus	
	(Onesimus) Philemon		
Philemon, Onesimus			

Perhaps more than most maps, this one calls for some interpretative commentary, especially because not all of the positions on it are permanent, but also because one set of positions does not belong there at all. The one that does not belong is the parenthetical relationship of indebtedness between Philemon and Onesimus, which I have included for comparative purposes. This relationship does not belong among the others because it exists in the domain of the world, not of the church, like all of the others we have mapped out

167

thus far. Nevertheless, we need to keep it in mind for two reasons. One is that it shows Philemon to be in the same position of inferiority to Paul as Onesimus is to Philemon. In our story, the master and his slave are equally inferior as debtors. The second reason is that while Onesimus's indebtedness to Philemon has effectively been removed from the map by Paul's payment of the slave's debt, Philemon's relationship of indebtedness to Paul is "outstanding" and now called in by Paul. If Philemon does as Paul "asks," he will erase both the debt and this position of inferiority to Paul from the map. But comparison also leads us to realize that while Paul employs the metaphorical relationship of indebtedness between himself and Philemon as an anti-structural expression of their structural relationship as apostle and Gentile, the relationship between debtor and debtee can only be terminated, not mediated. There is no other set of relations between Paul and Philemon that can mediate their relationship of indebtedness. In addition, unlike Paul's intervention into the relationship of indebtedness between Onesimus and Philemon by paying Onesimus's debt, only Philemon can pay his debt to Paul. The erasure of his debt and of this set of relations from our map is contingent upon his response to Paul's appeal.

But there is also another contingency and other possible erasures that hinge on Philemon's response, for, as we have seen, if he does not respond as Paul wishes his name can be erased from every position on the map! Especially important in the story are his positions as Paul's fellow worker and partner, on the one hand, and as brother, on the other. His position as a Gentile is already both mediated by his being a brother and transcended by his being a fellow worker and partner, which are the only positions of superiority he enjoys in the map of the church's social structure. He can *erase* his position as an inferior debtor by accepting Onesimus's position as his brother and in the process *confirm* his position as brother, fellow worker, and partner.

As for Paul, it is noteworthy that he slides up and down the slope that mediates his superiority. Depending upon where he positions himself, he stands in a more intimate or more anonymous relationship with others, yet only he is never subordinate to any of the others. From his position of superordinacy, even as a brother, which never fully masks *his* structural role, Paul seeks to preserve, or better, secure, the social structural integrity of the anti-structural church—with or without Philemon. Anti-structure must continue, but not at all costs, for Paul employs his structural authority to see that it does continue.

Our map of the social terrain of Paul's narrative world, at least in the story of Philemon, would not be complete without the worldly positions of master and slave being recorded on it. In the domain of the world, this set of relationships is, like that of literal debtors and debtees, unmediated by any other set of relations between the parties involved.[185] *Map 5* represents both the structural and anti-structural relations of the church and the corresponding structural relations of certain characters in the domain of the world.

Map 5

	Church		World
Structure	*Anti-Structure*		*Structure*
apostle			master/lord
debtee			debtee
	father, etc.		
	fellow worker		
		brother	
	child		
debtor			debtor
Gentile			slave

Thus far, we have been reading our maps from left to right. To appreciate *this* map, however, we have to read it from right to left, for in this way we can see how the church opposes its anti-structural system of mediations to some of the world's unmediated social structures. But reading the map in this way also reveals the way in which the church's anti-structures *invade* the world's social structures in the story of Philemon. In the world, Philemon and Onesimus are related in terms of two unmediated hierarchical structures, those of master and slave and of debtee and debtor. These relationships are, through Paul's letter, invaded by the church's ultimate mediation, the relationship between brothers, and brotherhood is anti-structurally opposed to the worldly social structures in such a way as to permit no other mediation, only a decision by Philemon as to which domain he is to occupy. Paul's letter to him, therefore, provokes the very crisis the letter is written to address.

Map 5 also represents the full range of churchly roles that Paul brings to bear on Philemon. Brotherhood is the church's anti-structural face towards the world, but it is backed up by all of the other relationships that appear to the left of "brother" on the map. Thus, Paul allows Philemon to maintain a position of superiority within the church as his fellow worker and partner, while also insuring Philemon's awareness of his, Paul's, superordinate position over him as the anti-structural "ambassador" and "foundation layer," and ultimately as the structural "apostle." Moreover, looking at the map as a whole in the light of our explorations of the letter to and story about Philemon, we can now see, too, that in addition to relating to Philemon as apostle to Gentile, debtee to debtor, foundation layer to fellow worker, and as brother to brother, Paul also relates to him as a structural superior in one domain to a structural superior in another domain—as apostle to master. As we have seen, Paul cannot secure his goals with Philemon by pitting superior against superior across domains unless and until he ensures Philemon's acknowledgment of his own participation in the domain of the church. The strategy of Paul's approach is therefore to ensure Philemon's acknowledgment of this by addressing him as a fellow worker, brother, and partner, and in the process disclosing to him the apostolic authority that lies behind his anti-structural address. Paul, therefore, implicitly acknowledges Philemon's position of structural superiority in the world but attacks it through his employment of anti-structural masks.

Our social structural studies have given us a number of insights into the social relations of the actors in Paul's narrative world, and our studies of their social relations have given us as many insights into the social structures of that world. At a number of points, however, we have found it necessary to refer not only to sociological constraints upon the actors' actions, but also to cognitive constraints, namely, to the symbolic universe within which the actors understand their actions and from which they derive their motivation to act in one way rather than in another. Our next task, therefore, is to explore the relations between Paul's symbolic universe and the actions of the actors in Paul's narrative world.

NOTES

1. Lévi-Strauss, *Structural Anthropology*, 1:289. On the various notions of social structure in anthropology, see further the chapter from which this epigram comes, "Social Structure," and its "Postscript," pp. 277–345; Hugo Nutini, "Some Considerations on the Nature of Social Structure and Model Building: A Critique of Claude Lévi-Strauss and Edmund Leach," in E. Nelson Hayes and Tanya Hayes, eds., *Claude Lévi-Strauss: The Anthropologist as Hero* (Cambridge, Mass.: M.I.T. Press, 1970), 70–107; and Neville Dyson-Hudson, "Structure and Infrastructure in Primitive Society: Lévi-Strauss and Radcliffe-Brown," in Richard Macksey and Eugenio Donato, eds., *The Structuralist Controversy* (Baltimore: Johns Hopkins Univ. Press, 1970), 218–46. French and British structural anthropologists differ in their notion of structure largely in terms of its degree of abstractness from the

concrete. Lévi-Strauss is more abstract, the British more concrete. My own use of the term, as illustrated in this chapter, falls somewhere between the two poles, since my "structures" are inferred from the social relations represented in Paul's letters and their stories. Lévi-Strauss's model of mediations is dealt with in the concluding section of this chapter, and Victor Turner's theory of structure and antistructure is discussed and applied in the section preceding the last one. In the concluding section I will also bring their contributions together in connection with some maps (i.e., models) of the social positions and relations found in Paul's narrative world.

2. In focusing on the actors' knowledge I am indebted to the contributions to the sociology of knowledge made by Berger and Luckmann, *The Social Construction of Reality*, by their mentor, Alfred Schutz, and less directly by Clifford Geertz. Berger and Luckmann provide the theoretical framework within which I read the work of both field and armchair anthropologists.

3. Following Berger and Luckmann, a "role" will be understood as "a collection of reciprocally typified actions" performed by a type of actor (*The Social Construction of Reality*, 56, 74–79). As indicated above, evidence for types of actors and typified actions comes both from the role-names Paul gives to actors and from other language, usually verbs, representing actions typical of them. While roles are the prerequisite for institutionalization, I will not presuppose the extent of the institutionalization of roles in Paul's narrative world but rather seek to show when possible where the roles are located in the process of institutionalization. For a survey of the history of biblical scholarship on the institutionalization of the early church, together with several classic essays on the subject, see Karl Kertelge, ed. *Das Kirchliche Amt im Neuen Testament* (Darmstadt: Wissenschaftliche Buchgesellschaft, 1977). See also Jean Delorme, ed., *Le ministère et les ministères selon le Nouveau Testament. Dossier exégétique et réflexion théologique* (Paris: Éditions du Seuil, 1974); and for more recent sociologically informed studies John H. Schütz, *Paul and the Anatomy of Apostolic Authority*, SNTSMS 26 (Cambridge: Cambridge Univ. Press, 1975); Holmberg, *Paul and Power;* and Meeks, *The First Urban Christians*, 131–39. Hainz's *Ekklesia* is a veritable commentary on sociological issues in each of Paul's letters, although it is not informed by contributions from sociology or social anthropology. It is, nevertheless, a study to which I am indebted, especially for its representations of previous research. Unavailable to me at the time of writing were *Neotestamentica* 10 (1976) on *Ministry in the Pauline Letters;* Robert Banks, *Paul's Idea of Community: The Early House Churches in Their Historical Setting* (Grand Rapids: Wm. B. Eerdmans, 1980); Walter Kleiber, *Rechtfertigung und Gemeinde: Eine Untersuchung zum paulinischer kirchenverständnis*, FRLANT 127 (Göttingen: Vandenhoeck & Ruprecht, 1982).

4. In view of John Gager's reminder about the important historical distinction between class and status in Roman society, it should be noted that I refer to status in a phenomenological rather than historical sense. That is

to say, I seek to determine the relative hierarchical status of actors by identifying relations of superiority, equality, and inferiority as these are represented in their social relations or actions. In so doing, I hope to establish the hierarchical status of the roles the actors play within the domain of the church, and for the purpose of understanding their actions. This approach will lead us to potentially historical conclusions, which is a reversal of the usual procedure of moving from what is historically known to the actions represented in individual texts. Historically, we can note that as a slave Onesimus belongs to the lowest social class in Roman society, and Paul and Philemon belong to a middle class located above that of slaves and freedmen. Status, which is bound up with personal achievement in social, cultural, or economic areas, is another matter. Philemon seems to have achieved a reasonable status because he owns at least one slave and has a home large enough to have guest rooms. Of Paul's status we know little, except that he is a self-employed free man and a Jew with Roman "citizenship." See further Gager's "Shall We Marry Our Enemies? Sociology and the NT," and his review article in *RSR* 5/3 (1979): 174–80. On Paul's "trade," see Ronald Hock, *The Social Context of Paul's Ministry: Tentmaking and Apostleship* (Philadelphia: Fortress Press, 1980); and E. A. Judge, "The Early Christians as a Scholastic Community. Part 2," *JRH* 1 (1960): 125–37. For Hock, Paul was a tentmaker, for Judge a "sophist."

5. The plural "our" refers to Paul and to Timothy who, while only called a brother in v. 1, is referred to as Paul's "fellow worker" in Rom. 16:21. In v. 2, Paul refers in a related way to Archippus as "our fellow soldier," which in light of Phil. 2:25 appears to be a synonym for "fellow worker." On the other hand, contrary to the RSV translation Paul does not refer to Timothy as "our brother" (v. 1), to Apphia as "our sister" (v. 2), or to Philemon as "my brother" (v. 7; cf. v. 20). Timothy is called "the brother" (*ho adelphos*), Apphia "the sister" (*tē adelphē*), and Philemon is addressed in the vocative as "brother" in both v. 7 and v. 20. This is similar to Phil. 2:25, where Paul identifies Epaphroditus as "*the* brother and *my* fellow worker and fellow soldier." It appears that in using the definite article and the vocative rather than the possessive pronoun, Paul is focusing on the social positions of brother and sister, not on personal relationships with him, even though that relationship is implied in v. 16. Just what may or may not be implied by the use of the definite article with "brother(s)" and "sister(s)" is unclear, but its frequent occurrence in Paul's usage suggests that it is synonymous with being a believer. In this sense, it is therefore an egalitarian identification applicable to all members of the church, whereas the use of the possessive pronoun has, as we will see below, a hierarchical connotation because it links those of whom it is used to *Paul's* position. I am not persuaded by E. Earle Ellis's view, in an otherwise fine paper, that "the brother(s)" sometimes designates a particular role like that of "fellow worker(s)." See Ellis, "Paul and His Co-Workers," *NTS* 17 (1971): 437–52, for discussion and further literature. A brother may *also* be a fellow worker, but "brother" never clearly denotes a fellow worker, only the position of a sibling among

siblings (so also Wolf-Henning Ollrog, *Paulus und seine Mitarbeiter: Untersu-chungen zu Theorie und Praxis der paulinischen Mission*, WMANT 50 [Neukirchen-Vluyn: Neukirchener Verlag, 1979], 78, n. 92).

6. "Of Christ Jesus" may also qualify "ambassador/old man" (*presbytēs*), on which see below under *Ambassador and Prisoner of Christ Jesus*.

7. On the moral reference of holiness/sanctification (*hagiasmos*), see e.g., 1 Thess. 3:11—4:8. In chap. 3 "holiness" will be considered in relation to the form of the children of God. But it should be noted here that because believers, who are "sons of God"–to–be, are also called "saints," the two designations refer to the same people, as they do in Wisd. of Sol. 5:5, where such "people" are immortal and, therefore, divine beings.

8. These positions are all implied in the semantics of the terms involved. Relational complications will be dealt with below when we consider the terms in their literary contexts.

9. Reasons for translating *presbytēs* by "ambassador" rather than "old man" are given below in the section on *Ambassador and Prisoner of Christ Jesus*.

10. In the articles by Gager cited in n. 4 above, he makes a similar distinction between the social description and the sociological interpreta-tion or explanation of social facts, and he also rightly sees these as different aspects of a single task. But because my own approach is oriented to estab-lishing the social facts through a dialectic of description and interpretation, his distinctions may be difficult to apply to this study. For purposes of clarity, therefore, let me say that when I use the word "social" I am refer-ring to concrete social contexts and relations represented in Paul's letters, and when I use the word "sociological" I am referring to the abstract structures implied by and underlying social relations. "Social structure" is therefore a sociological category.

11. For further discussions of the relations between laws and social structures, see, e.g., Vilhelm Aubert, ed., *Sociology of Law* (New York: Pen-guin Books, 1969), 14–67; and for the historical system of Roman slave law and its enforcement, see Thomas Wiedemann, *Greek and Roman Slavery* (Baltimore: Johns Hopkins Univ. Press, 1981); Bartchy, *Mallōn Chrēsai;* and Lohse, *Colossians and Philemon*, whose comments on the Letter to Phile-mon provide references to legal information pertinent to that letter. See also the papyrus notices concerning runaway slaves printed in Moule, *Co-lossians and Philemon*, 34–37.

12. As commentators observe, Paul's reference to Onesimus's debt to Philemon may be to something stolen or simply to damages suffered by Philemon by virtue of his slave's flight. While this may indicate that Onesi-mus's debt is metaphorical rather than literal, as I am treating it, we have to remember that Paul in effect paid Onesimus's debt to Philemon. Conse-quently, regardless of whether the debt is literal or metaphorical Paul im-poses the structure of indebtedness on the relationship, and in so doing suggests that Philemon has suffered literal damages which he, Paul, is literally paying for. Onesimus's debt is, therefore, only metaphorical if we

think of it solely in terms of the borrowing of money or its equivalent. I am not thinking in those terms.

13. On the emplotment of Onesimus's indebtedness in relation to Philemon's, see chap. 1, above. In both the plot of the story and the poetics and rhetoric of the letter, the closure of Onesimus's debt serves, in Paul's mind, as a motive for Philemon to close his debt. See further, below.

14. In addition to the commentaries, see for recent discussions of "in Christ" and "in the Lord," Hans Conzelmann, *An Outline of the Theology of the New Testament*, trans. John Bowden (London: SCM Press, 1969), 208–12; Werner G. Kümmel, *The Theology of the New Testament*, trans. John E. Steely (Nashville: Abingdon Press, 1973), 217–20; and E. P. Sanders, *Paul and Palestinian Judaism: A Comparison of Patterns of Religion* (Philadelphia: Fortress Press; London: SCM Press, 1977), 453–61. Kümmel sees Philemon 16 as distinguishing between Christians and non-Christians (p. 218), while Conzelmann and others rightly note that "in Christ/the Lord" in such contexts means "in the church," since believers had yet to employ the word "Christian" as a means of identifying themselves. But Conzelmann and others also see "in the flesh" as meaning "as a man" in contrast with being a Christian (ibid., 174). Usually, the social implications of the expression "in the flesh" are missed. I believe, however, that the social connotations of both sets of terms in Philemon 16 must be acknowledged. Support for this conclusion comes from the relations between several texts. In 1 Cor. 5:9–13 immorality is clearly a defining feature of the *social* world outside the church, namely, and in terms of 1 Thess. 4:3–6, the world of the "Gentiles who do not know God." But 1 Cor. 5:10–11 lists other vices, too, and these are among the vices that are identified in Gal. 5:16–26 as *works of the flesh* in contrast with works of the spirit performed by those who are "in Christ" (5:6, 25). In this light, "in the flesh," when contrasted with "in the Lord," connotes the social as well as the moral "space" of the world. "Walking according to the flesh" is a description of behavior in the Lord, i.e., in the church (cf. Rom. 8:1–17). Believers are of course still "in the flesh" anthropologically speaking, but they do not "walk according to the flesh" (cf. 2 Cor. 10:3; Gal. 2:20; Phil. 3:3; 1 Cor. 1:26); and they are still in the world, too, but their life in the church is "in the Lord" (1 Cor. 5:9–13). The social connotation of "in the Lord" is perhaps best indicated in a series of texts beginning with Gal. 3:26–28, where Paul says that as many as were baptized into Christ are one in Christ; there is neither male nor female. Similarly, in 1 Cor. 12:12–13 the church is depicted as one body into which believers have been baptized, and this body is "Christ." However, within the *social* body there is also a hierarchy of positions (12:27–31), and in 1 Thess. 5:12 Paul refers to the occupants of certain of these positions as being over the community, i.e., they are "over you in the Lord." In this chapter we are concerned with the social aspects of being "in the Lord"; in the next chapter we will consider the symbolic aspects.

15. The passive of the verb "parted" may, as Lohse suggests, refer to "God's hidden purpose," but there is also here an element of *Paul's* purpose

since he avoids saying outright that Onesimus left Philemon of his own choice. Similarly, when Paul suggests that God's purpose in the brief separation was that Philemon might have Onesimus back forever, if Paul has *his* way, Philemon will not have him back as a slave, but as a brother. Despite Paul's rhetoric and his recourse to his symbolic universe (i.e., "God's hidden purpose"), the social relations at issue are clear: Onesimus has run away; Paul intervenes in his behalf to secure a specific response from Philemon; Philemon must respond. Paul displays his symbolic universe in order to explain these relations, and he employs it in his rhetoric in order to achieve his goal.

16. The word "as" in v. 16a appears to govern grammatically both "a slave" and "a beloved brother." The word is not used in v. 17, where Paul says, "if you consider me a partner." The RSV adds, "as" in vv. 16b and 17.

17. See, e.g., Lohse, *Colossians and Philemon*, 203 and n. 59, where he quotes von Soden: " 'as' (*hōs*) expresses the subjective evaluation of the relationship without calling its objective form into question . . . therefore the line of thought found in 1 Cor. 7:20–24 is not exceeded."

18. It is important to note that because 1 Cor. 7:21–24 does *not* address the role of masters, it does not address the relationship between masters and slaves. Neither does it address the relations between slaves and free men in the church. The focus of 1 Corinthians 7 is on the relationship between an individual's social identity in the world and her or his identity in the church. In any event, Paul does not tell Philemon that he who is master in the world is a slave of the Lord. (See further below on "The Structure of the World and the Anti-Structures of the Church.")

19. "Brother" and "partner" connote social structural equality. In v. 17, Paul is not asking Philemon to receive Onesimus as a partner, but as an equal, which is also expressed in v. 16 when Paul says that Philemon will have Onesimus back as a brother.

20. Col. 3:18—4:1, Eph. 6:5–9, and 1 Tim. 6:1–2 are examples of how Philemon and Onesimus might work out their new relationship, but Paul conspicuously does not employ these solutions in his Letter to Philemon.

21. Contrast Lohse, *Colossians and Philemon*, 206 and n. 7, who quotes Dibelius-Greeven: "The legal side of the matter is not in view at all" (see also p. 187). Needless to say, commentators have not previously entertained the sociological implications that we have been exploring. For surveys of other views, see Stuhlmacher, *Der Brief an Philemon*, 52–54; and Hainz, *Ekklesia*, 206–8.

22. Cf. Stuhlmacher, *Der Brief an Philemon*, 40–41. Legally, a slave was the property of a master and as such he could be dealt with as the master wished. He could be bought, rented, or sold, and doubtless lent out. See Bartchy, *Mallōn Chrēsai*, 38–39.

23. Although Colossians is probably not written by Paul, it is of interest to note that the cognate verb of *to anēkon*, *anēkō*, is used in 3:18 to describe what is "fitting in the Lord" in terms of the obedient subordination of individuals to their superordinates—wives to husbands, children to par-

175

ents, and slaves to masters (3:18–22; on the household context of such instructions, see Lohse, *Colossians and Philemon*, 154–63). In the undisputed letters of Paul we do not find such household rules, but in the Letter to Philemon and his house church we can see that in this house church certain behavior is "fitting" and that it is to be achieved by "obedience" (v. 21). Here, however, obedience is due a nonresident, Paul, who is, as we will see, Philemon's superior.

24. See the next section, below, on Paul's use of his authority to correct such deficiencies.

25. After his initial greetings to the collective addressees in v. 3, Paul speaks in the first person solely to Philemon until v. 22b, when he expresses his hope that the collective prayers of the community will speed him on his way to them. In vv. 23–24, however, he sends greetings from his fellow workers to Philemon alone, and then offers his benediction upon the whole community (v. 25).

26. On the public rather than private character of the letter, see Wickert, "Der Philemonbrief—Privatbrief oder apostolisches Schreiben?"; and Hainz, *Ekklesia*, 199–209. The public character of the letter no longer requires justification, but my statement that we must assume public knowledge of its content does. The statement is not describing a historical fact, namely that the letter *was* received and publicly read, but a literary fact that is central to both Paul's letter and his story. He wrote the letter with a view to its reception, as the epistolary aorist shows, and its story comprehends a series of events whose historical occurrence is unknown to us. In assuming public knowledge of the letter's content we are, therefore, assuming what Paul assumed, and we are doing so in order to understand his intent, strategies, and tactics. Historically, on the other hand, our analysis should show us what should or might have happened upon the letter's arrival and the church's reading of it.

27. See especially Hans-Josef Klauck, "Die Hausgemeinde als Lebensform im Urchristentum," *MTZ* 32 (1981): 1–15, which includes bibliography.

28. In addition to Klauck, n. 27, above, see Floyd Filson, "The Significance of the Early House Churches," *JBL* 58 (1939): 105–12; Abraham J. Malherbe, *Social Aspects of Early Christianity*, 2d ed., enlarged (Philadelphia: Fortress Press, 1983), chap. 3, "House Churches and Their Problems"; idem, "The Inhospitality of Diotrophes," in *God's Christ and His People, Studies in Honor of N. A. Dahl*, ed. Jacob Jervell and Wayne Meeks (Oslo: Universitetsforlaget, 1977), 222–32 (chap. 4 in *Social Aspects*); Theissen, *Social Setting*, 83–87; Meeks, *The First Urban Christians*, 75–77, and his index, s.v., "household"; and Judge, "The Early Christians as a Scholastic Community. Part 2."

29. See n. 5, above.

30. See n. 25, above.

31. See Alfred Schutz's important essay, "Equality and the Meaning Structure of the Social World," *Collected Papers*, 2:226–73. See further

Theissen, *Social Setting*, 145–74, on social integration and the Lord's Supper in Corinth; and on the notion of *societas* in Roman law and in Paul, J. Paul Sampley, "Societas Christi: Roman Law and Paul's Conception of the Christian Community," in *God's Christ and His People*, 158–74, neither of which have the advantage of familiarity with Schutz's essay.

32. See further chap. 3, below, on the role of these ideas and their relationship to equality in Paul's symbolic universe.

33. This reality is the symbolic universe that Paul represents to his churches and seeks to make theirs. His appeals to and arguments with the churches are as much illustrations of the ways he communicates this universe to them as are his preaching and teaching.

34. Whatever churchly relations may have obtained between Paul and Epaphras, they also related as prisoners because they were prisoners; as such they shared the sphere of relevance designated by "imprisonment," as Paul did with his guards according to Phil. 1:12–14.

35. That is, we have to wonder both what he thought Philemon's response would be to his imprisonment and how he used this. I suspect that Paul's self-representation as an "ambassador and prisoner of Christ" reflects his thought to the extent that while using the language of worldly positions ("ambassador," "prisoner"), he also absorbs them into his churchly position ("of Christ Jesus") and thereby overcomes the reversal of status suggested by his imprisonment. As I will suggest later, this ameliorated reversal is also probably related to the reversal Paul expects from Philemon, namely, from being Onesimus's master in the world to being his brother in the church. Because the worldly distinctions are not to be made in the church, the loss entailed by their reversal is erased. By erasing any loss that might be imputed to his experience, Paul sets himself as a model for Philemon.

36. Cf. Hainz, *Ekklesia*, 200–202, for further discussion and literature.

37. See ibid., 199–209.

38. This will be dealt with more fully at the end of this chapter. For now, it will suffice to say that when, for example, Paul represents himself as a father and speaks as such, he speaks as to children. Thus, those to whom he is speaking are put in the position of construing themselves as his children, at least for the rhetorical moment.

39. See the literature cited in n. 3 above.

40. As the literature cited in n. 3 suggests, there is a virtual consensus on this point. The question today, rather, concerns where the several social roles referred to by Paul are to be located in the process of institutionalization. The answer to this question will differ from role to role.

41. Although uninformed by sociological literature, the best discussion to date on this interactional process is Annie Jaubert's "Les épitres de Paul: Le fait communautaire," *Le ministère et les ministeres selon le Nouveau Testament*, 16–33. See also the more extensive and sociologically informed study by Schütz, *Paul and the Anatomy of Apostolic Authority*. Schütz is oriented largely to the work of Max Weber and does not deal with the

sociology of knowledge. Holmberg's *Paul and Power* has a broader sociological base, but he, too, does not find much assistance in the sociology of knowledge. Alfred Schreiber's *Die Gemeinde in Korinth: Versuch einer gruppendyamischen Betrachtung der Entwicklung der Gemeinde von Korinth auf der Basis desersten Korintherbriefes*, NTAbh 12 (Münster: Aschendorff, 1977) approaches the development of the Corinthian church from the perspective of group dynamics. This volume was unavailable to me at the time of writing.

42. See n. 5, above.

43. See Walter Bauer, *A Greek-English Lexicon of the New Testament and Other Early Christian Literature*, 2d ed., trans. and adapted by W. F. Arndt, F. W. Gingrich, and F. W. Danker (Chicago: Univ. of Chicago Press, 1979) 439–40.

44. Titus is, of course, one of Paul's traveling colleagues, not a residential functionary like Philemon. See further, below, on the similarities and differences between itinerant and residential fellow workers.

45. In Phil. 2:22 Epaphroditus is called "the brother and my fellow worker and fellow soldier." The shift from the definite article to the possessive pronoun distinguishes between the last two roles and "the brother." See n. 5, above.

46. See also Hainz, *Ekklesia*, 51–54; and Ollrog, *Paulus und seine Mitarbeiter*, 77–79, for further historical-philological discussion and related literature. Because of the difference between this approach and mine, I will not attempt to debate issues with Hainz and Ollrog, which would require a virtual commentary on both of the above-mentioned volumes. Nevertheless, I wish to acknowledge my indebtedness to both of them.

47. The connective "therefore" (*oun*) refers back to the entire appeal begun in v. 8. However, because the appeal initiated in vv. 8–10 is interrupted by comments in vv. 11–16, v. 17 becomes the statement of appeal proper. This statement begins with a conditional clause which assumes that Philemon considers Paul a partner, and it ends with a clause that begins with an imperative of command or request. This command or request—"receive him as you would me"—states the behavioral condition that will prove the initial assumption to be real or unreal, true or false. Commentators are unusually silent about the significance of this conditional sentence and the condition it posits.

48. While the connective "therefore" refers back to the beginning of Paul's appeal in vv. 8–10, it does so because of the interruption in vv. 11–16. But it also introduces a conclusion based on what was said in the interruption. In vv. 11–14 Paul speaks from his own perspective on Onesimus, and in vv. 15–16 he speaks from Philemon's perspective, depicting Onesimus's absence as being for the purpose of Philemon having him back forever as a brother, a term Paul has already used to describe Philemon (v. 7), and a term which he uses to describe his own relationship with Onesimus (v. 16, "especially to me"). Thus Paul, Philemon, and Onesimus are "brothers," and Paul and Philemon are "partners" (v. 17). Consequently, when Paul tells Philemon to receive Onesimus as he, Philemon, would re-

ceive Paul, the relationship of brothers is as much at issue as the relationship of partners. *Paul* focuses on the relationship between the three brothers in vv. 15–16, but in his conditional sentence in v. 17 he assumes that Philemon's focus is on his partnership with Paul. Paul is, therefore, implying that Philemon cannot have the one relationship without the other.

49. I do not think that anyone doubts that Paul is Philemon's (and Titus's) senior partner, but no one has demonstrated this by an analysis of the social relations represented in Paul's rhetoric. Usually, it is a more theological assessment of Paul's apostolic role that leads to the conclusion of Paul's superiority, but that is not a sociological argument. If the degree of Paul's authority is to be determined, we have to see both what authority he claimed and how this claim translated into power by the consent of those over whom he claimed it. We do not know what power Philemon granted Paul, but we do know that others did grant it to him, as we will see in the course of this chapter. Minimally, we can cite 2 Cor. 1:3—2:13 and 7:5–16 as evidence that Paul's authority was acknowledged by the Corinthians, and also Rom. 15:26 as evidence that his authority in the matter of the collection enjoined in 1 Cor. 16:1–4 and 2 Corinthians 8 and 9 was also acknowledged; Achaia finally contributed to the collection.

50. Like many commentators, Lohse, *Colossians and Philemon*, 199 and n. 23, sees the preposition *peri* as meaning "for, on behalf of," not "about, with reference to." And he, too, dismisses Knox's idea that Paul was making a request *for* the gift of Onesimus (on which, see further Moule, *Colossians and Philemon*, 21). See also Bjerkelund, *Parakalō*, 118–24. However, I am rather inclined to see the preposition as a topical indicator meaning "about, with reference to," for Onesimus is the topic of Paul's appeal as the one whom Paul wants Philemon to receive as a brother. The frequently cited example of 1 Cor. 16:12 is but one of several in which topics are introduced by this preposition. Indeed, it is one of a number of topics to which Paul responds in 1 Cor. 7:1—16:18, which is itself introduced with the topical indicator *peri:* "Now concerning the matters about which you wrote . . . " (7:1a). Individual topics are introduced with the same preposition in 7:25; 8:1; 12:1; 16:1, and 16:12. See also 1 Thess. 4:9, 13, and 5:1. Each of these is a topic about which Paul makes an appeal or provides direction. It should also be noted that the use of *hyper* to introduce a topic of appeal in 2 Thess. 2:1 is as foreign to Paul's usage elsewhere as the *eucharistō* formula which appears *twice* in this letter, at 1:3 and 2:13. On topics in Paul's letters, see further David G. Bradley, "The *Topos* as a Form in the Pauline Paraenesis," *JBL* 72 (1953): 238–46.

51. For similar formulas without the topical indicator see 1 Cor. 16:15–18; Phil. 4:2 and 3; Rom. 15:30–33, 16:17–20. See also the formulaic beginnings of *parakalō* sections in Rom. 12:1–2, 1 Cor. 1:10, 2 Cor. 10:1–2; 1 Thess. 4:1, and for a comprehensive study of *parakalō*, Bjerkelund, *Parakalō*.

52. The Greek word here rendered as "authority" is not *exousia*, the more usual term, but *parrēsia*, which is usually translated as "boldness," "frank-

ness," or "openness." However, as Lohse notes (*Colossians and Philemon*, 198), the linking of *parrēsia* both to Paul's position "in Christ" and to its warrant for him to command Philemon lends to this instance of the word the connotation of authority. See also Schütz, *Paul and the Anatomy of Apostolic Authority*, 222–24. For a recent survey of usage and further literature, see Stanley B. Marrow, "Parrhēsia and the New Testament," *CBQ* 44 (1982): 431–46. Abraham Malherbe convincingly demonstrates Cynic philosophical influences in the use of *parrēsia* and other terminology in 1 Thess. 2:1–8, but he does not address Paul's assimilation and transformation of the terminology (" 'Gentle as a Nurse': The Cynic Background to 1 Thess. 2," *NovT* 12 [1970]: 203–17).

53. On the social connotation of "in Christ/the Lord," see n. 14, above. The Letter to Philemon contributes to this social connotation by speaking about the sharing of faith and the promotion of "the knowledge of all the good that is ours in Christ" (v. 6). Both the knowledge that is shared and the good that is possessed in Christ are social facts pertinent to life "in Christ" as distinct from life in the world. In addition, Paul's speaking in v. 7 of Philemon's having refreshed the hearts of the saints is related to v. 20, where Paul says: "I want some benefit from you in the Lord. Refresh my heart in Christ." "In the Lord" and "in Christ" define the social space in which the behavior referred to takes place. And Paul's expression of his confidence in Philemon's "obedience" (v. 21) is related to his claim to have the authority "in Christ" to command Philemon to do what is required (v. 8).

54. Within the social space of the church, "love" is both a symbolic value, i.e., an object of knowledge and value, and its behavioral forms. In vv. 4–7 Paul praises Philemon for behavior that embodies and enacts this value.

55. For a fuller discussion of the relationship between motives, rhetoric, and social structure, see below on *Commanding and Appealing*.

56. See the preceding section of this chapter on the implications of Paul's actions for the relationships between Philemon and Onesimus in the world.

57. See n. 5 above, on the relationship between "brother" and "fellow worker."

58. See n. 49 above, and below on metaphors of work. A single example from other letters concerns Timothy, who is described as Paul's fellow worker in Rom. 16:21 (cf. 1 Thess. 3:2) but as his "child" in Phil. 2:22, where he is said to have served with Paul in the gospel "as a son with a father." Similarly, in 1 Cor. 4:17 Paul says that he is sending Timothy, his beloved and faithful child in the Lord, to remind the Corinthians of *his* ways in Christ (cf. 16:10–11).

59. Philemon 4—7 is complicated by some grammatical and stylistic features, but these points about Philemon's work are nevertheless clear. On the grammatical and translational problems posed by v. 6, see Moule, *Colossians and Philemon*, 142–43; Lohse, *Colossians and Philemon*; Stuhlmacher, *Der Brief an Philemon*, 33–34; Wickert, "Der Philemonbrief—Privat-

SOCIAL STRUCTURES AND RELATIONS

brief oder apostolisches Schreiben?", 230–31, n. 2; and Gordon P. Wiles, *Paul's Intercessory Prayers: The Significance of the Intercessory Prayer Passages in the Letters of Paul*, SNTSMS 24 (Cambridge: Cambridge Univ. Press, 1974), 221–25. Stylistically, the entire thanksgiving section is chiastically composed. In v. 5 Paul refers to Philemon's love (A) and faith (B), and then he elaborates on them in reverse order, faith (B) in v. 6 and love (A) in v. 7. Cf. Lohse, *Colossians and Philemon*, 192–95. On "refreshing the heart," see 2 Cor. 2:12–13 and 7:5–16; Lohse, *Colossians and Philemon*, 195; Helmut Koester, "splangchna," *TDNT*, 7:555–56; and Church, "Rhetorical Structure and Design in Paul's Letter to Philemon."

60. On the role of hosts in the house churches, see the literature cited in n. 28, above.

61. As noted in my introductory chapter, it would be equally profitable to go beyond Paul's narrative world, but for methodological reasons we are confining ourselves to Paul's letters.

62. For a more historical approach to Paul and work, see the references to Hock and Judge in n. 4. See also Ollrog, *Paulus und seine Mitarbeiter*, 171, and for further discussion of the passages treated in the text see the comments on them by Ollrog and by Hainz, *Ekklesia*.

63. In addition to the references cited in n. 62, see the articles on "ergon" by Georg Bertram in *TDNT*, 2:635–55, and on "kopos" by Friedrich Hauck in *TDNT*, 3:827–30; see also Adolf von Harnack, "kopos, (kopian, hoi kopiōntes) in frühchristlichen Sprachgebrauch," *ZNW* 27 (1928): 1–10.

64. On 1 Corinthians 9 see Hainz, *Ekklesia*, 69–73; Hans Conzelmann, *1 Corinthians*, Hermeneia (Philadelphia: Fortress Press, 1975), 151–63; Günther Bornkamm, "The Missionary Stance of Paul in 1 Corinthians 9 and in Acts," in *Studies in Luke-Acts*, ed. Leander Keck and J. Louis Martyn (Philadelphia: Fortress Press, 1980), 194–207; and Holmberg, *Paul and Power*, 86–93.

65. Besides the commentaries, see the observations of Ollrog and Hainz on the passages to be discussed in this section. While I will concentrate on 1 Cor. 3:5–17, both 3:18–23, which concludes the argument in 1:10—3:23, and the bridge sentence in 4:1 are also pertinent. Because our focus is on sociological matters, I will not entertain historical and theological issues dealt with by others. See, e.g. Schütz, *Paul and the Anatomy of Apostolic Authority*, 187–203.

66. God is the principal in focus in this section, but 1 Cor. 3:5 refers to "the Lord" as having "given" (*edōken*) Apollos and Paul their jobs, which appears to be synonymous with the grace (*charis*) given (*dotheisan*) to Paul by God in 3:10. A similar confusion between God and the Lord as agents of the same enterprise is found in 1 Cor. 7:17 and Rom. 12:3. In 1 Cor. 7:17, Paul refers to the life "the Lord" assigned (*emerisen*) to individuals as also being the life into which God has called (*keklēken*) them, and in Rom. 12:3 he refers both to God as having assigned (*emerisen*) measures of faith to each person and to himself as having been given (*dotheisēs*) grace (*charis*). Nevertheless, in 1 Cor. 12:18 and 24 it is God who arranged (*etheto, syn-*

181

ekerasen) the members of the body which is Christ, and in 12:28 it is God who has placed (*etheto*) in the church first apostles, second prophets, etc. In light of all of these texts, the role of "the Lord" in 1 Cor. 3:5 and 7:18 is unclear, unless here "the Lord" refers to God, which is unlikely because for Paul "the Lord" refers to Christ (cf. 12:12; Phil. 2:11). Thus, except for 1 Cor. 3:5, in both the work metaphors and the body metaphors it is God who has assigned social positions to members of the church, i.e., "in Christ/the Lord."

67. Commentators are of divided opinion on the meaning of the genitive construction, "fellow workers of God" (cf. also 1 Thess. 3:2; 2 Cor. 6:1), some understanding it to mean "fellow workers with God," and others "fellow laborers in the service of God" (cf. Bauer, *A Greek-English Lexicon of the New Testament*, 788; Conzelmann, *1 Corinthians*, 74 and n. 53; Hainz, *Ekklesia*, 49 and n. 3). I agree with Ollrog, *Paulus und seine Mitarbeiter*, 68, and Victor Paul Furnish, "Fellow Workers in God's Service," *JBL* 80 (1961): 364–70, in preferring the second meaning. See further Furnish's article and Ollrog, ibid., 70–72 and 162–82. Ollrog's theological emphasis is, however, made at the cost of sociological insight.

68. On both this metaphor and the metaphor of the body, see further Hainz, *Ekklesia*, 256–66.

69. The term "job" is not an attested meaning of *charis*. I use it because it fits the system comprised by Paul's metaphors of work and distinguishes this connotation from that of "the power to" which is represented by *charisma*, usually translated as "gift." The distinction between these terms is discussed further, below. On it, see Hainz, *Ekklesia*, 333–51; Schütz, *Paul and the Anatomy of Apostolic Authority*, 249–80; and Holmberg, *Paul and Power*, especially pp. 137–92.

70. In 2 Cor. 10:13–18 Paul again employs the metaphor of a field of labor seen in 1 Corinthians 3, and he does so in order to indicate that God has assigned Corinth to him as his field. He does not, he says, wish to preach the gospel in someone else's field. But this statement is rhetorically related to his complaint in 2 Corinthians 10—13 that others are trespassing on *his* field by preaching in it. Cf. 1 Cor. 9:1, and also the possibility that Apollos had been competing with Paul as well. On the other hand, Paul returns to the construction metaphor of 1 Corinthians 3 in Rom. 15:15–21, and he does so in order to make the same point as in 2 Cor. 10:13–18: he does not wish to preach the gospel "where Christ has already been named," lest he "build on another man's foundation" (15:20). Thus Paul's "work" in 1 Cor. 9:1 is both the project God gave to him—to lay a foundation in Corinth—and the product of his labors—the foundation and the edifice built upon it.

71. Although we found some confusion in Paul's identification of his employer in 1 Cor. 3:5 (see n. 66), there is no fundamental confusion in his identification of his project as "the work of God" (Rom. 14:20), "the work of Christ" (Phil. 2:30), and "the work of the Lord" (1 Cor. 15:58; 16:10). God's project is for Paul to preach the gospel of Christ, who is the Lord, and therefore Paul's work can be said to be God's, Christ's, and the Lord's.

Despite having different specific jobs, the work performed by Paul and his fellow workers, and even by individual church members (1 Cor. 15:58), is one in that it is in the service of the gospel (cf. 1 Cor. 3:5–9, 11; 1 Thess. 3:2; Phil. 2:25, 30; 4:3; Rom. 16:3, 9, 12). In addition to preaching and exhortation, this work consists of acts of faith and love (cf. 1 Thess. 1:3; Philemon 4—7). See also Ollrog, *Paulus und seine Mitarbeiter*, 70–72, 162–74.

72. Regardless of how symbolic concepts or theological arguments may represent the social composition of a community, from a sociological perspective every community has to have structures of super- and subordination in order to endure. While it is valid to study the relationships between communal order and communal theology, as e.g., Hainz, *Ekklesia*, admirably does, the communal order itself cannot be fully understood without some appreciation of its underlying social structures. Indeed, because symbolic concepts and theological arguments function to legitimate communal order, knowledge of its underlying social structures can help us to appreciate more fully the concepts and arguments.

73. In addition to the more general statements in 1 Cor. 15:58, 1 Thess. 1:3, and 5:11, see, e.g., Rom. 14:17—15:7; 1 Corinthians 8, 10:23–24, 12—14.

74. The "neighbor" referred to here is clearly a "brother" (cf. 1 Cor. 10:1, 14; Gal. 5:13–14), but Paul's comments about nonbelievers in 1 Cor. 10:27–33 suggest that he also envisions his rule as applying to those outside the church, so that they might be saved. On the other hand, in Rom. 12:14–21 Paul appears to be referring to outsiders as enemies and urges that their needs be met, but now in order to "heap burning coals" upon their heads! Consequently, seeking the good of the outsider can result in their eschatological salvation or damnation. Nevertheless, the principal focus of Paul's comments about good deeds is upon the inhabitants of God's building. To edify or be edified, one has to be in the building.

75. This is certainly Paul's claim. However, the claim is sociologically empty if the churches do not grant him the power to exercise his rule over them. See further below, and for other approaches that do not disagree in essentials see Ollrog, *Paulus und seine Mitarbeiter*, 175–82; Hainz, *Ekklesia*, 267–310; Schütz, *Paul and the Anatomy of Apostolic Authority*, passim; and Holmberg, *Paul and Power*, 15–121.

76. It is worth noting that although Paul speaks about not wanting to build on another man's foundation (Rom. 15:20), his letter to Rome, whose churchly foundation was laid by someone else, sounds remarkably "constructive," especially if 16:17–20 is addressed to Rome, which many including myself doubt. But regardless of whether or not Romans 16 was originally destined for Rome, the letter to Rome suggests that Paul assumed that his authority among the Gentiles extended even to Rome (cf. 15:14–33). It is difficult to imagine the person who wrote this letter passing through Rome as no more than a religious tourist, especially if he found things there not to his liking. On the problems posed by this letter see the excellent collection of essays edited by Karl P. Donfried in *The Romans*

Debate (Minneapolis: Augsburg Pub. House, 1977); and Harry Gamble, Jr., *The Textual History of the Letter to the Romans*, SD 42 (Grand Rapids: Wm. B. Eerdmans, 1977).

77. I agree with Funk that Paul's emissaries and letters are forms of *his* apostolic presence. See Robert W. Funk, "The Apostolic *Parousia:* Form and Significance," in *Christian History and Interpretation: Studies Presented to John Knox*, ed. William R. Farmer, C. F. D. Moule, and Richard R. Niebuhr (Cambridge: Cambridge Univ. Press, 1967), 249–68.

78. See Schütz, *Paul and the Anatomy of Apostolic Authority*, 165–86, and Hainz, *Ekklesia*, 127–71.

79. For a fuller treatment of the relationship between Paul's gospel and his experience, see, e.g., Schütz, *Paul and the Anatomy of Apostolic Authority*, 84–186; and Hainz, *Ekklesia*, 62–69 and 109–13. I should add that in claiming that Paul's experience is the *ultimate* criterion of his judgment I do not deny that the gospel he preached (1 Cor. 15:3–6/7) was also a criterion, for it is both the foundation he laid and a tradition he received from others. However, in 2 Corinthians 10—13 he never tells us what the gospel preached by the "false apostles" contained, only that it was different; nor does he say that the "gospel" he preached is the basis of his judgment. Throughout, he refers to his experience and his confidence in it.

80. Whether or not 2 Cor. 12:1–5 refers to Paul's commissioning experience, which is debatable, in 12:6–10 (cf. 12:7) he makes it clear that it refers to a confirming experience of his own.

81. See Meeks, *The First Urban Christians*, 127–31, and Adela Yarbro Collins, "The Function of 'Excommunication' in Paul," *HTR* 73 (1980): 251–63.

82. Here I am in agreement with Günther Bornkamm's arguments concerning the compositeness of 2 Corinthians in "Die Vorgeschichte des sogenannten Zweiten Korintherbriefes," *Sitzungsberichte der Heidelberger Akademie der Wissenschaften, Phil.-hist. Klasse,* (1961):2. 2 Cor. 2:14—7:3/4, minus the interpolation in 6:14—7:1, is from the earliest letter in a series of letters represented in 2 Corinthians; 2 Corinthians 10—13 is the hortatory section of the second letter in the series; and 2 Corinthians 1—7/8, minus 2:14—7:3/4 is from the last letter. 2 Corinthians 9 was probably originally addressed to other churches in Achaia. For a brief account of the arguments in English, see Dieter Georgi, "Corinthians, Second," in *The Interpreter's Dictionary of the Bible Supplementary Volume* (Nashville: Abingdon Press, 1976), 183–86. For other views on the integrity of 2 Corinthians, see Kümmel, *Introduction to the New Testament*, 279–91.

83. Paul's problems with Jewish influences in Galatians and in Philippians 3 represent more symbolic than sociological problems, although the symbolic problems did have *social* consequences.

84. See, e.g., Rom. 16:3–4a, 9; Phil. 4:3; cf. also those who labor in the Lord referred to in Rom. 16:6, 12.

85. Because the Greek text lacks a grammatical subject for the noun "will," we do not know whose "will" it was that Apollos not go to Corinth.

However, because Apollos is the subject of the last verb in the sentence ("he has an opportunity"), it appears that it was his own will that he not go. See further Ollrog, *Paulus und seine Mitarbeiter*, 37–41, 215–19; Hainz, *Ekklesia*, 96–97; and Holmberg, *Paul and Power*, 66–67.

86. See on Timothy, 1 Cor. 4:17 and 16:10–11, and on Stephanas, 1:16 and 16:15–18, both of whom are discussed further below.

87. See Holmberg, *Paul and Power*, 59–60, 66–67; and Hainz, *Ekklesia*, 302–6.

88. See generally, C. K. Barrett, *Essays on Paul* (Philadelphia: Westminster Press, 1982), 118–31; and Ollrog, *Paulus und seine Mitarbeiter*, 33–37.

89. On the emissary as a form of Paul's presence, see the reference to Funk in n. 77.

90. On Timothy's tour of duty with Paul, see Ollrog, *Paulus und seine Mitarbeiter*, 20–23.

91. On these fellow workers see Ollrog, *Paulus und seine Mitarbeiter*, 24–33, 41–62; and Holmberg, *Paul and Power*, 57–65.

92. On the length of tours and spheres of activity see Ollrog, *Paulus und seine Mitarbeiter*, 9–62; and Judge, "Early Christians as a Scholastic Community: Part 2," 131–35.

93. On Stephanas, see further Ollrog, *Paulus und seine Mitarbeiter*, 42, 96–98; and Hainz, *Ekklesia*, 97–101. My view of Stephanas's role in Corinth originated in a paper by a former student, R. Bruce McColm, who rightly identified Stephanas's critical role in some of the social problems addressed in 1 Corinthians.

94. While Paul says that they "set themselves" (*etaxan heautous*) to this task, implying that they initiated the undertaking themselves, he does not mention in 16:15–18 what he says parenthetically back in 1:16, namely, that *he* baptized these first converts in Achaia. In view of the problem of "parties" in Corinth, Paul may in both passages be playing down his own initiative with regard to the commitment made by Stephanas and his household. Paul's rhetoric in 2 Corinthians 8 concerning his "appeal" to Titus, and the rhetoric of his "appeal" to Philemon, reflect a similar tendency in Paul to gloss over his own authoritative initiative in the actions of others. In any event, however, Paul not only baptized Stephanas and his household, but Stephanas also came to Paul, presumably about the problems in Corinth. And if Stephanas's service had to do with the collection (cf. 16:1–4; on this see further, below), it is doubtful that his involvement with it was self-initiated.

95. Although Paul does not say exactly why Stephanas and his companions visited him, the visit is one of three events that immediately preceded the writing of 1 Corinthians, the other two being Paul's reception both of a report from "Chloe's people" (1:11) and of a letter from Corinth (7:1). It seems probable that the visit was linked to either or both of these sources of information concerning Corinth.

96. See Hainz, *Ekklesia*, 101, n. 6, and also 96, n. 5, where he notes that the topical formula in 16:12 suggests that the Corinthians had also inquired

about or even requested a visit by Apollos. Judging from Paul's comments about Apollos here, it seems probable that both Paul and some Corinthians felt a visit by Apollos might alleviate the tensions in Corinth. If so, and if Apollos also declined Paul's strong appeal that he go to Corinth, one has to wonder about his motives for refusing to act as a mediator.

97. This verb is synonymous with *parakalō*, as is evident in their interchangeable deployment in 1 Thess. 4:1—5:22. See 4:1, 10 (18); 5:(11), 12, 14.

98. It is not clear from 1 Thess. 5:12–13 whether or not the three successive functions referred to in the three successive participial clauses of 5:12 designate different jobs. However, in Rom. 12:3–8 those who exhort and stand over the community are treated as performing separate tasks. On these two texts see Hainz, *Ekklesia*, 37–42 and 181–93.

99. The function (*praxis*) of members is referred to in Rom. 12:4 but not in 1 Corinthians 12, where it is the differentiation of and relations between "members" that is focal. On these passages and the body metaphor, see further Hainz, *Ekklesia*, 73–74, 78–88, 181–93, 259–66, and 322–45. See further Holmberg, *Paul and Power*, 95–201; Schütz, *Paul and the Anatomy of Apostolic Authority*, 249–80; Conzelmann, *1 Corinthians*, 211–15; Käsemann, *Commentary on Romans*, trans. and ed. Geoffrey Bromiley (Grand Rapids: Wm. B. Eerdmans, 1980), 331–42; and for lists comparing the functions represented in Romans 12 and 1 Corinthians 12, Meeks, *The First Urban Christians*, 134–36.

100. On the use of the word "job" to render *charis*, see n. 69, above. This rendering also helps to avoid the notion of *charis* as "office" and its institutional implications (see further the references to Hainz, Holmberg, and Schütz cited in n. 99). These implications are wrongly read into the texts in question when *charis* is viewed as "office." By starting with the idea of "jobs," we can then seek to determine from sociological and historical analysis the degree to which the various jobs have become institutionalized in any given community and in any given letter.

101. Unlike 1 Thess. 5:12–13, these functions are differentiated from one another as (1) jobs, (2) gifts, and (3) "members." For our purposes, it is more important to observe the differentiation of and relations between jobs than it is to differentiate their job descriptions, for which see, e.g., Hainz, *Ekklesia*, 37–42, 181–93, and the commentaries.

102. Cf. Rom. 1:1–6 and 15:15–21 for a further representation of Paul's job description, which contains different particulars from those of the "apostles" sent by individual churches (2 Cor. 8:23; Phil. 2:25). The particulars of Paul's job description also differ from those "apostles" referred to in 1 Cor. 15:7–11 at least in terms of the "field" God assigned to him.

103. Paul does not question the source of the gifts but rather concentrates on their underlying unity in the spirit and in their origination with God, in contrast with the Corinthians' emphasis (1) on the differences between the gifts and (2) on the baptizers who mediated the gifts to them (cf. 1 Cor. 2:12).

104. On 1 Cor. 11:17–34 see Theissen, *The Social Setting of Pauline Christianity*, 145–74, and also 121–43.

105. The spirit manifest in the Corinthians' "gifts" may also be involved in their "arrogant" or "puffed up" (*physioō*) attitude (1 Cor. 4:6, 18–19; 5:2; 8:1). In light of the metaphor of drinking the baptismal spirit (12:13), 10:1–13 may also reflect an arrogant self-confidence deriving from the baptismal "ingestion" of the spirit (cf. 10:4, 7, 12). For some further possibilities see Birger A. Peason's *The Pneumatikos-Psychikos Terminology in 1 Corinthians*, SBLDS 12 (Missoula, Mont.: Scholars Press, 1973).

106. Paul does not explicitly say that women were involved in speaking in tongues, but at the end of his argument in 1 Corinthians 12—14 he commands that women should keep silent in the churches (14:33b–36). However, this command may be an interpolation (Conzelmann, *1 Corinthians*, 246). But if it is not an interpolation, women prophesying would not be an issue because Paul acknowledges their doing so in 1 Cor. 11:5. For this reason, and also because it is only women and speakers in tongues (14:28) who are expressly enjoined to keep silent, if 14:33b–36 is original to Paul it is women speakers in tongues who are in view. For another interpretation see Meeks, "The Image of the Androgyne," 197–206 and more recently, *The First Urban Christians*, 70–71, and 125.

107. See Hainz, *Ekklesia*, 78–88 and 181–93.

108. Hans von Campenhausen, *Ecclesiastical Authority and Spiritual Power in the Church of the First Three Centuries*, trans. J. A. Baker (Stanford, Calif.: Stanford Univ. Press, 1969), 64 n. 54, notes the parallel between the treatment of secular authorities in Rom. 13:1–7 and "ecclesiastical authorities" in 1 Thess. 5:12–13. On Rom. 13:1–7, see further Käsemann, *Commentary on Romans*, 350–59.

109. For a discussion of previous research see, e.g., Schütz, *Paul and the Anatomy of Apostolic Authority*, 1–83 (and also 204–80), and Hainz, *Ekklesia*, 267–94.

110. The accusation against Paul, that he is a "man-pleaser" (Gal. 1:10), is answered both by Paul's denial that he received his message from human agents and by his affirmation that it came from God through a revelation of Jesus Christ (1:11–16). Paul further responds to this accusation by showing autobiographically his longstanding independence of the Jerusalem authorities he was alleged to be pleasing (1:17—2:10), and by showing even his opposition to them (2:11–21), which nicely turns the tables on his pro-circumcision accusers by pointing out that the Jerusalem leaders' position on circumcision was the same as *theirs*. The accusers are closer to the very Jerusalemites they accused Paul of pleasing than Paul is! Paul's relations with the Jerusalem leaders are dealt with further below at the end of the section on *Commanding and Appealing*.

111. Philemon 13 and Phil. 1:13 show that Paul's imprisonment is "*for* the gospel." However, the genitive construction "prisoner *of* Christ Jesus" in Philemon 1 and 9 represents both a construction and a conception that

goes beyond imprisonment for the gospel. Indeed, the construction represents a conception that denies the worldly status implied by imprisonment; Paul, during his imprisonment, is not a prisoner of the state but of Christ. As we will see shortly, this conception is related to Paul's representation of himself elsewhere as a *slave of Christ*, in which the worldly free man is a slave of Christ. Paul does not deny that he is either a free man or a prisoner, but these worldly realities are transformed for him by virtue of what he is in Christ. His symbolic universe gives a new and different meaning to his worldly experience, so much so that we have to say that the reality of the world as seen from within the world is replaced by the reality seen from within the church. For Paul there is only one reality.

112. Lohse, *Colossians and Philemon*, 199; cf. Stuhlmacher, *Der Brief an Philemon*, 37–38.

113. See the references in the preceding note for bibliography on those who take which position. Lohse and Stuhlmacher opt for "old man" because they see "ambassador" as contradicting Paul's alleged abdication of his apostolic authority in favor of appealing. Among other things, this rationale overlooks the fact that throughout the letter Paul's authority is only very thinly masked by his rhetoric.

114. In addition to the literature cited by Lohse and Stuhlmacher (n. 112, above), see also the recent arguments concerning Paul as ambassador in Robert Jewett, "Romans as an Ambassadorial Letter," *Interpretation* 36 (1982): 5–20, and esp. 10–12.

115. See further the discussion in chap. 1, above, of the process of composition in which Paul apparently came up with some new ideas for his "appeal" while dictating vv. 17–18. This suggests that in putting together his thoughts about his appeal he did so in terms of contrasts—until he got to vv. 17–18.

116. The word "also" (*kai*) is missing in some manuscripts but, as Lohse notes, it is adequately attested to in others (*Colossians and Philemon*, 200 n. 33). Lohse, however, does not address the parallelism between this construction and that in v. 9, and for this reason he also misses the contrastive relationship between the term separated by the "but now also" construction.

117. See Moule, *Colossians and Philemon*, 144, who translates v. 9 as follows: " . . . Paul the ambassador, yes, and now also the prisoner, of Jesus Christ." Although I see no reason for the definite article in this translation, I agree that the genitive construction "of Christ Jesus" qualifies both nouns. Paul is not only a prisoner of Christ (Philemon 1, 9) but he is also an ambassador of or for Christ (2 Cor. 5:20).

118. See further the discussion in chap. 3 of the metaphor of slavery in Paul's symbolic universe.

119. For further observations on the role of debtee, see the final section of this chapter. On the relationship between Paul's "paternity" and spiritual paternity in the ancient world, see Gutierrez, *La Paternité Spirituelle selon saint Paul.* Contrary to Gutierrez, p. 168, I see all of Paul's references to

himself as "father" as metaphorical, except for the similes in 1 Thess. 2:11 and Phil 2:22 (see n. 122, below). See further Holmberg, *Paul and Power*, 77–80, and Gottlob Schrenk and G. Quell, "patēr," *TDNT*, 5:945–1022. On the notion of Christian "patriarchalism" see Ernst Troeltsch, *The Social Teachings of the Christian Churches*, 1:76–82. Theissen now calls this "love patriarchalism" (*Social Setting*, 37, 107–10, and 139–40; see also the comments by Schütz in his introduction to Theissen's essays, 14–15). On God's paternity, see chap. 3, below.

120. It should be noted that there is no evidence in Paul's letters as to whether or not his "children" called him "father," but neither is there any evidence of their calling him anything else. We simply do not know if others addressed Paul as anything other than "Paul."

121. In both 1 Cor. 6:5 and 15:34 he "shames" the Corinthians for lacking knowledge they should have had. Cf. 4:17, on Timothy's mission to *remind* the Corinthians of Paul's ways and teachings. Clearly, Paul's symbolic universe had not been adequately internalized by the Corinthians. On internalization, see Berger and Luckmann, *The Social Construction of Reality*, 129–83.

122. Note that Paul employs here the notion of father in the form of a simile (cf. 2:7 and Phil. 2:22) rather than in the form of a metaphor. This may be related to the fact that he also uses the first personal plural ("we"), presumably to represent the co-writers of the letter, Silvanus and Timothy, "apostles" (2:6/7) who had been with him at the founding of the community (cf. 2:1ff.). The use of the plural is troublesome for the metaphor because it would imply that all three missionaries acted like fathers (and nurses, 2:7), which is something Paul never suggests elsewhere. Indeed, in Phil. 2:22 Paul uses the paternal simile (contrast the metaphor in 1 Cor. 4:17) when he describes the same Timothy as one who served (*douleuō*) with him in the gospel "like a child with his father" (*hos patri teknon syn emoi*). Timothy is Paul's "child," not a fellow father. For this reason we have to consider that although the use of the plural in 1 Thessalonians 1ff. derives from the presence of co-writers, Paul in fact is referring to himself without suggesting that these fellow-worker "children" are his equals. There is some evidence supporting this interpretation of the plural "we." While we cannot make too much out of Paul's use of the singular noun "father" in conjunction with the plural subject in "we were like a father" (2:11–12; cf. 2:7, "we were like a nurse"), we have to take seriously his slip in 3:2–5. In 3:2 he says "we sent Timothy," which could be understood as a reference to himself and Silvanus. However, in 3:5 Paul says that *he* sent Timothy. Thus 3:2 and 5 illustrate a difference between social reality and rhetoric that helps to explain the singular social reality behind the rhetorical plural in 1 Thess. 2:1ff. Be this as it may, it is nevertheless clear from 1 Thess. 2:11 that whether in the form of a metaphor or in the form of a simile, Paul is thinking in terms of kinship relations in which *he* is more than a brother (cf. 1:4; 2:1, 9, 17; 3:7; 4:1, 9, 10, 13; 5:1, 4, 12, 14).

123. This is clearly the case in 2:9, but it is more problematical in 2:5–6,

where the "burden" (*en barei*) referred to in v. 6 may not have to do with the community's obligation to support apostles but with a more authoritarian *attitude* that Paul contrasts with gentleness. Malherbe, " 'Gentle as a Nurse': The Cynic Background to 1 Thess. 2," makes a strong case for the latter interpretation by locating the "burden" in the context of terminology used to characterize Cynic preachers. But Malherbe does not consider that Paul may be using such terminology differently. The concept represented in 2:6 is quite similar to 1 Cor. 9:14, and Paul elsewhere uses words with the same *bar* root to refer to obligations for support (cf. 2 Cor. 11:9, *abarē;* 12:16, *katabareō;* see also *katanarkao* in 11:9 and 12:13, 14). See further Holmberg, *Paul and Power,* 87–89. Holmberg sees 1 Thess. 2:5–6 as an allusion to financial obligation.

124. Whatever other connotation the idea of imitation may have, here it is clearly associated with a child's imitation of his father. See similarly Holmberg, *Paul and Power,* 78. In addition to the bibliography cited by Holmberg on imitation, see also Schütz, *Paul and the Anatomy of Apostolic Authority,* 226–32; and Boykin Sanders, "Imitating Paul: 1 Cor. 4:16," *HTR* 74 (1981): 353–63.

125. See further Holmberg, *Paul and Power,* 77–80.

126. Contrast the behavioral expectations of the later "household rules," on which see Lohse, *Colossians and Philemon,* 154–63. In these rules order replaces affection as the focus of "family" life.

127. On the language of commanding and appealing, see Bjerkelund, *Parakalō,* 13–19, 24–28, and 188–90; and Holmberg, *Paul and Power,* 83–86. For other approaches to Paul's social style see von Campenhausen, *Ecclesiastical Authority and Spiritual Power,* 30–75; Schütz, *Paul and the Anatomy of Apostolic Authority,* 204–48 (on "The Rhetoric of Apostolic Authority"); and Holmberg, *Paul and Power,* 183–88.

128. Cf. Schütz, *Paul and the Anatomy of Apostolic Authority,* 221: "In this little verse in Philemon Paul parades a theoretical apostolic authority unmatched elsewhere in his letters." While the parade may be unmatched, Philemon 8—9 shows that *whenever* Paul "appeals" he does so as a rhetorical substitute for his authority to command, and Paul *does* parade the carrot and the stick elsewhere (e.g., 1 Cor. 1:10 [appeal/by the name of the Lord]; 4:14, 21; 7:6; 2 Cor. 11:8; 13:10). See further Holmberg, *Paul and Power,* 83–86; Bjerkelund, *Parakalō,* 188; and Hainz, *Ekklesia,* 199–209. Bjerkelund and Holmberg miss the persistent masklike nature of Paul's language of appeal, but Hainz does not. Contrary to Bjerkelund and Holmberg, I find little if any semantic difference between Paul's terminology for either his appealing or his commanding. The differences are more stylistic than semantic.

129. See Kümmel, *Introduction to the New Testament,* 314–20; and Donfried, ed., *The Romans Debate.* Galatians lacks any positive feedback on that community's response to Paul.

130. Among recent sociological studies of Paul, Holmberg, *Paul and Power,* emphasizes Paul's authority as represented in his administrative

activities, while Schütz, *Paul and the Anatomy of Apostolic Authority*, concentrates on his authority in relation to the gospel he preaches. From a non-sociological perspective, James I. H. McDonald, *Kerygma and Didache: The Articulation and Structure of the Earliest Christian Message*, SNTSMS 37 (Cambridge: Cambridge Univ. Press, 1980), surveys the major forms of early Christian preaching and teaching but he is not concerned with the question of authority.

131. To Funk's observation that letters and emissaries are forms of Paul's apostolic presence ("The Apostolic Parousia: Form and Significance"), we can add that all three forms of presence consist of two sequential parts—preaching or confirming the faith and exhortation (appeal). According to 1 Thessalonians, the activities of Paul (2:9–12) and Timothy (3:2) are divided in this way, and so also are Paul's letters, namely in terms of their *eucharistō/parakalō* structure. The *eucharistō* (extended thanksgiving) sections deal with the gospel and its reception (faith), and the *parakalō* (extended hortatory) sections with exhortation and appeal, and not infrequently with commands. To relate this observation to our earlier reflections on the composition of Paul's letters, we can say that the content and maintenance of faith is the conceptual premise (the "indicative"). In addition, the *eucharistō* section has a narrative dimension to the extent that Paul updates his relationship with the community addressed and in the process establishes the premise for writing. The *parakalō* section represents a new stage in the relationship in two ways, one being Paul's new instructions and the other the community's actions in response to them. Romans deviates from the norm only to the extent that there has been no previous relationship between Paul and Rome.

132. Despite the linguistic and perhaps conceptual differences between these expressions (on which, see Hainz, *Ekklesia*, 33–34), Paul and his fellow workers are the ones who do the speaking. By claiming to do so "through" or "in the Lord Jesus," they legitimate their words by anchoring them in a symbolic universe that locates the authority of their speech outside of themselves, depersonalizing their speech, as it were.

133. I use this word in the technical (sociology of knowledge) sense defined by Berger and Luckmann, *The Social Construction of Reality*, 92–128. The notion will be discussed further in chap. 3.

134. Being people "taught by God" (*theodidaktoi*) stands in contrast with being taught by men or "in words of human wisdom" (*en didaktois anthrōpinēs sophias logois*, 1 Cor. 2:13). This is but another manifestation of the same phenomenon discussed in n. 132, above. Socially, it is Paul who speaks but who in speaking says that his words (unlike those of certain other speakers) come from elsewhere. Consequently, the source of the authority of his words is displaced from himself onto God or the Lord, neither of whom are social actors in the *sociological* sense of "actor." *Theological* interpretations tend to blur this distinction because by definition they seek to explicate and thereby maintain Paul's symbolic universe. For the theologian, Paul's symbolic universe is usually *the* universe even when demythologized.

191

However, it is also fair to say that the theological critics have not traditionally thought in terms of symbolic universes—because their attention has been more on Paul's ideas than on the "world" they represent. On the relationship between theology and symbolic universes see the discussion in chap. 1 on the sociology of the letter.

135. In the examples to be discussed, we will only be interested in "words" that Paul attributes to "the Lord," not in the more general notion of God as the ultimate speaker, on which see, e.g., Holmberg, *Paul and Power*, 74–75. On words attributed to the Lord, see the classic essay by Oscar Cullmann, "The Tradition," in *The Early Church* (Philadelphia: Westminster Press, 1956), 59–99, and Archibald M. Hunter, *Paul and His Predecessors* (Philadelphia: Westminster Press, 1961), 45–51.

136. Cullman, *et al.*, see 1 Thess. 4:15 as containing a quotation of something Jesus said, thus making "the Lord" both the subject and the object of these words (*The Early Church*, 65; cf. 69).

137. On 1 Cor. 11:23–25/26, see Cullmann, *The Early Church*, 67–75; and on the entire section, 11:17–34, see Theissen, *Social Setting*, 145–74; and Conzelmann, *1 Corinthians*, 192–203.

138. 1 Cor. 11:26 is probably a Pauline addition. See Conzelmann, *1 Corinthians*, 192–203.

139. Cullman perceived the social connotation of speaking "in the Lord" but concentrated more on its theological significance than on the sociological significance of activity "in the Lord." On the latter, see n. 14, above.

140. The distinction between the social and the symbolic connotations of being "in the Lord" is discussed in n. 14, above, and in chap. 3, below.

141. E.g., from an institutionalized chain of transmitters like the Jerusalem authorities who may have received the traditions from Jesus and passed them on to the likes of Paul or his predecessors in Antioch. For other arguments concerning institutional influences on Paul, see Cullmann, *The Early Church*, 55–99; Hainz, *Ekklesia*, 239–50; Holmberg, *Paul and Power*, 15–56; and Schütz, *Paul and the Anatomy of Apostolic Authority*, 84–158, all of whom provide references to yet further literature.

142. In 1 Cor. 15:1–11, neither the temporal sequence of witnesses to the risen Lord nor the tradition naming them reflects a social sequence of transmitters. Moreover, Paul himself focuses on the witnesses' *common* experience and on their *common* preaching. He may be the last one in the list to have seen the Lord, but he is not the last in a series of transmitters of a tradition of the Lord's appearances. The tradition is one affirmed by all who have seen him.

143. Although the rhetorical character of Paul's speech in Romans raises questions concerning how much of what he says refers specifically to those in Rome, those in Rome are included in his comments in 6:17 because they have become obedient to the traditions, as Paul acknowledges in 1:8–12.

144. On the suggestion that 1 Cor. 7:1b represents the position of some Corinthians, see Conzelmann, *1 Corinthians*, 115 n. 10.

145. See further notes 127 and 128, above. On commanding, see 1 Cor.

SOCIAL STRUCTURES AND RELATIONS

7:6, 25; 2 Cor. 8:8 (*epitagē*) and Philemon 8 (*epitassō*); on directing, see 1 Cor. 7:17, 9:14, 11:34, 16:1 (*diatassō*); and on instructing, see 1 Thess. 4:2 (*parangelia*), and 1 Cor. 7:10; 11:17; 1 Thess. 4:11 (*parangelō*).

146. Cf. Holmberg, *Paul and Power*, 84, for discussion and further literature. See also Cullman, *The Early Church*, 73–74.

147. The "Lord's" instruction is represented by the infinitival imperative preceded by a negative, while Paul's instructions are in the form of a verb in the imperative mood. However, these grammatical differences do not affect the binding force of Paul's instructions.

148. Because the compositeness of 2 Corinthians (see n. 82, above) makes it unclear just when 2 Corinthians 8 was written, we cannot be certain that it was written after Paul's visit. Neither is it clear that the visit to Corinth by Titus referred to in 12:17–18 refers to the beginning of Titus's work referred to in 8:6. However, these problems do not affect the year's time between the writing of 2 Corinthians 8 (see 8:10) and the beginning of work on the collection in Corinth, which dates either from the time when 1 Corinthians was written (see 16:1–4) or from Paul's founding visit (16:1 presumes that the Corinthians already know about the collection and had queried Paul about it, and Stephanas may have begun work on the collection as a local agent following his conversion as the first convert in Achaia). But the important point is that if Paul visited Corinth between the time of writing 1 Corinthians and the sending of Titus referred to in 2 Corinthians 8, this would indicate that neither the letter nor the visit succeeded in getting the collection moving. See further Georgi, *Die Geschichte der Kollekte*, 51–67.

149. See Georgi, ibid., 56–58 and 67–79.

150. On the use of the priestly metaphor for both the mission and the collection, see Georgi, ibid., 75–76.

151. The anger of the Jews is directed at Paul's assertion that uncircumcised Gentiles (on which see below) have become Israelites and children of Abraham and of God by virtue of their faith in God's promise to Abraham and in its fulfillment in both Christ and the Gentiles who have accepted Christ as its initial fulfillment. See Romans 4, 9, Galatians 3—4, and the discussion of Abraham and Christ in chap. 3, below. In this light, the presentation in Jerusalem of the collection from the Gentiles is public testimony to their conviction that through Christ God has adopted them as his children, and therefore as Israelites. For Paul, the offering of the Gentiles is proof that God has fulfilled his promise. The Jews, on the other hand, are angry not at God but at what Paul says God has done. From what we can learn from Paul, it is apparent that many Jews, probably most of them, do not accept what he says God has done, but rather see him, Paul, as having betrayed both his people and their God. Paul's problem with the Jews, his own people, is to get them to see that he is only God's agent and that it is God who is behind the events they deplore. While we have no record of Paul's communications with his fellow Jews, we can see from the letter to Rome that his strategy is to show them how the conversion of the Gentiles fits into the Jewish symbolic universe—as the result of God's fulfillment of

193

his promise to Abraham. Paul's presentation of the collection in Jerusalem is a public demonstration of this "fact." Our present concern is more with sociological matters than with Paul's symbolic universe, on which see chap. 3.

152. In Rom. 1:13–14 Paul describes the Gentiles, i.e., non-Jews, as consisting of Greeks and "barbarians," i.e., non-Greeks, and subsequently he uses "Greek" to refer to Gentiles. His national distinction between Jew and Greek is interesting for two reasons. First, the distinction breaks down two prior ethnocentric distinctions, those between Greeks and barbarians and between Jews and Gentiles, in which others, barbarians and Gentiles, are contrasted with one's own group, Greeks and Jews. In other words, non-Greeks and non-Jews would not identify themselves as barbarians or Gentiles, unless they were legally or politically forced to do so—by Greeks or by Jews. Therefore, when Paul puts "Greeks" and "Jews" together, he cancels out the pejorative ethnocentric habit of viewing others in contrast with one's own group. In the process, he creates a different understanding of the relations between the two groups. Second, this new understanding is theocentric rather than ethnocentric. In his letter to Rome the new understanding has two aspects. One is the equality of Jews and Greeks in terms a) of being equally under the power of sin, b) of having the same God, and c) of having the same possibility of being justified before this God by faith in Christ the Lord. This equality is reflected when Paul speaks of "both Jew and Greek" (3:9–30; cf. 10:12 and 1 Cor. 1:22–24). We should also note that in the church the distinction between Jew and Greek does not obtain (cf. 1 Cor. 12:13; Gal. 3:28), and thus Paul can distinguish between Jews, Greeks, and the church of God (1 Cor. 10:32). The second aspect of the new understanding is represented in temporal terms when Paul speaks about "first the Jew, and also the Greek." In Rom. 1:16 the gospel is said to be the power of God for salvation to everyone who has faith, "to the Jew first and also to the Greek," and in 2:10 Paul says that God's judgment will be upon "the Jew first and also the Greek." Because 2:10 refers to an eschatological sequence, it is the missionary sequence represented in 1:16 that is of most interest to us. But in order to understand it we have to look at other parts of Romans in which the terms Jew and Greek are not brought together so formulaically. The first text is 5:12–21. In it Paul represents the history of God's creation from Adam through Moses to Christ, all "Jews." This history is updated in the second text, 11:17–24, the parable or allegory of God's olive tree. Here the Jews are the tree and the Gentiles are a wild olive shoot that God has grafted into the tree after removing some of the natural branches. The old Jew/Gentile (cf. "Gentile" in 11:11–14, 25–26) distinction is baldly represented in the contrast between the cultivated tree and the wild olive tree, but the point of most interest is that it is only after some Jews were cut off because of their unbelief (11:20) that some Gentiles were grafted into the cultivated tree by virtue of their belief. "The Jew first" corresponds to the events that occasioned the disbelief of some Jews, while "and also the Greek" corresponds to the occasion that led to the belief of

some Gentiles. The third text, 15:8–12, brings together the first two texts and supplies a motive for the process represented by the expression, "to the Jew first and also to the Greek." Christ became a servant to the Jews, Paul says, in order that the Gentiles might glorify God for his mercy. That is to say, even before some Jews rejected Christ it was God's plan to include the Gentiles among his people. That plan is laid out in Romans 9—11, which is discussed above, and Paul's role in that plan, also discussed above, is indicated in Rom. 1:1–15 and 15:14–33. This role has to be read into the plan of Romans 9—11 because it is not explicitly mentioned here.

153. Paul does *not* see the movement from Jew to Gentile as causally related in terms of God's sending him to the Gentiles only because some Jews rejected the gospel (as in Luke-Acts). For Paul, God's intent for the inclusion of the Gentiles was announced by or in connection with Moses, Abraham, David, and the prophets (Romans 4; 9:22–23; 10:18–21; 11:7–10), and it was already a motive for God's giving his son up to death (Rom. 15:8–12; cf. Gal. 3:13–14; 2 Cor. 8:9).

154. Cf. Georgi, *Die Geschichte der Kollekte*, 84–87.

155. This point raises a number of issues that I cannot deal with here because they would take us too far beyond our present concerns. Probably the principal issues have to do with the form of Paul's thought, with his symbolic universe, and with the development of both his thought and his symbolic universe. We do not "have" either of the latter in any one letter, and each letter either or both has or lacks things we find in other letters. Moreover, Paul seems to have drawn elements from his symbolic universe, perhaps even added them to it, as the occasion demanded, and then thought about them in an equally ad hoc manner. Patterns can be observed when he repeats himself, as in Romans and Galatians, but it is exceedingly difficult to know what patterns are primary (or "central") and what secondary, or whether it makes any sense at all to speak of primary or secondary (or of a "center"). What, for example, does it really mean to speak about the development of Paul's thought? Development presupposes a base to which some things are added and others perhaps altered or even dropped. But what is the base? What is added to it, altered in it, or subtracted from it? Some of these issues will concern us in chap. 3, but one of them requires attention here. That the Gentiles cannot become Jews if the Jews are to become jealous presupposes some frame of reference which establishes both the necessity of the Gentiles remaining Gentiles and the role of the Gentiles in making the Jews jealous. We see in Romans 9—11 one frame of reference, but this is from a late letter, possibly the last extant letter from Paul. When, therefore, did Paul arrive at this frame; for example, before or after the episode in Antioch in which he took a position against the Gentiles having to become Jews? Similarly, the notion of the collection which looms so important in Romans 15 only arose at the meeting in Jerusalem just prior to the episode at Antioch and fourteen or seventeen years after his call to preach Christ to the Gentiles. When did Paul come to link the mission to the collection, and when did he come to view the presentation of the collec-

tion in Jerusalem as an occasion for provoking the Jews to jealousy? And last but not least, does Paul's notion of justification by faith derive from his sense of the provocative role of the Gentiles or produce it? Too often, I think, we presume that Paul had a constant encyclopedic knowledge of Jewish biblical and postbiblical texts and ideas, and a constant and coherent "theology" of his own. In this we surely presume too much.

156. For a recent suggestive and controversial attempt to describe an aspect of Paul's symbolic universe (its "pattern of religion") in relation to contemporary Judaism, see Sanders, *Paul and Palestinian Judaism*, and as an example of responses to his effort, see the reviews by Nils A. Dahl and Samuel Sandmel in *RSR* 4 (1978): 153–60. For the numerous and ongoing responses that are often less appreciative than those of Dahl and Sandmel, see the listing of reviews in *NTA*.

157. The three year difference derives from the uncertainty of whether Paul's reference to "after fourteen years" in Gal. 2:1 (cf. 2 Cor. 12:2) means fourteen years after the time of his call or fourteen years after the trip to Jerusalem three years after his call. See Kümmel, *Introduction to the New Testament*, 252–55; and Robert Jewett, *A Chronology of Paul's Life* (Philadelphia: Fortress Press, 1979), 47–104.

158. Nickle, *The Collection*, 70, thinks Paul's representation of the collection was a success, and Georgi, *Die Geschichte der Kollekte*, 87–90, suggests that it was received without enthusiasm (p. 89). We do not know from Paul's letters what happened upon his arrival, let alone how he responded to its reception. Acts 21:10–30 describes Paul's arrival and arrest but says nothing about the collection, which is only referred to in a speech attributed to Paul in 24:16–21. In this speech Paul indicates that while he was presenting "alms and offerings" some Jews expelled him from the temple and tried to kill him until some Roman soldiers intervened (in 24:16ff. Paul breaks off his description when he comes to mention the Jews; I have filled in the gap from 21:27ff.). However, the reliability of Acts is highly questionable for a number of reasons bearing on the presentation of the collection. Three points deserve mention. First, Luke does not reflect any awareness of the relationship between the mission and the collection that obtained from the time they first clearly came together in the meeting at Jerusalem, which in Acts 15 is described in terms very different from Paul's. In his entire description of Paul's activities from that meeting until after Paul's arrest there is no mention of the collection. Second, related to the different terms in which Luke and Paul describe the meeting at Jerusalem is Luke's rather systematic attempt to show the harmony between the different groups of Christians. If disharmony existed, as Paul suggests it did, Luke does not represent it. Third, corresponding to Luke's rendering of the harmonious relations within the church is his characterization of the Jews as being responsible for any disharmony associated with the church, as in Acts 21 and in the speech attributed to Paul in Acts 24. To be sure, Luke's report of Paul's words about the collection in 24:17 seem out of place, but they seem this way because the collection is not referred to previously.

Consequently, because Acts offers no indication that the hopes Paul envisioned in Romans 15 were fulfilled, I conclude that at least in Paul's terms his service failed, certainly among the Jews and probably also among the saints. If they had been fulfilled, Luke would have been the first to publicize this demonstration of harmony within the church.

159. On 1 Corinthians 9, see the references cited in n. 64, above.

160. This is especially evident in the Corinthian correspondence, Philippians 3, and Galatians.

161. See Bjerkelund, *Parakalō*, 13–23, 177–78; and from another perspective, Betz, *Galatians*, 253–55.

162. We should also note that Gal. 4:31 begins with a conclusive "therefore" (*dio*), which is the same word used in the transition to the hortatory section of the letter to Philemon (v. 8), where we would normally expect the transitional "therefore" (*oun*). See further Betz, *Galatians*, 251. Bjerkelund missed the whole process of redistribution described above because he concentrated on the hortatory sentence in Gal. 4:12.

163. See also Paul's use of his own name in the opening of the *parakalō* section of Philemon (v. 9). Betz, *Galatians*, 258 and n. 48, sees Paul's words in Gal. 5:2 as a mobilization of "his whole authority as an apostle." But while Betz refers to Philemon 9 as another instance of Paul's use of his name, he does not identify the combination of apostolic mobilization and rhetorical masking presented in this verse, a combination also found in a more sarcastic tone in 2 Cor. 10:1, which also introduces a *parakalō* section, 10:1—13:10.

164. See further Betz, ibid.

165. I refer specifically to ideas presented in Turner's *The Ritual Process*. For a more sociological than social anthropological view of certain phenomena that Turner calls "anti-structural," see Bryan Wilson, *Religious Sects* (New York: McGraw Hill, 1970), 22–35 and especially 36–47, on sectarian responses to the world. Under the heading of "deviant responses" Wilson describes many of Turner's "anti-structural" phenomena. For a review and bibliography of Wilson's work, see Donald E. Miller, "Sectarianism and Secularization: The Work of Bryan Wilson," *RSR* 5 (1979): 161–74. Meek's *The First Urban Christians* represents numerous insights drawn from both Turner and Wilson. It should be acknowledged, too, that Turner's notions are not accepted by all anthropologists because many of them are wary of global explanatory concepts in comparative studies (see, e.g., T. O. Beidelman, "The Moral Imagination of the Kaguru: Some Thoughts on Tricksters, Translation, and Comparative Analysis," *American Ethnologist* 7 [1980]: 27–42). In this regard, however, I am convinced that if Turner had not created the concepts of structure and anti-structure, we would have had to invent them ourselves in order to account for what we see in Paul's letters. Looked at from another angle, Paul's letters lend further support to many of Turner's ideas.

166. Simmel, *The Sociology of Georg Simmel*, 181–303. Cf. Schütz, *Collected Papers*, 2:270.

167. The views summarized here come from Turner, *The Ritual Process*, 94–203. See also the list of oppositions between structural and anti-structural categories on 106–7.

168. Cf. Wilson's definition of a sect: "The term *sect* is applied broadly to all religious movements that emphasize their separateness and distinctiveness of mission, regardless of their organizational character" (Wilson, *Religious Sects*, 16). See also Meeks, *The First Urban Christians*, 84–107 and 159–62.

169. On 1 Cor. 5:9–13 see Wayne Meeks, " 'Since then you would need to go out of the world': Group Boundaries in Pauline Christianity," in *Critical History and Biblical Faith: New Testament Perspectives*, ed. Thomas J. Ryan, The Annual Publication of the College Theology Society (Villanova: The College Theology Society, 1979), 4–29; and more recently, Meeks, *The First Urban Christians*, 94–105.

170. See Robin Fox, *Kinship and Marriage: An Anthropological Perspective* (Baltimore: Penguin Books, 1967); and more briefly, Malina, *The New Testament World*, 94–121.

171. See Turner, *The Ritual Process*, 104 (on sexual continence). Libertinism or promiscuity can be equally anti-structural (pp. 112–13), and this may be a position taken by some who misconstrued Paul's teaching about freedom (cf. Gal. 5:10), especially some in Corinth who considered all things lawful (1 Cor. 6:12; 10:23—11:1; cf. 5:1–5). Indeed, Paul's anti-structural teaching about marriage (1 Corinthians 7) follows immediately upon his repudiation of anti-structural immorality (6:12–20). The hermeneutical significance of Turner's notions are readily evident in both cases, because in each case anti-structural behavior is not entertained merely for its own sake, for its intrinsic value, but as a means of demonstrating the difference between life in Christ and life in the world. Anti-structural behavior is therefore symbolic behavior.

172. Contextually, 1 Cor. 7:17–24 seems to form a conclusion to 7:1–16. However, this "conclusion" also appears to have helped Paul reshape his previous comments when he proceeded to give instructions to the unmarried in 7:25–40. First Cor. 7:26–27 is clearly influenced by the idea of remaining in the state in which one was called (7:17–24), but 7:28–38 repeats in another form much of what Paul said in 7:1–16.

173. For a full discussion of these verses see Bartchy, *Mallōn Chrēsai;* and more briefly Conzelmann, *1 Corinthians*, 127–28.

174. See also Col. 3:11 and Lohse, *Colossians and Philemon*, 143–46; Betz, *Galatians*, 182–201; and Meeks, *The First Urban Christians*, 88 and 150–57. Meeks describes this as a "reunification formula," which is discussed in chap. 3, below.

175. In addition to Meeks, ibid., see especially Käsemann, *Commentary on Romans*, 227–28; and also Betz, *Galatians*, 210–11.

176. See Conzelmann, *1 Corinthians*, 246, and n. 106, above.

177. I use the notion of segmentation to indicate nonhierarchical social distinctions. See Turner, *The Ritual Process*, 131; and Berger and Luck-

mann, *The Social Construction of Reality*, 82 and n. 52, and p. 199. The notion of segmentation is also used by anthropologists in a narrower sense to refer to the formation of sub-lineages within large descent groups (Fox, *Kinship and Marriage*, 122–31). For a hierarchical interpretation of the segmentary distinctions, see Madeleine Boucher, "Some Unexplored Parallels to 1 Cor. 11:11–12 and Gal. 3:28: The New Testament on the Role of Women," *CBQ* 31 (1969): 50–58 (especially 56); and Ben Witherington, "Rite and Rites for Women—Gal. 3:28," *NTS* 27 (1981): 593–604. Although in some contexts the individual distinctions may have a hierarchical connotation (e.g., 1 Cor. 11:11–12), in Paul's treatment of them in 1 Cor. 12:13 and Gal. 3:28 he contrasts the segmentary structural differences with their anti-structural unity. This is different from his anti-structural inversion of apparently hierarchical structures in 1 Cor. 7:22 and 9:19.

178. See further Meeks, *The First Urban Christians*, 87–89 and chap. 3, below, on the asexuality of "sons of God," which is seemingly contradicted by the idea of brothers *and sisters* in the church.

179. Ibid., 150–57 and his diagram on p. 160. On initiation rites see Turner, *The Ritual Process*, 94–97, and 102–8; and Arnold van Gennep, *The Rites of Passage*, trans. Monika B. Vizedom and G. L. Caffee (Chicago: Univ. of Chicago Press, 1960) 65–115.

180. For references see n. 81, above, and for further discussion, chap. 3, below.

181. See the discussion above on the metaphors of work and of the body.

182. See Turner, *The Ritual Process*, 131–65, 203.

183. See Lévi-Strauss, *Structural Anthropology* 1:206–31, and 224 for an example of the model employed below. Because Lévi-Strauss's thought is exceedingly complex, I will not complicate our discussion by elaborating further on it. The maps below will suffice to show how oppositions are mediated in certain areas of Paul's thought. A fairly simple introduction to the complexities of Lévi-Strauss's thought may be found in Edmund Leach, *Claude Lévi-Strauss* (New York: Viking Press, 1970), and especially chap. 2, "Oysters, Smoked Salmon, and Stilton Cheese." The model of mediations will also be employed in chap. 3, below.

184. In order to avoid cluttering up the map, I will omit "fellow soldier" and "fellow prisoner," which are probably synonymous with "fellow worker" (Ollrog, *Paulus und seine Mitarbeiter*, 76–77). In any event, the two omitted categories do not represent roles played by the principals in our story.

185. Here we must be careful not to confuse social structural or mythic mediations with the kind of ethical mediation we find in Col. 3:18—4:1, Eph. 6:1–9, and in Pliny's correspondence with Sabinianus (printed in Lohse, *Colossians and Philemon*, 196–97).

3

SYMBOLIC UNIVERSE AND SOCIAL RELATIONS IN THE STORY OF PHILEMON

The limits of my language mean the limits of my world.[1]

Ludwig Wittgenstein

[S]ymbolic universes . . . are sheltering canopies over the institutional order as well as over individual biography. They . . . set the limits of what is relevant in terms of social interaction.[2]

Berger and Luckmann

The Letter to Philemon has usually been found uninteresting because of its lack of "theological" content in comparison with others of Paul's letters. But it is precisely this lack that makes the letter and its story *sociologically* interesting, for the unexplained use of certain symbolic terms shows that those to whom Paul is speaking share with him knowledge about at least those aspects of his symbolic universe in which these terms function. He presumes that his addressees understand what it means to speak of God as their "father" (v. 3) and of themselves as "brothers" and "sisters" of one another (vv. 1, 7, 16, 20); and he presumes that they know what it means to speak of Christ as the "master" or "lord" (*kyrios*, vv. 3, 4, 16, 20, 25). Indeed, and more comprehensively, they know that "faith in Christ" entails "the knowledge of all the good" they possess by virtue of their being "in Christ" (v. 6). Being "in Christ" thus represents a comprehensive reality whose principal coordinates are Christ's lordship over them, which entails their faithful enslavement to him, and God's fatherhood, in relation to which they are all brothers and sisters of one another. All that is good for them is bounded by their being "in Christ," and this good is realized in their loving relations with one another as fellow children of God and fellow slaves of Christ (vv. 5, 7, 9). Their relations with God and Christ therefore define their ultimate social identities, limit and

200

motivate their behavior, and assure them of their goodness (vv. 6, 14). It is true that this knowledge is not "theology," but it is also true that it constitutes a "world," a symbolic universe. It is our task in the present chapter to explore this universe in order to understand more fully its implications for the social relations of the actors in the story of Philemon. This task is sociological because it poses problems that must be dealt with in the related terms of the sociology of knowledge and symbolic anthropology, but it is also literary because it is concerned with the construction of Paul's narrative world. Narrative worlds, like other worlds, also have symbolic universes.

In order to prepare ourselves for this stage in our exploration of Paul's narrative world, we might best begin by answering the question of why the knowledge Paul shares with his addressees is not "theological." The answer is important because we will be dealing with matters that are usually thought of as being theological. For this reason, we need to develop further the distinction we made earlier between theology and symbolic universes.[3]

Theology can take many forms, but traditional theological *criticism* usually does one of two things, and on occasion it does both. One is to describe Paul's thought as Paul's *theology*, thereby assuming that his thought is theological and that he is a theologian, even though the word "theology" did not mean in Paul's time what it means today, and even though in his time there was no recognizable social role called "theologian."[4] In addition, following one approach Paul's "theology" is usually treated in historical and comparative terms, in which his ideas or "doctrines" are related to those of other contemporary "Christians" (a word also not yet invented, or at least not in currency as a self-identification), or to the history of "Christian," Jewish, or Greco-Roman ideas. As we can observe in any book on biblical theology or on Paul's theology, it is the content and logical relations of Paul's central ideas or doctrines that is the ultimate object and product of this form of criticism. But the same object and product is also found in the other type of theological criticism which tends, however, to be less historical and comparative and rather seeks to affirm the "theology" pieced together from Paul's letters. Thus the one form of criticism tends to be more historical, the other more normative. The one is interested in Paul's theology as something other than our own; the other is interested in it as something upon which our theology depends.[5]

It is in this context that we must answer the question of why the knowledge Paul shares with his addressees in the Letter to Philemon is not "theological." It would be too simplistic, but not altogether inaccurate, to respond that because Paul *could* not have been a theologian, since there was no such role in his world, his thought cannot have been theological unless we reckon him to be the first theologian. More to the point is the response that regardless of whether or not there was such a thing as a theologian in Paul's world, or whether or not Paul was the first one, *theology is a form of systematic reflection upon prior knowledge.*[6] From the point of view of the sociology of knowledge and of its forms and functions, this prior knowledge collectively constitutes a symbolic universe and theology is a form of systematic reflection upon it or its parts. The Letter to Philemon is sociologically interesting, therefore, because in the knowledge Paul communicates to his addressees in the letter, he is not theologizing *about* his and their symbolic universe but referring to it directly in language and concepts taken from it. The shared knowledge cited above is not itself in the form of theology, but neither does it refer to a theological system. Although the knowledge is expressed in the form of concepts or ideas that *can* refer to a theology, here they refer to a reality that is defined, shaped, and represented by the knowledge Paul and his addressees have of it. This reality is their symbolic universe.[7]

The distinction between theology and symbolic universes as two different forms of knowledge is fundamental for our exploration because we will be concentrating on segments of Paul's symbolic universe, not of his theology. Our exploration can be successful only if we remember what it is that we are exploring, for we will quickly find ourselves tempted to follow the wrong path. The reason for the temptation is already suggested in the definition of theology as a form of reflection upon a symbolic universe, for the same symbols will appear in both the symbolic universe and the theological reflection. Thus, when we come to a given symbol we can follow it along the path of the symbolic universe or along the path of the theology. We will be taking the former path, and if we come across a symbol in the context of Paul's "theologizing," now understood in terms of the sociology of knowledge, we will have to work through the theologizing to the symbol's context in his symbolic universe. The critical point, however, is the context, because the same symbol may well have one context in the theology and another in the symbolic universe.[8] Indeed, the difference between these contexts further differentiates theologies from their symbolic universes.

The knowledge of which symbolic universes are comprised is, like the knowledge contained in an encyclopedia, virtually inexhaustible and subject to change over time, both for individual persons and for total communities. No one person can possess the totality of this knowledge and, encyclopedias notwithstanding, there is no one communal repository for it.[9] The knowledge is possessed in the form of pieces or clusters of pieces, or of frames, and as inherited communal products they are subject over time to alteration and rearrangement by individuals like Paul as well as by communities like, for example, Corinth. Like the words in a dictionary, the pieces of knowledge can be put together to form different messages, but always within the constraints of a grammar of structuring principles. In this light theology is, as a *systematizing* form of reflection on the contents and structures of symbolic universes, one means of introducing *a new or revised order,* and therefore new meaning, to certain segments of the universes, or even to the whole. Consequently, when we come to a theological statement we have to work back from *its* order, to the order it is reshaping. For example, when Paul addresses the idea of freedom in 1 Corinthians, he is dealing with the view of some Corinthians that their freedom is from all laws (cf. 1 Cor. 6:12–20; 10:23—11:1). However, this view seems to represent a systematic misinterpretation of a prior notion of freedom they learned from Paul, a notion that is part of the symbolic universe he presupposes in his letter to Galatia, where freedom is from the Law of Moses and cosmic powers, not from *all* laws (cf. Gal. 4:1—6:6). Thus, we have one symbolic notion in two contexts. But there is also a third context, for in his letter to Rome Paul reflects more systematically on the idea of freedom than he did in the letter to Galatia and now sees freedom as liberation from the "law" of sin and death to which he relates the Law of Moses (cf. Romans 5—8). This example well illustrates a point made in chapter 2 concerning the problem of identifying constants both in Paul's thought and in his symbolic universe, given the lack of their full appearance in any one letter and the probability that they changed somewhat during the period from his call to be an apostle to the time of his last extant letters (e.g., the idea of the collection for Jerusalem). But the example also illustrates a possible constant or base-system in Paul's symbolic universe, because it suggests that Galatians rather than 1 Corinthians or Romans represents the most basic image from his symbolic universe, and that the other two letters contain reflections upon it, first by the Corinthians, who got the image wrong, and second by Paul, who theologically elaborated on it in Romans. On the other hand, however, in all three textual contexts we can see that the idea of freedom is a symbol bound up with the ideas of slavery, of Christ as the one through whom men have been freed from slavery, and of Christ as the new master of his "free slaves." The symbol of freedom is, therefore, bound up with several other

203

symbols to form a system within Paul's symbolic universe, one we will call the master-slave system. It is with such systems as this that we are concerned. The example itself will be taken up again below in our more extended exploration of this system. For now I wish only to add that while it will not be our task to show in every case the relationships between such symbolic systems and Paul's "theology," we frequently will be moving from the latter to the former. As in the case of "freedom," we will be confronted with statements that are not direct representations of his symbolic universe. Even a hasty reading of his letters reveals that Paul represents his knowledge of his symbolic universe in a variety of ways, sometimes directly in the form of proclamation, teaching, or even quotations, and sometimes in more systematizing and reflective forms of argumentation *about* that knowledge. Nevertheless, as in the story of Philemon it is the knowledge of the symbolic universe in which the actors live that now concerns us, not the rhetoric or the conceptual forms through which that knowledge is communicated.

Because our point of departure is in the shared knowledge represented in the Letter to Philemon, we have the advantage of starting with two fundamental features of Paul's symbolic universe, the kinship system and the master-slave system. These are among the most stable systems we can find in his letters and they are landmarks in the symbolic universe of his narrative world. As in our exploration of social relations, we will limit ourselves to the knowledge communicated by Paul in his letters, and we will not seek historical-comparative knowledge from other sources. Similarly, as in our exploration of social relations, we will begin with the language Paul uses, only now we will be looking for the symbolic systems in which this language functions, not systems of social relations or their structures. Because the language is symbolic, integrating the social realities of everyday experience into realities that transcend that experience, like the fatherhood of God and the lordship of Christ, we will, as it were, be viewing everyday social realities from above rather than from below, in terms, that is, of cognitive rather than of sociological systems and their structures. Ultimately, however, the two views come together because social existence always takes place within a symbolic universe. An illustration of this based on information drawn from Paul's letters may help us to appreciate both the unity of the two views and the peculiar character of the one with which we are presently concerned.

The total social-symbolic universe represented in Paul's letters is like a theater featuring a play in which the audience has a part. The theater is the spatial framework of his symbolic universe; the audience consists of the social actors with whom Paul relates; and the play enacted on the stage is the temporally and dramatically shaped aspect of his symbolic universe.[10] Paul is a member of the audience who claims that his role has been given to him by one of the actors on the stage ("God"), and his role is both to inform others in the audience about the play and the roles assigned to them, and to assist them in their performances. Importantly, the production is one in which the audience, and we ourselves, only know from the likes of Paul what has happened, is happening, and will happen both on the stage and in the theater. Neither the audience nor we readers can see what is taking place on the stage; we only know about it from what Paul tells us. We are all totally dependent upon him, or upon others who say the same or similar things, for our knowledge about the audience's roles and about the play itself.[11]

By distinguishing between the theater that encompasses the whole, the on-stage play, and the audience, we can grasp both the whole and the relations between its social (audience) and symbolic (on-stage) parts. But most importantly, the distinctions help us to understand the difference between Paul's symbolic universe and what he says about it. As indicated earlier, his communications about it take many forms. Some things he simply describes in narrative form (*diēgēsis*), like what God, Abraham, Moses, or Christ have done, are doing, or will do; some things he merely refers to as events, persons, or states already known to his audiences, like the fatherhood of God and his promises to Abraham, and like the death, resurrection, and lordship of Christ; and some things he merely quotes, like words of David, Moses, or Christ, all actors on the stage. Yet other things, however, are the objects of theoretical or moral reflection, and the communications that follow from such reflection serve, on the one hand, to explain or interpret on-stage activities, and on the other hand, to secure behavior by the play's audience that is consistent with these activities. In all cases, the knowledge that Paul communicates serves to motivate behavior. Those in the audience respond by doing some things *because* of this knowledge, and they also do the same or other things *in order to* achieve ends the knowledge defines.[12]

In this light, then, we can say that in the previous chapter we were concerned with the parts assigned to the audience, and on occasion with some of the explanations Paul offered about the parts. For example, his work and body metaphors and his explanation of relations between Jews and Gentiles all represent his reflection on the play as a whole, or upon certain of its scenes and acts, or upon some of the patterns governing the roles of actors both on the stage and in the audience. In the present chapter, on the other hand, our concern is to concentrate on the play on the stage. Our goal is to determine the plot of the play and the way it shapes the behavior of the participant audience. In other words, we are shifting our focus from the social relations of the audience to the symbolic universe of the theater. Because we are taking our point of departure from the story of Philemon, our first task is to consider the principal actors in Paul's symbolic universe, God and Christ, and the symbolic systems of social relations in which *they* participate. In subsequent sections, we will explore these systems further, and in the process attend to the emplotment of the actors' actions and their relevance to the audience. Needless to say, Paul's symbolic universe is as sociologically structured as his world of social relations, a world where social distinctions are determined by the symbolic universe. Believers are sons of God, slaves of Christ, brothers and sisters of one another, and fellow slaves.

THE KINSHIP AND MASTER-SLAVE SYSTEMS: A PRELIMINARY SURVEY

Within Paul's symbolic universe, the metaphoric images of God as "our Father" and of Christ as "the" or "our Lord" are what one anthropologist, James Fernandez, has called "organizing metaphors," for they "provide images in relation to which the organization of behavior can take place."[13] The possessive pronoun "our" indicates that believers relate to God and to one another as *his* children, and to Christ and to one another as *his* slaves. Terminologically, the foundational significance of these identifications of God, Christ, and the believer is suggested by Paul's formulaic references to them. On the one hand, as firm parts of his epistolary style he always greets his addressees by invoking "grace and peace from God our father and the Lord Jesus Christ" (Rom. 1:7; 1 Cor. 1:3; 2 Cor. 1:2; Gal. 1:3; Phil. 1:2; Philemon 3; cf. 1 Thess. 1:1, where the formula appears in the address rather than in the greeting),[14] and he consistently addresses them as "brethren" or "brothers" (*adelphoi*). On the other hand, from some of his letters we also find both that all believers ritually acclaim God by crying "Abba! Father!" (Rom. 8:15; Gal. 4:6), using *both* the Aramaic and the Greek words for "father," and that they all ritually confess Jesus' lordship by speaking of him as "Lord" (Rom. 10:9–13; 1 Cor. 12:3; Phil. 2:11), in one case summoning his presence by using the Aramaic *marana tha,* "Come, Lord!" (1 Cor. 16:22; cf. Rev. 22:20).[15] Because there are no other comparable descriptions of God or Christ, this formulaic evidence leaves no room for doubt about the centrality of kinship and master-slave metaphors in Paul's symbolic universe. However, this evidence does raise the interesting question of how the two metaphoric systems can *both* be central and equally "organizing," for in none of the texts just cited are the two systems related to one another. One of our principal problems is, therefore, to determine how they are related.

One possibility for relating the systems is found in a comment by Paul in 1 Cor. 8:1–7a.[16] Here the fatherhood of God and lordship of Christ are referred to as matters of communal knowledge that Paul contrasts with the popular belief, in the world outside the church, in many "gods" and many "lords" (8:5). Paul and the Corinthians *know* "that 'there is no God but one' " (8:4), and that "for us there is one God, the Father (*heis theos ho patēr*), from whom are all things and for whom we exist, and one Lord, Jesus Christ (*heis kyrios Iēsous Christos*), through whom are all things and through whom we exist" (8:6).[17] The prepositional clauses following the identification of God and the Lord suggest a relationship between them in which the Lord Jesus Christ mediates ("through whom") to believers what God the Father has created and predetermined ("from whom," "for whom"). But because Paul does not elaborate on this connection either here or elsewhere in precisely these terms,[18] this possibility remains undeveloped. However, Paul does develop another possibility for relating the kinship and master-slave systems in connection with the notion of "sons of God." Indeed, this notion is developed in two related ways, one associated with Christ, the other with believers. First, when focusing on Christ, Paul identifies God as "the father of our Lord, Jesus Christ" (Rom. 15:6; 2 Cor. 1:3; 11:31; cf. Eph. 1:3; Col. 1:3), or, conversely, when he focuses on God he speaks of Christ as God's "son, Jesus Christ our Lord" (1 Cor. 1:9; cf. Rom. 1:3–4).[19] One bridge between the kinship and master-slave systems is therefore the identification of the Lord as God's son. Second, when Paul focuses on believers we find him saying that through Christ's death they cease to be "slaves" and become "sons" or "children of God."[20] That this is part of the same bridge as the first one is confirmed by Rom. 8:29, where Paul refers to Christ, God's son and our Lord (cf. 8:39), as "the firstborn (*prōtotokon*) among many brethren," for here *the* son of God, Christ, is depicted as the eldest among the "children of God," indeed as the son *through whom* others become sons or children of God and with whom they are "fellow heirs" (cf.

8:17).[21] There is, however, one final twist in the bridge between the two metaphoric systems, for while Christ as the son of God made it possible for believers to become free from one form of enslavement, he also entered them into another, namely to himself as their Lord. Thus, Christ is both son of God and Lord, and through him believers become both children of God and slaves of Christ.

There is, therefore, no question *that* the kinship and master-slave systems are related in Paul's symbolic universe through the notion of the children of God, but there still remains the question of exactly *how* the two systems are related to form a single system. Despite the relationship, there are still two metaphorical systems and they cannot each be central and equally organizing. How, then, does the relationship between the two systems address this problem? To answer this question, and also to provide a framework for our more detailed exploration of Paul's symbolic universe, we can be aided by a "map" that we can follow in our exploration. Because the kinship notion of "sons/children of God" bridges the kinship and the master-slave systems, let us begin with the kinship system.

For the anthropologist, Paul's symbolic kinship system appears to be a strange one indeed, for while it has a father and children of both sexes (brothers and sisters), it lacks a mother, except for Gal. 4:21–31, where "the Jerusalem above" is called "our mother" (4:26),[22] and it has no term for daughters.[23] Even more distinctively, the kinship system consists of only two generations, those of the father and of his children, for after the firstborn male Jesus Christ, the son of God, all of the rest of the children of God are generated through Christ without a spouse.[24] We will find other peculiarities than these, especially in connection with the role of Abraham, but these are quite sufficient to show that while Paul conceives of the relationship between God and his people in kinship terms, he does so with extreme symbolic freedom. And it is especially important for us to recognize this freedom because Paul explicitly and persistently contrasts his symbolic system with literal biological genealogies like those with which the anthropologist works (cf. Rom. 9:1– 13 and below on Abraham, Adam, and Christ). Since Paul is self-conscious about the difference between literal and symbolic kinship structures, we can profit from a comparison of them based on the anthropological shorthand for representing the structures of kinship relations. The shorthand language is simple: a triangle represents a male, a circle a female, an equal sign a reproductive relationship between them (e.g., marriage or concubinage), and a line descending from the equal sign represents the link to their offspring, as in the diagram below.

male   female

=

males   females

This diagram represents two generations, one of a father and mother, the other of their four children. To indicate another generation proceeding from the offspring of the first one, we have to add another set of parents and, for example, their daughter in order to provide a wife for a second generation male. Because we will have to explore later the contrast Paul makes between his symbolic kinship system and the literal kinship relations of Abraham, Hagar, Sarah and their descendants (Romans 4; 9:6–13; Gal. 4:21–31), we can use this family to illustrate multiple generations.

Hagar   Abraham   Sarah   Rebeccah's parents

=   =   =

=

Ishmael   Isaac   Rebeccah

Jacob   Esau

Finally, in order to represent the relationship of kinship *descent* between Abraham, Isaac, and Jacob, with which Paul is also concerned, the shorthand can be adapted to a slightly different format.

Abraham   =   Sarah

Isaac   =   Rebeccah

Jacob

Viewed on this backdrop of normal or literal kinship relations, Paul's symbolic kinship system is singularly anomalous, as we can see in the next diagram.

209

God

Christi   other children of God

Our anthropological shorthand points to two anomalies in this diagram, each of which requires explanation. The first concerns the generation of the firstborn son of God from God alone; the second concerns the generation of other children of God from the son of God. Later we will see that both anomalies are bound up with the direct creation of an image (*eikōn*) of the creator. For now, it is necessary to focus on the relationship between the firstborn and subsequent children of God, and for this we have to go beyond the shorthand system and recognize that for Paul those who become children of God after the firstborn son do so through *a process of adoption* (Rom. 8:12–24, 29; Gal. 4:4–7).[25] Subsequent children of God are not "generated" by even a symbolic reproductive process, and that is why the language of kinship shorthand cannot represent it. Paul's symbolic kinship system therefore has to be represented in some other "language," and in order to discover that language we have to survey in a preliminary way the process of adoption as Paul represents it.

The adoption process is first and foremost a *process* because it has a beginning, middle, and end, all of which Paul envisions as taking place within the lifetime of his generation (cf. 1 Cor. 7:25–31; 15:51–52; 1 Thess. 4:13–17). The process begins with Christ's death, following which the children-to-be are baptized "into Christ," that is, symbolically into his death and socially into the church. But baptism is also symbolically into Christ's resurrection from the dead, for Paul says that having been united with Christ baptismally into a death like his, the child-to-be looks forward to being united with him in a resurrection like his (Rom. 6:5–11) when he returns (e.g., 1 Corinthians 15). Consequently, until Christ's return the child-to-be is "in Christ," and when Christ returns, the adoption process will end because those who have died will be raised from the dead like Christ was, and then all will have their physical bodies transformed into a new form, the form of the children of God, which completes the adoption process (Rom. 8:18–25; 1 Corinthians 15; 2 Cor. 5:1–19; 1 Thess. 4:13–17; Phil. 3:20–21). At baptism, too, the children-to-be receive a "spirit of adoptive sonship" (Rom. 8:15–17) which is a down-payment on or a guarantee of the completion of the process (2 Cor. 1:22; 5:5; cf. 1 Cor. 15:20). And it is this spirit that enables the child-to-be to cry, "Abba! Father!", in anticipation of the process's completion (Rom. 8:12–17; Gal. 4:4–7). Prior to baptism into Christ, candidates for adoption are merely human beings, "men," not only because they live "in the flesh," but also because they live *in terms of the flesh (kata sarka)*. But after baptism and prior to the redemption of their physical bodies, the children-to-be are "in Christ" the son of God, and they have symbolically died to the flesh with Christ and now live in terms of the spirit (*kata pneuma*, cf. Rom. 6:5–11; 8:1–39; Gal. 5:16–25). To be sure, Paul says that the children-to-be *are* sons and children of God by virtue of their baptism, but the symbolic and rhetorical character of such statements is established both by his repeated references to the process described above and by explicit statements, often made in the same breath as the others, that the adoption process is only completed with the future redemption of the children-to-be's bodies (e.g., Rom. 8:9–25). In addition, while the adoption process thus has a beginning, middle, and end for the children-to-be, it also has an end for Christ's role in it. His role in the process began with his being sent as God's son, and after his death and resurrection the children-to-be live "in him." But Paul also says that when Christ returns he will deliver the kingdom of God to the Father and, as God's son and the Lord to whom all things have previously been subordinated, he will subordinate *himself* to God, "that God may be everything to everyone" (1 Cor. 15:24–28). Therefore, when *as* children of God the believers assume "the image of the man of heaven" (15:19–50), that is, of Christ's glorious body (Phil. 3:20–21), which is the form of the sons of God (Rom. 8:29), there will only be the Father and his children. The firstborn among many brethren will take his place among the other children of God in the presence of their Father.

At this juncture we need to observe further that the master-slave system coincides with the limited duration of the superordinacy of Christ, God's son. Because in social terms being "in the Lord" is synonymous with being "in Christ," the believer is, in the interim between baptism and the eschatological redemption from the physical body, a slave to Christ Jesus the Lord. We will find that the kinship and master-slave systems therefore both overlap and interpenetrate at a number of points during this period, but for now the most noteworthy point is one that also differentiates the two systems. The two overlap in terms of their common negative judgment about the physical body, but they differ in their focus. The kinship system focuses on the completion of adoption as children of God as a *future* event associated with the redemption from and the transformation of the body, while the master-slave system focuses on the

211

present form of bodily existence as a condition of enslavement (cf. Phil. 2:7–8; Rom. 6:15–23; 8:19–21). Prior to baptism one is enslaved to the sinful body of flesh (Rom. 6:5–23) and to cosmic powers (Gal. 4:1–11; 5:1), but after baptism one is free from these bonds and is enslaved to Christ as Lord (1 Cor. 7:21–23; cf. 6:20). And once again, because the lordship of Christ pertains to the time of the believer's life in bodily form, Christ's lordship, like his superordinacy as the firstborn son of God, ends when this form is "redeemed." His lordship functions only as long as the believer remains in the body, for one is a "slave," whether to sin or to Christ as Lord, only by virtue of being in bodily form, which is the form of enslavement. When this form is eliminated, there are no longer slaves or masters, only children of God, and for this reason the master-slave *system* ceases to function when the body is finally redeemed. Thus *the master-slave system is related to the kinship system as one symbolic representation of a stage within the process by which God adopts his children.*

We are now in a position to return to the question of whether or not the two symbolic systems form a single system within Paul's symbolic universe. We have just seen that they combine within a single system because the master-slave system is relevant to but one stage in the temporal aspect of the kinship system and its adoption process. The kinship system provides the structure of Paul's symbolic universe, while the master-slave system is mapped onto one of its parts. But can we take this affirmative answer a step further by drawing a "map" of this single system? Again, we must answer affirmatively, but to do so we have to abandon the anthropologists' kinship shorthand because it is inadequate to the task of representing the process of adoption. Indeed, the idea of a *process* now becomes critical, for it introduces a temporal dimension to our "map" and a plot to Paul's symbolic universe. In addition to the adoption process having a beginning, middle, and end, it also has a "before," a "now," and a "then"—a time before one enters the process, the time of the process itself, with its beginning and middle, and the future time of the completion of the adoption process. In this light, when we remember that each of *these* three stages also entails a different relationship between the individual ("man") and God, the shape of our map begins to come into focus. For while the anthropologists' kinship shorthand fails to help us with Paul's symbolic kinship system, their model of mediations once again comes to our assistance.[26] This model can represent both the structure of the symbolic kinship system with its adoption process and the place of the master-slave system within it, and in so doing it reveals the adoption process to be part of *a process of mediation.* We have seen that Paul's symbolic universe has the character of a drama become narrative, because the drama is known in the form of story. Now we will be able to see that the plot of this story, and therefore the dramatic structure of Paul's symbolic universe, is based on a system of temporally sequential mediations, mediations achieved by the adoption process.

The model of mediations that governs Paul's symbolic universe has three temporally sequential stages. *In the first stage,* prior to Christ's death and the believer's baptism as the entry into candidacy for adoption, the individual person, "man," *is in a position radically opposed to God.* As a result of the transgression of the first man created by God, Adam, "man" is both alienated from and opposed to God by "sin," and "he" is subject to death, that is, mortality (cf. Romans 5—8; 1 Cor. 15:42–57; 2 Cor. 5:1–5).[27] God is immortal, "man" mortal, and therefore mortality is the boundary line that separates God the Father from "man" whom he created. In the second stage, this opposition between God and "man" is objectively mediated in Paul's symbolic universe by the death and resurrection of God's son, through which God reconciled "man" to himself (Rom. 5:6–11; 2 Cor. 5:16–21). This act of reconciliation is subjectively, that is, personally mediated for individuals by their internalizing of it through faith in what God has done, is doing, and will do to bridge the gap between himself and "man" (cf. Rom. 5:1–21; 10:8–13). In turn, one's internalization of God's mediation is *socially* expressed by baptism "into Christ," God's son, and by behaviorally conforming to Christ by walking according to the baptismal spirit. Thus, *in the second stage the beginning of the process of adoption is the beginning of the process of mediation, a process graphically represented by the lesser and temporary opposition between Christ as God's son and those who are "in him."* Despite the unity between Christ and the children of God–to–be that is implied by the notion of being "in Christ," Christ the son of God has fully experienced what the believer has experienced only in part, and what the believer can only fully experience by remaining in Christ. Christ has overcome the body of sin and death in *his* death and resurrection, and he has reassumed the glorious body that the believer will only assume at the end of the processes of adoption and mediation. Christ is the firstborn among many brethren, but their "birth" has yet to be accomplished; being "in Christ" they are, as it were, in the womb of their brother! For this reason, the terms "son of God" and "those in him" remain opposed. But while this opposition is somewhat obscured by the temporal peculiarity of the sibling relations between the firstborn son of God and those who *will become* other children of

God, the structural opposition is more clearly evident in the symbolic master-slave system.

As we have seen, the master-slave system applies to the same stage as the beginning and middle of the process of adoption because being "in the Lord" is synonymous with being "in Christ." Thus, the lordship of Christ and the believers' enslavement to him serve as another representation of the first stage in the mediation of the opposition between God and "man." That this system represents the beginning of a process of mediation is significant because in the previous chapter we saw that the literal master-slave relationship in the world was one that lacked any *structural mediation.* The symbolic form of the master-slave system differs because it *is* mediated precisely by its temporary character, for it obtains only during the period in which the believer inhabits the form of flesh and blood. This period ends, and along with it the applicability of the master-slave system, when Christ returns from heaven to bring the dead back to life and to change the lowly bodies of all believers into the likeness of his glorious body (Phil. 3:20–21). The symbolic master-slave system is, therefore, designed to be mediated by being structurally superseded. Thus, *in the third stage the redemption of the body constitutes the completion of the processes of adoption and mediation, for the fleshly form of enslavement will be replaced by the glorious form of the children of God* (Rom. 8:18–25). Becoming a child of God in this way is the ultimate mediation between God and "man" because "man in Christ" is now in the form of Christ which, we will find, is the form not only of all children of God, but also of God himself, for Christ's form is God's (cf. Phil. 2:6, 3:20–21; Rom. 8:29; 1 Cor. 15:47–50; 2 Cor. 4:4, 14).[28] Becoming a child of God in this way is, therefore, the ultimate mediation also because the mortal nature *has put on immortality* (1 Cor. 15:53), thereby erasing the boundary line of mortality that separated "man" from God.

Let us now plot the coordinates of this structure of mediations on a "map" that will guide us in our deeper exploration of Paul's symbolic universe.

(1)	(2)	(3)
God the Father		
	Jesus Christ, son of God/Lord	
		sons of God
	"man in Christ"/"in the Lord" as sons of God-to-be and as slaves of Christ	
"man"		

214

Three observations about this map conclude our preliminary survey. First, because the model of mediations begins with the creation of "man"[29] and ends with the radical transformation of this creation, the global structure of Paul's symbolic universe is shaped by a process of mediations that is based on the kinship relations obtaining between God as Father and "men" as his children. The relations between these kin are temporally dramatized through the process of mediations represented on the map. Second, the adoption process begins the process of actual mediations by partially mediating, that is, by reconciling, the initial opposition between God and "man." This stage of the process of mediation is partial because the adoption process is not completed during it. And third, the master-slave system coincides with one stage in the processes of adoption and mediation, the stage represented in the central column on our map. In other and more historical terms, the map above represents the structure of the total "history" of "man" as Paul envisions it. The first column represents "man's" past up to the sending of God's son as Jesus Christ. The central column represents the present of Paul and his fellow believers from the time of Christ's appearance until his return. This period is a stage in the adoption process during which the believer is enslaved to Christ. And the third column completes the processes of adoption and mediation by representing the near-future goal of the "history" of mediations. "History" thus proceeds through a period of alienation which is followed by a time of reconciliation which eventuates in redemption and adoption. In subsequent sections of this chapter we will go more deeply into some of these temporal moments by exploring both elaborations of them and additions to them. Our explorations will not result in a complete encyclopedia of Paul's knowledge of his symbolic universe, but they will contribute articles on some of its most fundamental features.

KINSHIP RELATIONS IN PAUL'S
SYMBOLIC UNIVERSE

Since we are ultimately concerned with the effects knowledge has on behavior, but largely "have" only the knowledge, we have to ask what it means to Paul and his "children" to know and understand themselves as God's children.[30] In some cases, like Paul's behavior and that of others he refers to (cf. Philemon 4–7), we can see concretely how knowledge has affected behavior, and in chapter 2 we considered a number of such cases. However, apart from Paul's own activities we saw more knowledge than behavior because *he* was describing the behavior of others in terms of *his* knowledge and, indeed, what he described was heavily loaded on the side of his own administrative concerns. Nevertheless, what we saw often also revealed gaps between his children's knowledge and their behavior, and that should make us cautious about assuming that in Paul's stories the other actors will always behave according to what they know or should know. For example, while we want to know what Paul and Philemon understood by the knowledge which Paul implies they shared, we cannot assume that in the story of Philemon our hero *acted* as the knowledge and rhetoric prescribed. But what we *can* do with somewhat greater confidence and fewer assumptions is show the meaning for Philemon of the options his knowledge defined for him. Because these meanings are to be inferred from the knowledge he and Paul share, we begin with the knowledge Paul communicates in his several letters about being a child of God. But why begin with this particular body of knowledge?

Of the possible starting points we might take within Paul's complex kinship system, we begin with the notion of the children of God not only because it bridges the kinship and master-slave systems but also because it is the one notion that refers to the individual actor's most fundamental identity in relation to all others, be these others social or symbolic actors. To make this individual actor concrete, let us call him "Philemon." Knowing God as the Father of all believers and Christ as his son,[31] and therefore as another child of God, serve as reference points for Philemon's understanding of himself, of all other believers, and even of all nonbelievers who, by virtue of their unbelief, are not children of God. Knowing God as Father, and Christ and oneself as his children is not like the knowledge we might have of Cleopatra, George Washington, or Babe Ruth, none of whom directly affect our understanding, let alone our deepest understanding, of ourselves, even if we are Egyptologists, patriotic Americans, or avid baseball fans. These comparisons are, of course, absurd, but they nevertheless point to the force of Paul's kinship language, a force that derives its power from its anchoring of the believer's identity within a closed symbolic and social system, a system in which all actors are bonded together as kin and separated from those who do not belong to the family. It is in this light, then, that having explored the social relations between brothers and sisters in chapter 2 we now turn to the symbolic relations between the children of God–to–be, God's first child, Jesus Christ, and God as their common Father. In the next section we will explore the symbolic relations between the Lord Jesus Christ and his slaves, and in the last section we will consider the effects of all of this symbolic knowledge on the behavior of actors like Philemon and Paul.

As we saw in our preliminary survey of the kinship and master-slave systems, the most distinctive feature of the knowledge associated with the believer's being a child of God is that being such is the end-result of a process of adoption, not of biological descent. Christ's status as the firstborn son of God is another matter, since it is not the result of adoption, and this will concern us in due course. Of more immediate importance for the believer's self-knowledge as a child of God–to–be is the distinction between the process of adoption and biological descent, because for Paul the process of adoption is a metaphor for the process of mediation. Adoption is a form of symbolic descent which Paul contrasts with biological descent. Although Philemon and other believers may not have shared all of the knowledge Paul communicates about this contrast, he is so consistent in making it that we have to assume at least their knowledge of the contrast itself, otherwise they could not have understood what he meant by identifying them either as God's children or as brothers and sisters of one another.[32] The contrast between symbolic and biological descent is made in three separate contexts in Paul's thought, each of which represents knowledge derived from separate segments of his symbolic universe. This separateness reflects Paul's failure to integrate thoroughly either the contexts or the segments, but by working through them sequentially we can gain a sense of their place both in his symbolic universe and in his thought. The three contexts and segments concern Adam and Christ, Abraham and Christ, and Jesus Christ and the son of God. In each case we will have to work through Paul's theologizing and rhetoric to the symbolic systems behind them, and in the process of working through the three cases we will have to reiterate many observations made in our preliminary survey in order to expand upon them.

Adam and Christ[33]

For Paul, the relationship between Adam and Christ is one of contrast, and the contrast is between two genealogies, the genealogy of sin and biological death that began with Adam's act of transgression, and the symbolic genealogy of righteousness and life that began with Christ's righteously obedient death. Strictly speaking, both genealogies are "symbolic" because both are cognitive representations of matters that are not a part of everyday experience. Nevertheless, we can distinguish between them because the genealogy of death interprets a biological aspect of the history of "man" from Adam to Christ—people die—while the genealogy of life repre-

217

sents a comparable concreteness that has been realized only in Christ's past death and resurrection. Believers participate in the genealogy of death because they are still subject to biological death, but they participate in the genealogy of life through their hopeful anticipation of being enrolled in the genealogy of the sons of God— when with the redemption of their bodies upon Christ's return they are adopted as sons. Thus, from the time of the believers' baptism, which marks their enrollment as *candidates* for adoption, until Christ's return, their place in the genealogy of life is symbolic, for some of them may die in the interim (cf. 1 Thess. 4:13–17; Phil. 1:19–24; 1 Cor. 15:52). Believers still bear the image of the man of dust, Adam, but they believe that they will bear the image of the man of heaven, Christ, the firstborn son of God.

Paul develops his understanding of Adam and Christ in Rom. 5:12–21 and 1 Cor. 15:20–57. The two texts are oriented to different points, the first to the origins of and contrasts between sin and death on the one hand, and righteousness and life on the other, and the second to the bodily forms of existence derived respectively from Adam and Christ. Paul does not fully represent the significance of Adam and Christ in either text, or even between the two together, and therefore other texts, especially Romans 5—8, are needed even minimally to complete the conceptions represented in them.

In Rom. 5:12–21 Paul speaks about Adam, Moses, and Christ in terms of their historical sequence, but he also represents a contrast between Adam and Christ that both breaks up the historical continuity between them and links Moses to Adam. "Sin,"[34] Paul says, entered the world through the transgression of one man, Adam, and through sin death was introduced for all men, because after Adam all men sinned (5:12–14, 17, 20). Sin and death are therefore inherited traits in the genealogy of "man" that began with the first man, Adam, and Moses is linked to him because the Law introduced by Moses served to increase the power of sin. By naming sins the Law aroused sin to new heights (5:13; cf. 7:4–23). Thus, sin, death, and the Law characterize the genealogy of man from Adam to Christ.[35] With "the one man," Christ, however, sin was displaced by righteousness through *his* righteously obedient death, and death was displaced by eternal life *through him*, that is, through his resurrection from the dead (5:12–21; cf. 6:4–11).[36] Elsewhere, Paul also says that Christ's death brought an end to the time of the Law's reign, thus terminating the power of the Law as well as the power of sin and death over believers (Rom. 7:4–6; 8:3–4; 3:19–26; Galatians 3). The believer, therefore, knows that the Law is no longer valid, that sin has been condemned, and that death has been conquered.

Through Christ's death and resurrection the believer has been freed from all of them.

In Rom. 5:12–21 Paul only alludes to the future realization of the life made possible through Christ (cf. 5:17–21), but earlier in Romans 5 he speaks about the believers' "hope of sharing the glory (*doxa*) of God" (5:2), and later he describes the realization of this hope as being united with Christ in a resurrection like his, as living with him (6:5–11), and as being glorified with him (8:17, 30; cf. Phil. 3:20–21). The moment of realization will occur when the sons of God are revealed (8:19), when creation will be set free from its bondage to decay and obtain the freedom of the glory of the children of God (8:21). This is the moment when believers will be adopted as sons and have their bodies redeemed (8:23), the moment when they become conformed to the image of God's firstborn son and become his brothers (8:29–30). This emphasis on the future transformation of the believer's body is the focus of Paul's comments on Adam and Christ in 1 Corinthians 15.

In the course of explaining to the Corinthians the meaning of the resurrection from the dead, Paul twice refers to Adam and Christ. The first time, his comments sound like Rom. 5:12–21, although they differ from it because they refer to Christ's resurrection, not his righteousness. Nevertheless, in referring to his resurrection they also explain the meaning of eternal life, which was not explained in Romans 5. Thus, after affirming that Christ was raised from the dead as the first fruits of those who have fallen asleep (1 Corinthians 15—20), Paul says,

> as by a man came death, by a man has also come the resurrection of the dead. For as in Adam all die, so in Christ shall all be made alive. But each in his own order: Christ the first fruits, then at his coming those who belong to Christ. Then comes the end, when he delivers the kingdom to God the Father after destroying every rule and every authority. For he must reign until he has put all his enemies under his feet. The last enemy to be destroyed is death (15:21–26; cf. 1 Thess. 4:13–17; 2 Cor. 4:13—5:5).

Eternal life is what is left after death has been conquered. The beginning of the conquest was in Christ's resurrection from the dead, and the end will come when Christ returns and those in Christ "shall be made alive." Paul does not systematically treat all of the questions one might want to ask about this statement. He does not, for example, spell out what happens to those who are *not* in Christ after death is finally and absolutely conquered. On the other hand, however, he is concerned to spell out what it means to say that those in Christ, "shall be made alive," and it is in this connection that he once again takes up the contrast between Adam and Christ.

Responding to his own rhetorical question concerning the body (*sōma*)[37] with which the dead are raised (15:35), Paul contrasts the earthly, physical (i.e., "psychic," *psychikos*) body inherited from Adam, "the man from the earth, a man of dust," with the heavenly, spiritual (*pneumatikos*) body of Christ, "the man of heaven" (15:45–50). Adam was only a "living being" (Gen. 2:7), made from earth or dust, a creature of perishable flesh and blood, above all mortal. The man of heaven, on the other hand, is a "life-giving spirit" from heaven, not earth, and he is made of imperishable, immortal, and glorious stuff (cf. 15:42–44, 52–55). Believers, as everyone since Adam, bear the image (*eikōn*)[38] of the man of dust, but they will, at Christ's return, come to bear the image of the man of heaven, for "flesh and blood cannot inherit the kingdom of God, nor does the perishable inherit the imperishable" (15:49–50). The exchange of images appears to come with the second of two moments following Christ's return, for prior to the transformation of all, those who have died, and obviously only they, have to be raised from the dead:

> We shall not all sleep, but we shall all be changed (*allagēsometha*), in a moment, in the twinkling of an eye, at the last trumpet. For the trumpet will sound, and the dead will be raised imperishable, and we shall be changed. For this perishable nature must put on[39] the imperishable, and this mortal nature must put on immortality (15:51b–53; cf. 1 Thess. 4:13–17; 2 Cor. 4:13—5:5; Phil. 3:20–21).

Then death will have been conquered (1 Cor. 15:54–57).[40] Paul is unclear as to the relationship between the resurrection body and the transformation body, or rather, while he seems to think of one imperishable, immortal body, he does not indicate what those who are raised imperishable are changed *from* when "all" are changed. Here, as elsewhere, Paul fails to resolve inconsistencies of detail, but this does not mean that behind the inconsistencies there is no fundamental conception of his own. In the present case, for example, there can be no question but that Paul envisions a radical transformation of the believer's bodily form, regardless of the inconsistency between resurrection and transformation. He understands the transformation body to be the resurrection body but fails to recognize that those who have died are, in his terms, doubly transformed but have nothing to be transformed into after the first transformation in which they are "raised imperishable." The point, I think, is therefore to concentrate on the conception Paul is operating with, not the inconsistencies, and this conception comes out clearly in the texts we have been considering: there will be a radical transformation of the believer's body.

Paul's comments on Adam and Christ in Romans 5 and 1 Corinthians 15, together with the supporting texts from Romans 5—8, represent a general conception containing an opposition between the genealogies associated with them. The genealogies describe the origins of the respective images borne by the believer, the image of Adam, the man of dust, and the image of Christ, the man of heaven. Sin, death, and the Law originate in the genealogy of Adam, the first man, while righteousness, life, and grace originate in the genealogy of Christ, the firstborn son of God.

Having considered the temporal and dramatic framework within which the believer is transformed from one image to the other, let us look at the contrasting characteristics of the two images, for these show us the states the believer is adoptively transformed both from and into.

Image of the Man of Dust	*Image of the Man of Heaven*
Rom. 8:19–23, 29, the distinction between states:	
bondage to decay (*phthora*) or perishability	revealing of the sons of God; liberty of the glory of the children of God; adoption as sons; the redemption (*apolytrōsis*) of the body; conformity to the image of the firstborn son of God; transformation (*allassō*, 1 Cor. 15:51–52)
1 Cor. 15:42–54, the distinction between bodies:	
perishable (*phthora*)	imperishable (*aphtharsia*)
dishonor (*atimia*)	honor or glory (*doxa*)
weakness (*asthenia*)	power (*dynamis*)
physical or psychic (*psychikos*)	spiritual (*pneumatikos*)
living being (*psychēn zōsan*)	life-giving spirit (*pneuma zōopoioun*)
flesh and blood (*sarx kai haima*)	
from the dusty earth (*gēs choïkos)*	from heaven (*ex ouranou*)
mortal (*thnēton*)	immortal (*athanasia*)

Later, in our consideration of Paul's distinction between Jesus Christ and the son of God, we will explore further the transformation of the believer from the one image into the other. For now, it will suffice to conclude that the distinction between Adam and Christ entails a contrast between two forms of existence and their genealogies, one "earthly," that of the sons of men, and the other "heavenly," that of the sons of God. For this reason, Paul's kinship system contains ideas that cluster on two axes. The horizontal genealogy originates on earth with the first man, Adam, and it is broken into in time by the vertical axis that originates in heaven with God and his firstborn son, Jesus Christ. From the time between Christ's appearance on earth and in human history in human form, until the time of his return, the believer lives on earth, in human history and in human form, the image of the man of dust. However, the genealogy of the believer in the image of the man of dust is symbolically canceled by being "in Christ," and the believer lives through this and related symbols in the hope of being enrolled in the genealogy of the children of God upon Christ's return to transform the believer's body into the likeness of his own glorious body, whereupon the believer will become an adoptive son of God. Consequently, to know oneself to be a child of God *means* knowing that one is in the process of transformation from a radically negative form of existence into a radically positive and antithetically different form. Therefore, to be a "brother" to a "brother" is vastly more than a matter of social relations. In Paul's terms, it is a matter of life or death. Within his symbolic universe, the everyday experience of life is viewed as death, and real life can only be attained by dying, in the first instance symbolically through baptism (Rom. 6:3–11), but also in some cases literally (cf. Phil. 1:21–24; 2 Cor. 5:1–6). The believer's behavior while in the mortal image of the man of dust is, accordingly, motivated by the goal of becoming transformed into the image of the man of heaven. Failing to treat a brother as a brother is therefore to risk not only social disapproval and rejection, indeed exclusion from the brotherhood, but it is also to risk losing the ultimate reality for which one has joined the group. The ultimate equality of believers both in the church and in the kingdom of God is not merely a good social idea, it is a reality that supersedes all other realities. And in this sense, to fail to be a brother to a brother is to do the unthinkable, to give up eternal life, the hope and reality of immortality.

The genealogies of death and life are accompanied in Paul's symbolic universe by two other genealogies in which biological and symbolic descent are contrasted in a quite different way. For these we have to turn to Paul's understanding of the relationship between Abraham and Christ.

Abraham and Christ[41]

With the relationship between Abraham and Christ we move from the genealogies of sin and death and of righteousness and life to the genealogy of faith and promise. Here it is not Abraham and Christ who are contrasted, but two parallel genealogies, both of which originate in Abraham, a genealogy of the flesh and a genealogy of promise. There is no direct connection between these and the genealogies of Adam and Christ, although in the genealogy of promise Paul elaborates on certain themes found in them, for example, the themes of Law, righteousness, and the children of God.

The opposition between the parallel genealogies of the flesh and of promise are best represented in Rom. 9:2–13 (cf. vv. 14–18), where Paul speaks about his Israelite "brothers," his "kinsmen according to the flesh" (*syngenōn . . . kata sarka*, 9:3). "To them," he says, "belong the adoptive sonship (*huiothesia*),[42] the glory (*doxa*), the covenants, the giving of the Law, the worship, and the promises; to them belong the patriarchs, and to them belongs the messiah (*ho Christos*)[43] according to the flesh" (9:4–5a). In contrast with this biological and cultural, indeed ethnic, heritage of the Israelites, Paul says that neither Israel, nor descent (*sperma*)[44] from Abraham, nor the children of God are to be defined by genealogies of the flesh (9:6–8; cf. 4:1). To the contrary, they are defined on the basis of the genealogy of what Paul speaks of as the promise that God made to Abraham when he said: "Your seed (*sperma*) will be reckoned through Isaac" (9:7; cf. Gen. 21:12). Although this sounds like biological descent, and was, according to Paul, interpreted as such by his fellow Israelites, he does not understand it in this way. Rather, his polemical point is that his people have forgotten that it is God who determined what the line of descent from Abraham would be, namely, through Isaac rather than Ishmael, Abraham's firstborn son, and through Jacob rather than Esau, Isaac's firstborn son (cf. 9:10–13). Here our earlier kinship diagrams are helpful. Whereas kinship descent usually follows the law of primogeniture, succession or descent through the firstborn male, Paul points to God's rejection of this law in his decision to reckon descent through Isaac and Jacob rather than through Ishmael and Esau. According to Gal. 4:21–30, Hagar's son Ishmael was born according to the flesh, while Sarah's son Isaac was born through God's promise to Abraham and Sarah that *they* would have a son. From all of this, Paul draws the conclusion that *God's* determination of descent overrides cultural determinations like the law of primogeniture, and in support of this conclusion he also appeals to certain characteristics of God as an

223

actor, namely, to his purpose to elect his own people for his own reasons (9:11, 17), his mercy and his compassion (9:14–17), and his freedom to harden "the heart of whomever he wills" (9:18), even to display his wrath (9:22–24). Against the "clay" of biological and cultural genealogies, Paul sets the potter and his freedom to do with the clay what he wishes (9:20–21). The creator fully determines his own organization of his creatures despite their pretensions (cf. 1:22–25). He determines who is an Israelite; he determines who is a descendant of Abraham; and he determines who his children are. And his determinations are not biological, according to the flesh and its cultural ways, but symbolic, according to his promise to Abraham.

Integrally related to the genealogy of promise is the notion of faith, for faith is the means by which the believer participates in it. Paul develops his understanding of the relationship between promise and faith in Gal. 3:6—4:7 and in Romans 4 and 8, but because the texts in Romans evidence a higher degree of reflection and theoretical focus than Galatians, we begin with Galatians and supplement it with observations derived from Romans. Our concern here is with the *knowledge* Paul conveys about the relationship between God's promise and faith, not with the particular arguments he makes in these letters. Therefore, and in order to represent the system comprised by this knowledge, we can outline the sequence of propositions upon which his arguments are based.

(1) *God promised Abraham that in him all the nations, that is, Gentiles, will be blessed, making them "sons of Abraham," his descendants (sperma), and his heirs* (Gal. 3:7–8, 14, 16a, 29; 4:21–31; Rom. 4:13–21). Jews are to be blessed through Abraham, too, for he is also their "father," but they will be blessed on the same principle as the Gentiles (Rom. 4:16; cf. 9—11), the principle of faith, which we will consider under another proposition. For now, the more comprehensive form of the first proposition is that the sons of Abraham, his descendants, and his heirs are determined by God on the basis of their faith in God, regardless of whether they are ethnic Jews or ethnic Gentiles. The initial and more limited form of the proposition is rhetorically oriented to the Gentiles to whom Paul is speaking in both Romans and Galatians. However, both forms of the proposition, like all of the rest, are grounded in what Paul views as the historical actions of God and others, like Abraham. Thus, Paul does not think in terms of general principles alone, but in terms of principles he derives from historical events known to both Jews and Gentiles from Jewish Scriptures, here Gen. 12:3 (cf. Gen. 18:18). Adam and Abraham are for Paul historical actors whose relations with

God have a continuing relevance for subsequent generations, and it is Paul's concern to show his audiences this relevance.

(2) *"Abraham believed God and it was reckoned to him as righteousness"* (Gal. 3:6; Rom. 4:1–12; cf. Gen. 15:6). Abraham's "belief" in God's promise to him is for Paul an act of trust and faith, an act proceeding from the conviction that God was able to do what he had promised (Rom. 4:5, 12, 17–22). The promise referred to here, however, is not exactly the same promise referred to in the first proposition, although Paul appears to think of them as synonymous. Here the promise is that Abraham, who was in his old age and still childless, would become the "father of many nations" (Rom. 4:17, 18; cf. Gen. 17:5; 15:15), and these "nations" are Abraham's descendants. Abraham's faith or belief in God is, therefore, contrasted with the physical improbability that an aged and infertile Abraham and Sarah could produce even one son and heir, one descendant, let alone many nations (Rom. 4:17–22; 9:6–13). But in Paul's argument Abraham's faith is also contrasted with the fact that he became circumcised (Rom. 4:1–12; cf. Gen. 17:9–14). This fact raises for Paul the question of whether God considered Abraham righteous because of his faith or because of his circumcision.

The question of the basis upon which God reckons one righteous is for Paul as social as it is "theological." It concerns not merely how God wants his people to relate to him, but equally importantly how God's people are to relate to one another. The fact that Abraham and his successors were circumcised (Gen. 17:9–14) is a social fact that became a criterion for being a Jew, a son of Abraham, because Jews require both born Jews and Gentile converts to become circumcised according to the Law of Moses, in which book of laws are the stories of Abraham, including the story of God's introduction of the law of circumcision to him. Thus, the people of God who organize their lives according to the Law of Moses relate to would-be Gentile converts by requiring them to become circumcised. Paul's rejection of this requirement, and of life according to the Law generally, is therefore a rejection of circumcision and the Law both as a means of relating to God and as a requirement for entry into the church, for membership in the Israel of God, for being a son of Abraham, and for enrollment as an adoptive son of God, in a word, for the relations between the people of God.[45] Paul's answer to the question of the basis upon which God reckons one righteous is, therefore, a statement of the conditions for inclusion in the genealogy of the sons of God.

His answer to this question begins with a description of the "historical facts." Simply, God pronounced Abraham righteous because

225

of his faith *before* he was circumcised (Rom. 4:10), and thus his circumcision was only "a sign or seal of the righteousness he had by faith while he was still uncircumcised" (4:11a). In other words, Abraham was declared righteous in an episode described in Genesis 15 and had the law of circumcision introduced to him in a later episode described in Genesis 17! Historical facts are also at issue in Gal. 3:17, where Paul says that in fact the Law of Moses came with Moses himself, who appeared on the scene of history 430 years after God made his promises to Abraham. Paul then moves from fact to interpretation. God's

> purpose was to make him [Abraham] the father of all who believe without being circumcised and who thus have righteousness reckoned to them, and likewise the father of the circumcised who are not merely circumcised but also follow the example of the faith which our father Abraham had before he was circumcised (Rom. 4:11b–12).

Because Paul distinguishes between the book of the Law and the history represented in it, he can not only say that promise, faith, and righteousness are historically prior to the Law, but he can also contrast them with the Law in such a way as to repudiate it. Righteousness did not come with the Law of Moses but with Abraham's faith in God's promise to him, and the Law, which in connection with Adam and Christ we have seen to be associated with sin and death, only brought God's wrath upon his people (Rom. 4:15). The Law did not annul God's promise to Abraham, because the law was only a temporary custodian. God never intended to use the Law as a measure of righteousness (Gal. 2:16; 3:11–12, 15–25). Consequently, those in Christ who become circumcised are not only bound to keep the whole Law, but they are also severed from Christ (Gal. 5:2–4). Those who live according to the Law live under its curse, for those who do not "abide by all things written in the book of the Law" will be cursed by God's wrath (Gal. 3:10–12). Blessing, on the other hand, is to be had only in the righteousness God accords to faith in his promise and its fulfillment.

Abraham's faith in God's promise to him of many offspring is the beginning of both the genealogy of the promise and the genealogy of the sons of God, although Abraham himself is not identified as a son of God. The connection between the two genealogies is not clearly drawn by Paul,[46] but it is clearly asserted. Abraham is the father of all who have faith in God's promise to him (Rom. 4:11b–25), and the children of the promise are the children of Israel, of Abraham, *and of God* (Rom. 9:6–8). And as we have seen, these genealogies are contrasted with the children and genealogy of the flesh. Thus, Paul tells

Gentile believers in Christ that they are sons of God through faith, and that as such they are Abraham's offspring and heirs according to the promise (Gal. 3:21—4:7; cf. Rom. 8:12–25, 29). In Christ Jesus the blessing of Abraham has come upon the Gentiles and they have received the promise of the spirit through their faith (Gal. 3:14).[47] This is the spirit of adoptive sonship (*huiothesia*) which enables the believer to cry, "Abba! Father!" (Rom. 8:15), the spirit of God's son (Gal. 4:6; cf. 4:4–7 and Rom. 8:12–27), the firstfruits of the spirit of adoptive sonship (Rom. 8:23; cf. 8:18–30).[48] However, by introducing the fulfillment of the promise to Abraham we are getting ahead of ourselves (see propositions three through six, below). More directly relevant to the present proposition is the idea that as a descendant of Abraham and a child-to-be of God, one is also an heir (*klēros*).

Abraham's children are God's children because they are the children of God's promise to Abraham, not of the flesh. But Abraham's descendants are also said to be heirs according to promise: if one is a son, he is also an heir of God's promise to Abraham and an heir, therefore, of God (Gal. 3:29; 4:7; Rom. 8:14–17). Shortly, we will consider the heirs, that is, the children of Abraham and God. Now we need to understand just what the *inheritance* (*klēronomia*) is. In Rom. 4:13 Paul says that God promised Abraham and his descendants (*sperma*) that they would "inherit the world" (*kosmos*). Exactly what this means is not altogether clear from Romans, although it may be related to the eschatological notion expressed in 1 Cor. 6:2, that "the saints will judge the world." But Rom. 4:13 is in any event eschatological, and so are others of Paul's references to the inheritance. Three times he refers to the fact that "the unrighteous will not inherit the kingdom of God" (1 Cor. 6:9–10; Gal. 5:21), and in 1 Cor. 15:50 he says that "flesh and blood cannot inherit the kingdom of God, nor does the perishable inherit the imperishable." The inheritance of Abraham's descendants and of God's children is, therefore, the kingdom of God into which the believer is called. This is the heavenly commonwealth from which Christ will come to change the believer's abject body into the image of his own body of glory (Phil. 3:20–21; cf. "the Jerusalem above," Gal. 4:26, and the more individualized "heavenly dwelling," 2 Cor. 5:1–5). And this is the kingdom that Christ will deliver to God the Father "after destroying every rule and every authority and power," including death (1 Cor. 15:24–26). Thus, one receives the inheritance of the kingdom following the eschatological transformation of the physical body by which the process of adoption is completed (cf. 1 Cor. 15:42–57; 2 Cor. 4:16—5:10; Rom. 8:12–25; Phil. 3:20–21; 1 Thess.

4:13—5:11). However, in drawing this conclusion we must not over-emphasize the sequential relationship between transformation, adoption, and the receiving of the inheritance, for the last two moments are the simultaneous results of the process of transformation: if a son, then an heir (Gal. 4:7; Rom. 8:17). Receiving the inheritance and being adopted as sons are two ways of expressing the same eschatological state. This is also evident in Paul's remark that God has called believers into his kingdom *and* glory (1 Thess. 2:12), for the believer shares God's glory through adoption (Rom. 5:2, 8:12–30) and God's kingdom through inheritance.

Finally, because Paul considers the inheritance of the kingdom of God to be the ultimate fulfillment of God's promise to Abraham (Rom. 4:13; Gal. 3:18), the coming of Abraham's blessing upon the Gentiles (Gal. 3:8, 14) is both a *partial* fulfillment of that promise and a stage in the eschatological reception of the inheritance of the kingdom.

(3) *It is men of faith who are sons of Abraham* (Gal. 3:7). In Clifford Geertz's terms, Abraham is a symbolic model both *of* faith by his enactment of it and *for* faith, in the sense that he is a model to be followed (cf. Rom. 4:11b–12).[49] Following his model for faith one participates in the genealogy of the promise, and therefore just as God considered Abraham to be righteous because of his faith, so will he consider others righteous because of their faith (Rom. 4:23–25; Gal. 3:9, 11). But for Paul faith is not merely a general quality of behavior or an attitude of faithfulness in general. Faith is inseparable from the promise of descendants for Abraham, because those who have faith *are* his descendants and as such *they* are fulfillments of God's promise. Indeed, the object of their faith is both the promise and its fulfillment. This means, however, that before *they* can participate in the fulfillment of God's promise they have to have faith in its fulfillment. How can this be?

(4) *Jesus Christ is the offspring promised to Abraham, and therefore he is its fulfillment* (Gal. 3:16). Paul makes a critical point when he asserts that God's promise was made to Abraham and his "offspring" (*sperma*), in the singular, not to his "offsprings," in the plural (Gal. 3:16–17),[50] and that *Christ* is the promised offspring. Once again, Paul does not seem to have clearly thought through everything that he says, for he ignores the fact that Isaac is the first son of the promise (Gal. 4:28; cf. Rom. 9:9–12). Similarly, and more importantly, although he says that it is men of faith who are the sons of Abraham, Christ does not appear in the genealogy of the promise by virtue of *his* faith (nor does Isaac!), but by virtue of his being God's fulfillment of his promise to Abraham.[51] Because it is in Christ Jesus

that the blessing of Abraham has come upon the Gentiles, so that they might receive the promise of the spirit through faith (Gal. 3:14), Christ, as the initial fulfillment of God's promise, becomes the new object of faith. As such, it is through faith in Christ that others become children of Abraham and of God, and as such heirs. This, then, is the answer to the question with which we concluded proposition three. Gentiles are fulfillments of God's promise only by virtue of their faith in Christ as its fulfillment (see further, proposition six).

(5) *Faith has come or been revealed in Christ precisely as faith in Christ, and therefore those who believe or have faith in Christ will be reckoned righteous by God* (Gal. 3:14, 22–25; Rom. 4:23–25). What is believed about Christ in addition to his being Abraham's offspring is that he is Lord, that God raised him from the dead (Rom. 10:9–10), and that he was put to death for our trespasses and raised for our justification (Rom. 4:24–25). Exactly what these things signify is spelled out in various ways throughout Paul's letters,[52] but genealogically the critical point is that "Christ," and all that that term signifies, is now the sole object of the act of faith which God will consider righteous. Besides the juridical connotations of being reckoned righteous, knowing one's self to have been considered righteous because of one's faith is also to know that one is a son and heir of Abraham and of God. Knowing that one has been justified by faith, one is able to hope for one's glorification as a son of God (cf. Rom. 8:30).

(6) *Those who are in Christ are Abraham's descendants, sons of God, and heirs* (Gal. 3:26—4:7, 28; Rom. 4:16–25; 8:12–25, 28–30). With this proposition we come to the end of Paul's understanding of the relationship of faith to the genealogy of the promise, and with it we see the merger of this genealogy with the genealogy of the sons of God, for faith in Christ as Abraham's offspring enrolls one as a child of Abraham, a child of God's promise to him, and therefore as a child of God. However, this merger is not complete because Paul has much more to say about the sons of God in connection with Christ as the firstborn son not of Abraham but of God. And in this connection no mention is made of Abraham or his children. For Paul, being in Christ appears to have attracted ideas, and indeed whole complexes of ideas, like those associated with Adam and Christ and Abraham and Christ, which are, in his mind, united by their orientation to Christ without being systematically related to one another as complexes of ideas. Each complex or system of ideas appears to have had a particular function to play in Paul's dealings with his people, but with little or no systematic relationship between them either in

his thought or in his symbolic universe. For example, in the case of Adam and Christ he is concerned with the contrast between the old person and the new, while in the case of Abraham and Christ he is concerned with the place of Gentiles in the genealogy of the children of Abraham—with, that is, the relationship between Jews and Gentiles in the Israel of God (cf. Romans 9—11; Galatians, *passim*). The most comprehensively systematic representation of the symbolic universe upon which Paul's thoughts depend is to be found in his comments on the relations between Jesus Christ, the son of God, and the sons of God, to which we now turn.

Jesus Christ and the Son of God

Although as Abraham's "offspring" Jesus Christ is theoretically *God's* son, because Abraham's offspring are children of God's promise to him, Paul does not draw this conclusion because he knows Christ to be God's son in a very different way and, indeed, in a way that is once again contrasted with biological descent. In biological terms, he knows that Jesus Christ was "born of woman" (Gal. 4:4), that he was a descendant of David (Rom. 1:3), that as such he is the Israelite "Christ," that is, messiah, according to the flesh (Rom. 9:5), and that he had a biological brother named James (Gal. 1:19). And Jesus died. In symbolic terms, on the other hand, Paul also knows that Jesus Christ was God's son before, during, and after his biological life, and that as God's son he is responsible for enabling others to become sons and children of God. This son of God is "the man from heaven" (1 Cor. 15:28, 47–49) whom God sent, "born of woman, born under the Law, to redeem those under the Law, so that we might receive adoption as sons" (Gal. 4:4). Symbolic and biological descent, therefore, intersect at the point where he who was "sent" was "born of woman," and for this reason Paul can say both that God sent his son in the likeness (*en homoiōmati*) of sinful flesh (Rom. 8:3) and that Christ was born in the likeness (*en homoiōmati*) and shape (*schēma*) of men (Phil. 2:6–7).[53] Before he was sent, he was in the form (*morphē*) and image (*eikōn*) of God, and equal (*isos*) to him, and after his death in human form he was raised from the dead in a spiritual body of glory, enthroned son of God in power,[54] and exalted in heaven as Lord over all in heaven and on earth and under the earth (cf. Phil. 2:5–11; 2 Cor. 4:4; 1 Cor. 15:35–50; 2 Cor. 3:18; Phil. 3:20; Rom. 1:4; 1 Thess. 1:10; 4:13–17). The son of God thus began, indeed, he was "born," in the form and image of God as *his* firstborn son. Later, he was also "born" as Jesus Christ in the form and image of man, and after completing his work in that form he reassumed his original form. The symbolic biography of the son of God, therefore, interprets the "biological" biography of the man Jesus Christ (cf. 2 Cor. 5:6). This much is clear. However, the question posed for us by it concerns its significance for the generation through adoption of other sons and children of God. How does the firstborn son of God make it possible for others to become children of God? The intersection of the son of God's contrasting forms of existence suggests that we can best begin to answer this question by exploring Paul's understanding of *the form of the children of God*, the prototype of which is the form of the firstborn son of God.

In our discussion of Adam and Christ we saw that the children of God–to–be are to be transformed from the image (*eikōn*) of the man of dust, Adam, into the image of the man of heaven, the firstborn son of God, Jesus Christ. This means that the process of adoption is a process of transformation *from* human form and *into* the form of the firstborn son. Because Christ was "born" in this form, he is *not* an adopted son,[55] and because he is the *first*born son his form is the prototype of the form into which others will be adoptively transformed. All children of God, are, therefore, of one form. But Paul also goes a significant step further when he says that Christ is the image (*eikōn*) of God (2 Cor. 4:4), for this suggests that believers are being transformed into the image of God at the same time that they are being transformed into Christ's image.[56] Clearly, in order to understand the form of the children of God and the process of adoptive transformation, we have to understand the relationship between forms and images.

In Paul's usage, the terms "body" (*sōma*), "form" (*morphē*), and "shape" (*schēma*) refer to the configuration of something,[57] while the term "image" (*eikōn*) defines the configuration in relation to something else of which it is a replication.[58] "Image," therefore, denotes a formal configuration but also a relationship of some kind of identity between what is shaped according to an image and the shape of the image's prototype. The question is, what kind of identity does Paul envision when he speaks of a person being or bearing[59] the image of someone else, like Adam, Christ, or God? The clearest answer to this question comes from 1 Cor. 15:42–54, where Paul contrasts the believer's bearing the image of the man of dust with his coming to bear the image of the man of heaven (15:49). His comments show that the identity between the image bearer and the image's prototype (the man of dust, the man of heaven) is one of substance rather than of mere external resemblance, like the idols alluded to in Rom. 1:23, where Paul speaks of them as the likeness of the image of mortal men (*homoiōma eikonos phthartou anthrōpou*).[60] Those who bear the image of the man of dust share with him both a perishable, weak, and mortal physical body and the infection of sin (cf. Rom. 5:12–24, 19).[61] Similarly, when believers come to bear the image of the man of heaven, the firstborn son of God, they will share with him an imperishable, glorious, powerful, and immortal spiritual body that is not infected by sin. As Paul says, "As was the man of dust, so are those of the dust; and as is the man of heaven, so are those who are of heaven" (15:48). What, then, of the relationship between the firstborn son of God, as God's image, and God as this image's prototype? That Paul could have said, "As is God, so is the son of God," is evident from Phil. 2:6, where he asserts that Christ, before taking human form, was in the form (*morphē*) of God and equal (*isos*) to him. It is therefore clear that when Paul speaks of a person being or bearing the image of someone else, he is speaking about their having in common a form that is comprised of certain qualities.[62] Indeed, Paul uses the idea of image to suggest a kinship relation between the prototype and the copy. This is especially significant not only because in the examples just cited the qualities of the man of heaven are qualities of the form of God, but also because these are qualities of God's children. Ultimately, therefore, *God's* form is the prototype for the image, and therefore also for the form, of his children, from the firstborn to the last. For this reason, in our attempt to understand the form of the children of God we have to consider God's form as well. Let us therefore inquire more closely into what Paul has to say about both God and his image.

Second Cor. 3:1—5:21 is immensely rich in ideas relevant to the form of both God and his children, and for our purposes 4:6 serves as a focal point. There Paul says that it is the God of creation, "who said, 'Let light shine out of darkness' [Gen. 1:3], who has shone in our hearts to give *the light of the knowledge of the glory (doxa) of God in the face of Christ.*" When we analyze this statement, we find that it is God's glory, which has the quality of light, that is the link between God, Christ, and the believer, between, that is, God and his children. The believer, who is not yet fully a child of God, knows God's glory from "the face of Christ," and the knowledge of it illuminates the believer from within. But Christ's possession of this glory is such that Paul can also speak of "the glory of the Lord" (3:18) and "the glory of Christ" (4:4), and it is precisely in this connection that he identifies Christ as the image (*eikōn*) of God. Parallel to his reference to "the light of the knowledge of the glory of God in the face of Christ," is his reference to "the light of the gospel of the glory of Christ, who is the image of God" (4:4). Through the gospel of Christ the believer, therefore, has both access to "the face of Christ" and the knowledge of God's glory, and in beholding, that is, knowing, Christ's glory the believer is in the process of being transformed (*metamorphoō*) into his image, that is, from the believer's mortal glory into Christ's glory (3:18).[63] God's glory is the prototype for the glory of his children, whose glorious form is the image of God's glory. However, this form also has other qualities.

In 2 Cor. 3:7—4:6 "glory" has the quality of radiant light, and in 1 Cor. 15:40–41 light is also a quality associated with the glory of heavenly "bodies" like the sun, moon, and stars. But "glory" also connotes "power" (*dynamis*). In 2 Cor. 4:7, the believer's possession of the light of the knowledge of the glory of God in the face of Christ is referred to as God's "transcendent power" (*hē hyperbolē tēs dynameōs*) within the believer, and in Rom. 6:4 and 1 Cor. 6:14 God's power and glory are even synonymous: Christ was raised from the dead through the glory (*dia tēs doxēs*) of the Father; God raised the Lord through his power (*dia tēs dynameōs autou*).[64] But this association of power and glory with the resurrection of the dead is not limited to *Christ's* resurrection, because the believer will participate in it, too. The firstborn son of God is not only the firstborn *among many brethren*, but in his resurrection from the dead he is also the first to be raised from among *those who have died*, and it is through him that *others* will be raised and transformed when he returns (1 Cor. 15:20–24, 51–57). When we observe the parallelism between the formulations of these two themes,

firstborn son among many brethren (Rom. 8:29)
firstfruits   of those who have fallen asleep (1 Cor. 15:20)

it becomes apparent that they are fundamentally related, for in Paul's view it is in connection with the resurrection of the rest of the dead that others will become children of God. Part of this view is described in 1 Corinthians 15 in such a way as to help us see the intimate relationship between the qualities of the form of God and the qualities of the form of his children.

In his discussion in 1 Corinthians 15 of the kind of body (*sōma*) with which the dead are raised, and into which they and others who have not died will be transformed,[65] Paul distinguishes between different kinds of bodies and their correspondingly different "glories" (15:35–42). Peculiar to the resurrection body are the qualities of imperishability (*aphtharsia*), glory (*doxa*), power (*dynamis*), spirituality (*pneumatikon*, in contrast with physicality, *psychikon*), and immortality (*athanasia*, 15:42–44, 50–53). Because all of these qualities are also associated either directly or indirectly with both God and his firstborn son, these qualities belong to the form of God and the form of his children. They belong to the firstborn son both by virtue of his own resurrection and by virtue of his being God's son. As God's son he was "born" in the form of God, and after his mortal death he was, through his resurrection, reinstated as son of God in power and glory.[66] His fleshly body died, but in his resurrection he assumed a spiritual, glorious, powerful, and immortal body (cf. Rom. 1:3–4; Phil. 3:20–21). But the qualities of the resurrection body are also qualities of God. Although Paul does not speak explicitly about God's body or form, the attributes of the resurrection body are attributes of God. It was through *his* glory and power that he raised Christ, and he is also imperishable (Rom. 1:23), the source of the spirit (e.g., Rom. 8:1–27; 1 Cor. 6:19; 12:3, 4–13), and immortal (cf. Rom. 1:20, 23; 2:7, he gives eternal life; 1 Thess. 1:9).

The resurrection body is thus the body of God and his children, and Christ's body is the glorious image of God into which believers are being transformed. In sinning, man had fallen short of the glory of God (Rom. 3:23) and become conformed to the image of the man of dust, but after Christ's death and resurrection men are called into God's kingdom and glory (1 Thess. 2:12). Those who accept this call are foreknown by God and predestined by him to be conformed (*symmorphos*) to the image of his son (Rom. 8:28–30), which means being glorified with him (8:17, 30) and with him sharing the glory of God (5:2). When Christ returns from heaven to deliver his people into the heavenly commonwealth, he will alter (*metaschēmatizo*) their abject bodies and bring them into conformity (*symmorphos*) with the body of his glory through the energy (*energeia*) which empowers (*dynamai*) him to subject all things to himself (Phil. 3:20–21; cf. 1 Cor. 15:20–57). Then will the sons of God be revealed, for then believers will obtain the freedom of the glory of the children of God, their adoption as sons, the redemption of their bodies (Rom. 8:19–23).

Before we turn our attention to other aspects of the process by which the believer is transformed into the image of Christ and becomes a child of God with him, we need to consider a troublesome but important text in which Paul says that man *is* the image and glory of God (1 Cor. 11:7). The passage is troublesome because it is inconsistent with what we have just observed about man's *present* condition of bearing the image of the man of dust, but it is important because it leads to further insights into Paul's notion of the children of God. We will consider these insights first and then attend to the inconsistency.

First Corinthians 11:7 must be approached through its immediate context in the letter for it is one of three related statements in Paul's argument in 1 Cor. 11:3–16.[67] The first statement concerns a hierarchical series consisting of God, Christ, man (male), and woman. Each term but the last is said to be the "head" of the one following it, so that God is the "head" of Christ, Christ the "head" of every man, and man the "head" of woman (11:3). Paul does not explain what he means by "head," although the context clearly indicates that it connotes authority and superordinacy over someone else. On the other hand, he is also inconsistent in his use of the word "head." Whereas in 11:3 "the head of" someone is a metaphor for someone else, in vv. 4–16 the "head" is the literal head of the person being spoken about. Be this as it may, the second statement concerns another series, this time of God, man (male), and woman. Here man is said to be the image and glory of God, while woman is identified as the glory of man, and no "image" is mentioned for the woman (11:7). Paul explains this series in terms of the order in which man and woman were created by God—man first, and then woman out of the man. He does not refer to man being created out of dust, as he does later in 15:45–49. Finally, the third statement is that "in the Lord" man and woman are *not* independent (*chōris*) of one another, "for as woman was made from man, so man is now born of woman" (11:11–12).

Taken together, these three statements represent three sequential stages of male-female relations: at the creation of the first man and woman; during the time of procreation that began when the first woman gave birth to the first child to be "born of woman"; and "in the Lord." All three statements represent the order in which the first man and woman were created: God created man in his own image and glory and then created woman out of the man and in *his* glory. The notion of "image" is focal here, and woman is, as it were, "out of focus" because she is *not* created in God's image. Thus, and importantly for Paul's total kinship system and its adoption process, there *can* be no "daughters of God," only sons of God,[68] a fact we will return to shortly. In addition to the original created order— "woman was made from man"—the third statement also refers to the procreated order—"man is now born of woman." In order to appreciate the role of this procreated order in Paul's kinship system, we have to do something that he did not do, namely relate it to his discussion of the first man, Adam, in 1 Cor. 15:45–49. For 1 Corinthians 15 shows that procreated man, now presumably including women, differs from the created first man because procreated man is created in the first man's image, not, like the first man himself, in the image and glory of God.[69] Procreated man bears the image of the man of dust and inherits from him both sin and mortality (cf. Rom.

5:12–21). Through sin, both the first man and procreated men (including women) have fallen short of the glory of God (Rom. 3:23). They have exchanged the glory and truth of the immortal God for images resembling mortal man, and they serve the creature rather than the creator (Rom. 1:22–25). Thus, after the first man had been created in the image and glory of God, this man's transgression (Rom. 5:12–21) led to the procreation of subsequent human beings in *his* earthly image, and it is therefore from the form of this alienated image that man is to be transformed by having his form brought into conformity with the image and glory of Jesus Christ, the son of God who is himself the image of God. The closest Paul comes to acknowledging the parallelism between the first man and the firstborn son of God, both of whom are the image of God, is in his comments on Adam and Christ. However, those comments focus on the *contrast* between Adam and Christ and ignore the "history" represented by the sequence of the three stages we are tracing. It appears that Paul never arrived at the point of clearly relating these two segments of his symbolic universe, although in connection with the third stage we find additional evidence that suggests he could have done so with further reflection.

The third stage of male-female relations, "in the Lord," is one in which men and women are not independent (*chōris*) of one another. Although it is not by any means clear what Paul intended by his explanation of this statement—"for as woman was made from man, so man is now born of woman"[70]—the statement itself seems to be an expression of ideas more clearly represented in Gal. 3:26–28.[71] There he says that in Christ Jesus, that is, in the Lord, "all are *sons* of God" (cf. Rom. 8:12–30), there is "neither Jew nor Greek, there is neither slave nor free, *there is no male and female.*" Since there is no male and female in the Lord, men and women are not to be distinguished from one another in the church, and the notion of *sons* of God thus loses its customary sexual connotation of masculinity. Sexual distinctions do *not* obtain among God's children who are, like the first man, asexually or presexually "male." For Paul, sexual distinctions appear to derive from the procreated order rather than from the created order, and for this reason the third stage in the history of male-female relations appears to replicate the first stage, in which God only created "man" in his image and glory, and then woman out of the man. What is more, it also appears that there is a parallelism between this first presexual man and the asexual firstborn son of God, since both are created in the image of God. Indeed, the asexuality of the sons of God requires that the firstborn son be asexual, even if Paul does not explicitly say so.

Although Paul does not draw all of these connections, they are, nevertheless, there to be drawn, and drawing them helps to make sense of some of his kinship conceptions. In particular, they help us to understand what he means when he refers to the children of God—to-be as *"sons* of God" and *"brothers,"* for these terms, which have distinct sexual connotations in the realm of the procreated order, are asexually contrasted with the sexual differentiation obtaining in that order. In the Lord, there is neither male nor female. In the Lord/Christ believers are sons of God–to–be and as such they are in the process of becoming conformed to the image of the firstborn son who is properly speaking the firstborn among many *brothers* (*adelphoi*), although "brethren," as we have previously rendered *adelphoi*, happily blurs the masculine sexual connotation of "brothers." Thus, and paradoxically to be sure, it is not the lack of daughters of God in Paul's kinship system that is striking, but the presence of "sisters" *in the Lord!* That is either a slip on Paul's part or a concession to procreated realities. But whatever the reason may be, our consideration of 1 Cor. 11:3–16 shows that *the ultimate peculiarity of Paul's symbolic kinship system is its rejection of the very sexual distinctions upon which kinship is based.* That he succeeded to the extent he did in maintaining the kinship metaphor while totally reshaping the idea of kinship is nothing short of marvelous.

Less marvelous is the obvious inconsistency in Paul's treatment of the first man, which at least needs to be noted so that it does not interfere with our exploration. As we have seen, man cannot at the same time *be* both the image and glory of God (1 Cor. 11:7) and the bearer of the image of the man of dust (15:47–49). For whatever reasons, Paul disregarded two facts: in 1 Cor. 11:7, the bearer of the image of God is the first man whom God created (cf. Gen. 1:26), and in 1 Cor. 15:47–49 the bearer of the first man's "image" is procreated man. If Paul had attempted to deal with these facts, and with the help of the ideas about Adam expressed in Rom. 5:12–21, he would have arrived at connections like those referred to above. But he did not do so, and therefore the parallelism between Adam and Christ as images of God is not fully reconciled with what we may call the history of sexuality, which is a major aspect of the history of the form of the children of God–to–be. However, if the first stage in that history remains only vaguely connected to the subsequent stages, the last two stages are clearly linked together by the process of bodily transformation from the sexually divided image of the man of dust into the asexual image of the man of heaven. Let us, therefore, turn to this process of transformation and complete our consideration of Paul's kinship system, for the moment of transformation is the moment of adoption as sons of God.

According to Paul, it was God's purpose to summon "men" into his kingdom and glory (1 Thess. 2:12; cf. 1 Cor. 2:7; Rom. 8:28–30), and their glorification is synonymous both with their adoption as God's sons and with the redemptive transformation of their bodies (Rom. 8:18–30). In anticipation of this moment believers call God "Father" and live in the hope of sharing his glory (Rom. 5:3), which they know from the gospel and "see in the face of Christ" (2 Cor. 3:18—4:6). As we have seen, the realization of this hope is in the believer's apparently near future, but about the actual moment of realization all Paul says is that when Christ, the son of God, returns he will transform the believer's body into the likeness of his own body. Until then, the believer is in the process of being transformed into the image of Christ, the son of God, who is being "formed in them" (Gal. 4:19), but about this aspect of the process Paul only says that it *is* taking place, presumably through proper behavior of a moral, social sort, like that considered in the last chapter.[72] There remains, then, the beginning of the process, which is both objective, in terms of when and how it became possible to hope for one's glorification, and subjective, in terms of when and how one enters into the hope of glorification.[73]

Although Paul expresses himself in terms derived from a number of different systems, which makes his terminology resistant to a simple description oriented to but one system, one fundamental conception nevertheless seems to underlie his various expressions.[74] This conception is that man's (as with Paul, the term is used generically) relationship to God was objectively changed by the death and resurrection of Jesus Christ, through which God reconciled man to himself and overcame the state of alienation that had existed between them. Reconciliation is the beginning of the process of glorification as adoptive sons of God.[75] Objectively, the believer's hope is grounded in the belief-knowledge that in Christ's death and resurrection in the form of man, Christ brought an end to the reign over man of the Law, sin, and death and began the process of bodily transformation. In his death in mortal flesh, Christ terminated the time of the Law's custodianship over man by taking upon himself man's obligation to God under it (Gal. 3:10—4:7). Thereby, he redeemed man from the Law and reconciled him to God, who can now consider man righteous if man believes in what God has done through Christ (Rom. 3:19–26; 5:6–21). In addition, by terminating the Law through his death, Christ deprived sin of the power it enjoyed over man through the Law (Romans 5—8; 1 Cor. 15:56), and through his resurrection as the first to have been raised from the dead, Christ began both the conquest of death itself and the process of bodily transformation which will be completed after the rest of the dead have been raised and death's conquest thereby made complete (1 Cor. 15:20–57). All of these things are considered by Paul to be objective facts, and therefore by believing them one has a new objectivity, a new world, and in believing them one has a new regard for oneself as well (2 Cor. 5:15–19; cf. Romans 5—8). New knowledge creates a new reality, and thus a new identity.

Subjectively, one can participate in this new relationship with God by believing that through Christ God has in fact called one into the new relationship with himself (cf. Rom. 10:8–12; 8:28–39). But belief alone does not provide full participation, nor is belief alone sufficient to enable one to become a son of God. One must also participate "in Christ" by being baptized into his death, and together with others seek to become conformed to his image through proper social behavior (sanctification; edification). In Paul's view, from the very beginning God had "many brothers" in mind, hence individual participation in the new relationship with God is through participation in the community of those whom God has called. Baptism is, therefore, not only into Christ as an individual actor, but also into the community of those who are called, namely, the church. Baptism into Christ entails the believers' affirmation of the symbolic meaning of their new understanding of themselves, and baptism into the church entails the public affirmation of this new understanding as an understanding shared with others. Individually, the believers receive at baptism the experiential power called "the spirit," but it is collectively that they call upon God as Father and anticipate becoming his sons. Thus, in baptism the legacy of birth in the image of the man of dust is symbolically, that is, cognitively, canceled by the believers' coming to a new understanding of themselves. They know themselves to have been crucified and buried with Christ, and they believe that they will also live with him from the time of their baptism into eternity. They know that because Christ was raised from the dead he will never die again, that the death he died canceled the power of both death and sin over all who are in him, and that the life he now lives he lives to God. And on this basis they consider (*logizomai*) themselves dead to sin and alive to God through their relationship with Christ (Rom. 6:3–11). Indeed, they no longer "know" any one in the old human (*kata sarka*) terms (2 Cor. 5:16), and they no longer construe life in those terms (Rom. 8:5–8). Their perspective and their behavior is now governed by new terms, by new knowledge, and by a new conviction of what is really real. They have entered into a new reality. They have a new world, a new identity, and new motives for their behavior in this world. Their former individual identities, together with the world that defined them, has been replaced. Their former individuality is absorbed into their unity in Christ, into whose image they are being shaped during the process that leads to their becoming sons of God with him. This process begins with their reconciliation to God through Christ's actions in human form and it ends with their adoption as sons. Christ is thus in his human activity the agent of their reconciliation, while in his identity as the firstborn son of God he is the model, the image, of what they will be when, once again as an agent, he comes to transform their bodies into the likeness of his own body, the form of the sons of God.

MASTER-SLAVE RELATIONS IN PAUL'S SYMBOLIC UNIVERSE

In exploring kinship relations in Paul's symbolic universe, we began by asking what it means to Paul and his "children" to know and understand themselves as *God's* children. We posed this question in order to gain information that, in the last section of this chapter, will help us to determine the behavioral options such knowledge defined for people like Paul and Philemon. Since our exploration of master-slave relations in Paul's symbolic universe has the same goal, we can rephrase our earlier question and now ask what it means to Paul and his children to know Jesus Christ as their common master or Lord and themselves as his slaves.

The positions of master and slave are as fundamentally relational as the positions of parents and children, for each position only exists in relation to the other.[76] Believers, therefore, know themselves to be slaves of Christ because they know him as their Lord. This point is especially important because Paul only very rarely speaks of believers as slaves of Christ (1 Cor. 7:22),[77] and otherwise identifies them as slaves of righteousness and of God (Rom. 6:18, 22; cf. 1 Thess. 1:9).[78] For these reasons, we must presuppose that Philemon knows himself to be a slave of Christ because Paul refers not only to Jesus Christ as "the Lord" (Philemon 3, 5, 20, 25), but also to Philemon's love and faith toward the Lord (v. 5) and to their being "in the Lord" (vv. 16, 20a), which is synonymous with being "in Christ" (vv. 6, 8, 20b, 23), both of which mean being in his service or belonging to him. Indeed, Philemon's love and faith toward (*pros*) the Lord are qualities of the slave's relationship with his master as, from the other side, the "grace" (*charis*) of the Lord that Paul both sends to and invokes upon the church is a quality of the master's relationship with his slaves (vv. 3, 25).[79] Regardless of whether or not these terms represent qualities of worldly master-slave relations, they are qualities of the relations between the Lord Jesus Christ and his slaves because he is their Lord and they are his slaves. Be this as it may for the moment, the common knowledge of the lordship of Christ that is only minimally present in the Letter to Philemon requires us to examine Paul's other letters in order to construct a fuller picture of master-slave relations in Paul's symbolic universe.

Paul's master-slave system depends for its structure and much of its terminology and values on the economic master-slave system of the world outside the church.[80] He refers to the worldly system when he speaks of himself as a free man (1 Cor. 9:1, 19), of Onesimus as a slave (Philemon 16), of slaves, free men, and freedmen who have become members of the church (1 Cor. 7:21–22; 12:13; Gal. 3:28; 4:1–7, 21–31; cf. Phil. 2:22), and of masters (Rom. 14:4).[81] And although he uses certain terms symbolically, his usage reflects knowledge of their worldly significance. He knows about the purchase (*agorazō*) of slaves and about the purchase price (*timē*, 1 Cor. 6:20; 7:23), about the "redemption" (*apolytrōsis*, Rom. 3:24; 8:23)[82] or "buying" (*exagorazō*, Gal. 3: 13; 4:15)[83] of a slave for purposes of freeing him, and therefore about both a buyer or redeemer (1 Cor. 1:30) and the freeing (*eleutheroō*) or manumitting of slaves (Rom. 6:5–23; 8:2, 21; Gal. 4:4–7; 5:1). Paul also knows that a slave receives wages (Rom. 6:23), that to be a slave means to be obedient (Rom. 6:16) and self-humbling (Phil. 2:8), that a slave stands or falls before his master (Rom. 14:4; Phil. 2:9–11), that he must await the master's commendation without commending himself (2 Cor. 10:18), that he must accept the master's decision as to what is sufficient for him (2 Cor. 12:8–10), and that he can only exhort his master to intercede on his behalf (2 Cor. 12:8–10; cf. Rom. 8:27, 34 in view of Christ's lordship and of his identification with the spirit, as in 2 Cor. 3:17). The good slave boasts only about his master (1 Cor. 1:31; 2 Cor. 10:18), the one to whom he belongs (cf. 1 Cor. 1:12; 3:4–5, 21–23; Rom. 7:4; 14:7–9),[84] the one whom he "fears" (2 Cor. 5:11; cf. 1 Thess. 4:6). And above all, the slave is not his own person because someone has purchased him (1 Cor. 6:19b–20; 7:23; Rom. 14:6–9). Usually, much of this knowledge is viewed as "Christian" because it refers to Christ or believers in him, but to view it this way is to put the cart before the horse. Such knowledge is *now* Christian because Paul and others view things in terms of Christ's lordship over them, but the structure, terminology, values, and not least the sentiments conveyed by the knowledge are anti-structurally appropriated from the master-slave system of the world outside the church.[85] Even when we cannot prove such a derivation of individual terms, their appearance in *Paul's* master-slave system suggests that they probably come from its worldly counterpart.

What Paul says about the relations between the Lord Jesus Christ and his slaves often represents typical and even ideal master-slave relations. This is especially evident, as in most of the examples just cited, where the behavior of the actors derives from their *roles* as master and slave rather than from personal qualities that are independent of the roles. As we might expect, the actions of the "slaves" are usually role-specific, allowing for little if any influence from the actors' personal qualities, for they are not free to be themselves because they belong to someone else. The actions of slaves are therefore highly typified, relatively lacking in individuality. Matters are quite different, however, with the role of master, for he who plays it is both legally and personally free. While his role places certain constraints upon his actions, he is relatively free to act as he will and for whatever motives that move him. Paul's characterization of the slave Onesimus and the master Philemon well illustrate this contrast between typical and individual behavior, but for our purposes his characterization of Jesus Christ as master is far richer and more pertinent to our present concerns. The actions of Jesus Christ as Lord are informed not only by the typifications associated with a master, but also by this master's peculiar personal biography. Thus, Paul's "Lord" is the historical person Jesus Christ, who is himself the firstborn son of God. As God's son, he was originally in the form of God and equal to him, but in becoming Jesus Christ he humbly assumed the form of a slave by being born of woman, born in the likeness and shape of man, and in this form he obediently died on a cross. After his death and resurrection as Jesus Christ, God exalted him and named him master over all that is in heaven and on earth and under the earth (Phil. 2:5–11). Since then, he is in heaven, but he is expected to return soon (cf. 1 Thess. 2:19; 3:13; 4:15–17; 5:2, 23; 1 Cor. 1:7–8; 4:5; 5:5; 11:26; 15; 2 Cor. 1:14; 4:5; Phil. 3:20–21). After he has subordinated all things under himself and defeated all his enemies, he will return to earth, gather his people, transform their bodies, deliver them to God, and then subordinate himself to God, relinquishing the role of master that God had given to him (cf. 1 Cor. 15:24–28).[86] The double biography of Paul's Lord as both the firstborn son of God and Jesus Christ defines the individuality of *this* master, and it is accompanied by the motives for his actions, for example, by the fact that he was sent to do what he did. We will return to both of these points later. For the moment, two conclusions have to be drawn about the individuality of Paul's Lord. The

242

first is that as we attempt to understand Paul's symbolic master-slave system we should be sensitive to the distinction between traits that are specific to the *role* of master and traits that are specific to the biography of *this* master. Although he is both a typical and even ideal master, he is also a distinct individual. The second conclusion is that the primary identity of the actor who is Paul's Lord is that of the firstborn son of God, for he is the one who became the man Jesus Christ, who in turn was appointed by God as master of all, for a time.[87]

The knowledge of Christ's lordship that Paul shares with his children is also at least as substantially and as widely shared as knowledge about the kinship system.[88] Both the fatherhood of God, which is communally acknowledged in the ritual cry "Abba! Father!" and the sonship of believers appear to belong to the initiatory rite of baptism, and as such they represent public knowledge among all believers. But the master-slave system permeates *all* aspects of the believers' communal life because the present lordship of Christ is the principal focus of that life.[89] Paul describes as the content of his preaching the announcement that Jesus Christ is Lord (2 Cor. 4:5), and believers are called into the fellowship of God's son, "Jesus Christ our Lord" (1 Cor. 1:9). They are baptized "in the name of" the Lord Jesus Christ (1 Cor. 6:11; cf. 1:9, 13, 15), and "into" him (Rom. 6:3), into one body which is Christ (1 Cor. 12:12–13, 27), and thereafter they are "in Christ" or "in the Lord," both socially and symbolically. Because they have been baptized in the name of the Lord, they can be identified as those who "call upon" (*epikaleō*) his name (Rom. 10:12–13; cf. 1 Cor. 1:3), which they ritually confess (*homologeō*), saying, "the Lord is Jesus" or "Jesus is Lord"[90] (Rom. 10:9; cf. 1 Cor. 12:3; Phil. 2:9–11). Paul thus preaches as Christ's the name "Lord," which God gave to Christ, and the believer confesses this identification and calls upon Christ by using it of him. Moreover, the ritual meal of the community is called "the Lord's table" (*trapexa kyriou*, 1 Cor. 10:21) or "the Lord's supper" (*kyriakon deipnon*, 1 Cor. 11:20), for the Lord is its symbolic host and his slave-guests symbolically share in his body and blood both in remembrance of his death and in demonstration (cf. 1 Cor. 11:26, *katangellō*) of their expectation of his return (11:23–26; cf. 16:22b). The tone of such meals is solemn because improper behavior at them is a profanation of the body and blood of the Lord, which brings one under the Lord's judgment and even leads to illness and death (11:27–34). And last, but certainly not least, it is in the authoritative name of the Lord that community discipline is enforced by the likes of Paul (cf. 1 Cor. 5:3–5; 16:22; Gal. 1:8–9).[91] Obedience to the Lord and his agents is required of all, for "salvation" from judgment is dependent on it (cf. Phil. 2:12–13; Rom. 10:8–13, 21; 1:5, 16; 15:18).[92]

Because this knowledge of Christ's lordship is so institutionalized in the communal life of Paul's churches, his allusions to it in letters like the one to Philemon convey to their readers vastly more meaning than we might expect from the allusions themselves. Paul's statement about his authority in Christ/the Lord to command (v. 8) and compel (v. 14) Philemon, and his expression of confidence in Philemon's obedience to his wishes "in the Lord/Christ" (vv. 20–21), are ultimately and fully meaningful only in the context of what it means for Philemon and Paul to belong to the Lord. The knowledge that is clearly institutionalized in the baptismal and meal rituals and in disciplinary aspects of church life contributes heavily to our understanding of this meaning, but equally important is the knowledge found in Paul's interpretations of and elaborations upon the institutionalized knowledge. It is not clear just how institutionalized this supplementary knowledge is, yet it is evident that if Paul has his way the very sharing of it will institutionalize it as communal knowledge. Nevertheless, it is probably not as institutionalized as the ritual and disciplinary knowledge (but cf. 1 Cor. 7:17b; Rom. 6:17), for the latter is a fixed part of the social life of every church while Paul's supplementary knowledge is largely offered only when he feels that individual churches need it. So, for example, it is only in Galatians and Romans that he contrasts being a slave with being a son of God, only in Romans that enslavement is to sin and death, only in 2 Corinthians that he contrasts the glory of the Lord with the glory of Moses, and only in Philippians that he cites Christ's slavelike humility and obedience as a model for believers who now acknowledge him as their Lord. Nevertheless, despite the difference in the degree to which the institutionalized and more personalized kinds of knowledge are shared among Paul's churches, the more individualized supplementary knowledge forms a simple system of ideas, values, and sentiments representing Paul's understanding of the institutionalized knowledge. His letters do not contain everything that he said to each church, but his system of master-slave knowledge is such that he cannot help but to have communicated it in explaining the institutionalized knowledge to his churches. Consequently, precisely because his ideas, values, and sentiments do form a coherent system, we must be concerned with the distinctive features of that system.

The two most distinctive features of Paul's master-slave system are its universalization of the two roles, master and slave, and its representation of the very form of human existence as the form of a slave. To be human is to be a slave.

The first feature is rather simple because Paul depicts Christ as having been designated by God as Lord over all in heaven and on earth and under the earth (Phil. 2:10). He will remain Lord until he has destroyed every rule and authority and power, the last enemy being death, and when all things have been subordinated to his lordship he will turn both his role and those whom he has subordinated over to God (1 Cor. 15:24–28).[93] In the meantime, he is the link between the love of God and those who belong to him as his slaves. Neither "death, nor life, nor angels, nor principalities, nor things present nor things to come, nor power, nor height, nor depth, nor anything else in all creation" can, under his lordship, separate the believer from the love of God (Rom. 8:38–39; cf. 1 Cor. 3:21b–23). For the believer, "there is one God, the Father, from whom are all things and for whom we exist, and one Lord, Jesus Christ, through whom are all things and through whom we exist" (1 Cor. 8:6). Through the lordship of Christ, the believer is victorious against all powers, both real and imagined, that might threaten him (Rom. 8:17–39; 1 Cor. 15:57; cf. 2 Cor. 4:7—5:5). Christ is thus in the process of securing his own universal and cosmic lordship, and all of those who belong to him are his slaves, totally dependent upon him. In the world there are many lords, each having his own slave, but in Christ there is only one Lord and all who are his are his slaves.

More complex is the second distinctive feature of Paul's master-slave system, the understanding of the form of human existence as being the form of enslavement. With this notion, Paul radically universalizes the meaning of "slave" by defining the human condition as such as a condition of enslavement. The "form of a slave" (Phil. 2:7) is to the master-slave system what the form of the children of God is to the kinship system, and indeed the two intersect in Paul's symbolic universe because it is the form of the children of God that replaces the form of a slave: "Through God you are no longer a slave but a son, and if a son then an heir" (Gal. 4:7). The condition of enslavement and the process of liberation from it are, therefore, focal points for another representation of the process of mediations that governs Paul's symbolic universe. In order to establish the coherence of the ideas, values, and sentiments comprising this representation we can once again employ the format of a series of propositions.

(1) *The shape (schēma) and likeness (homoiōma) of man has the form of a slave (morphē doulou,* Phil 2:7[–8, RSV]). The description of man as having the form of a slave is found only in Philippians 2,

but the ideas, values, and sentiments associated with it are found in several other descriptions that we have already observed in dealing with Paul's kinship system. That all of these are most closely related becomes evident when we see that each of them belongs to a set of contrasting terms. Thus, in Philippians 2 "the form of a slave" is contrasted with "the form of God" (*morphē theou*, 2:6), and Christ's behavior in the form of a slave is appropriately characterized as both humble (*tapeinos*, 2:8; cf. 2:3) and obedient (*hypēkoos*, 2:8; cf. 2:12). Humility and obedience are qualities characteristic of slaves in general and not merely of Christ's behavior in human form. But because *he* was humble and obedient to the point of giving his life, *his* behavior was exemplary both *of* slavelike behavior and *for* his own subsequent slaves (cf. 2:3–5, 12–13). More to the point of our present concerns, however, is the contrast between Christ's two forms and the qualities associated with his form as a slave.

The slavelike qualities of humility and obedience provide links to other passages in Paul's letters that on the face of it do not seem to be related to the idea of the form of a slave. One important example comes from Phil. 3:21, where Paul contrasts the believer's "humble" or "abject" body (*to sōma tēs tapeinōseōs*) with Christ's "glorious body" (*sōma tēs doxēs*),[94] here referring to Christ's body in the form of God, not in the form of a slave (on which see further, below). Phil. 3:21 is synonymous with 2:6, 7 because having "the form of a slave" means having a lowly or humble body, while having a body of glory means having the form of God.[95] But Phil. 3:21 is also important for two other reasons. One is that even the believer is considered to be in the form of a slave until he or she is finally transformed into the form of God. Human existence, both before and after one becomes a believer, is in the form of a slave. This point will prove to be fundamental for understanding the apparent paradox that the believer has been liberated from one form of enslavement only to be temporarily enrolled in another, namely to Christ as Lord (see proposition 3, below). The other reason Phil. 3:21 is important is that it links 2:6–8 both to a number of other texts we considered in connection with the form of the children of God, and to the contrasts we observed between characteristics of the image of the man of dust and characteristics of the image of the man of heaven (1 Cor. 15:47–49).[96] Indeed, the contrast between these two images, as well as between their characteristics, is homologous with the contrast between the form of God and the form of a slave. Believers not only bear the image of the man of dust until Christ returns, but all of the characteristics of the image of the man of dust are defining features of the form of a slave, of man as such. Believers are, like nonbelievers, enslaved (*douleia*) to decay or perishability (*phthora*, Rom. 8:21); they are "sewn" in dishonor (*atimia;* cf. *tapeinōsis*, Phil. 3:21) and weakness (*astheneia*, 1 Cor. 15:43); they have a physical or psychic body (*sōma psychikon*, 1 Cor. 15:44); they are living beings (*psychēn zōsan*, 1 Cor. 15:45) of flesh and blood (*sarx kai haima*, 1 Cor. 15:50), made from the dusty earth (*ek gēs choïkos*, 1 Cor. 15:47); and they are, finally, mortal (*thnēton*). It is enslavement to the perishable body that renders the form of human existence as that of a slave.

Enslavement to the perishable body of flesh raises a number of other issues concerning the form of a slave. On the one hand, they have to do with enslavement to sin and death, and on the other hand they have to do with enslavement both to the Law of Moses, which stimulates sin, and to the "elemental spirits of the universe" (*stoicheia tou kosmou*, Gal. 4:3, 9).

For Paul, enslavement to the "sinful body" (*to sōma tēs hamartias*, Rom. 6:6) is the same as enslavement to "sinful flesh" (*sarkos hamartias*, 8:3). "Body" and "flesh" are synonymous when Paul is referring to the mortal body as being in the image of the man of dust, so that sin can be said to dwell both in the flesh (7:18) and in the body (6:12), in both cases meaning "in the person" (cf. 7:20) who is in the form of a slave. It is the perishable body of flesh that is "sold" into enslavement to sin, which is a power within the body that commands one's obedience (*hypakoē*) to the body's passions (6:12; cf. 6:6, 13, 16), to the desires of the flesh (13:14; cf. Gal. 5:16–17, 24). Sin was, it will be recalled, historically introduced into the genetics of humankind through Adam's transgression, and once introduced it remains as a powerful component within the biological and moral constitution of human beings. But with sin also came death, which like sin was historically introduced and, like sin, remains a constitutional characteristic of the species: people die (Rom. 5:12–21). Thus, because of sin humans are enslaved to death as well as to sin. Although Paul speaks of sin and death as "reigning" (*basileuō*), using a royal metaphor (cf. Rom. 5:14, 17, 21; 6:12), this metaphor operates within his master-slave system, for people are also "enslaved to sin" and "freed" from it (6:6–7, 22), and they are "set free" from "the law of sin and death" (8:2). This liberation is the subject of another proposition, but in connection with the present one we should note that it entails a process, the end of which will be the full liberation from the bondage to decay when the mortal body is redeemed and the believer obtains the full freedom of the glory of the children of God, the adoption as sons. This "redemption" (*apolytrōsis*) is, as we have seen, a metaphor drawn from the master-slave system, and when it takes place all forms of enslavement will end, and so will the master-slave system itself. Without the perishable body of sinful flesh there is no enslavement, only freedom.

"While we were living in the flesh, our sinful passions, aroused *by the Law*, were at work in our members to bear fruit for death" (Rom. 7:5). Because the Law, sin, and death form an unholy trinity of notions in Paul's symbolic universe, the Law of Moses is a part of the enslavement to which people are subject. In Romans, Paul speaks about the Law as a captor from which the believer has been discharged (7:6), but in the context of 7:1–3 being a captive is synonymous with being enslaved (7:1), just as being discharged or released is synonymous with being set free (7:3). Whatever the metaphor, however, the Law itself is not evil but only an unwitting accomplice to sin. Sin found in it an opportunity to do its work because the Law made man conscious of sin by naming sins (7:5–24), and thus the Law aroused sinful passions in the weakened flesh (8:2). In his letter to Galatia, Paul also refers to the Law in terms of enslavement and liberation. There he speaks of the Law as a yoke of slavery from which Jews had to be "redeemed" (*exagorazō*, Gal. 3:13; 4:5) and from which Christ has set them free (*eleutheroō*, 5:1).[97] In Galatians Paul also depicts the Law as a temporary constraint, a custodian like a child's guardian or trustee (Gal. 3:19–25; 4:1–2), but master-slave metaphors dominate, as we can see in his allegorical interpretation of the story of Abraham's two sons. One was the son of a slave, the other the son of a free woman. The slave woman Hagar and her slave son stand respectively for the covenantal Law of Moses and "the present Jerusalem, for she is in slavery with her children," while the free woman Sarah and her free son stand respectively for the promise to Abraham and the heavenly Jerusalem: "the Jerusalem above is free, and she is our mother" (4:21–27). Developing his lesson from this interpretation, Paul quotes from the original story, in which it is said: "Cast out the slave and her son; for the son of the slave shall not inherit with the son of the free woman" (4:30; cf. Gen. 21:10–12). Applied to the Galatians, this means that they are the children not of the slave but of the free woman, and therefore they should not submit to the yoke of slavery, the Law, which Jewish teachers are requiring of them (5:1b; cf. 2:4–5). With a veritable shout Paul says, "For freedom Christ has set us free" (5:1a), and the act of liberation (*eleutheroō*) to which he refers is virtually synonymous with the act of redemption (*exagorazō*) he has twice cited previously (3:13; 4:5). Thus, in Romans Paul addresses the problem of enslavement to sin, death, and the Law, while in Galatians he concentrates on enslavement only to the Law (but see Gal. 5:13–26

248

and 6:8). However, the emphasis in Galatians is related to the problem of Jewish teachers who are seeking to get Gentile believers in Christ to submit to the Law of Moses. In response to this problem Paul identifies the Jews as being enslaved to the Law and contrasts their enslavement with the freedom of those who are in Christ, whether Jews or Gentiles, and who, being in Christ, are true sons of Abraham. But having addressed the enslavement of Jews apart from Christ, Paul also addresses the enslavement of Gentiles apart from Christ.

While the Jews have been enslaved to the Law, Gentiles have been enslaved to "the elemental spirits of the universe" (*ta stoicheia tou kosmou*, 4:3, 9).[98] Although it is not clear how these "spirits" are related to the idols worshiped by Gentiles (cf. Rom. 1:21–25; 1 Thess. 1:9–10), they are apparently construed by Gentiles as divine beings or principles associated with calendrical divisions and their corresponding ritual observances (Gal. 4:8–10). But whatever these spirits are, and regardless of their relationship to the Jewish teachers in Galatia, the reason for enslavement to them is ignorance of God (4:8–9), and the consequence of this enslavement is immorality, indulgence in the sinful passions of the flesh (cf. Gal. 5:13–24; Rom. 1:21–31; 1 Thess. 1:9–10; 4:3–8). The consequence is familiar to us, but not its premise, the ignorance of God. Paul does not explain this ignorance, or its consequence, in terms of his notion of perishable man mortally affected by sin but in terms of the Gentiles' foolishness and stupidity in *choosing* to worship the creature rather than the Creator (Rom. 1:21–31). Although this act seems analogous to Adam's transgression (cf. Rom. 5:12–21), Paul does not draw this connection or otherwise seek to relate these comments about the Gentiles to what he says about Adam, sin, death, and the Law. In Galatians the Law is to the Jews what the "elemental spirits" are to the Gentiles, but these "spirits" are not said to stimulate sin like the Law. Indeed, in Romans the Law, coming *after* sin and death, stimulated sin but did not introduce it, whereas idolatry appears to have produced sinning. So once more we find that Paul has not gotten around to resolving differences or drawing relationships between various pieces of his symbolic universe. Perhaps the closest he comes to doing so in this connection is his assertion that *all* have sinned and fallen short of the glory of God (Rom. 3:23; cf. 3:9), two manifestations of which failure are enslavement to sin and to objects that are not God. Enslavement is therefore the defining characteristic of that form of human existence which is in the image of the man of dust, and liberation entails being set free from both the form and its image. In other words, the image of the man of dust has the

249

form of a slave, and liberation entails a transformation into another image. But whatever the words, for Paul freedom is of considerably higher value than enslavement. Indeed, within the master-slave system God's purpose is to liberate his creatures from their form as slaves.

(2) *Sent by God the Father, the firstborn son of God was born in human form, the form of a slave, to free men from that form and transform them into the form of the sons of God* (cf. Phil. 2:5–11; Gal. 3:26—4:7; Rom. 8:2–30).[99] Because this and the rest of the propositions include all of the knowledge we have already considered in connection with Jesus Christ and the son of God, we can presuppose that knowledge and focus on those aspects of the propositions that are more specifically related to Paul's symbolic master-slave system. In addition, our concern in this proposition is principally with the liberating acts of the son of God in the form of Jesus Christ, not with the acts of Jesus Christ as Lord. Here we must remember that the primary identity of the actor we are concerned with is that of the firstborn son of God, for he was the one who was born, lived, died, and rose as Jesus Christ, and who, following his resurrection from the dead was named Lord of all by God. Strictly speaking, the liberating acts associated with Christ's death and resurrection are therefore *not* the acts of the Lord Jesus Christ *as Lord*, because he only became Lord after having accomplished them. They are *the acts of Jesus Christ as a slave.* Similarly, the final liberating act associated with the return of the Lord Jesus Christ does not appear to proceed from his role as Lord but from his role as son of God. Although Paul says that the Lord Jesus Christ will transform bodies of humiliation into the body of his glory by the same energy (*energeia*) that enables him to subordinate all things to himself (Phil. 3:20–21; cf. Rom. 14:4), the body of glory is the form of the sons of God, and the transforming energy is a product of the firstborn son's power and glory, not of his authority as Lord. This energy combines with the Lord's authority in his conquest of death (cf. 1 Cor. ,15:25–26), but the transformation of the body of humiliation appears to be an act of the son of God. Admittedly, however, Paul is not unequivocally clear at this point, at least in part because this is the point of transition between the end of the master-slave system and the full realization of the kinship system. Nevertheless, despite the lack of clarity the focus of the second proposition is on those acts by which it becomes possible for people to be freed from the form of enslavement. Christ clearly only becomes Lord after the initial liberating acts associated with his death and resurrection, and his lordship only becomes effective when others enter into his service as slaves.

For these reasons, we will deal with Christ's lordship under the next proposition, which concerns the liberation and re-enslavement of the believer. Our focus now is on what Paul considers to be the objective facts of liberation achieved by Christ's death and resurrection, for these are the basis for their subjective appropriation by the believer.

Christ's birth in the likeness (*homoiōma*) of man and his assumption of the shape (*schēma*) of man (Phil. 2:7), and his being born of woman (Gal. 4:5) and his being sent in the likeness (*homoiōma*) of sinful flesh (Rom. 8:2), are all to be subsumed under the notion that he who had been in the form of God took the form of a slave (Phil. 2:7a). According to Paul, God sent his son in this form to free (*eleutheroō*) people "from the law of sin and death" and make them sons of God (Rom. 8:2–3, 12–30). However, included in this purpose is also the redemption (*exagorazō*) of Jews from the curse of the Law (Gal. 3:13; 4:4–5; cf. Rom. 7:1–6) and the liberation of Gentiles from servitude (*douleuō*) to beings that by nature are not gods (Gal. 4:8–9). Both these nongods and the Law, for Gentiles and Jews respectively, stimulated sin due to the weakness of the flesh; all people, both Jews and Greeks, are under the power of sin (Rom. 3:9; cf. 3:23). Paul does not say exactly how Christ's actions could free the Gentiles from enslavement to their nongods, but he does say that both Jews and Gentiles can be free from the Law because Christ, in his death, "redeemed (*exagorazō*) us from the curse of the Law" by becoming a curse for us (Gal. 3:13). In the death of Christ, God condemned sin in the flesh in order to fulfill the just requirement of the Law which others could not fulfill for themselves (Rom. 8:3–4). "Christ was put to death for our trespasses" (Rom. 8:25a), he died for the ungodly, for us (Rom. 5:6, 8), and for our sins (1 Cor. 15:3), reconciling us with God and justifying us before him (Rom. 5:9–10) by acquitting all who were under the Law through his righteous and obedient death on their behalf (cf. Rom. 5:18–19). Christ's death was therefore under the Law, but *for* those who could not themselves be righteous before God under it. His death under the Law was God's means of bestowing the possibility of righteousness upon those who could not achieve it themselves by doing the Law, which was never designed to produce righteousness anyway, but only to identify sins to be avoided (cf. Gal. 2:15–16; 3:19–25; Rom. 5:12–21; 7:1–24). As we saw earlier, by introducing this means of being considered righteous before God, and therefore of being reconciled with him, God also terminated the Law of Moses as the form of mediation between himself and his people, the Jews, and therefore for everyone else as well. Christ's death as a slave satisfied all of the require-

251

ments of the Law for others who could not meet them, and in the process it brought an end to the time of the Law's custodianship over God's people. In a different and more strained argument, Paul also suggests in master-slave terms that because the Law is binding, that is, is lord over (*kyrieuō*) people, only during their life, Christ's bodily death freed (*eleutheroō*) him from the Law, and therefore also all of those who are baptized into him (Rom. 7:1–6; cf. 6:3–11, and below). The Law itself still exists and functions as usual for those who have not heard about Christ's death, or have not accepted it, but since his death it has no claim either upon him or upon those who are "in" him. But whatever argument Paul makes, it is clear that for him Christ's appearance in the form of a slave was necessary for the liberation of all who have that form because it was by his death in that form that he made their liberation possible. After his death and because of it, the Law, which serves to stimulate sin, ceases to function both for him and for those who identify with him. Yet, the Law is still only an accessory to the criminal lordship of sin, the currency of whose wages is death. Those who are in the form of a slave are fundamentally enslaved to the lordship of sin and death, and Christ's death in that form liberated people from them as well.

In addition to fulfilling and terminating the Law, Christ's death in the likeness of sinful flesh condemned sin itself in the flesh (Rom. 8:3),[100] and the "death he died he died to sin, once for all" (6:10a). Christ's death is therefore doubly for others, because it fulfilled the requirement of the Law that others could not fulfill and because it condemned sin *itself.* Like the Law, sin remains in the world, but also like the Law sin has lost its absolute lordship over people. How? Just as the Law has lordship over a person only during his life (Rom. 7:1), so is sin's lordship effective only during one's life— because sin works through the passions of the *mortal* body (6:6–7). When this body dies, sin loses its power over it, and therefore "he who has died is freed (*dedikaiōtai*) from sin" (6:7). It is immediately understandable from this why Christ's death freed *him* from the Law and sin, but it is less clear why *his* death also qualifies their absolute lordship over others. The only explanation for this is that Jesus Christ was the son of God whom God sent for precisely this purpose (Rom. 8:3–4; cf. 3:21–26; 5:6–11; 2 Cor. 5:14–19; Gal. 4:4– 5; 5:1a).

With the elimination of the absolute lordship of the Law and sin, only death remains of the unholy trinity. Its lordship (*kyrieuō*, Rom. 6:9) is historically and anthropologically derived from sin's lordship, for death was the consequence of sin, and both sin and death derive their power from the perishable body of flesh. Because Christ died and was raised from the dead, death no longer has lordship over him because he will never die again. Therefore, like the Law and sin, death remains in the world, but like them its absolute lordship has also been qualified for all (Rom. 6:8–10), for Christ's resurrection is but the first. When he returns God will raise from the dead those who belong to him, and they, together with those who are still alive, will have their bodies transformed into the likeness of the glorious body of the sons of God (1 Cor. 15:20–23, 51–57; 2 Cor. 4:13–14; Phil. 3:20–21; 1 Thess. 4:13—5:10).

Thus, in Christ's death and resurrection the son of God has made it possible for others to be freed from enslavement to the Law, sin, and death. Prior to the sending of the son of God in the form of a slave, people had only the image of the man of dust, but after Christ's liberating acts on their behalf they have on the horizon of their own possibilities the image of the man of heaven, the form of the sons of God. In addition to this, however, after Christ's death and resurrection God also named *him* Lord over all and called people into fellowship with him. Through this fellowship, through belonging to *this* Lord and being "in" him, one participates in his personal victories over the Law, sin, and death and orients one's self to the image of this man of heaven, into which one considers one's self as being transformed. The process of transformation will be completed when this Lord completes his subordination of all things under himself and destroys his resistant enemies, the last of which is death itself (cf. 1 Cor. 15:20–57). The Law has been terminated, sin condemned and weakened, and death mortally wounded, all by Christ's death and resurrection. The end is near.

(3) *Those who accept the call into fellowship with God's son, Jesus Christ the Lord, are freed from the lordship of sin and death by the spirit of life that is "in Christ" and become slaves of Christ as Lord, for his death was the price God paid to buy, that is, redeem, them from their former masters* (1 Cor. 1:9; Rom. 8:2; 1 Cor. 7:21–23; 6:19b–20a; Rom. 6:3—8:17). This proposition has two aspects. One concerns the freeing of the believers from their former masters, sin and death,[101] and the other concerns their re-enslavement to a new master, Jesus Christ. Before we take up these aspects separately, we should remember that their common ground is Paul's understanding of the present form of human existence as the form of a slave. As long as one exists in the mortal body, one can never be anything but a slave. The question therefore is, "A slave to what?" After Adam, the first man, and before and apart from Christ, people have no choice but to be a slave to sin and death. But after Christ one can be a slave to him as Lord—and hope to become a son of God like him

through the transformation of the mortal body. The wages of sin is death, says Paul, but the return one receives from the holiness or sanctification[102] made possible in Christ is God's gift of eternal life in Christ Jesus the Lord (Rom. 6:20–23). This gift, and the completion of the process of liberation from the form of a slave, will come with the redemptive transformation of the enslaved body in the adoption as sons of God. The common ground of liberation and re-enslavement is expressed in master-slave terms when Paul says that God purchased (*agorazō*) the slaves of sin and death from these masters,[103] with Christ's death as the price, and then he assigned the redeemed slaves to the risen Christ whom he named as their master. They do not belong to themselves, but to the master Jesus Christ (cf. 1 Cor. 6:19–20; 7:23; 1:30; Rom. 14:7–9).[104] He is Lord of their bodies, and their bodies are in his service (1 Cor. 6:13 end), and it is he who now determines their status, roles, and jobs (1 Cor. 7:17; cf. 7:1–40; 3:21–23; 12:4–30).[105]

Paul says that the believer has been set free from the lordship of sin and death by the law of the spirit of life in Christ Jesus (Rom. 8:2; cf. "Lord" in 7:25, and see also 2 Cor. 3:17). However, because the spirit becomes effective for believers only with their baptism, baptism provides the wider context within which we must view their liberation from sin and death (cf. 1 Cor. 12:13; 2:12; 6:11; Gal. 3:2–3, 5, 27—4:7; Rom. 8:12–17).[106]

Being baptized into Christ Jesus is for Paul a baptism into Christ's death, a burial with him in which the believer is symbolically united with Christ in a death like his. Under the previous proposition, we saw how Christ's actions *could*, objectively speaking, have efficacy for others. Now we have to see how they actually, that is, subjectively become efficacious for them. The key here is the notion of symbolic union.[107] Consistent with the understanding of symbol in the sociology of knowledge, the symbolic character of union with Christ is confirmed both by the fact that the believer does not literally die and by Paul's conclusion that after baptism one *knows* or *understands* one's self in a different way. "We know (*ginōskontes*) that our old self was crucified with him so that the sinful body might be destroyed, and we might no longer be enslaved to sin" (Rom. 6:6). "If we have died with Christ, *we believe (pisteuomen)* that we shall also live with him" (Rom. 6:8; cf. 1 Thess. 4:14–17; 2 Cor. 4:13–14). "So *you* also *must consider yourselves (hymeis logizesthe heautous)* dead to sin and alive to God in Christ Jesus" (Rom. 6:11). Therefore, knowing that they participate in Christ's victory over sin and death, believers *set their minds (phroneō; to phronēma)* not on the things of the flesh but on the things of the spirit (Rom. 8:5; cf. vv.

5–8). All of this "knowledge" is symbolic because it pertains to things "that are not seen" in the world of everyday life (cf. 2 Cor. 4:18; Rom. 8:24–25). They are things that enable the believer to understand the world of everyday life in a different way. But this knowledge is only a small sample of the symbolic universe adopted by the believer at baptism, for everything associated with it that Paul describes as *fact* (e.g., in Romans 5—8) is, in fact, symbolic knowledge.

For Jewish believers baptismal knowledge tells them that they have been freed from the Law of Moses, and in social terms they are actually free from it. The same is true of the Gentiles who have been freed from idols and the elemental spirits of the universe. But regardless of whether believers are Jews or Gentiles, their baptismal knowledge also tells them that they are in the process of being freed from sin and death. The authority and lordship of the Law has already been canceled, and the last enemy to be destroyed is death, and therefore neither of these is or should be focal for the believer, whose central concern once baptized is the war with sin. Because it dwells within the believer, it has an experiential immediacy which both the Law and death lack. The Law is a social "yoke" that can be put on or taken off, and one's own death is always in the future, but never in the present. Sin, however, daily, even momentarily, demands obedience from those whose form is the form of enslavement. *Knowing* that sin itself has been mortally wounded by the death of the son of God, that sin has been condemned, is a powerful force. But sin remains as a power that requires of mortals more than knowledge to resist its demands. Sin is a law dwelling within fleshly bodies, and it seeks to enslave people as long as they are in that body (cf. Rom. 7:7–24). Knowledge of sin's wounds helps, but a counterbalancing power, a counteracting law, is needed to resist sin's undiminished power. It is not knowledge that is the liberator from sin's lordship, but "the law of the spirit of life in Christ Jesus" (Rom. 8:2).

The spirit received by believers at baptism is much more than an object of knowledge, much more than a symbol, because it is experienced by them as a power within them. The power of the spirit is probably best indicated by the acts attributed to it in 1 Corinthians, where its power is clearly experienced by those who through it prophesy and speak in tongues (cf. 1 Corinthians 12—14; Rom. 15:19). But it is also and more significantly evident in the ritual cry "Abba! Father!" which Paul attributes to the spirit "himself"[108] as "bearing witness with our spirits that we are children of God" (Rom. 8:15–16; cf. Gal. 4:6). Similarly, it is evident in Paul's understanding of the believer's prayers because "the spirit helps us in our weakness; for we do not know how to pray as we ought, but the spirit himself intercedes for us with sighs too deep for words" (Rom. 8:26). Usually, Paul speaks of this spirit as being God's, but he can also refer to it as the spirit of God's son (cf. Gal. 4:6; Rom. 8:9; 2 Cor. 3:17). But just whose spirit it is, is not the point, for God and his firstborn son share the same form, glory, power—and doubtless "spirit." The point is rather that the spirit which is experienced within the believer is understood as the form of the *Lord's* presence within the believer. Not only *is* the Lord the spirit, but it is also the case that "where the spirit of the Lord is, there is freedom" (*eleutheria*, 2 Cor. 3:17).[109] The experience of the spirit is, therefore, understood as the sign and power of one's liberation from the form of a slave and from its masters, sin and death, as we can see in Paul's words that immediately follow those just quoted: "And *we* all, . . . beholding the glory of the Lord, *are being changed into his image* from one degree of glory to another; for this comes from the Lord who is the spirit" (3:18). Thus, the spirit that is experienced within is also understood as the power (cf. Phil. 3:20–21, "energy") by which one is being transformed from one form into another, from the form of a slave and into the form of the sons of God. The spirit is the experiential guarantee that the still mortal self will be "swallowed up by life" (2 Cor. 5:1–5; cf. 1:22), and as in the cry "Abba! Father!" it is also the guarantee that one is "no longer a slave but a son, and if a son then an heir" (Gal. 4:7), for it is "the spirit of adoptive sonship" (Rom. 8:15), the spirit of God's firstborn son (Gal. 4:7), the spirit of God himself (Rom. 8:9–10). All "who are led by the spirit of God are sons of God" (Rom. 8:14). Paul's comments in 2 Cor. 3:17–18 and 5:1–5 are, therefore, intimately related to the ritual cry "Abba! Father!" because the spirit that produces this cry is experienced as the liberator from slavery and both the guarantee of sonship and the power that leads one on the way to it.

The full realization of freedom and sonship are, however, still in the believers' future, and for as long as they remain in the mortal body they are still subject to sin's demands. Paul comes at this problem from two angles, enslavement to God and the Lord Jesus Christ, and obedience to the law of the spirit of life. Together, these two themes represent the paradox in which the believer is a free slave or, like Paul himself, an enslaved free man: believers have been set free from sin and have become slaves of righteousness (Rom. 6:18; cf. 6:22; 7:1–6). The metaphorical character of this new enslavement is fully acknowledged by Paul, who claims that in saying this he is speaking in human terms (*anthrōpinon*) because of the weakness of the believers' flesh (*dia tēn astheneian tēs sarkos humōn*, Rom. 6:19).[110] But precisely because the believers are still in the flesh the metaphor is profoundly apt. Believers have a choice—to yield themselves as obedient slaves to sin or to yield themselves as obedient slaves to God and the master whom he has appointed over them (Rom. 6:12–23). Apart from the Lord believers had no choice because they were unable to resist the power of sin at work within them. But in the Lord the power of the spirit is also at work within them, for those who belong to the Lord have the spirit of the Lord (Rom. 8:9). In the Lord, believers therefore have both a choice *and* the power to act upon it, and they can demonstrate that they belong to the Lord by setting their minds on the spirit and by following its directions, by "walking according to the spirit," not "according to the flesh" (cf. Rom. 8:2–17; Gal. 5:16–26). Believers know that by walking according to the spirit they will demonstrate in humble and obedient action (cf. Phil. 2:1–13) their confession of Christ's lordship over them, and that in doing so they will put to death the deeds of the body and live (Rom. 8:13). Of course, in addition to this internal guidance they also have the external guidance of Paul, his fellow workers, and local church leaders, whose roles we examined in the last chapter. Together, these symbolic forms and social arrangements shape the lives and sustain the faith of both individuals and communities.

(4) *Through God believers are no longer slaves but sons, and if sons then heirs. However, they will fully obtain the freedom of the glory of the children of God only when they are set free from the form of a slave and its bondage to decay. Only with the redemption of their bodies will their adoption as sons of God be complete* (Gal. 4:7; Rom. 8:21, 23). When Paul speaks about the believer no longer being a slave but a son, he is employing the rhetoric of faith and hope. That much is clear from all that we have seen in connection with both the image of the man of dust and the form of a slave. We can, therefore, conclude our exploration of Paul's symbolic master-slave system by pointing to its conclusion, its termination for believers in their departure from the form of a slave and putting on of the form of the sons of God, and its termination for the Lord Jesus Christ when he delivers the kingdom to God the Father and subordinates himself to God (1 Cor. 15:24–28). Then there will no longer be either slaves or masters, even the lordship of Jesus Christ, but only God the Father and his sons.

MEDIATION, INTERNALIZATION, MOTIVATION, AND ACTION

The symbolic knowledge we have been exploring comprises a system of mediations between the individual and God. This system defines individual and social existence in the world in radically negative terms, but it also provides people with a basis for transcending their situation, symbolically in the present and literally in the near future. The relevance of the system for the everyday life and behavior of individuals, that is, its power to motivate behavior consistent with it, depends upon the degree to which individuals internalize the system and make it their own, upon the degree to which they accept it as true, upon the degree to which it expresses their own sentiments about themselves and their world. Related to this contingency, we have observed in both this and the preceding chapter that not every individual member of Paul's churches may have had all of this knowledge, nor if they had it need they either have understood it as Paul does or acted upon it.[111] Thus, the contingencies attending the internalization of symbolic knowledge make it difficult for us to predict the behavior of an actor like Philemon on the basis of the knowledge he shared with Paul. Bearing this limitation in mind, however, we can nevertheless point to certain facts about that knowledge which bear on the behavioral options it sets for such actors.

The first fact is that because the major features of this knowledge are bound up with fundamental ritual and disciplinary activities in which every believer participates, the knowledge is sustained by institutionalized forms of social relations—the baptism of each new believer, the periodic meetings for communal meals and worship in relatively small house churches, and the emerging system for insuring communal order and discipline. The second fact is that the knowledge propagated in connection with these institutions, including Paul's own interpretations of and elaborations upon it, is totalistic, constituting a symbolic universe. It embraces the whole of the believers' social life, beginning with their most fundamental identities as particular human beings and extending to their understanding that the present shape of the world is passing away, soon to be replaced by a totally different form of existence and therefore by a totally different reality, one in which they can participate only by acting according to their new knowledge. What is more, precisely because this knowledge is totalistic, its meaningfulness for individuals depends on its representing their own sentiments about themselves and their world, regardless of whether they had these sentiments before joining the church or had them generated in them by

the preaching that led them to join it. The shared knowledge, therefore, represents internal realities, the sentiments, as well as external
realities, men, women, and their world. The individuals' decisions
to join the church are motivated both by their acceptance of the
reality represented in this knowledge and by their sentiments about
it. Their decisions entail a felt commitment to its representation of
what is really real and therefore of paramount value. They are in
every way caught up in a process of resocialization, not of secondary
socialization.

In addition to the institutionalization and comprehensiveness of
this body of knowledge there is also a third fact to be considered, for
at the very beginning of the believers' membership in the church
their new knowledge is experientially reinforced by their experience
within themselves of a power which they are told *is* the Lord,
namely, the spirit received at baptism. However the social scientist
may explain this experience, the social scientist knows (1) that
something *is* experienced, (2) that this experience personally validates what one has learned and now "knows," and (3) that this
knowledge both interprets the experience and structures the individual's life.[112] The experience confirms the claims of the knowledge
and the knowledge interprets the experience. Thus, by institutional
means knowledge is given, experientially confirmed, interpreted,
and then acted upon.

Unencumbered by social scientific distance, believers do more
than believe, they *know*, and they know because they believe: " . . .
we too believe, and so we speak, knowing that he who raised the
Lord Jesus will raise us also with Jesus and bring us with you into
his presence" (2 Cor. 4:13b–14). Those who are in Christ are therefore not of two minds, not split between two worlds.[113] By adopting
the church's totalistic knowledge they have departed from one
world and entered into another. There is, however, one complicating factor, for while believers *understand* themselves to be participating in a new reality, we have seen that the old one remains and
that believers also participate in it both as social beings and as
mortal beings. It is precisely for this reason, that the old has not yet
fully passed away or the new yet fully come, that believers have
behavioral options which they would not have if the new had fully
come. Indeed, if there were only the new reality there would be no
options, for all would be sons of God, whose very form lacks the
social distinctions that create social options. Because the old has
not fully passed away, believers like Philemon *have* options, the
possibility of choice. These options now concern us, and they are
informed both by the several facts about the believers' knowledge

that we have just observed and by the content of that knowledge which we have been exploring throughout this chapter.

Although our concern is ultimately with the options Philemon has before him, let us first consider Paul, for what he represents about his own choices will help us to understand the options from which Philemon has to choose. Because Paul is both a model *of* a good believer and *for* being a good believer, he serves as a model for Philemon.

Of all the characters in Paul's wider story, except for Christ in the form of a slave, Paul has most fully internalized his new knowledge even though he has not fully integrated it in his thought. To be sure, we can only say this because *he* is the storyteller and because he has revealed more about himself than he has of others. Nevertheless, what he has revealed about himself, both directly through self-conscious statements and overt verbal actions and indirectly through how he says what he says or does what he does, discloses more about what it means to be in Christ than what he says about anyone else. Indeed, the indirect forms of disclosure are as important as the direct because Paul represents being in Christ to others in the forms of his presence to them as well as in the form of his words, be they hortatory or "theological."[114] For Paul, the central reality about being in Christ is *being* in Christ, and the principal forms of this being are those of a slave of Christ the Lord and of a son of God—to-be. He, Paul, is an exemplary model of each.

Although in the last chapter we found that Paul's representation of himself as a slave of Christ is an anti-structural mask for his apostolic role, we also found that it is, nonetheless, a mask that he opted to wear in enacting that role. In the last chapter, however, we were concerned to identify the role behind the mask; now we are concerned with the choice of *this* mask both as a form of his self-representation to others and as a model for them to imitate. These others must know what we know from 1 Cor. 9:1 and 19, that in the social system of the world Paul is a free man, but they also know from him that in the church he has assumed the role of Christ's slave (Rom. 1:1; Gal. 1:10; Phil. 1:1; cf. 1 Cor. 7:22b), and that as such he is a slave "to all" (1 Cor. 9:19; 3:21–23; 2 Cor. 1:24; 4:5; cf. Gal. 5:13). Doing the work of the Lord means working as the Lord's slave, and even when he represents himself as an apostolic "father," he speaks of himself as a fellow slave with his fellow workers (Phil. 1:1a; 2:22; 2 Cor. 4:5). In addition to these explicit representations of himself, we need also to realize that everything Paul says about the believer being a humble and obedient slave of Christ is an expression of his own understanding of *his* enslavement to Christ (cf. Romans 6—8; 14; Phil. 2:1–13). Christ's own humility and obedience in the form of a slave is the ultimate model of and for the enslavement of believers to him as Lord, but Paul's obedience to Christ and his imitation of Christ's suffering as a slave is a more immediate model for other believers as well (cf. Phil. 2:1–13; 3:4–17; 1 Cor. 4:16;[115] 10:32—11:1; 1 Thess. 1:6–7).[116] All who do the work of the Lord are his slaves (cf. 1 Cor. 16:10 and 15:58), but in his own mind Paul is the workman-slave *par excellence* (cf. 1 Cor. 4:8–13; 2 Cor. 4:7—5:10; 6:1–11; 10:1–18; 11:16—12:10; Phil. 1:19–26; 3:4—4:1, 11–13). He is so persuaded of his identification with Christ in the form of a slave that he is willing to die like Christ in his service to him as his Lord, honoring Christ in his body, "whether by life or by death," knowing that in life he is in the Lord, while in death he is with the Lord (Phil. 1:20; cf. 1:19–26; 3:10–11; 2 Cor. 4:7—5:10; Rom. 8:35–39).

In his Letter to Philemon, Paul does not represent his obedience to Christ, although that may be implied by his imprisonment for Christ and the gospel, but he does clearly represent his humility as a model for Philemon to follow in making his decision about how to respond to Paul's "appeal." As we saw in our discussion of Paul's administrative style in chapter 2, both his preference to act out of love rather than out of authority, that is, his decision to appeal rather than to command (Philemon 8–10, 14), and his putting aside of his own desire to keep Onesimus with him illustrate the humble style of a slave of Christ who does not act as a master over others, even though he is their superior (cf. 2 Cor. 1:24). Paul's choice of this humble behavioral option serves, as we saw, as a model for Philemon because Paul does not want him to act out of his position of authority over Onesimus, nor does he want Philemon to act out of his personal desires concerning his slave.[117] The situation rather requires (*to anēkon*, v. 8) another act of brotherly goodness (*to agathon*, v. 14) by Philemon which will represent *his* obedience (*hē hypakoē*, v. 21) not simply to Paul but "in the Lord" (v. 20; cf. vv. 4–7, 16). Philemon's obedience to Paul's "appeal" will, therefore, demonstrate Philemon's enslavement to Christ. Indeed, by freely choosing (v. 14) to obey Paul, Philemon will, like Paul, show that he, too, is a free man in the world who has opted to become a slave of Christ. Of course, the fact that *this* free man is also a master in the world is a complicating factor in his decision, which we will attend to in a moment. But if he who is a superior chooses to treat his inferior as an equal both in the flesh and in the Lord, he will be imitating his own superior, Paul, who has treated his inferior, Philemon, like an equal. For all of these reasons, Paul's Letter to Philemon shows that his slave-mask represents both his profoundest sentiments about what it means to be in Christ and also, therefore, a model for other believers to imitate.

Paul is also an exemplary son of God–to–be, a brother among brothers, and this, too, is attested by his rhetoric, his style, and his representations of what it means to be a son of God. This role is not as conspicuous in his letters as the role of a slave of Christ, but that is because in the present time one is in the form of a slave. The form of the children of God is something that is to be obtained only in the future. Nevertheless, Paul consistently addresses the members of his churches as sibling brethren, appeals to them as a brother even though he is their "father," and he knows that he, too, is being changed from one degree of glory to another. In addition, the behavior he teaches and expects from his brothers cannot be other than his own behavior, nor can the motives he supplies for so behaving be other than his own motives. Perhaps the most profound example of Paul's status as a son of God–to–be is his celibacy (1 Corinthians 7), for it anticipates the erasure of sexual distinctions that characterizes the form of the sons of God. This example is especially interesting because what Paul says about celibacy and sexuality in 1 Corinthians 7 discloses the kinds of options that exist because the old has not yet passed away or the new fully come. His own option for celibacy is one he would like others to follow, but because of the passions of the present fleshly form of existence celibacy is not possible for all (7:6–9). Thus, Paul spells out the options he considers valid until the form of this world has passed away. But while he makes concessions in the matter of celibacy, he does not do so in the matter of Philemon's reception of Onesimus. Let us turn, therefore, to Philemon and his options.

In order to understand Philemon's options we first have to have an appreciation of both his knowledge and the situation in which he finds himself.

Although in this chapter we have been treating Philemon as a typical believer, in previous chapters we found him to be exceptional because he is a fellow worker of Paul, the head of the house in which a church meets, and a master in the world outside the church. The last of these requires that he know the laws and customs pertaining to the ownership of slaves, but the first two suggest that he also is fairly advanced in his knowledge of Paul's symbolic universe. As a typical believer he must share at least the institutionalized knowledge that is bound up with communal life in the church, and his decision to accept the call into the church suggests that he has found his own sentiments about the meaning of life in the world expressed and articulated in the church's symbolic universe. But the exceptional aspects of Philemon's position in the church imply much more. As one of Paul's fellow workers, he should know more than the minimal institutionalized knowledge, and as an apparent leader of a local church he must be presumed to have internalized this knowledge to a significant degree for him to have communicated it to others as Paul says he has (Philemon 4–7). Philemon, therefore, knows a lot, and what he knows contributes to both the definition and the intensity of his situation.

Given the totalistic nature of the knowledge associated with being in Christ, every believer has both a social position in the church and a personal position in its symbolic universe. Knowledge of this universe has motivated the believer's entry into the social unit, and behavior commensurate with the community's knowledge is a condition for remaining in it because behavior is monitored or judged by both peers and superordinates. On the other hand, Philemon's superordinate position in the church, and the greater knowledge associated with it, defines his position more sharply than that of others by making his behavior more publicly visible and by giving him greater responsibility for behaving in a manner consistent with the church's symbolic universe. But Philemon's social position is not simply within the church that meets in his house, because he is also one of Paul's fellow workers and partners. If the members of his house church did not know this before Paul's Letter to Philemon and them, they surely knew it after they received it. It is likely, however, that Philemon's association with Paul is public knowledge, for in the opening of the letter two other members of Philemon's circle are named as addressees along with him and his church. Apphia and Archippus also know Paul, and so also do five others who are with Paul and are named in the letter's closing greetings know Philemon to be one of Paul's associates. Philemon's social position in his own church is therefore bound up with his position in the wider network of Paul's associates, and this is all the more conspicuously public if Paul has appointed him to his position in the local church. But regardless of how he attained his position, his relationship with Paul and his associates places him under their watchful eyes as well as his church's. Philemon's behavior is subject to the approval of both groups, and according to Paul's letter he has, up to the time of writing, won the approval of each group. Paul praises him for his demonstrated faith towards the Lord Jesus and his acts of love among the saints or brethren, who in turn have had their hearts put to rest by his activities (vv. 4–7). And because Paul has received his information from others; it is clear that Philemon has a good reputation both in the church and among Paul and his associates.

Because Philemon's demonstrations of faith and love have won public approval on all fronts, these symbolic values, faith and love, are also disclosed as the norms by which behavior is judged. Philemon's behavior is both motivated by these values and judged by them. Consider, however, the implications of a behavioral failure and a negative judgment upon it. If a believer's behavior is *not* commensurate with being a faithful slave of Christ or a loving brother, it will demonstrate that he or she is not a slave of Christ or a brother or a sister, and such a demonstration has a number of social consequences. For the community, it poses both a social problem and a threat to the community's symbolic universe that must be attended to. For the individual offenders, on the other hand, their situation is in jeopardy for they stand to lose both their social position in the church and their personal position in its symbolic universe. This situation is intensified for such individuals and their community because of the totalistic nature of their symbolic universe, and it is all the more intense when a) the offender is a superordinate in the local church, and b) when he or she is also a subordinate in the wider network of church leadership beyond the local church. Up to the time when Paul wrote his Letter to Philemon and the church in his house, Philemon's situation was secure, the social life of his church was stable, and their symbolic universe was unthreatened.

Philemon's situation is further defined by his relationship with his slave Onesimus prior to the slave's return as a brother. Although we do not know how Philemon treated his slave before he ran away, we do know two facts about their relationship that are acutely significant for understanding Paul's story. The first is that Onesimus was not a believer and that he chose to run away from his believing master. The second and more important fact is that prior to Onesimus's unlawful departure, his believing master did not free or manumit him. It is dangerous to speculate about Onesimus's motives for running away, since we have no clues to them, but it is less dangerous to speculate about the implications of what Philemon did *not* do, because they are self-evident. On the one hand, because he did not free Onesimus we can safely infer that while he had the legal right to free his slave he had neither the desire nor the need to do so. Being a believer, being in Christ, did not motivate him to free his unbelieving slave. On the other hand, while Philemon did not choose to free his slave it also appears that neither his church, nor Paul, nor other fellow workers pressured him to do so. Thus, Philemon's position in the church did not require him to change or question his institutional role as a master in the world outside the church. From this, then, we can infer further that Philemon was able to compartmentalize his life in such a way as to be both a good churchman and a good man of the world.[118] He was able to relate to members of his church in churchly terms and to nonchurch members like Onesimus in worldly terms. Apparently the question had yet to arise in his church as to what a believing master is to do with his unbelieving slave. Thus, Philemon's situation prior to Onesimus's return as a brother and prior to the arrival of Paul's letter was also one in which he led a double life, which leads us to Paul's motives for writing his letter and thereby changing Philemon's situation.

In addition to the fact that Philemon led a double life, we also have to reckon with the fact that Paul wrote *what* he did in interceding for Onesimus with his master. These two facts are related because in writing what he did and as he did Paul shows that he was not all that confident about how his fellow worker would receive Onesimus. If he had been confident a simpler note would have sufficed, for he could have assumed that because the converted Onesimus *is* no longer a slave but a son, and as a son a brother, Philemon would acknowledge this and act accordingly, at least by receiving him as a brother, if not also by freeing him (cf. v. 21). Instead, we find Paul appealing to Philemon's faith and love, presenting his own humble behavior as a model, but from the very beginning of his appeal also disclosing his thinly veiled authority, and at the end, after v. 19a, abandoning his original strategy, sharply changing his tone, and even suggesting a potentially ominous visit by himself in the near future. Paul would not have needed such a wide array of manipulatory techniques if he had been as confident of Philemon's response as he claims (v. 21). To be sure, we do not know whether Paul's qualms about Philemon's reception of Onesimus were motivated by his knowledge of the particular history of the master's treatment of his slave, which he learned from the slave, or by the possibly new *issue* he saw posed by a runaway slave being converted and then returning to his believing master, in whose house a church congregated. Nevertheless, whatever Paul's motives may have been it is clear from his letter that the particular case became for him a case in point, for the letter treats the case in terms of the wider issue it poses, however obliquely it may seem on the surface.

How does Paul represent the issue posed by this particular case? Although he directly refers to the case of Philemon's reception of Onesimus, in one sense Paul makes an issue out of it by making it public in his letter to the community. But he also does so by setting the case in the context of communal values that are threatened by the case, by treating a particular instance of social relations within the framework of the community's symbolic universe. Indeed, he makes these values the ultimate issue by citing them as the only acceptable basis for Philemon's response to his appeal: the brotherhood of believers in faithful service under the Lord is realized only through selfless acts of love among the brethren. The failure of a brother to act like a brother not only upsets the social order, but it also violates the symbolic universe. In the Letter to Philemon, as in all of Paul's other letters, a "good" act in relation to a fellow believer is an act of selfless love, an act which is good, selfless, and loving because it "builds up" (*oikodomeō*) the other person and thereby also the community as a whole. In the Letter to Philemon this is expressed in terms of loving acts that refresh or bring rest to the hearts of the saints (v. 7; cf. vv. 9, 14, 16, 20b), and in the particular case of Philemon's reception of Onesimus the act in question is a social requirement (*to anēkon*, v. 8) to which obedience could be commanded (vv. 8, 14, 21), which testifies to the magnitude of the issue. Self-interest cannot be an acceptable motive for behavior; rather, in an act of love one should act as though one were the other's slave (Gal. 5:13). Thus, while the case of Onesimus's return as a brother creates a social problem for the local church, Paul sees this problem as one of maintaining a social order commensurate with the church's symbolic universe. The problem for him is not that a slave has inconveniently returned as a brother, but that the brotherhood cannot be preserved if brothers do not act like brothers. The idea of being brothers, which derives from the idea of believers being sons of God–to–be, is a fundamental idea in Paul's symbolic universe. And for this reason any breach in the social fabric of the brotherhood entails a breach in the symbolic fabric of Paul's universe, which determines what is required in social relations.

The issue of the integrity of the brotherhood and its symbolic universe is sharpened in Paul's letter by his failure to offer Philemon any alternatives or to make any concessions, and it is further sharpened by his representation of the issue as one which requires obedience, related to which are implicit threats of administrative consequences if Philemon does not respond appropriately. There is only one response that will meet what is required, only one response that will be "good," and that is Philemon's reception of his slave as an equal, both in the flesh and in the Lord. Regardless of what else Paul may have had in mind, like the freeing of Onesimus (cf. v. 21b), this alone will demonstrate Philemon's obedience. While Paul does not offer Philemon any alternatives to this, the fellow worker can clearly choose to remain a master and superior to his slave, but in this case Paul suggests that being a fellow worker and a master over a brother are as mutually exclusive as being both the slave and a brother of a brother. We can see this in Paul's threats of administrative consequences should Philemon choose to be disobedient. Clearly, it is Paul who will decide whether or not Philemon's response is obedient, good, and in fulfillment of the requirement posed by the situation. Equally clearly, Philemon's relationship with Paul is contingent upon his response. The climax of Paul's appeal (v. 17) suggests that Philemon's status as one of Paul's fellow workers and partners is at stake, and this is made known to both other members of Philemon's church and others of Paul's fellow workers. Because Paul has made a public issue of the case, he will also have to react publicly to any failure by Philemon to respond as he should. Although the apostle never specifies what administrative consequences might follow from Philemon's disobedience, he does specify a time and a place for a public reckoning should that prove necessary. Given both the case and the issue it poses, Paul's reference to his coming to visit Philemon at his house/church in the near future (v. 22) again only thinly veils sentiments such as those he openly expressed to the Corinthians: "What do you wish? Shall I come to you with a rod, or with love in a spirit of gentleness?" (1 Cor. 4:21). That Paul's visit could turn out to be the occasion for administrative action cannot have escaped the notice of anyone who was party to his letter. Philemon's relationship with Paul is clearly on the line in his response to the apostle's "appeal." Less clear, on the other hand, is Philemon's position in his own church. Or is it not perhaps the case that it is the clearest point of all because it is the most fundamental? For if Philemon refuses to receive his brother as a brother, he will demonstrate that *he* is not a brother. Paul's rhetoric plays on Philemon's "official" relationship with him as a fellow worker and partner, but both the particular case and the issue it poses have to do with being brothers. If Philemon is not a brother, he cannot be a fellow worker, and he is a fellow worker only because he is a brother associated with Paul. Consequently, when Paul comes to visit the church at Philemon's house, it is the fellow worker's status as a brother that is principally at stake. What might happen should Paul have to come with a rod?

We have seen that at baptism one symbolically separates oneself from the world, publicly ceases to be a slave to the flesh and the law of sin and death, and becomes a son of God—to—be, by virtue of which one also becomes the brother or sister of other believers. We have also seen that one remains a brother or sister by acting like one, principally through acts of selfless love for one's siblings, and that when believers fail to act like brothers or sisters by acting out of self-interest one returns to enslavement to the self-centered flesh. When this happens, believers are not only failing to act like brothers or sisters, indeed, to *be* a brother or sister, but they are also placing in jeopardy their social status and personal identity as sons of God–to–be. Their behavior is, as it were, an anti-confession, a denial of the church's symbolic universe, and they will have personally reversed the effects of the baptismal process. It is in this light that we also have to remember that Paul's churches had a ritual by which they could publicly acknowledge the individual's reversal. If baptism is the communal rite of entry into the brotherhood, excommunication is the corresponding rite for departure from it. In 1 Cor. 5:1–5, which interestingly enough follows immediately upon Paul's threat to come to Corinth with a rod, although in connection with a different problem, we see an example of the communal procedure for excommunication. Although absent, Paul pronounces judgment on the offender in the name of the Lord Jesus, and in communal assembly the church delivers the offender "to Satan for the destruction of the flesh." Whatever this delivery actually entails is not clear, but in view of 1 Cor. 5:9–13, which is on the same subject of immoral brothers addressed in 5:1–5, the wicked brother is cast out of the brotherhood. Most interesting for our purposes, however, are the offenses Paul cites as a basis for excommunicating the offender. While it is not clear whether the "rod" he threatened to bring in 1 Cor. 4:21 is a rod of judgment leading to excommunication, it is of interest that the offense is at least nominally "arrogance" (4:18, but see also 1:10—4:21). Quite clear, on the other hand, are the offenses listed in 5:1–13: immorality, greed, idolatry, reviling, drunkenness, robbery (cf. 5:11). Is failing to be a brother to a brother an any less egregious offense than these that lead to excommunication? If not, Philemon stands to lose both his social position as a brother and fellow worker and his symbolic position as a son of God–to–be, and the loss will be publicly decided in his own house.

Needless to say, Paul's letter dramatically alters Philemon's situation from what it was before Onesimus's return. When Onesimus and Paul's letter arrive on his doorstep, he is confronted both with his runaway slave and a letter which in effect tells him that his slave is now his brother, that he must receive him as such, and that if he does not he will have to face Paul in person. What is more, everyone in his church, not to mention others of Paul's fellow workers, know all about it, if not from Philemon's sharing of the letter, from Onesimus, and ultimately from Paul who could show up at almost any time. Philemon is on a very public spot.

If Onesimus's conversion and return pose for Paul and the church at Philemon's house the issue of the integrity of the brotherhood and its symbolic universe, for Philemon the issue entails a decision between two symbolic universes, two social worlds, and most of all two identities. In Paul's mind, Philemon has only one option, but in Philemon's mind there are two because prior to Onesimus's running away he lived in two worlds. Previously, he could be "in Christ" while still being and acting like the master of a slave "in the world." Now he finds that "being in Christ" makes a totalistic claim upon him from which there are no exceptions. *If he is to remain in the service of Christ the Lord, he cannot be "in Christ" only when he is "in church."* Thus, what we suspected in chapter 2 in connection with the social relations between Philemon and Onesimus is confirmed by our considerations of Paul's symbolic universe. Because they *are* in Christ, Onesimus cannot *be* both Philemon's slave and his brother, and Philemon cannot *be* both Onesimus's master and his brother. A believer can act *as though* he were his brother's slave, but his brother can neither act like nor be his master. Philemon made a choice of worlds once before; now he finds that he has to make the same choice once again. The difference between the two times is that the price of being a slave of Christ has gone up; it now costs a "master." On the other hand, Philemon can look at things differently; by paying a "master" he can become a son of God. The agonizing question that we must share with him is, "How much is it worth to become a son of God?" We share the question with him because we do not know how much *he* thinks it is worth. But all of the evidence and all of the arguments we have arrayed suggest that if one understands and accepts Paul's symbolic universe, being a son of God is worth any price at all. The only reason we have to question Philemon's decision is that Paul was not all that confident about it.

Through his Letter to Philemon, Paul therefore engineers a crisis for his fellow worker in which he has to make a decision about which of two worlds are to be his. When he is confronted with Onesimus's presence on his doorstep, and after having read Paul's letter, he is confronted not only with having to decide whether or not he will receive his slave as his brother, but also whether or not *he* is and wants to be a brother, a slave of Christ, and a son of God. Paradoxically, the critical decision to be made concerns himself, not Onesimus, for Onesimus *is* a brother, a slave, or rather a freedman of Christ, and a child of God–to–be regardless of what he, Philemon, decides. But the paradox is also not without irony, for the doorstep on which Philemon and Onesimus stand is the threshold of the church that meets in Philemon's house. If Philemon slams the door of his house in Onesimus's face in rejection of Paul's "appeal," he will be tacitly excluding himself from the house church into which he has retreated. Onesimus stands on the threshold of Philemon's house, waiting to be invited into his, Onesimus's, church, but Philemon stands on the same threshold with the choice of making the invitation or of having himself be invited to leave. For at least a fleeting moment, perhaps Philemon wonders just whose house it is. A good question, but whether or not he asked it, one thing is certain. Standing there on his own doorstep, Philemon is a man on the threshold between two worlds.

NOTES

1. Cited by Mary Douglas, ed., *Rules and Meanings*, 201.
2. Berger and Luckmann, *The Social Construction of Reality*, 102.
3. See above, intro. pp. 28–30 and chap. 1, 57–59.
4. The word "theology" is not used in the New Testament, and in its earliest appearance, in Plato (Republic, 379A), it refers to the composition of myths (see Hendrikus Boers, *What is New Testament Theology?* [Philadelphia: Fortress Press, 1979], 15–16). Deissmann, *Light From the Ancient East*, 348–49, refers to "theologians" in the imperial cult of Asia Minor at the end of the first-century c.e., but even here the role name has the sense of "prophet" rather than of a doctrinal specialist. Deissmann's point was to show that the later Christian notion of theology as doctrinal speculation is foreign to the New Testament period, in which we have largely to do with direct forms of religious expression rather than with theoretical speculation. The New Testament writings are religious, not theological (ibid., 378–83). See further the literature cited in n. 5, below. On the pre-Christian idea of "theology," see Werner Jaeger, *The Theology of the Early Greek Philosophers*, The Gifford Lectures, 1936 (Westport, Conn.: Greenwood Press, 1974, 1960).
5. For a brief survey and references to the abundant literature on New Testament theology, see Boers, *What is New Testament Theology?* For further discussion and translations of two classic texts by W. Wrede and A. Schlatter that are discussed by Boers, see Robert Morgan, *The Nature of New Testament Theology*, SBT 2d Series, 25 (London: SCM Press, 1973). See also James M. Robinson, "The Future of New Testament Theology," *RSR* 2 (1976): 17–21. On the history and problems of Paul's "theology," see for discussion and further literature, e.g., Boers, *What is New Testament Theology?*, 75–84; J. Christiaan Beker, *Paul the Apostle: The Triumph of God in Life and Thought* (Philadelphia: Fortress Press, 1980), 3–19 and passim; and E. P. Sanders, *Paul and Palestinian Judaism*, 431–542.
6. See Berger and Luckmann, *The Social Construction of Reality*, 104–16, on "theology" as a form of "machinery" used for maintaining symbolic

universes. I consider this understanding of theology to be a development of the "history of religions" method associated with Wrede, Deissmann, Bousset, Bultmann, etc. (see Werner Kümmel, *The New Testament: The History of the Investigation of its Problems*, trans. S. MacLean Gilmour and Howard C. Kee [Nashville: Abingdon Press, 1972], 206–405). My approach differs from it in two ways. First, unlike the history of religions method I am not presently concerned with comparing, e.g., Paul's thought with other systems of religion and thought in his time nor, therefore, with the historical context of his thought. Second, and related to the first point, my concern is with the body of knowledge that Paul thought about and as we can reconstruct it from what he wrote. The history of religions school distinguished between systematic reflection and the religion or beliefs reflected upon, but I am concerned with the *knowledge* that was reflected upon. See Bultmann, *Theology of the New Testament*, trans. Kendrick Grobel (New York: Charles Scribner's Sons, 1955), 2:237–51, and his introduction to Wilhelm Bousset's *Kyrios Christos: A History of the Belief in Christ from the Beginnings of Christianity to Irenaeus*, trans. John E. Steely (Nashville: Abingdon Press, 1970), 7–9. In this respect, my approach comes closest to the concerns for the coherence, patterns, or structures of religion and thought addressed in different ways by such recent critics as Sanders, Beker, and Meeks. I differ from them principally because my orientation is to the sociology of knowledge. I did not receive Daniel Patte's *Paul's Faith and the Power of the Gospel: A Structural Introduction to the Pauline Letters* (Philadelphia: Fortress Press, 1983) until after my manuscript was completed. But his concern for the "systems of conviction" underlying Paul's thought is related to those of Sanders, Beker, and Meeks, yet different from mine for the same reason mine differ from theirs. Suffice it to say that I see the sociology of knowledge as providing the means for continuing and developing one aspect of the history of religions approach.

7. While social scientists have long distinguished between social facts and theological facts, the sociology of knowledge as set forth by Berger and Luckmann treats theology as a social fact also because it is a social form of knowledge that is dependent upon another social form of knowledge, a symbolic universe, not some "real" universe that is directly accessible apart from prior knowledge. We only "have" reality in the form of knowledge, and knowledge is dependent upon both social conventions—language—and cultural traditions.

8. This distinction helps to distinguish further between my approach and those of Sanders, *Paul and Palestinian Judaism;* Beker, *Paul the Apostle;* and Meeks, *The First Urban Christians.*

9. In addition to Berger and Luckmann, *The Social Construction of Reality,* see on dictionaries, encyclopedias, and frames as kinds of knowledge, Umberto Eco, *The Role of the Reader,* 3–43. Although Eco does not cite Berger and Luckmann, nor they him, his form of semiotics (theory of signs and communication) represents a technical elaboration of their fundamental insights. In my judgment, Eco's work is as much of an extension and development of the sociology of knowledge as *it* is of earlier sociological and anthropological insight. In addition, Eco's work has the further merit of being heavily informed by literary criticism and hermeneutics. See further

Eco's *Semiotics and the Philosophy of Language,* Advances in Semiotics (Bloomington: Univ. of Indiana Press, 1984), 46–86; "Metaphor, Dictionary, and Encyclopedia," *New Literary History* 15 (1984): 255–71; and John Haimann, "Dictionary and Encyclopedia," *Lingua* 50 (1980): 329–57. It should also be noted that biblical studies has tended to be "dictionary" oriented rather than "encyclopedia" oriented, as is evident in Kittel's *Theological Dictionary of the New Testament* and in Bultmann's remarkable chapters on Paul's theology in his *Theology of the New Testament.* On the other hand, however, it is also fair to say that Bultmann is more encyclopedic than dictionary-like in his discussion of pre-Pauline thought. The difference is that in an encyclopedia-type article a given notion provides the basis for bringing together a wide range of dictionary-like information. In encyclopedia knowledge one gathers together all information related to a single notion, not merely the lexical meanings of the notion itself. "Frames," on the other hand, are items of knowledge which lead us to supply other knowledge, as for example in what we imagine when one speaks of taking one's car to the garage or of going to a supermarket. We know that certain kinds of things happen in such places and use this knowledge to understand what one says about going to them. So, for example, when Paul says, "When you assemble as a church" (1 Cor. 11:18), the readers *know* that they can expect certain things because they are typical of such assemblies. "Assembling as a church" is a Pauline "frame." Our problem in this case, of course, is that we do not know as much about what the Corinthians associated with such assemblies as we do about our own. The notion of "lord" or "master" is perhaps more useful because it has a dictionary meaning, "one who owns another," an encyclopedia "meaning," which concerns the nature and history of master-slave relations, and "meaning" as a frame, because when one calls another his master a frame of expectations is generated about both him and his master.

10. The idea that the play on the stage is the temporally and dramatically shaped aspect of Paul's symbolic universe calls for some comment. By it I mean that Paul views the activity on the stage mimetically, as the representation of actors in action over a period of time. This is another, and I think better, way of saying that he thinks historically or also mythologically about God's relations with man. It is better because Paul does not distinguish between historical and mythological actions, but only between the actions of different actors over time (cf. Käsemann, *Commentary on Romans,* 47). But we must also distinguish between the way Paul *views* these actions and the ways in which he verbally represents them. As I will suggest below, sometimes he narrates them, i.e., shows them, other times he alludes to or refers to them, i.e., tells about them or talks about them. This means that when *we* reconstruct his symbolic universe from the forms in which Paul represents it, we have to envision the play on the stage and find our own language for representing it. Finally, Berger and Luckmann say that symbolic universes order history (*The Social Construction of Reality,* 103). Because "history" is itself a fiction and as such a social fact (see

272

the introduction, above, on "History as Story"), I prefer to say that "history" is an aspect of every symbolic universe, more developed and more significant in some, less so in others, but always there in some form.

11. In Paul's letters we can see that some members of the audience have a different idea of what is happening on the stage, and therefore of their own roles (cf. 1 and 2 Corinthians, Galatians, Philippians 3). This, together with Paul's responses to them, reveals that Paul is active in the process of securing one symbolic universe in the face of competition from other symbolic universes. While we are concentrating on his symbolic universe, comparative study should do the same with the competition and then attempt to show how all of the competitors, including Paul, are related or opposed. The history of religions school made an impressive beginning in this regard, but its achievements need to be continued in more contemporary terms.

12. On because-motives and in-order-to-motives, see Schutz, *The Phenomenology of the Social World*, 86–96. See also Geertz, *The Interpretation of Cultures*, 94–98.

13. James W. Fernandez, "Persuasions and Performances: Of the Beast in Every Body . . . And the Metaphors of Everyman," *Daedalus* 101 (1972): 42.

14. In 2 Thess. 1:1–2, the opening formula appears both in the address, like 1 Thessalonians, and in the greeting, like all the other letters. The more typical appearance in the greeting is also found in Eph. 1:2; 1 Tim. 1:2; and 2 Tim. 1:2. Col. 1:2 lacks "and the Lord Jesus Christ," and in Titus, Christ is identified as "savior" rather than as "Lord." In general, these deutero-Pauline letters are of interest because they show the influence of Paul's style, as well as the continuing significance of the metaphors of "father" and "lord." On the adjectival use of the pronoun "our" in the formula, see Werner Kramer, *Christ, Lord, Son of God*, trans. Brian Hardy, SBT 50 (London: SCM Press, 1966), 219–22, and on the whole formula, 151–56. Of sociological interest is Klaus Berger's argument that because Paul sends his addressees greetings from the Father and the Lord he is placing himself in the sequence of Father-Son/Lord-Apostle and thereby legitimating his apostleship. ("Apostelbrief und apostolische Rede/Zum Formular frühchristlicher Briefe," *ZNW* 65 (1974): 190–231, and on this argument, 202–4).

15. On the cultic contexts of the title "Lord," see Bousset, *Kyrios Christos*, 129–38; and for "Father" also see the recent study by Meeks, *The First Urban Christians*, 140–70. On "Lord," see further Kramer, *Christ, Lord, Son of God*, 65–107; and on "Father," Käsemann, *Commentary on Romans*, 227–28; and Betz, *Galatians*, 209–11. Käsemann does not see the acclamation of God as "Father" as baptismal, Betz is uncertain, and Meeks confident (121, n. 34, and p. 152). While the acclamation may not be limited to baptism, Rom. 8:15 and Gal. 4:6, in their contexts, suggest that it is part of the baptismal ritual. The reception of the spirit is part of the ritual, and because it is the force that cries "Abba! Father!" thereby identifying the initiates as God's sons, it is likely that it is at baptism that this cry is uttered through them for the first time.

16. On this text, see Conzelmann, *1 Corinthians*, 139–47; and Kramer, *Christ, Lord, Son of God*, 94–99.

17. However much the greeting formula referring to God as Father and Jesus Christ as Lord may be Paul's creation, 1 Cor. 8:1–7a supports the idea, which should not need support, that these two identifications are fundamentally related in the communal knowledge of Paul's churches.

18. Cf. Rom. 11:33–36, and Käsemann, *Commentary on Romans*, 318–21.

19. Bousset already noted that Paul uses the notion of son of God to bridge the notions of God as Father and of Christ as Lord (*Kyrios Christos*, 205–10). Bousset did not, however, go beyond the notions to the systems of which they are parts. On the notion of son, see further Kramer, *Christ, Lord, Son of God*, 108–28 and 183–94. Rom. 1:4 suggests that Christ only became son of God in connection with his resurrection, but 1:3 speaks of him as being God's son before his human birth, which is consistent with Paul's view that Jesus Christ is the human form of a previously existing divine being (cf. Phil. 2:5–11). This means that the emphasis in Rom. 1:4 is not on Christ becoming son of God, but on his becoming son of God *in power*. Cf. Käsemann, *Commentary on Romans*, 10–13, and below on "Jesus Christ and the Son of God."

20. It is evident from a comparison of Gal. 3:26—4:7, where Paul only speaks of "sons" (*huioi*), with Rom. 8:12–23, where "sons" and "children" (*tekna*) are synonymous, that there is no difference between the referents of "sons" and the referents of "children." Each of these two texts, on the other hand, also refers to the baptismal participation in Christ's death by which one becomes a son of God. The asexual character of God's children is discussed later in connection with the relationship between Jesus Christ and the son of God.

21. Although Kramer (*Christ, Lord, Son of God*, 188) rightly sees that Paul was particularly interested in the relationships between God, his son, and other sons, Kramer's method and purpose lead him far short of seeing the systems of thought with which Paul operated. His method is of interest to us because he, too, is concerned with what Paul thought about. The difference between our concerns is that he reduces the objects of Paul's thought to pre-Pauline formulas. Thus, in part one of his book he deals with pre-Pauline formulas and in part two with Paul's use of them. This method has both the strengths and weaknesses of redaction criticism in gospel studies. Indeed, Kramer's method is redaction critical. Its strength is limited in the degree to which it can empirically distinguish between a writer's hand and the hand of sources the writer used. Its weakness is that it *reduces* evidence of the writer's hand to what is *not* source material and then looks only at the writer's "theology." (This is a common criticism also of Bultmann's *Theology of the New Testament*, in which Paul's theology is sharply separated from pre-Pauline thought and religion.) Redaction criticism is therefore doubly reductionist. Be this as it may, Kramer's study of "Christ," "Lord," and "Son of God" focuses on these titles and not on the conceptions they represent. When he deals with Paul, Paul's conception of the person represented by these titles is lost behind the three titular masks,

which Kramer sees Paul as deploying without "working together the ideas which underlie them" (p. 191). For Kramer, the underlying ideas are pre-Pauline, and because Paul does not wrestle with the pre-Pauline ideas associated with the formulas he appears to use them indiscriminately. What is missing in Kramer but focal in our enterprise is a concern for *Paul's* ideas and the systems they participate in.

22. In Paul's allegorical interpretation of Gal. 4:21–31, "the Jerusalem above" that is referred to as "mother" is associated with Sarah and God's promise to her and to Abraham. Because Paul ultimately sees the "mother" here as the promise (cf. 4:28, "children of promise"), "she" is not a proper kinship partner for God as Father, at least in *kinship* terms. See further below on the differences between kinship and adoption and the relationship between promise and adoption (see under "Abraham and Christ").

23. The word for daughters occurs only in 2 Cor. 6:18, in reference to the sons and daughters of God the father. However, this reference is not only anomalous in Paul, but it is also part of a non-Pauline interpolation, 2 Cor. 6:14—7:1. See Joseph A. Fitzmyer, "Qumran and the Interpolated Paragraph in 2 Cor. 6:14—7:1," *CBQ* 23 (1961): 271–80 (reprinted in Fitzmyer, *Essays on the Semitic Background of the New Testament*, Sources for Biblical Study 5 [Missoula, Mont.: Scholars' Press, 1974], 205–17); and Hans Dieter Betz, "2 Cor. 6:14—7:1: An Anti-Pauline Fragment?" *JBL* 92 (1973): 88–108.

24. In the Deutero-Pauline letter to Ephesus, the church is likened to a wife and Christ to her husband (Eph. 5:21–33). But the subject there is subordination and superordination (cf. 1 Cor. 11:3), not kinship. On Paul's view of normal kinship relations, see further below, and also the discussion below of Abraham and Christ.

25. The noun "adoption" (*huiothesia*) is used in connection with both the believer's entry into the process of adoption (Gal. 4:5; Rom. 8:15) and the completion of the process (Rom. 8:23). Commentators usually observe that this legal term is used "religiously," but I know of no study that has dealt with adoption in terms of its full role in Paul's thought. (On the meaning of *huiothesia*, contrast Käsemann, *Commentary on Romans*, 227, with Betz, *Galatians*, 208–9.) See further below, and n. 42 for further comments on the translation of the word for adoption.

26. On the model of mediations see the concluding section of chap. 2.

27. On death as a problem to be dealt with in all symbolic universes, see Berger and Luckmann, *The Social Construction of Reality*, 101–3. See also Geertz, *The Interpretation of Cultures*, 98–108, on the interpretability of death, and Lévi-Strauss, *Structural Anthropology*, 1:219–30, on the mediation of the opposition between life and death.

28. On the notions of the form of the children of God and of man and Christ as the "image of God," see the discussion below of Jesus Christ and the son of God.

29. On the lack of clarity attending Paul's comments on the relationship between the creation of man and Adam's transgression, see below on Adam and Christ, and Jesus Christ and the son of God. Suffice it to say in the

275

present context that while creation is not for Paul identical with man's "fall," the state of human alienation from God is traced back to the first created man. The emphasis is therefore on this man, not on creation itself.

30. I consider this question to be a development of the kinds of questions asked by the history of religions school. For example, Bousset inquired into what early Christians believed about Christ (*Kyrios Christos*), and Bultmann self-consciously took the further step of inquiring into what such beliefs meant to them (*Theology of the New Testament*). I differ from Bultmann because rather than using an extrinsic key to this meaning (existential phenomenology), I am trying to reconstruct in intrinsic terms the symbolic universe of meaning in which individual "beliefs" function (e.g., titles and other representations of Christ or "man"). See the references cited in n. 6 above.

31. Although Christ is not referred to as God's son in the Letter to Philemon, his being such is so prominent a feature in the symbolic universe represented in his other letters that we must presuppose Philemon's knowledge of it. It is dangerous methodologically to assume that Philemon knows everything that Paul communicates in other letters about his symbolic universe, but it is also foolish to think that Philemon, for example, knows only what is referred to in Paul's letter to him. Thus, he may not know what Paul communicates elsewhere about Adam and Abraham (on whom, see below), but some of what Paul says about them is so basic for his understanding of what it means to be a child of God that at least it must be presupposed as knowledge shared by Philemon. In the next sections we will therefore explicate *Paul's* knowledge, and in the concluding section we will address the question of what Philemon knows.

32. Excluded from discussion here are the kinship relations between Paul and his children, and Abraham and his children. Paul does not relate his paternity or his children either to God's or to Abraham's although in the last section of this chapter we will see that he does represent himself as a son-to-be of God. On the relationship between Abraham's paternity and children and God's, see below on Abraham and Christ.

33. On Adam and Christ, see for an extended discussion, Robin Scroggs, *The Last Adam: A Study in Pauline Anthropology* (Philadelphia: Fortress Press, 1966); and for narrower exegetical commentary, Käsemann, *Commentary on Romans*, 139–58; and Conzelmann, *1 Corinthians*, 267–69, and 281–88.

34. On Paul's notion of sin, see Romans 5—8, Käsemann, *Commentary on Romans*, 131–252, and below, on master-slave relations to Paul's symbolic universe.

35. Cf. 1 Cor. 15:56. In addition to Käsemann's exegetical discussion in the reference cited in n. 34, see Bultmann's classic statement on Law, sin, and death in his *Theology of the New Testament*, 1:227–69 and 330–52.

36. Just how these displacements were achieved will be dealt with below in our discussion both of Jesus Christ and the son of God and of Paul's

master-slave system. See generally, Bultmann, *Theology of the New Testament*, 292–306, "Christ's Death and Resurrection as Salvation-occurrence."

37. On Paul's understanding of "body" and "flesh," see Bultmann, *Theology of the New Testament*, 1:191–203 and 232–46.

38. The notion of "image" is discussed below in connection with the relationship between Jesus Christ and the son of God.

39. Metaphors having to do with garments are found in 1 Cor. 15:53–54 and 2 Corinthians 1—5 (putting on and taking off) and in 1 Cor. 15:49 (wearing). Meeks, "The Image of the Androgyne," 183–84, and *The First Urban Christians*, 155–57, identifies a baptismal context for the imagery of disrobing and robing, but he does not refer to these texts which, in any event, are oriented to the "putting on" of heavenly garments *when Christ returns*, as also in the metaphoric "wearing" of the image of the man of heaven. I do not see baptismal allusions in these texts. The metaphors seem rather to be a variation on Paul's notion of bodily transformation and conformity to the image of Christ, on which see below.

40. The unholy trinity of Law, sin, and death, which are central to the discussion of Adam and Christ in Rom. 5:12–21, are mentioned only briefly in 1 Corinthians 15 (15:56), which is focused on death and the conquest of it. Nevertheless, the very presence of a reference to this trinity in 1 Corinthians 15 is significant because it shows that their presence in Romans 5—8 is not an ad hoc matter, but a set of relationships about which Paul had given some thought. Thus, too, others than the Romans may have known about his ideas, and the Corinthians may have known more about them than 1 Cor. 15:56 might suggest.

41. On Abraham and Christ see, e.g., Ernst Käsemann, *Perspectives on Paul*, trans. Margaret Kohl (Philadelphia: Fortress Press, 1971), "The Faith of Abraham in Romans 4," 79–101; idem, *Commentary on Romans*, 105–29; and Betz, *Galatians*, 137–60, 181–201, and 238–52.

42. "Adoptive sonship" or "adoption as sons" (RSV) renders the Greek word for "adoption" (*huiothesia*), in Rom. 8:23; 9:3, and Gal. 4:5, but in the RSV rendering of this noun in Rom. 8:15, "adoption" is totally displaced by "sonship." While "sonship" is clearly the end-result of the process of adoption (cf. Rom. 8:14–17, 19, 21; Gal. 3:25—4:7), the RSV translation obscures the reference to the process itself.

43. Rom. 9:5, "the messiah," is the only clear titular use of the word "Christ" in Paul's letters. As Kramer and others have argued, "Christ" has become a proper name for Paul and is not a title (*Christ, Lord, Son of God*, 203–14). For a moderately dissenting view, see Nils A. Dahl, "The Messiahship of Jesus in Paul," in *The Crucified Messiah and Other Essays* (Minneapolis: Augsburg Pub. House, 1974), 37–47. The merit of Dahl's study is that unlike Kramer, Dahl has a sense of Paul's conception of the actor who is referred to in various ways, e.g., as Christ, Lord, and son of God. In any event, Dahl has shown more that the conception of "messiah" has informed Paul's understanding of "Christ" than that his use of the word retains a titular character.

44. *"Sperma"* refers to a person's genealogical seed or offspring and hence to descendants. Paul, however, is concerned with two factors that are not always clearly reflected in translations of *sperma*. One is the distinction between the singular "descendant" and the plural "descendants," in which Paul sees Christ as *the* descendant of Abraham (cf. Gal. 3:16 and Rom. 9:6–8). In this case, using the plural "descendants" (RSV) to render the Greek singular obfuscates Paul's point. The second factor is that Paul's concern about who is a descendant of Abraham is expressed in terms of how *descent* is to be reckoned. For this reason I will on occasion render *sperma* by "descent" in order to avoid the misleading connotations of the English plural, "descendants," and of the more archaic notion of "seed."

45. The whole of the letter to Galatia and Philippians 3 deal with problems raised by Jews who wish to have Gentile believers become circumcised. The more theoretical discussions of circumcision and the Law of Moses in Romans concerns the same problem. See further the discussion in chap. 2, above, of Paul's understanding of the collection for Jerusalem.

46. The connection is unclear because Paul does not harmonize what he says in Romans 9 with the idea that Christ is the firstborn son among many brethren (8:29; cf. Exod. 4:22 [LXX] for Israel as God's firstborn son). Christ is not the firstborn son because he is Abraham's "offspring" (Gal. 3:16), but because he is the first to bear the image of God (cf. 2 Cor. 4:4; Phil. 2:5–9, and below on Jesus Christ and the Son of God). We will also see that the idea that man was created in the image of God (1 Cor. 11:7) could have led him to begin the genealogy of the sons of God with Adam (cf. Luke 3:23–38). For these reasons, the genealogy of the promise and the genealogy of the sons of God can only be said to begin with Abraham when Paul identifies the sons of Abraham with the sons of God.

47. On the identification of the promise to Abraham as "the promise of the spirit," see Betz, *Galatians*, 152–53.

48. On the first fruits of the spirit, see also 2 Cor. 1:22, 5:5; Gal. 5:5, and below on the master-slave system.

49. Geertz, *The Interpretation of Cultures*, 93–94.

50. See n. 44, above, and proposition 5, below.

51. See n. 46, above, on Paul's failure to relate his assertions that Christ is both the firstborn son of God and Abraham's offspring.

52. On the total framework of beliefs, see 1 Thess. 1:9–10; on Jesus' death, see Galatians 3 and Rom. 3:21–26; and on Jesus' resurrection, see 1 Corinthians 15.

53. In these texts Paul uses the word "likeness" to mean "form," but it is difficult to determine the degree of identity between the form and that which it is like. On this problem, see J. Schneider, *"homoiōma," TDNT*, 5:191–98.

54. "Since 'power' and 'glory' can be synonymous (cf. Rom. 6:4 with 1 Cor. 6:14), so 'spirit' is also related to 'glory,' the life-giving power from heaven'; the 'spiritual body' (1 Cor. 15:44) is the 'body of glory' or 'glorious body' of Phil. 3:21; the resurrection of 'the spiritual body' is a raising up 'in

glory' and 'in power' (1 Cor. 15:43)." Bultmann, *Theology of the New Testament*, 1:156.

55. Despite the probably "adoptionist" christology of the tradition behind Rom. 1:3–4, Christ's preexistence as son of God rules out any adoptionist notions in Paul's christology. See Käsemann, *Commentary on Romans*, 10–14.

56. On 1 Cor. 11:7, where "man" is said to be the image and glory of God, see below.

57. The "something" is the essence of the thing so shaped. On these terms and related verbs, see Bultmann, *Theology of the New Testament*, 1:192–93.

58. On the relationship between an image as copy and its prototype, see Conzelmann, 1 Corinthians, 186–88 and 287–88. See also *"eikōn," A Greek-English Lexicon*, 2d ed.; Gerhard Kittel, *"eikōn," TDNT*, 2:395–97; and n. 53, above.

59. See n. 39, above.

60. See the literature cited in nn. 39 and 58, above, and Käsemann, *Commentary on Romans*, 44–45.

61. Sexuality also appears to be part of the image of the man of dust through procreation rather than creation, on which see below in connection with 1 Corinthians 11.

62. That is to say, they have a common "nature." Cf. Bultmann, *Theology of the New Testament*, 1:193, and the literature cited in n. 58.

63. While 2 Cor. 3:18 only says that the believer is being transformed "from glory into glory" (*apo doxēs eis doxan*), they are being transformed from the degree of glory they possess by virtue of being in the form and image of the man of dust into the glory which characterizes Christ's form and image as the son of God. Basic to this process is the idea that different bodies have different degrees of glory (cf. 1 Cor. 15:38–50).

64. Bultmann, *Theology of the New Testament*, 1:156.

65. On the lack of clarity concerning the relationship between the resurrection body and the transformation body, see above, under Adam and Christ.

66. Paul does not explicitly draw these connections but they represent the implicit conception underlying his statements about the biography of the firstborn son.

67. On 1 Cor. 11:3–16, see Conzelmann, *1 Corinthians*, 181–91; and Meeks, "The Image of the Androgyne."

68. In addition to the image of the androgyne discussed by Meeks (see above, n. 67), see also the notion that sons of God are angels and as such both immortal and asexual (cf. Luke 20:34–36). The image of the androgyne, i.e., of "man" as originally a masculine-feminine unity, is oriented to creation, while the idea that sons of God are angels is oriented to the eschaton. The latter seems to govern Paul's understanding of sons of God. (Cf. the sons-to-be of God speaking in the tongues of angels, 1 Cor. 13:1 and 14:2, but see also 13:8, speaking in tongues will cease!) Paul, however, has

difficulty relating this idea to the idea that man was created in God's image, which is associated with creation of the first man. Once again, therefore, Paul has not fully integrated the considerable knowledge he possesses.

69. The problem we have in trying to relate 1 Corinthians 11 to 1 Corinthians 15 results from Paul's failure to realize that "man" in Paul's time cannot be both in the image of God (1 Cor. 11:7) and in the image of the man of dust (1 Cor. 15:49; Rom. 5:12–21). The first man's transgression introduced sexuality, sin, and death, and that is not accounted for in 1 Cor. 11:7, which is therefore to be considered anomalous in Paul's thought. For further problems resulting from 1 Cor. 11:7, see below.

70. I.e., how does "for as woman was made from man, so man is now born of woman," explain their unity "in the Lord"? Paul seems to suggest that men and women are derivative of one another, whether in the form of creation or of procreation. But if this is what he means, it is not the same point made in his other comments about the unity of males and females "in the Lord," on which see below.

71. See also Meeks, "The Image of the Androgyne," 200–203 and 180–89. However, Meeks ignores the role of sons of God and their form, because he is a) interested in the pre-Pauline baptismal formula of "re-unification," in which "sons of God" may have been absent (but see p. 181 n. 78), and b) in the cultic re-unification of what was separated after creation. In any event, the notion of the form of the sons of God which believers will assume when Christ returns, i.e., eschatologically, is at least a Pauline notion, and it is one which he clearly shares with his churches.

72. In terms of Paul's symbolic universe, the concept of holiness or sanctification (*hagiasmos; hagiosynē*) refers to the overall process of transformation and is the moral aspect of the process of adoption as sons. In baptism, the believer is washed, sanctified, and justified in the name of the Lord Jesus Christ and in the spirit of God (1 Cor. 6:11), but it is only those who remain holy, i.e., morally pure, who will inherit the kingdom of God (cf. 1 Cor. 6:9–11). Believers are called to be "saints" or "holy ones" (*hagioi*, Rom. 1:7; 1 Cor. 1:2; 1 Thess. 4:7), called into God's kingdom and glory, and in order to enter his kingdom one must lead a life worthy of God (1 Thess. 2:11–12; 3:12—4:8). In this light, and in relation to the believer being in the process of becoming a son of God, the identification of believers as "saints" or "the holy ones" in Philemon 5 and 7 refers to the moral quality of the sons-to-be of God. In other words, a son of God is, morally speaking, holy. Sanctification and adoption, therefore, represent different aspects of the same process. On the concept of holiness see Bultmann, *Theology of the New Testament*, 1:84–85. Christ's sacrificial death for sins is expressed in terms of the forgiveness of sins, release or deliverance (redemption), justification, sanctification, and reconciliation, pp. 101–2 and 136–37, and baptism is both sanctifying and purifying. See also pp. 338–39, for a summary of Paul's understanding of holiness. Bultmann does not draw the connection between sanctification and adoption or between "the saints" and the "sons of God."

73. Cf. Bultmann's discussion of "Christ's Death and Resurrection as Salvation-occurrence," *Theology of the New Testament*, 1:292–306.

74. See Bultmann, ibid., 295–300, on the derivation of Paul's terminology from "a number of different thought complexes" (p. 295). We will come at this issue from another angle in the next section in connection with another "thought complex," the master-slave system. Suffice it to say that Bultmann did not attach the same significance I have to either the kinship or the master-slave systems. I suspect that he did not do so because he was concentrating on the presence of other than Pauline thought complexes in Paul's thought, not on Paul's own thought as an independent entity. This is yet another example of the difference between moving from context to text (Bultmann, *et al.*) and from text to context. We are only beginning the latter process because we are focusing on the "text" of Paul's symbolic universe.

75. Reconciliation, justification, redemption, and forgiveness of sins all refer to the effects of Christ's death both as objective and subjective facts of a one-time character, in contrast, for example, with sanctification, adoption, and salvation which, although beginning at a single point in objective and subjective (personal) history, designate a process. However, redemption refers also to another one-time event, the eschatological redemption of the body (Rom. 8:23). See Bultmann, ibid., 84–85 and 292–306.

76. Our focus on the system of relations between masters and slaves, and between parents and children, differentiates our approach from traditional christologies and theologies, which virtually ignore the role of slaves or the relationship between the firstborn son and other sons of God and rather concentrate on Christ as Lord or as son of God.

77. On the use of the verb for serving Christ as his slave (*douleuō*), see Rom. 12:11, 14:18, and 16:18.

78. Apparently one is a slave of God in the sense that God is the one who has appointed Christ as master over all. See proposition 3, below, and n. 104.

79. The unusual preposition *pros* in Philemon 5, instead of *eis*, both of which can be rendered by "in," is also found in connection with faith in (*pros*) God in 1 Thess. 1:8. Interestingly enough, when Paul elaborates on the Thessalonians' faith in 1:9–10, their relationship to God is described as "serving as a slave," *douleuō*. This is not much to go on, but it does support the idea that Philemon's faith in (*pros*) the Lord Jesus represents a slavelike quality. Also, in 1 Thess. 5:12–13 love is a quality associated with the behavior of subordinates to superordinates, and in Gal. 5:13 Paul tells the Galatians to serve (*douleuō*) one another through love. And last, in 2 Cor. 12:8–9a the *Lord* responds to Paul's appeal by saying, "My grace (*charis*) is sufficient for you. . . . " In each of his letters Paul begins by sending to his addressees grace and peace from God the Father and the Lord Jesus Christ, and he concludes by invoking the grace of the Lord upon his addressees (1 Cor. 6:23; 2 Cor. 13:14; Gal. 6:18; Phil. 4:23; 1 Thess. 5:28; Philemon 25; the ending of Romans, which lacks the invocation, is disputed).

80. On master-slave language in Paul's letters, see Deissmann, *Light*

From the Ancient East, 318–30, and both for criticism of Deissmann's theory of Paul's dependence on an institution of sacral manumission and for an independent approach to Paul's knowledge of slavery, see Bartchy, *Mallōn Chrēsai*, passim (the critique is on pp. 121–25). I have not had access to the dissertation by Kenneth C. Russell, "Slavery as Reality and Metaphor in Pauline Letters" (Diss., Pontifical Univ., Rome, 1968), on which see Bartchy, ibid., 15–17.

81. In Rom. 14:4a, b, Paul uses worldly master-slave relations as an analogue for behavior in the church.

82. While Käsemann, *Commentary on Romans*, 96 and 237, finds no reflection of redemption from slavery in Paul's use of *apolytrōsis*, and Conzelmann, *1 Corinthians*, 52 (and n. 31), finds the word rare, both a) argue their position against Deissmann's theory concerning sacral manumission, and b) ignore the evidence for Paul's master-slave system that we are considering here. Although the word *apolytrōsis* is rare and is used metaphorically by Paul, its lexical meaning is clear. It refers to the buying back of a slave or captive, making him free by payment of a ransom (Bauer, *Greek-English Lexicon*, 2d ed., p. 96, and for the related terms *lytron, lytroō, lytrōsis, lytrōtēs*, pp. 482–83). For evidence of such redemption and the role of third parties as redeemers in the process of manumission, see Bartchy, *Mallōn Chrēsai*, 80 n. 289 and 99–103.

83. See Betz, *Galatians*, 148–52 and 208–9.

84. "I belong to" in 1 Cor. 1:9, 13–15 (cf. 3:4, 21–23) is related to baptism, and for Paul to baptism in the name of or into Christ the Lord. Cf. Bultmann, *Theology of the New Testament*, 1:136–38: in baptism the believer becomes the property of Christ the Master/Lord.

85. On the anti-structural character of Paul's orientation to the world, see the concluding sections of chap. 2, above.

86. In 1 Corinthians 15, Paul refers to Jesus as "Lord" (vv. 31, 37–58) and as "son" (v. 28), but his focus is on the death and resurrection of Christ and he only briefly alludes to Christ's relinquishing of his lordship (vv. 24–28). The allusion is recognizable because the terminology of subordination in 15:27–38 is drawn from the role of Lord as seen in Phil. 2:9–10; Rom. 10:9–13, and 14:11. The allusion is somewhat obscured, however, by 15:25, where Paul refers to Christ's lordship as his "reigning," using the royal term "to reign" or "to rule" (*basileuō*). Because Paul does not elsewhere speak about Christ's reigning over a kingdom (*basileia*, 15:24), this text is exceptional. Nevertheless, because it is exceptional we should observe that elsewhere he uses the verb "to reign" synonymously with the verb *kyrieuō*, meaning "to have dominion" or "lordship" (Rom. 6:12, 14). Thus, he says that death "reigns" (*basileuō*) over man (Rom. 5:14, 17, 21; 8:2), but then claims that man has been "set free" (*eleutheroō*) from sin and death (6:6–7, 22; 8:2), and that death no longer "has dominion" or "lordship" (*kyrieuō*) over man (6:9). In this context, therefore, the verb "to reign" functions within the master-slave system, and so also, I think, in 1 Cor. 15:24–28, although the presence of the noun "kingdom" in 15:24 is difficult to

explain. On the subordination of Christ to God, see also 1 Cor. 3:23 and 11:3.

87. The second conclusion describes the most fundamental features of the character, Jesus Christ, and as such it responds to the fragmentation of this actor's identity that results from the study of christological titles and models. Paul may not always succeed in coherently integrating what he says about this character, but he does have a substantially coherent conception of him.

88. The kinship and master-slave systems provide a conceptual framework for comprehending different aspects and phases of the biography of the son of God.

89. The classic description of the pre-Pauline cult of the Lord is by Bousset, *Kyrios Christos*, 129–38. His treatment of Paul's contribution, on the other hand, is marred by its preoccupation with the idea of Christ-mysticism (pp. 153–210, on which see Bultmann's introduction to *Kyrios Christos*, 7–9). Bultmann, *Theology of the New Testament*, 1:121–29, 133–64 (cf. 92–108) provides a more extensive, nonmystical description of the pre-Pauline church, in which he includes comments on Paul's contribution to it. See also Kramer's analysis of the different aspects of church life in which the lordship of Christ is central, *Christ, Lord, Son of God*, 65–107, and his discussion of Paul's elaboration of traditional ideas, 151–82.

90. See Kramer, *Christ, Lord, Son of God*, 65–84; and Conzelmann, *1 Corinthians*, 204–6. Although "Lord" precedes "Jesus" in the Greek of 1 Cor. 12:3, which is a ritual acclamation, "Jesus" is the subject and "Lord" the predicate. The point is that Jesus is identified as the Lord/Master, which parallels the account in Phil. 2:9–11 of God's giving Jesus this title and role.

91. See, e.g., Kramer, *Christ, Lord, Son of God*, 169–73.

92. On obedience, see chap. 2, pp. 131–151, which are concerned with Paul's language of commanding and appealing. Ultimately, "salvation" is from the eschatological wrath of God (cf. Rom. 2:5–10; 6:9–11; 9:27–28; 1 Thess. 1:10; 5:9–10).

93. See n. 86, above, and on 1 Cor. 15:24–28, Conzelmann, *1 Corinthians*, 269–75.

94. The Greek literally says "body of humiliation" and "body of glory," but the adjectival use of "humiliation" and "glory" refers to the nature of the body as lowly or glorious, as composed of lowly or glorious "stuff."

95. See further above on "Jesus Christ and the Son of God," and on the role of obedience in the image of "slave," see below on Romans 6.

96. See above on "Adam and Christ."

97. On Gal. 3:13 and 4:5, see Betz, *Galatians*, 148–52 and 208–9. On freedom, see propositions 2 and 3, below.

98. On "the elemental spirits of the universe," see Betz, *Galatians*, 204–5 and 215–17; and Lohse, *Colossians and Philemon*, 94–99.

99. On this and the next proposition, see Bultmann, *Theology of the New Testament*, 1:292–306, "Christ's Death and Resurrection as Salvation-occurrence," and 330–52, "Freedom."

283

100. Cf. Käsemann, *Commentary on Romans*, 216–19.

101. On liberation from the law and the elemental spirits of the universe, see proposition 2, above.

102. See 1 Cor. 6:11, where in connection with baptism one is said to have been "washed," "sanctified," and "justified," which indicates the synonymity obtaining between these terms. See further nn. 72 and 75, above.

103. Conzelmann, *1 Corinthians*, 113 and 128, notes the metaphors but does not see them as developed because Paul does not say either who received the purchase price or from whom the believer was bought. Bultmann, however, rightly observes that the context of 6:12–20 shows that one has been bought from sin (*Theology of the New Testament*, 1:297). This is confirmed by the wider context of the master-slave system in Paul's symbolic universe, for man is freed from sin and death by the ransom price of Christ's death. Nevertheless, Conzelmann's point is valid to the extent that for Paul the significance of the purchase price is that it was *for* the slaves, not *to* their former masters. His concern with the former masters is expressed in terms of Christ's *victory* over them, not of the value they received from his death. Thus, once more Paul fails to follow through on the various implications of his symbols.

104. In view of the preceding note, we should observe that Paul's thought moves from Christ's death as the currency with which slaves have been bought from sin and death to the paradox that because of his death in the form of a slave God made *him* Lord/Master over those whom he, God, purchased with that death. Also, because it is God who redeemed the former slaves of sin and death and made Christ their Lord, we can understand the apparently anomalous statement in Rom. 8:22, that believers have become "slaves of God." God is the ultimately authoritative master and Christ is his appointed agent who, after a time, will turn those in his trust over to God (cf. 1 Cor. 15:24–28).

105. On the status and jobs of believers, see chap. 2, esp. on Paul's work and body metaphors.

106. See above on "Jesus Christ and the Son of God"; Bultmann, *Theology of the New Testament*, 1:153–64, 311–13, 330–39, 348–52; and Meeks, *The First Urban Christians*, 150–57.

107. For discussion of this notion and the related idea of participation, and also for further literature, see Robert C. Tannehill, *Dying and Rising with Christ*, BZNW 32 (Berlin: Töpelmann, 1966); and E. P. Sanders, *Paul and Palestinian Judaism*, 433–74, 518–23.

108. The noun "spirit" (*to pneuma*) and its modifier (*auto*) are neutral rather than masculine in form, but apparently because it is God's spirit (Rom. 8:14) or Christ's (Gal. 4:5) translators refer to the spirit as masculine (cf. "himself," *auto*, in Rom. 8:16 and 26).

109. On the problematical identification of the Lord with the spirit, see E. Schweizer, "*pneuma*," TDNT, 6:418–20; and Kramer, *Christ, Lord, Son of God*, 165–68.

110. Bultmann sees the formula, "I speak in a human way" (Rom. 3:5; 6:19; 1 Cor. 3:3; 9:8; Gal. 3:15), as indicating that the form of statements

about things divine is really inappropriate to their content, but that the form is necessary because of the weakness of man's flesh (*Theology of the New Testament*, 1:232). At least in Rom. 6:19; 1 Cor. 3:1–3; 9:7–8a; and Gal. 3:15, when Paul speaks in this way he is being analogical or metaphorical.

111. In addition to the Corinthian correspondence and the letter to Galatia, we can also see the diversity of understandings of Paul in such Deutero-Pauline letters as Colossians, Ephesians, and 2 Thessalonians. As the author of 2 Peter 3:16 said, there are some things in Paul's letters that are hard to understand, which the ignorant and unstable twist out of shape. For our purposes, however, the diversity of understanding reflected in the undisputed letters is more important because it shows that despite the presence of institutionalized knowledge, understanding varied significantly from church to church and from believer to believer. This fact makes it very difficult to infer from certain knowledge that certain behavior followed. Since certainty about the knowledge and behavior is not to be had, the best we can do in our project is to establish the probabilities and let them govern our predictions of behavior. At least the sentiments represented by knowledge that should be possessed by believers are such as to render the actors' options with a stark clarity.

112. Cf. Geertz, *The Interpretation of Cultures:* "It is in some sort of ceremonial form—even if that form be hardly more than the recitation of a myth, the consultation of an oracle, or the decoration of a grave—that the moods and motivations which sacred symbols induce in men and the general conceptions of the order of existence which they formulate for men meet and reinforce one another" (p. 112). Ritual activity entails, "both the formulation of a general religious conception and the authoritative experience which justifies, even compels its acceptance" (p. 118). See further the entire essay from which these quotations come, "Religion as a Cultural System," 87–125. As for the baptismal experience, one is told in advance of baptism both what it means and that one will receive the spirit. During baptism, one experiences internally a power which is understood to be the spirit, and after baptism this experience becomes the experiential reference point for subsequent behavioral direction and teaching about the group's symbolic universe.

113. In saying that believers are not of two minds, I mean that they have committed themselves to viewing experience within the framework of the church's symbolic universe. In addition to one complication of this to be dealt with below, it should be noted that this is different from Paul's references to being of two minds in Philippians 1—2, where he is concerned with different interpretations within the church of its symbolic universe.

114. The priority for Paul of *being* in Christ over the verbal forms in which it is expressed is evident in the Corinthian correspondence where he expresses his disdain for fancy speech and worldly wisdom (cf. 1 Cor. 1:4—3:4; 4:1–21; 8:1—9:24; 12—14; 2 Cor. 1:12–24; 3:1—6:13; 7:2–3; 10—13).

115. In 1 Cor. 4:16, it is Paul's fatherly model that is to be imitated (cf.

4:15–17, 21), but in view of Phil. 2:22 (cf. 1 Cor. 16:10) even as a father Paul is a "slave" in bondage with his children.

116. On the imitation of Paul, the imitator of Christ, see further Bultmann, *Theology of the New Testament*, 1:304–5.

117. What Philemon is to imitate is Paul's slavelike inoffensiveness to others, his seeking to please them rather than seeking his own advantage. Cf. 1 Cor. 9:19–27; 10:23—11:1; Rom. 14:10—15:6. See also 1 Cor. 11:2, "remember me in everything and maintain the traditions even as I have delivered them to you." First Cor. 11:3 then represents a tradition concerning the subordination of individuals to their superiors.

118. Philemon is a good man of the world in the sense that he has fulfilled his worldly role as a master. Whether or not he was a good master from his slave's perspective is another matter, since Onesimus may have fled because he found Philemon to be a bad master. On this, however, we have no evidence.

CONCLUSION:
SOME REFLECTIONS ON
PAUL'S LETTER AND
ITS STORY

We can bring our exploration to a close by reflecting on another close, the closure of Paul's story about Philemon. Closure has to do with the satisfaction of the expectations generated by a narrator throughout his narration, and we have been exploring the literary, sociological, and symbolic means by which Paul has led us to expect certain things about the close of his story. By constructing this story from his letter, and by exploring the symbolic forms and social arrangements of its narrative world, we have seen confirmed Clifford Geertz's assertion that " . . . it is through the flow of behavior—or, more precisely, social action—that cultural forms find articulation."[1] Likewise, the corollary of this assertion has also been confirmed, for we have seen that these cultural forms, be they symbolic or sociological, are the social constructions that make social action meaningful both for the actors and for those of us who are trying to figure out what their actions signify to them.[2] The emplotment of the actors' actions in Paul's story, and the array of cultural forms that give them meaning, have generated in us certain expectations that must be satisfied by Paul's story. We have found, however, that like many another narrator Paul has left us with one of those "Did he, or didn't he?" endings.[3] Thus, as readers of his story we are left with the task of concluding—or closing—it. But for our purposes, unlike for example the historian's, the answer to the question we are left with, the closure itself, is not as interesting as the answer to the question of why we think Philemon—and Paul—did one thing rather than the other. It should be evident by now that I think Philemon responded affirmatively to Paul's appeal, and that if he did not he was excommunicated from the church. That, at least, is the closure I have found myself supplying on the basis of what I

287

have seen in our exploration. Let me reflect, therefore, on my reasons for supplying this ending, and in the process make a few observations about Paul's wider narrative world, for it informs the narrower world of his story about Philemon.

Paul's Letter to Philemon constitutes but one action in his story about Philemon, but it is the action by which he knowingly precipitates a crisis both for Philemon and for the community of which he is a, if not *the*, leader. Paul's thinly veiled command that Philemon receive back his runaway but now converted slave as a brother, and indeed that he do even more than this, represents an intentional confrontation between Paul and Philemon, but also between Paul and the church that meets at Philemon's house, for the church itself will also have to receive the converted slave as a brother and deal with Philemon should he fail to obey Paul. Philemon's situation is focal because the church will not *have* to react until Philemon has, but while the church will only have to take sides if Philemon does not obey Paul, its potential response is a factor that both Paul and Philemon have to reckon with. To establish the role of the church in his story, Paul wrote his letter in such a way as both to involve the church in the problem and to incline it to adopt his point of view. He addressed the letter to it as well as to Philemon, he praised its leader's efforts among its members and thereby expressed his pleasure with their behavior as well as his, and he placed them as well as Philemon under the watchful eyes of others of his fellow workers, letting the local church know that it is a part of a wider community and that the problem posed by Onesimus's return is one shared by Philemon, the local church, and the extended church. All are given to know that the integrity of the brotherhood and its symbolic universe is at issue in Paul's demand that Onesimus the slave be received as the brother he has become. The carrot is apparent but so also is the stick. Philemon is placed before the watchful eyes of his church, and the church is placed before the watchful eyes of Paul and his fellow workers, and through them probably before the eyes of other churches as well. And Paul will be coming to visit the entire church that meets in Philemon's house. Our expectations concerning Philemon's response to Paul are, therefore, informed by the role of the community of which Philemon is a member. Later we will develop this role further in connection with the sociology of authority in Paul's churches, including the church at Philemon's house.

Philemon's position is focal because Paul has placed him between the proverbial rock and hard place. By demanding that Philemon receive his runaway but now converted slave as a brother, Paul puts Philemon in the position of having to perform an action in the domain of the church that will necessarily affect his position as a master in the domain of the world. Paul's demand, therefore, transforms Philemon's previously comfortable double life in the two domains by rendering the institution of slavery in the domain of the world as a rock and the institutional domain of the church, whose support Paul has cultivated in his letter, as a hard place. The worldly responsibility for acting as a master with his slave is placed in conflict with the churchly responsibility for acting as a brother with a brother when Philemon's slave becomes his brother. To be sure, there is no a priori reason for there being a conflict between these responsibilities, as we can see in the Deutero-Pauline letters (cf. Col. 3:22—4:1; Eph. 6:5–9; 1 Tim. 6:1–2). However, in the Letter to Philemon Paul has both perceived a conflict and sharpened it by making it public and by calling for action in the church that has consequences for Philemon's life in the world. While the letter is written in Christ, and to Philemon as one who is in Christ, its message forces Philemon to step imaginatively outside of the church in order to assess his responsibilities in the two domains in which he has participated. And that is why he is *between* a rock and a hard place.

What is the conflict Paul has perceived? Significantly, he does not attack the institution of slavery as such, nor even the participation of a believer in it. Rather, he attacks only the participation in it of a believing master and his believing slave. The case of Philemon and Onesimus represents for Paul a conflict not only in personal relations but also and more fundamentally a conflict between identities. It is logically and socially impossible to relate to one and the same person as both one's inferior and as one's equal,[4] but these status terms show that the corresponding social relations are grounded in social identities. In Paul's view the ultimate issue is the identity of believers as sibling children-to-be of God, and therefore as equals. Because Onesimus is no longer a slave but a brother, both in the flesh and in the Lord, his *being* a brother to Philemon means that he cannot also *be* a slave to Philemon in any domain. In other words, *being* in Christ or *being* in the Lord is a state of social being that governs the relationships between believers even outside the spatial and temporal boundaries of the church. Being in Christ/the Lord, therefore, excludes all other forms of social being for those who are "in" him. And this state of being is the norm which determines the behavior, the form of social relations, that is appropriate, indeed required (*to anēkon*), between believers.

If Philemon acts as Paul demands, his action in the domain of the church will affect his institutional position in the domain of the world, at least with regard to his institutional relationship with Onesimus as his slave. While we do not know from what Paul explicitly says in his letter exactly how he expected Philemon to deal with his institutional position in the world, Paul's line of argument strongly suggests that the only acceptable action would be for Philemon to free his slave. This seems to be the only institutional action in the domain of the world that would satisfy the institutional reality of Philemon's and Onesimus's identities as brothers in the domain of the church, where they are totalistically "in Christ." And this seems, too, to be the only action that would warrant the kind of argument that Paul makes in his letter. The very fact *that* he wrote at all indicates the magnitude of the issue he envisioned, but the *way* he wrote represents a conflict between mutually exclusive positions on the issue. However, before we turn to this rhetorical aspect of Paul's argument, we need to observe that one of the strategies behind the argument is to allow, indeed require, Philemon and other readers to draw the appropriate conclusion from it. This is part of the open-endedness of his story as well. The focus of the argument is on Philemon's behaving in terms of what he and Onesimus now *are* by virtue of their being in Christ. It is on behavior that is commensurate with their institutional identities in the church, namely, as brothers. Thus, Philemon's problem is not so much one of *how* to act in the domain of the church, for that he surely knows, nor is the problem even one of whether or not to act like a brother to a brother, for the real problem must be resolved before he makes that decision. The real problem Paul's letter poses for Philemon is the decision he has to make about his responsibilities in the domain of the world. Before the arrival of Paul's letter, he had to be concerned about what to do with his delinquent slave should he be found or return. But with the arrival of Paul's letter he has to think not in terms of playing his role of master but of relinquishing it. His thoughts are forced to move from the punishment of his delinquent slave to the idea of freeing him and having him around as a brother. These observations about Philemon's concerns and thoughts are admittedly speculative, but there is nothing speculative about the fact that Philemon has to make a decision about his worldly responsibilities and even privileges as a master over a slave. And on this point we have to remember that a premise of Paul's letter is *his* apparently serious doubts about whether or not Philemon will draw the proper conclusion from his and Onesimus's status as brothers in Christ, through whom they will become sons of God like him. It is the *possibility* that Philemon will take his worldly identity and responsibilities more seriously than their churchly counterparts, and not only not free Onesimus but also not receive him as a brother, that motivates both Paul's writing of the letter and his writing it as he did.

The competing demands that Paul envisions for Philemon are fundamental to both his letter and its story because they supply the motive for the letter, including its rhetoric, and the plot of its story. How so?

The plot of Paul's story is structured around the theme of indebtedness.[5] This theme both links together and contrasts two story-lines, one concerning Onesimus's indebtedness to Philemon in the domain of the world, the other Philemon's indebtedness to Paul in the domain of the church. The story begins with Philemon's entry into metaphorical debt to Paul, and because this is probably a reference to Philemon's having been converted by Paul this relationship of indebtedness is located in the domain of the church. But before Paul develops Philemon's story-line further he shifts to Onesimus's. Onesimus's story-line begins with his running away from Philemon and in the process incurring a debt to his master in the domain of the world. This line is carried through to its closure as Paul tells about his converting Onesimus, his sending of the new brother back to Philemon, and his repayment of Onesimus's debt to his master. Onesimus's story-line is therefore closed because he has fulfilled his worldly responsibilities to his master. By the same token, however, it is also implied that *Philemon's* worldly responsibilities for disciplining his slave have been satisfied, for by representing Onesimus's relationship to his master as one of indebtedness the payment of the debt cancels the obligations of the parties to the relationship. Paul, at least, represents Onesimus's slate as having been wiped clean by his return and by the payment of his debt, and therefore any disciplinary action by Philemon would be unnecessarily punitive. Paul's emphasis is on Philemon's acceptance of the fact that worldly obligations surrounding Onesimus's flight have been met, and on Philemon's now fulfilling of his churchly obligations to his new brother. Having completed Onesimus's story-line in this way, Paul then turns back to Philemon's story-line by calling in Philemon's debt to him, the payment of this debt being in the form of the master's reception of his slave as his brother, both in the flesh and in the Lord (vv. 15–21). The total story, therefore, concerns Philemon's debt to Paul, within which Paul has embedded the story of Onesimus's debt to Philemon. The total story ends with Philemon's response—to pay or not to pay—and with Paul's announcement of his visit to Philemon and his church, a visit in which Paul will find out how Philemon has responded and act accordingly. Dis-

291

ciplinary action against Philemon is a clear possibility if he defaults on his debt, for if Paul has the authority to command Philemon's obedience in this matter he also has the authority to discipline him. What form that discipline might take is not hinted at in the letter or its story, but from other Pauline texts we have seen that excommunication is very much a possibility. More of this later.

The emplotment of the theme of indebtedness quite clearly represents the competing demands from the two domains in which Philemon participates, and it does so with no little irony. On the one hand, Onesimus's conversion is the occasion for the repayment and canceling of his worldly debt, while Philemon's conversion is the occasion for his incurring of a debt to Paul in the domain of the church. On the other hand, Paul pays Onesimus's worldly debt in the currency of the world, and Philemon must pay his own debt in the domain of the church in the church's currency. The irony here is that the church's currency is Philemon's freeing of his own slave. Because Onesimus is no longer a slave but a son of God, Philemon will, through the paying of *his* debt, be "buying" his slave as a brother. And last, these contrasting relationships of indebtedness are linked together because Paul's payment of Onesimus's worldly debt serves as a model and an incentive for Philemon to pay his churchly debt. Paul has acknowledged Onesimus's worldly debt and paid it. Now it is Philemon's turn to acknowledge his churchly debt and pay it. Paul has thus anticipated Philemon's worldly concerns and satisfied them, and thereby Paul forces Philemon to attend to churchly concerns and be as magnanimous in the domain of the church as Paul has been in the domain of the world. But this leads us beyond the story to the rhetoric of the letter. Suffice it to say that the emplotment of Paul's story leads us to expect that Philemon will accede to Paul's demand and that Paul's visit serves as an incentive for his doing so. Paul motivates Philemon's response by introducing the because-motive of his conversion by Paul, but also by introducing the in-order-to-motive of Paul's visit. Philemon should accede to Paul's demand *because* Paul converted him and *in order to* receive Paul's approval when he comes.

The competing demands of the world and of the church also motivate Paul's writing of the letter and his choice of rhetoric in it. He writes as he does because of his concern about how Philemon will respond to Onesimus's return and in order to secure Onesimus's reception as a brother rather than as a delinquent slave. Because Paul's reasons for writing *what* he did are to be found in *how* he wrote it, let us focus on the rhetoric of his letter. There are two aspects of its rhetorical composition, one having to do with the emplotment of referential actions in the poetic sequence of actions in the letter, the other having to do with its narrower rhetorical features.

In his letter Paul reveals his rhetorical strategy by referring to referential actions in such a way as to accentuate the positive and at least delay the negative.[6] He accentuates the positive by indicating his approval of Philemon (action 5) and by informing him of Onesimus's conversion (action 4) and return (action 6). Only after having done this does Paul allude to Onesimus's having run away (action 3), in connection with which he makes his "appeal" to Philemon and commits himself to repaying Onesimus's debt (action 7). Up to this point, therefore, both Philemon and Onesimus, and indeed Paul himself, are cast in a very positive light. Even Onesimus's delinquency, which is one of the fundamental premises of the letter and the story, is virtually ignored, for it has to be inferred from the facts that he is returning and that Paul is paying his debt. Only after these facts have been established does Paul introduce the matter of Philemon's indebtedness to him (action 1). Coming where it does in the letter, the reference to this, the first action in Paul's story, identifies Philemon's response to Paul's "appeal" as the payment of his own debt to Paul (action 9). But it also identifies the concluding action referred to, Paul's planned visit (action 10), as an encounter between the debtor and his debtee. Thus, the closural action referred to in the letter is rhetorically ambiguous. From it Philemon knows that if he accedes to Paul's "appeal" their meeting will be a pleasant one, but that if he does not it could be very unpleasant indeed, for he will confront Paul as one who has publicly defaulted on his profound debt to the ambassador of Christ Jesus. Paul therefore accentuates the positive and delays the negative, but he also lets Philemon know that he, Philemon, will be responsible for erasing the potentially negative tone of their meeting.

The poetic emplotment of actions in Paul's letter is closely related to his more narrowly rhetorical tactics in it. Formally, that is, in terms of the letter's overall rhetorical structure of greetings, thanksgiving, appeal, and close, Paul greets Philemon as his beloved fellow worker (v. 1b) and expresses his thanks to God for Philemon's previous demonstrations of his faith and love (vv. 4–7). Following this, Paul makes his own appeal to Philemon out of love and for another loving act of goodness (vv. 8–16). At least initially, therefore, the rhetorical tone and composition of the letter accentuates the positive—love, faith, and goodness among brothers. But underlying Paul's appeal there is also a backbone of authority and power that points to the utmost seriousness of the situation envisioned by him.

293

He begins his appeal by stating that the situation is one in which he has the authority to command Philemon to do what is required (v. 8), but that for love's sake he prefers to appeal to him (vv. 9–10) and secure his free consent in the matter rather than have him respond out of necessity, that is, as to a command (v. 14). Yet it is the line that runs from command through necessity that at the end dominates the letter, for Paul concludes his "appeal" by expressing his confidence in Philemon's *obedience* and more (v. 21).[7] The transition from the earlier positive tone of the letter to the tone of authority and power appears to begin already at the climax of Paul's "appeal" in v. 17. When Paul concludes by saying, "Therefore, if you consider me a partner, receive him as you would receive me," he is rhetorically allowing Philemon to act on the basis of his perception of his relationship with Paul, but Paul is actually setting up Philemon's response as a test which he, Paul, will grade. In fact, Philemon's response will prove to Paul whether *he* should continue to reckon Philemon as his partner, fellow worker, and brother.[8] Following v. 17, the tone of the letter changes dramatically.[9] In v. 18 he offers to pay any debt Onesimus owes Philemon and then in v. 19 takes up the pen to write a promissory note in his own hand (v. 19a). But no sooner has he written this than he turns the issue of indebtedness back on Philemon by reminding him that he owes Paul his "own self" (v. 19b). Now the rhetorical mask of appealing to Philemon's faith, love, goodness, and judgment about his relationship with Paul is dropped. Now Paul speaks openly as Philemon's apostolic debtee and superior, saying: "Yes, brother, *I* want some benefit from you in the Lord! Refresh *my* heart in Christ!" (v. 20). Then, somewhat more calmly but nevertheless firmly, he concludes: "Confident of your obedience, I write to you, knowing that you will do even more than I say" (v. 21). And by the way, prepare a guest room for me, for I am hoping through the church's prayers to be able to visit you (v. 22). This tone and style differs markedly from that of vv. 8–16 (cf. vv. 17–18) in yet another way, too, for vv. 8–16 are structured in terms of a series of contrastive statements representing different points of view on the same subject.[10] There Paul seems to be self-consciously reasoning his way through to Philemon's conscience rather than assaulting it with an apostolic command. But when he took up the pen himself to add vv. 19ff., he dropped this reasoned style and spoke like the authority figure he claimed to be in v. 8. He is, therefore, no longer reasonably above it all but in the midst of it, confronting Philemon rather than reasoning with him. He has ceased to be the reasonable and loving model for Philemon to emulate[11] and becomes the one who has the authority to command—and does.

Both Paul's initial rhetorical tactics and his sudden abandonment of them suggest that he viewed the Philemon affair as a very sensitive one indeed. The situation required the greatest of tact and care so as not to offend Philemon and his congregation, and we know this from the tact and care represented in the composition of the letter. But for all his care and tact Paul was also convinced that Philemon and his church had a nonnegotiable obligation to receive Onesimus for and as what he had become, not for and as what he had been. The shadow that hovers over both Paul's decision to write and how to write it is the possibility that Philemon and his church might not be sensitive to their obligation to their new brother. Initially, therefore, Paul's strategy was to communicate both his sentiments and his authority in the matter but to do so in such a way as to secure compliance on the basis not of personal sentiment or authority, but of the church's knowledge and values. Yet, Paul could not restrain himself when he got to the point of having fulfilled his and Onesimus's obligations to the worldly institution of slavery by returning Onesimus and paying his debt. At this point, Philemon's obligation to the institution of the church, and his indebtedness to Paul within that institution, made Paul's previous rhetoric seem so much pussyfooting about. Thus, Paul switched to sentiment and authority, telling Philemon what he wants and representing it as a matter of institutional obligation requiring nothing less than obedience. What Paul wrote and how he wrote it are motivated by his sense of the competing demands with which Philemon and his church would be confronted when Onesimus returned to them as a brother. His task was to bring them to the realization that in this case there can be *no* competition and, unlike the case of marriage in 1 Corinthians 7, no concessions.

The issues of Paul's authority and of the communal knowledge and values that shape his social style lead us not, as earlier, to Paul's wider narrative world for an appreciation of the symbolic forms and social arrangements that govern the social life of churches like the one at Philemon's house. These forms and arrangements contribute to the plot of Paul's story and its closure, and they also bring back into focus the role of the church in both the letter and its story. Our concern now is with the structures of institutional authority and the systems of institutional life that bear on Paul's story about Philemon. In particular, we are interested in the distinction and relationship between local institutional authority and life, as for example in the church that meets at Philemon's house, and the translocal authority of Paul and his itinerant fellow workers, like Timothy who is with him at the time of his writing to Philemon. Neither the letter

295

nor the story can be fully appreciated if we do not recognize that Paul's letter represents the intrusion of translocal authority into the authority structures of the local church. Let us begin with some general observations about structures of authority in Paul's churches and then consider Paul's letter to Philemon in that light.

Every local church has its own structures of authority and its own knowledge, values, and rituals, but each of these is substantially the same in all churches. The sameness, of course, results from the efforts of the likes of Paul who taught the churches these things, and that is a factor we will return to shortly. For now, the significance of the commonality between churches is that the church at Philemon's house must be presumed to practice rituals like baptism and the Lord's Supper, and to meet regularly for worship, which includes at least prophesying, teaching, and prayer, and probably also readings from Jewish Scriptures and homilies on them. Likewise, the church at Philemon's house must also be presumed to share with other churches the *knowledge* that in other letters is associated with the central rituals of baptism and the Lord's Supper. Thus, Philemon's church knows about such ideas as the fatherhood of God, the lordship of Christ, the sibling relationship between believers, and enslavement to Christ, and they know about the death, resurrection, and return of Christ, together with the meaning of these events for believers. And they also know about and indeed have experienced the power of the spirit, by which their behavior is guided in the direction of acts of mutually edifying love among the brethren. And so on. But in addition to these practices and to this knowledge, the church at Philemon's house also has structures of authority like those seen in other letters.

From such texts as 1 Corinthians 12—14, Rom. 12:3–8, and 1 Thess. 5:12–22 it is clear that structures of superordination and subordination are in each church determined by three factors: the sanctioning of local authority figures by outsiders who founded the church; the role of host played by the owner of the house in which the church congregates; and the ritual and administrative needs of the community. Whatever weight an apostolic sanction may have carried, because the outsiders who founded the churches did not impose on them a preshaped system of roles ("offices"), the structures of local authority emerged in connection with the different jobs performed by individual members. Members of the community owed deference, the granting of authority, to those who performed the different jobs for them. In time, authority became attached to the job itself, but in the beginning it appears that the job and the person who performed it were closely bound up together. Authority to do the job was granted by the community to the one who did it, whereas later authority inhered in the job itself and became the property of the performer when he took the job. In the early stages in the formation of the communities, local authority was, therefore, virtually in a constant process of negotiation between the workers and between them and those for whom they worked. But in this context of constant negotiation one role seems to have been more permanent and therefore of particular significance in the social life of each church, namely, the role of host played by the owner of the house in which the church congregated. This role is of especial significance in the letter to and story about Philemon.

To appreciate the role of host we need to remember that after the founding of a church by nonresident missionaries like Paul and his fellow workers, these outsiders moved on to other cities and left the local churches pretty much on their own, except for inspection visits by fellow workers, letters from Paul, or even visits by him if the situation demanded them. In founding a church, the missionaries would gather a following through their preaching, and after baptizing their followers they would teach them the symbolic forms and social arrangements by which they were to maintain their communal identity. But from among the followers the missionaries also authorized some individuals to run the shop, as it were. Although we do not know the means by which such individuals were selected and authorized, one type of person was always involved, the believing owner of the house in which the church met. Such people were always local residents and their social significance was guaranteed because their houses and their own activities within them were the most centrally conspicuous features of local church life. Deference is almost automatically due them in some, if not many, matters in a church's social life, for the host of a church is the only one in a fixed position literally to oversee all of the functions taking place in and originating from his or her house. To be sure, no individual host is guaranteed to have superordinate authority in a church, but the *position* of host is guaranteed to attract such authority should there be no other competition for it. Consider, now, Philemon's position as host of the church that meets in his house.

Whether it is by virtue of his being the host of his church or of other personal qualities, or both, Philemon the host is the leader, the resident authority figure in the church that meets in his house. Although Paul does not describe him as a "host," he is clearly such because he is the master of the house in which the church meets. It is in this capacity, therefore, that we must also understand Paul's praise for Philemon's active role both in the sharing of his faith in the Lord Jesus and in refreshing the hearts of the saints. And it is in this capacity, too, that Philemon is the first church member named in the greetings of Paul's letter. Yes, he is the one to whom Paul's appeal is specifically addressed, and that surely contributes to Philemon's name being mentioned first. But the one to whom the appeal itself is addressed is also the leader of the church. Paul gives no hint in his letter that there is any other leader superior to Philemon; he does not write to some other authority figure to have him or her deal with Philemon. No, it is Philemon to whom his church looked for a place to meet, for knowledge of the good that is theirs in Christ, and for comfort. Paul addresses Philemon first because he is both the church's leader and its problem, and those are facts that are fundamental to Paul's letter and story. But because the local authority figure is also the problem, Paul has to deal with the problem of authority, for by putting Philemon on the spot he is also challenging the loyalties of the rest of the congregation. Are they going to stand by the one to whom they have granted authority on a daily face-to-face basis, or are they going to reject his authority by acknowledging the superior authority of an outsider, a nonresident whom they only know from a distance and quite possibly have never met? Paul's intervention on Onesimus's behalf raises questions about the relationship between local and translocal structures of authority. To appreciate these questions and their significance for the Philemon affair, we have to return to some general considerations about the social life of a church in the absence of its founding father(s).

From what we have seen thus far, two factors played a role in the social life of each church. On the one hand, after founding a church Paul and his fellow workers moved on to form other churches, leaving the new community to hone the social arrangements of their communal life in a manner consistent with the symbolic universe it had been taught. On the other hand, because in each church there are a number of jobs to be performed by its members, the possibility of competition for authority and the necessity of ranking authority on some kind of a scale are built into the situation of each local church. Each church has to reckon both with its own structures of super- and subordination and with the problems of social relations attending the emergence of these structures. Thus, the individuals whom Paul had authorized as leaders begin by enjoying an authority derived at least in part from Paul's, but in his absence they are in the position of having to cultivate their own authority by securing the consent of the governed. Leaders are in the position of having to live up to the expectations both of Paul and of their own congregations, but their most concrete and immediate problems have to do with the negotiation of their own authority within their churches. Depending on the individual leader and on local circumstances, a leader can lean in one direction—Paul's—or another—the congregation's—but the absence of Paul's translocal authority and the presence of immediate needs within the church produce a gap between local and translocal authority. Paul's letters are replete with illustrations of this structural problem and its possible social consequences.

The gap between local and translocal authority *need* not be a problem for every church. As we can see in 1 Thessalonians and Philippians, the two could easily be in harmony though separated by distance. But we can also see from the Corinthian correspondence, Galatians, and Philippians 3 that in Paul's absence the young communities were vulnerable both to dissidents within and to other preachers who had come in from the outside, often creating the local dissidents. These letters show, too, that dissent could focus on Paul, on the fellow workers whom he sent back to churches they had founded, and probably also on those like Stephanas of Corinth whom Paul had authorized to be a local leader. The role of outside preachers is interesting because it represents a competition between translocal authorities for the allegiance of local churches, a competition fought out, moreover, within the local churches and not at some distant "summit." But for our purposes the general vulnerability of the young local churches and their potential for becoming alienated from Paul and his translocal entourage is more pertinent. In the Corinthian correspondence we can see that outside competition alienated some church members from Paul and his fellow workers, including the local leader Stephanas. But more importantly, we can see that some Corinthians came to resent Paul's authoritarian manner and therefore his authority (see especially 2 Corinthians). The Corinthian correspondence represents Paul's head-on confrontation with a local church that on more than one occasion disputed his translocal authority, showing both *that* the gap between local and translocal authority structures could be one of conflict between them and *how* Paul dealt with such conflicts. The Letter to Philemon represents the same two things, although from a different angle. Let us therefore look at the letter and its story in terms of the relationship between local and translocal authority.

The structures of authority in the church at Philemon's house prior to Paul's letter were not the subject of conflict. While we do not know who founded this church, it is evident from Paul's letter that he was more or less intimately involved in the process. He knows by name at least three members of the church: Philemon, Apphia, and Archippus. And Philemon knows Paul, Timothy, and five other fellow workers of Paul, and he is himself one of Paul's fellow workers and partners. So whoever founded the church, whether Paul, a fellow worker, or even Philemon as a fellow worker, the church at Philemon's house knows itself to be under the translocal authority of Paul, a fact of which he reminds them in v. 8 of his letter. On the local level, on the other hand, we have seen that Philemon is the principal authority figure in his church. Paul acknowledges his leadership by expressing his approval of it, but he also suggests that Philemon's position in the church is one that he has authorized, for he calls Philemon *his* fellow worker and partner. Thus, Philemon's authority is not in conflict with Paul's, and the relationship between local and translocal authority structures is one of harmony. Indeed, harmony also seems to have been the rule within the church under Philemon's leadership. Paul's letter provides no suggestion of any dissent within the church, and that is significant because it means that the congregation has had no reason to question Philemon's authority any more than Paul's. Authority has not been an issue for the church at Philemon's house. But with Paul's letter, the situation changes.

Paul's letter makes authority an issue because it puts the congregation in the position of having to become conscious of the gap between local and translocal authority, if not ultimately to decide for one authority rather than the other. It is Paul who introduced the problem of authority over them by claiming to have it, and although he promptly renounced his intent to impose it, all know that it, or at least the claim to it, remains despite Paul's rhetoric. And in v. 21 he openly describes the response he expects from Philemon as an act of obedience and more. But the issue of authority becomes immediately concrete for the congregation by Paul's announcement of his intended visit, for his arrival will be the occasion for a showdown on the question of whose authority ultimately governs the social life of this church. Paul's letter, therefore, sets up a test for both Philemon and his church, but as we have seen, when Paul sets up such tests for others he is also subjecting himself, and particularly his authority, to a test (cf. 2 Corinthians 8—9 and the presentation of the collection in Jerusalem).[12] If others pass his tests, so does Paul pass his, for his authority is confirmed by their actions. But if others fail Paul's tests, Paul does, too, and his authority is not only terminated among them, but it is also diminished among others observing the test. Paul's Letter to Philemon and his church is, therefore, ultimately a test of his authority over them as an ambassador of Christ, and that means that it is a test of his ability to do the work of Christ among them and perhaps among others as well.

By making the case of a believing master's reception of his newly converted slave a test of authority that could result in the loss of a congregation and a rejection of his authority, Paul reveals the magnitude of the case in his own mind. It is in this light, then, that we have to view the striking change of tone in Paul's letter after v. 17. The rhetoric with which he began his letter suggests that he was sensitive both to the issue of equality posed by the case and to the issue of authority posed by his intervention into the case. The issue of equality required his intervention, and he began to do so with care and tact. But in the process of intervening he seems to have perceived that his intervention required the very assertion of authority that he had initially sought to minimize. It is as though he initially envisioned the social problem of Onesimus's return, saw the shared symbolic values of faith, love, goodness, and personal judgment as the key to solving it with only a minimal show of authority, but then realized that the situation that had required his intervention, in however brotherly terms, ultimately raised the question of authority in the church at Philemon's house. With this realization, he decided to disclose the structures of authority in which Philemon and his church *had* to act. Thus, what began as in many respects a peculiar local problem became, by the end of his letter, a translocal problem, indeed a universal problem because it involved both the churches' symbolic universe and the social arrangements required by it. Hence the paradox that to defend the equality of brothers Paul had to exercise his superiority among them.

What, then, does this shift from equality to authority lead us to expect about the closure of Paul's story? Principally, by putting the case of the returning but converted slave in the context of his authority as an ambassador of Christ, Paul radically polarizes the options open to Philemon and his church. By representing the polar opposites as acting either in worldly or in properly churchly fashion, Paul forces Philemon and his church to think beyond narrow self-interest and local sentiments to what being in Christ is all about. But in putting the particular case on this cosmic level, it also becomes possible for Paul both to assert his authority and to renounce it, not now merely through rhetoric but through the symbolic universe in which both the church's actions and his are comprehended. By identifying his authority as being "in Christ," for whom he is presently a prisoner of the state, his authority is shifted

301

from his person to the symbolic universe which he shares with Philemon and his church, and in which all authority is grounded. Paul risks a conflict between local and translocal authority because he understands both to derive from the same symbolic universe shared by all believers. Through his letter, he seeks to make the church at Philemon's house consider their situation not in terms of authority figures, but in terms of the source of their authority, which is also the source of the responsibility of all parties to the case. Paul does not "theologize" with the church at Philemon's house; he appeals directly to the reality of their all being in Christ. Thus, like Philemon, the members of the church that meets in his house are confronted not with the question, "Who is Paul?", but with the question, "Who am I?" Paul, I think, felt more confident about the answers of the many than he did about the answer of the one, and that is why he played the hand that he did. Being in Christ is not just a good "game," it is the only "game," and one is either in it or out of it. Thus, when Paul comes to visit the church, if they did not know about it already its members may find out about another play in the "game," the ritual procedure of excommunication referred to in 1 Cor. 5:3–13. For it, too, is a part of the social reality of being in Christ. I suspect that Philemon knew about this, too, all of this, and that is why I think he acceded to Paul's appeal—and more.

Finally, to have entitled our exploration "Rediscovering Paul" is more than a little pretentious, for it suggests that somehow we have lost him and need to rediscover him. Perhaps the question of whether or not he has been lost can only be answered in terms of whether or not we have individually learned anything new, rediscovered anything, through our exploration. For myself, I wanted to find a social being named Paul whom I had lost behind the veils of theological criticism and comparative studies. For me the former had reduced Paul to an itinerant if not an armchair church intellectual, and the latter had dissolved his image into a kaleidoscope of "parallels." It is always nice to find what one is looking for, and I think I have found it. But having found what I was looking for, I must also now share the worry that I may have created the object I have found, not rediscovered the object I had lost. But then history *is* story. The question is, out of what shall we make up our stories?

NOTES

1. Geertz, *The Interpretation of Cultures*, 17. See further chap. 2, above.
2. Cf. ibid., 3–30, and chap. 3, above.

3. For another example of this kind of ending, see my "When is the End Not the End? Literary Reflections on the Ending of Mark's Narrative."

4. The issue of equality is entirely absent in the Deutero-Pauline letters cited above.

5. See chapter 1, above, pp. 65–78.

6. See chapter 1, above, pp. 72–75.

7. See chapter 2, above, pp. 131–151.

8. See chapter 2, above, pp. 139–145.

9. See chapter 1, above, pp. 73–78.

10. See chapter 2, above, pp. 131–134.

11. See chapter 2, above, pp. 133–135, and chapter 3, pp. 262–270.

12. See chapter 2, above, pp. 139–142.

307